HEALTHY
AND
DELICIOUS

HEALTHY
AND
DELICIOUS

400 Professional Recipes

Sandy Kapoor, Ph.D., M.P.H., R.D.

John Wiley & Sons, Inc.
New York | Chichester | Brisbane | Toronto | Singapore

This publication is designed to provide accurate and
authoritative information in regard to the subject
matter covered. It is sold with the understanding that
the publisher is not engaged in rendering legal, accounting,
or other professional services. If legal advice or other
expert assistance is required, the services of a competent
professional person should be sought.

Library of Congress Cataloging-in-Publication Data
Kapoor, Sandy, 1952–
    Healthy & delicious : 400 professional recipes / Sandy Kapoor.
      p. cm.
    Includes index.
    ISBN 0–471–13158–X (cloth : alk. paper)
    1. Quantity cookery. 2. Low-fat diet—Recipes. 3. Salt-free diet—Recipes. 4. Sugar-free diet—
Recipes. 5. Low-calorie diet—Recipes. 6. Low-cholesterol diet—Recipes. I. Title.
TX820.K348 1996
641.5′7—dc20   95-30430

Printed in the United States of America

10 9 8 7 6 5 4 3 2 1

To my best friends and sisters,
Susan Nordquist, Janet Kaiser, and Ellen Furuya.

Contents

Table of Recipes   xiii

Preface   xxi

Acknowledgments   xxiii

Introduction   xxv

Computing Nutrients in Recipes xxv

 Measuring Ingredients *xxv*
 Abbreviations *xxvi*
 Ingredient Specifications *xxvii*
 Nutrient Needs *xxviii*
 Calorie Needs *xxx*
 How Recipes Fulfill Nutrient Recommendations *xxx*
 Recipe Nutrient Analysis *xxx*
 Converting Recipes *xxxi*

RECIPES

1.

Stocks and Soups

1

Stocks 2
Soups 9

2.

Sauces

33

Hot (Warm) Sauces 34
Condiment Sauces, Salsas, Relishes, Chutneys, and Spreads 41
Rubs, Marinades, Glazes, and Spice Blends 57

3.

Meat

63

Beef 64
Lamb 82
Pork 93
Veal 105

4.

Poultry

109

Turkey 110
Chicken 122
Other Poultry and Game 141

5.

Fish and Shellfish   149

Fish   *150*
Shellfish   *165*

6.

Dried Beans, Peas, Lentils, and Vegetables   171

Dried Beans, Peas, and Lentils   *172*
Vegetables   *190*

7.

Potatoes, Grains, and Pastas   217

Potatoes   *218*
Grains   *233*
Pastas   *255*

8.

Salads and Dressings   269

Main Course Salads   *270*
Vegetable and Grain Salads   *275*
Fruit Salads   *291*
Oils and Vinegars   *298*
Dressings   *305*

9.

Egg and Cheese Dishes 321

Egg Dishes *322*
Cheese Dishes *327*

10.

Hors d'Oeuvres and Beverages 337

Snacks *338*
Dips and Toppings *352*
Beverages *360*

11.

Breads, Cakes, Frostings, and Sweet Sauces 365

Breads and Cakes *366*
Frostings and Sweet Sauces *385*

12.

Cookies, Bars, Pies, and Pastries 403

Cookies and Bars *404*
Pastry Crusts *411*
Pastry Fillings and Toppings *422*

13.

Puddings, Frozen and Fruit Desserts 437

Puddings *438*

Frozen Desserts   442
Fruit Desserts   454

APPENDIX 1
Substitutes to Reduce the Total and/or Saturated Fat and/or Cholesterol   468

APPENDIX 2
Substitutes to Reduce Sodium/Salt   476

APPENDIX 3
Substitutes to Increase Fiber   483

APPENDIX 4
Substitutes to Reduce Calories, Add Nutrients, or Increase Portion Size without Calories   487

APPENDIX 5
Healthy Cooking Procedures   491

APPENDIX 6
Sources for Food Ingredients in Healthy Cooking   495

APPENDIX 7
Healthy Cooking Tools, Equipment, and Sources   498

Glossary   500

Index   511

Table of Recipes

Stocks and Soups

Flavorful Vegetable Stock
Rich Brown Veal Stock
Rich Fish Fumet
Rich White Chicken Stock
Shrimp Broth

Black Mushroom and Pearl Barley Soup
Brown Lentil Soup Seasoned with Oregano
Butternut Squash Bisque Garnished with a
    Dollop of Chunky Apple Yogurt
Chicken Brown Rice and Vegetable Soup
    Flavored with Curry
Chilled Fresh Tomato, Bell Pepper, and
    Cucumber Gazpacho
Chilled Peach Soup Flavored with Cinnamon
    and Clove

Corn Chowder Garnished with Roasted Red Bell
    Pepper
Cream of Mushroom Soup Finished with Sherry
Cream of Tomato and Sweet Red Bell Pepper Soup
Fresh Corn Soup in Light Creamy Broth
    Accented with Cumin
Gingered Creamy Carrot Bisque
Lean Turkey Ball Soup with Garbanzo Beans and
    Vegetables
Mushroom, Beef, and Barley Soup
Oriental-Style Vegetable Egg Drop Soup
Shrimp Ball Soup with Vegetables
Split Pea Soup Laced with Spinach
Thick Vegetarian Minestrone Soup
Whole Wheat Chicken Noodle Soup with
    Vegetables

Sauces

Chicken Gravy Thickened with Blended
    Vegetables
Italian-Style Tomato Sauce

Low-Fat White Sauce (Medium Consistency)
Low-Fat White Sauce (light consistency)
Low-Fat White Sauce (heavy consistency)

Low-Fat Cheddar Cheese Sauce
Low-Fat Creamy Onion Sauce
Low-Fat Creamy Shrimp Sauce
Low-Fat Mustard Sauce
Low-Fat Swiss Cheese Sauce
Mushroom Sauce Thickened with Pureed
　　Vegetables
Tomato Coulis Seasoned with Garlic and Basil
Vegetable-Thickened Vodka Sauce

African-Style Spicy Hot Sauce
Cranberry Pineapple Relish
Fresh Mint and Cilantro Chutney
Fresh Tomato Salsa Seasoned with Cilantro and
　　Chilies
Homestyle Chunky Peanut Butter
Hot Red Chili Sauce
Lime Ginger-Garlic Sauce

Papaya Mango Salsa
Spicy Red Pepper Tomato Sauce
Sweet Spring Roll Sauce
Tomato Bell Pepper Salsa
Tomato Cucumber Relish
Tomato Relish Embellished with Fresh Basil and
　　Garlic
Vietnamese-Style Dipping Sauce
Whipped Creamy Cranberry Spread
Zesty Freshly Grated Horseradish and Yogurt
　　Sauce with Dillweed

All-American Barbecue Sauce for Fowl
Indian-Inspired Spice Blend
Orange-Rosemary Mustard Rub
Pineapple Yogurt Pepper Sauce
Red Wine Marinade for Game
Spicy Cajun-Style Seasoning Blend

Meat

Beef Cubes Braised in Mustard Beer Sauce
Beef Patties Studded with Pickled Beets and Capers
Beef Round Roast and Vegetables Braised in Red
　　Wine Broth
Cajun-Style Roast Tenderloin of Beef
Extra-Lean Ground Beef Burgers with Onions,
　　Bell Peppers, and Worcestershire
Flank Steak Topped with Mushrooms and Green
　　Onions
Homestyle Beef Stew Laden with Chunky Winter
　　Vegetables
Marinated Spicy Pot Roast with Gingersnap Gravy
Philippine-Style Spring Rolls Filled with Beef,
　　Tofu, and Shrimp
Sauteed Beef Tenderloin Strips in Stroganoff-
　　Style Sauce
Sauteed Beef Sirloin Steak Napped with Spicy
　　Red Pepper Tomato Sauce
Stir-Fried Strips of Beef Tenderloin in Soy Glaze

African-Inspired Lamb Stew with Vegetables and
　　Couscous
Broiled Herb-Marinated Leg of Lamb
Grilled Lamb Kebabs in Apricot Glaze
Roasted Leg of Lamb Seasoned with Ginger,
　　Mint, and Lemon

Rolled Leg of Lamb Roasted with Mint
Spicy Lamb Stew with Potatoes and Spinach in
　　Tomato Broth
Zucchini Slices Layered with Ground Lamb and
　　Cheese Sauce Moussaka-Style

Braised Pork Cubes Seasoned with Paprika
　　Finished with Yogurt Goulash-Style
Breaded Pork Cutlets with Mozzarella Cheese
　　Filling
Citrus-Flavored Pan Broiled Pork Chops
Lemon-Scented Grilled Pork Chops Seasoned
　　with Sage
Oriental-Inspired Roasted Pork Tenderloin
Pork Tenderloin Cubes in Soy and Sherry Glaze
　　with Green Onions
Pork Tenderloin Stuffed with Raisin and Ripe
　　Olive Studded Brown Rice
Roasted Tenderloin of Pork Seasoned with
　　Crushed Fennel Seeds

Roasted Veal Sirloin Napped with Vegetable-
　　Thickened Vodka Sauce
Veal Shanks Braised in Mediterranean-Style
　　Tomato Sauce

Poultry

Cajun Turkey-Tofu Burgers
Mini Turkey Balls with Hints of Allspice
  Turkey Balls with Hints of Allspice Braised in
  Pan Gravy
Sliced Moist Turkey Breast Napped with Creamy
  Cranberry-Enriched Sauce
Stuffed Bell Peppers Layered with Ground
  Turkey, Brown Rice, and Mozzarella Cheese
Tamale Casserole with Cornmeal Crust And
  Ground Turkey Filling
Turkey Tacos with Low-Fat Cheese and Fresh
  Tomato Bell Pepper Salsa

All-American Barbecue-Style Chicken
Chicken Breasts Braised in Tomato Port Wine
  Sauce
Chicken Breast Cubes Simmered in Creamy
  Coconut Sauce
Chicken Breasts Seasoned with Paprika, Braised
  Hungarian-Style

Chicken Breasts and Celery Seasoned with Fresh
  Herbs, Slowly Braised with Garlic Cloves
Chicken Croquettes Topped with Mushroom-
  Filled Sauce
Chicken Thighs in Crispy Cinnamon Crust
Chicken Thighs Simmered in Chunky Tomato
  Sauce with Mushrooms and Bell Peppers
Crispy Baked Mustard Chicken Breast
Grilled Chicken Drumsticks Tandoori-Style
Oregano Seasoned Chicken Breasts Topped with
  Melted Mozzarella Cheese
Spit-Roasted Chicken on the Rotisserie
  Oven-Roasted Chicken

Asian-Inspired Broiled Cornish Game Hens
Rabbit Braised in Chunky Tomato Wine Sauce
  Seasoned with Fresh Rosemary
Roasted Breast Of Guinea Hen Infused with Madeira
Roasted Farm-Raised Venison Napped with
  Mushroom-Filled Sauce

Fish and Shellfish

Crispy Crusted Orange-Scented Sole Fillets
Mackerel in Soy-Ginger Glaze Baked en Papillote
Marinated Broiled Shark Fillets Garnished with
  Papaya Mango Salsa
Red Snapper Simmered in Tomato Sauce
  Veracruz-Style
Salmon Baked in Parchment on a Bed of
  Vegetables with Fresh Tarragon
Shark and Vegetable Kabob Broiled with
  Pineapple Yogurt Pepper Sauce
Spicy Catfish with Garlic and Cilantro
  Corn bread Topping

Steamed Whole Sea Bass with Black Bean Sauce
Swordfish Steaks in Chunky Tomato Sauce
Yellowfin Tuna Burgers Coated with Teriyaki
  Ginger Glaze

Asian-Style Steamed Squid on a Bed of Shredded
  Lettuce
Barbecued Spicy Coconut Shrimp
Crab Cakes Peppered with Roasted Corn and
  Bell Peppers
Mediterranean-Inspired Shrimp

Dried Beans, Peas, Lentils, and Vegetables

Black Bean Patties Topped with Tomato Bell
  Pepper Salsa
Freshly Fried Pinto Beans Simmered in Broth
Garbanzo Beans in Ginger Sauce
Jamaican-Style Brown Rice and Kidney Beans
Kidney Beans Simmered in Spicy Tomato Broth
  Garnished with Bell Peppers, Carrots, and
  Celery
Pink Lentils Seasoned with a Roasted Blend of Spices

Pinto Beans Simmered in Vegetable
  Broth
Puerto Rican-Style Black Beans
Red Kidney Beans with Indian Seasonings
Smooth Lentil Sandwich Spread Seasoned with
  Asian Spices
Split Mung Beans Laced with Cauliflower and
  Spinach
Three Bean, Lentil, and Pea Stew

Baby Carrots in Fruit Glaze with Apple Slices
Beets Glazed in Orange and Red Wine Vinegar Sauce
Cauliflower Florets Coated with Cilantro and
    Onions
Cauliflower Stir-Fried with Tomatoes Accented
    with Turmeric, Ginger, and Cilantro
Citrus-Glazed Carrots Sprinkled with Minced
    Parsley
Corn-Stuffed Zucchini with Melted Cheese and
    Oat Flake Topping
Crispy Crusted Baked Eggplant
Greens with Freshly Ground Peanuts
Grilled Corn on the Cob
    Boiled Corn on the Cob
    Steamed Corn on the Cob
    Oven-Steamed Corn on the Cob
    Fresh Grilled, Boiled, Steamed, or Oven-
        Steamed Cream-Style Corn
Medley of Stir-Fried Vegetables

Sherried Chunky Puree of Green Peas
Shredded Green Cabbage and Apples Accented
    with Cinnamon
Sliced Gingered Orange Beets
Smoky Eggplant Puree Seasoned with Green
    Chilies
Snow Peas Stir-Fried with Bamboo Shoots and
    Shiitake Mushrooms
Spicy Coconut-Flavored Stir-Fried Vegetables
Stir-Fried Broccoli with Wine, Soy Sauce, and
    Ginger
Sweet Chunky Corn Cake
Sweet Potato Patties with Hints of Orange
Toasted Sesame Green Beans
Tomatoes Stuffed with Zucchini and Carrots
    Laced with Cheese
Zucchini, Bell Peppers, and Tomatoes Stewed
    with Turkey Ham
Zucchini Sauteed with Tomatoes and Herbs

Potatoes, Grains, and Pastas

Baked Russet Potatoes
    Baked Sweet Potatoes
Cheesy Mashed Potatoes with Green Onions
Creamy Garlic Sliced Potatoes
Golden Potato Slices in Cheese Custard
Italian Seasoned Potatoes Baked in Parchment
Mashed Golden Buttermilk Potatoes
Mashed Potato Pancakes Accented with Onion
    and Garlic
New Red Potatoes Adorned with Parsley and
    Chives
Onion-Flavored Mashed Potatoes
Oven-Roasted Potato Wedges Seasoned with
        Rosemary
    Oven-Roasted Garlic-Seasoned Potato Wedges
Potato Boats Stuffed with Cheesy Buttermilk
    Mashed Potatoes, Studded With Diced Bell
    Peppers
Potato Cubes Sauteed with Ginger, Garlic, and
    Fennel Seeds
Potatoes Speckled with Turkey Bacon and
    Seasoned with Rosemary
Sliced Potatoes Layered with Onions

Barley Risotto Garnished with Exotic Mushrooms
    and Spinach
Boiled Brown Basmati Rice
Brown Rice Simmered in Tomato Broth
Buckwheat Corn Bread, Spinach, and Ham Stuffing

Couscous Seasoned with Fresh Ginger and Soy
Crunchy Triticale Sprinkled with Dried Peaches
Fried Brown Rice Beaming with Vegetables
Paella-Style Brown Rice Strewn with Chicken,
    Seafood, and Vegetables
Spicy Brown Rice Pilaf Peppered with Bell
    Peppers, Celery, and Onions
Turmeric-Flavored Brown Rice Simmered with
    Tomatoes
Whole Grain Granola with Sunflower Seeds,
    Cashews, Almonds, Dried Apricots, and
    Raisins
Whole Grain Oat Porridge Flavored with
    Cinnamon and Cardamom
Wild Pecan Rice Speckled with Raisins and
    Vegetables
Wild Rice Embellished with Exotic Mushrooms
    and Toasted Almonds
Wild Rice Studded with Blueberries and Shiitake
    Mushrooms

Carrot-Flavored Angel Hair Pasta Pancakes
    Spotted with Bell Peppers
Macaroni Layered with Ground Turkey in Red
    Wine Mushroom Sauce
Manicotti Tubes Filled with Spinach,
    Mushrooms, and Cheeses, Covered with
    Tomato Sauce
Orzo Pilaf Flavored with Cloves and Cinnamon

Penne Pasta Baked in a Creamy Cheddar and
Swiss Cheese Sauce
Spinach Almond Lasagne with Whole Wheat
Noodles

Translucent Noodles, Beef, and Vegetables in
Soy Glaze
Whole Wheat Spaghetti Tossed with Lightly
Sauteed Vegetables

Salads and Dressings

Beefalo and Shrimp Thai-Style Cellophane
Noodle Salad
Cashew Chicken Salad with Grapes and Water
Chestnuts
Hot Potato, Sausage, and Broccoli Salad
Oriental Chicken Salad with Orange-Pineapple
Soy Dressing

Broccoli Marinated in Rice Wine Vinaigrette
Bulgur Salad Peppered with Garden Vegetables
Cucumbers and Onions Marinated in Sweet and
Sour Dill Dressing
Diced Cucumber, Red Onion, and Tomato Salad
Green Salad Tossed with Vegetables and Dressed
with Saffron and Basil Orange Vinaigrette
Grilled Summer Vegetable Salad
Jicama and Orange Salad Splashed with Freshly
Squeezed Lime Juice and a Sprinkle of Chili
Powder
Potato, Kidney Bean, and Bell Pepper Salad in
Oil-Free Vinaigrette
Quinoa Salad Decorated with Pineapple,
Mandarin Oranges, and Water Chestnuts
Red Beets Pickled German-Style
Shredded Cabbage with Corn and Bell Pepper
Tossed in Pineapple Tofu Dressing
Soba Noodle Salad Tossed with Red and Yellow
Bell Peppers, Snow Peas, Carrots,
Mushrooms, and Water Chestnuts
Spinach and Red Leaf Lettuce Dressed with
Walnut Vinaigrette
Vegetable Slaw Coated in Ranch-Style Dressing

Fresh Fruit Salad Tossed with Beets, Pomegranate
Seeds, and Roasted Peanuts
Fresh Peaches and Grapes Waldorf-
Style
Malaysian-Inspired Tropical Fruit and Crisp
Vegetable Salad

Naturally Sweet Fresh Fruit Medley
Pineapple Cubes, Orange Sections, and Jicama
Strips Glazed with Orange Pineapple Soy
Dressing

Basil and Garlic Scented Extra-Virgin Olive Oil
Chervil- and Other Tender Herb-Scented
Canola Oils
Orange- and Ginger-Flavored Safflower Oil
Garlic-Flavored Oil
Herb-Flavored Oil
Horseradish-Flavored Oil
Shallot-Flavored Oil
Raspberry-Infused White Wine Vinegar
Blackberry-Infused White Wine Vinegar
Blueberry-Infused White Wine Vinegar
Peach-Infused White Wine Vinegar
Pear-Infused White Wine Vinegar
Strawberry-Infused White Wine Vinegar
Rosemary- and Thyme-Infused White Wine
Vinegar
Rosemary-, Thyme-, and Garlic-Infused Red
Wine Vinegar

Asian-Inspired Lime Dressing
Balsamic-Rice Vinegar Dressing
Citrus-Flavored Cranberry Vinaigrette
Creamy-Peach Poppy Seed Dressing
Freshly Squeezed Lime and Vegetable Dressing
Nonfat Creamy Curry Dressing
Oil-Free Mayonnaise-Like Dressing
Orange Pineapple Soy Salad Dressing
Pineapple-Flavored Creamy Tofu Dressing
Ranch-Style Salad Dressing
Raspberry-Infused Honey Vinaigrette Dressing
Rice Wine Vinaigrette
Saffron and Basil Orange Vinaigrette Dressing
Sesame-Flavored Ginger Soy Dressing
Vegetable-Thickened Oil-Free Vinaigrette
Walnut-Flavored Vinaigrette Dressing

Egg and Cheese Dishes

Broccoli Timbales Enhanced with Swiss Cheese
Fiesta Scrambled Eggs
Spinach Mushroom Souffle

Bean- and Cheese-Filled Whole Wheat Tortillas
Fresh Low-Fat Milk Paneer Cheese
    Fresh Low-Fat Milk Chenna Cheese
Fresh Nonfat Milk White Cheese

Fresh Nonfat Yogurt Cheese
    Thickened Yogurt Flavored with Fresh Herbs
Green Peas and Fresh Cheese in Tomato Sauce
Spinach and Swiss Cheese Phyllo Strudel
    Broccoli, Corn, and Cheddar Cheese Phyllo
        Strudel
Toasted Open-Face Swiss Cheese Sandwich with
    Tomatoes and Caraway

Hors d'Oeuvres and Beverages

Crispy Whole Wheat Cheese Wafers
Cucumber Slices with Fresh Mint and Cilantro
    Chutney Sandwiches
Gingered Apricot Farm-Raised Venison Jerky
Ginger Sesame Chicken Wings
Grilled Portobello Mushrooms Glazed with Herb
    Marinade
Mushrooms Stuffed with a Chunky Mixture of
    Sauteed Fresh Vegetables
Roasted Corn Tortilla Chips
Roasted Idaho Potato Chips
    Cajun-Style Roasted Potato Chips
    Roasted Parsnip, Sweet Potato, or Yam Chips
Stone-Ground Whole Wheat Caraway Pretzels
Toasted Mustard Rounds

Buttermilk Sour Cream Potato
    Topping

Cannellini Bean Dip Adorned with Green
    Onions, Bell Peppers, and Tomatoes
Chili Cheese Dip with Tomatoes and Onions
Fruit-Sweetened Nonfat Strawberry Yogurt
    Strewn with Strawberry Chunks
    Nonfat Plain Yogurt
    Other Fruit-Flavored Nonfat Yogurt
Guacamole-Like Avacado Dip with Diced Red,
    Yellow, and Green Bell Peppers
Ranch-Style Chip Dip
Roasted Elephant Garlic

Chardonnay and Cranberry Spritzer
Freshly Prepared Spicy Tomato Cocktail
Spicy Minted Orange Iced Tea
Strawberry, Banana, and Kiwi Orange Shake

Breads, Cakes, Frostings, and Sweet Sauces

Angel Spice Cake
    Candy Cane Angel Cake
    Cocoa Angel Cake
    Coffee-Flavored Angel Spice Cake
    Licorice-Flavored Angel Cake
    Vanilla Angel Cake
    Angel Spice Cupcakes
    Fruit-Filled Angel Cake
Apple Crumb Cake
Banana Apricot Whole Wheat Cake with No
    Added Fat
Banana Bran Walnut Muffins
Buckwheat Stone-Ground Yellow Corn Bread
Carrot, Raisin, and Pineapple Whole Wheat
    Cake
Cornmeal Cake with Anise and Cinnamon
Cranberry Orange-Flavored Upside Down Cake

Gingerbread Cake Topped with Bananas
Hot Fudge Pudding Cake
Low-Fat and Low-Cholesterol Chocolate Cake
Peach Meringue Mousse Cake
Pumpkin Whole Wheat Pancakes
Whole Wheat and Onion Sage Drop Biscuits
Whole Wheat French Bread

Apple Syrup Flavored with Calvados
Apricot-Flavored Powdered Sugar Frosting
Buckwheat Honey Glaze
Butterscotch Sauce
Chilled Apricots in Light Fruit Juice Syrup
    Apricot Puree from Dried Fruit
Creamy Light Cheese Frosting
Date Puree
    Dried Plum and Raisin Purees

Fruit-Sweetened Strawberry Sauce
Granny Smith and McIntosh Applesauce
Naturally Sweetened Raspberry Sauce
Orange Fruit Glaze
Orange-Pineapple Yogurt Topping
Pineapple-Orange Flavored Seven-Minute
    Frosting

Pureed Fresh Pineapple Sauce
    Fresh Pineapple Juice
Raspberry Glaze Finished with Kirsch
Rhubarb Sauce with a Splash of Orange
Thick and Fluffy Maple Cooked Frosting
    Thick and Fluffy Flavored Frosting
Yogurt Honey Topping Dashed with Almond

Cookies, Bars, Pies, and Pastries

Apricot and Coconut Wheat Flake Cereal
    Bonbons
Candied Orange Zests
Crisp Spiced Ginger Cookies
Honey-Baked Whole Grain Bread Strips in
    Custard Coating
Little Almond Meringue Bites
Orange-Scented Custard Strips

Chocolate Meringue Shells
    Chocolate Meringue Sticks
Feathery Light Crepes
Graham Cracker Crust
    Vanilla or Chocolate Wafer Crusts
    Gingersnap, presweetened flaked or puffed type
        cereal, or toasted cake or muffin crusts
    Flaked or puffed type cereal or toasted
        unsweetened bread crumb crusts
Meringue Pastry Shells
Philippine-Style Spring Roll Wrappers
Phyllo Pastry Tart

Reduced-Fat and Cholesterol-Free Oat Pastry
    Crust

Baked Banana-Strawberry Alaska
Blueberry Dessert Topped with Oat Pastry
    Lattice-Style
    Blackberry, Currant, Gooseberry,
        Huckleberry, Loganberry, Raspberry, or
        Strawberry Dessert Topped with Oat Pastry
        Lattice-Style
    Berry-Filled Angel Cake
Fresh Fruit Melange Coated with Mimosa Sauce
    in Phyllo Pastry Shell
Hot Peach Tart on Oat Crust
Lemon Chiffon Angel Pie
Meringue-Topped Key Lime Pie
Meringue Topping for Pie
Old-Fashioned Pumpkin Pie in Oat Crust
Raspberry Snow Tart
Reduced-Fat Pumpkin Cheesecake in a Graham
    Cracker Crust

Puddings, Frozen, and Fruit Desserts

Baked Banana Whole Grain Bread Pudding
Baked Brown Rice Pudding Studded with Dried
    Cherries
Sweet Potato Whole Grain Bread Pudding

Apricot Frozen Yogurt Sweetened with Fruit
    Juice
Banana Split with Frozen Yogurt and
    Butterscotch Sauce
Chunky Pineapple Sherbet
Frozen Banana Bonbons
Frozen Banana-Strawberry Yogurt
Frozen Raspberry Popsicles
Papaya Banana Popsicles

Smooth Freshly Prepared Low-Fat Peach Sherbet
Tropical Mango Sorbet Sweetened with Fruit
    Juice
    Kiwi Sorbet Sweetened with Fruit Juice
    Strawberry Sorbet Sweetened with Fruit Juice

Apple and Currant Phyllo Strudel
    Apricot and Raisin Phyllo Strudel
    Cherry Phyllo Strudel
Apple Crisp with Raisins and Crumbly Oat
    Topping
Baked Bananas Coated in Graham Cracker
    Crumbs with Orange-Pineapple Yogurt
    Topping

Baked Peaches Stuffed with Grape Nuts and Walnuts
Berries Encased in Angel Cake
Cantaloupe Balls Laced with Ouzo
Glazed Apples Rolled in Feathery Light Crepes
Honeydew Melon Garnished with Ginger

Oranges, Cherries, and Raspberries Layered in
    Cherry-Flavored Syrup
Steamed Pears with Cinnamon and Honey
Sweet Cherry Crepes with Vanilla Frozen Yogurt
Warm Fruit-Sweetened Apricot Souffle

Preface

Now, more than ever before, Americans are interested in eating healthfully when dining out. At the same time, they want good-for-you food to be satisfying and appealing. The collection of recipes that I have created for this book will allow you to offer your guests lighter and healthier menu choices.

The six nutritional factors about which diners often express concern when eating away from home are:

1. Reducing the amount of total fat, saturated fat, and cholesterol.
2. Increasing the amount of complex carbohydrates and fiber.
3. Controlling sodium/salt.
4. Reducing the amount of sugar.
5. Moderating the amount of protein, with an emphasis on non-red-meat sources.
6. Controlling the amount of calories.

This book offers 400 healthier recipes designed to address these concerns. The recipes were developed also to serve as training tools for food service professionals seeking to offer more healthful selections on their menus. They may be used in food service operations in the exact form listed in this text; modified as appropriate to meet the needs of specific customer bases, following the substitution suggestions in Appendices 1 through 4; or simply provide inspiration for the creation of more healthful dishes in your own personal style. Each recipe is introduced with a few words about its features. Descriptions of healthy cooking ingredients are offered in recipes or the Glossary. Healthy cooking procedures, sources for healthy cooking ingredients, and healthy cooking tools, equipment, and sources are listed in recipes or Appendices 5, 6, and 7. A basic understanding of professional cooking is assumed.

Healthful food has gained a reputation for being tasteless and boring. This does not need to be the case. My criteria in developing the recipes for the dishes in this book were (1) that they be truly delicious and (2) that they be of a quality that would make guests want to return for more. The nutritional attributes were considered to be an added benefit.

These recipes were tested in three food service operations at California State Polytechnic University in Pomona, California—the Restaurant at Kellogg Ranch in the School of Hotel and Restaurant Management, Kellogg West Conference Center, and Los Olivos dining center. Several of the recipes were adapted from creations of Cal Poly Hotel and Restaurant Management student research assistants. Cal Poly student research assistants also assisted in the nutritional analyses and testing of the recipes. Individuals are recognized in the specific recipes for their contributions.

Most of the recipes are designed to serve 24. They include selections from appetizers, soups, and main course dishes to sauces, salads, starches, vegetables, and desserts. This collection includes many dishes with strong ethnic influences, and many inspired by the cuisine served in mainstream America. Some of the dishes are representative of contemporary California fare. The choices of ingredients range from ones readily available in the supermarket to some more easily found in ethnic or health-oriented food stores. Sources are suggested in cases where ingredients may need to be ordered or special purveyors sought out.

Each of the recipes is accompanied by its nutritional profile per serving: the nutritional chart provided with every recipe includes the amounts of

- calories
- protein (in grams and percentages)
- fat (in grams and percentages)
- carbohydrates (in grams and percentages)
- alcohol (in grams and percentages)
- fiber (in grams)
- cholesterol (in milligrams)
- sodium (in milligrams)

The values have been rounded. A note of caution: when modifications are made in the recipes or amounts of ingredients vary from those specified, the nutrition analysis will no longer be accurate and must be adjusted to indicate the changes.

Acknowledgments

The recipes in this book are the result of five years of development, testing and tasting, retesting and tasting, and retesting and tasting again and again, with ongoing nutrition analyses. There is only one word for the hard work of the many talented, creative, and diligent Cal Poly Hotel and Restaurant Management student research assistants who have participated in this project—awesome! I thank them all for their contributions: Tim Allison, Chris Carlson, Jackson Chuang, Chris Cuffari, Gary Dahl, Shelley Doonan, Sondra Dreis, Jeff Durham, Kathy Farnsworth, Paul Findly, Karen Fitzgerald, Christine Garboski, Leticia Gonzales, Cheryl Goodrich, Sean Grovier, Jeff Haines, Amber Ingram, Terry Jackson, Muliati Jeniawati, Katie Kehoe, Blair Kerley, KC Knauer, Brian Knirk, Diane Knirk, Anita Laksana, Bibi Leung, Derin Lewis, Genevieve Lorenzo, Rajeev Maini, Stacy Medrano, Lisa Milton, Karen Moses, Victoria Mylne, Kelly Potter, Saijai (April) Pradipnathalang, Alicia Rowan, Susan Serdarusich, Richard Shea, Will Soper, Byron Takeuchi, Vicki Tan, Amelia Toy, Robert Trummeter, Michele Tune, Sheri Yamasaki, Ira Widjojo, Paula Zahursky.

I also thank my husband and colleague, Professor Tarun Kapoor, for his suggestions and advice throughout the many stages of recipe development, and our friend and colleague, Professor Gary Hamilton, for tasting and retasting the recipes. In order to receive the approval of this pair's very critical and sensitive palates, it had to be good.

I am most appreciative of Jim Falconer and his staff at the Los Olivos Dining Center, Michael Casner and his staff at the Cal Poly Kellogg West Conference Center, and the faculty and students in the Restaurant at Kellogg Ranch, for sponsoring evaluation of the recipes in their facilities. The administration and staff of the School of Hotel and Restaurant Management and California State Polytechnic University have been most supportive of this project over the past six years.

I am indebted to the colleagues who reviewed hundreds of pages of manuscript and whose comments made the final product better: Professor Robert H. Bosselman, of the William F. Harrah College of Hotel Administration at the University of Nevada Las Vegas; Professor Nancy Graves, of the Hilton College of Hotel and Restaurant Management at the University of Houston; and especially Chef Stephen C. Fernald, Director of Education, the Educational Institute of the American Culinary Federation, for his very attentive commentary on the manuscript.

Finally, thank you to my editor Claire Thompson at Wiley for believing in the project.

SANDY KAPOOR

Pomona, California

September 1995

Introduction

Computing Nutrients in Recipes

Measuring Ingredients

Healthy cooking requires all ingredients to be carefully measured as specified in each recipe and for recipes to be divided into the number of servings indicated if nutrition analyses per serving are to be accurate.

Recipe ingredient lists describe how ingredients should be cut, whether peeled or washed, if any parts have been removed, and any other prepreparation required before being measured. For good product results and to provide correct nutrient information, the ingredients in recipes should be measured in the form listed. For example, if an ingredient in a recipe is listed as carrots, coarsely chopped, washed, and trimmed, the carrots should be weighed after trimming and chopping. Similarly, when 1 pound of skinless chicken drumsticks is listed as an ingredient, the drumsticks should be weighed after their skins have been removed.

In those cases where the amount of an ingredient is listed with its weight or measure followed by the words "as purchased," "canned," or "drained," weigh or measure the ingredient in the form specified. After weighing or measuring the ingredient, complete any prepreparation directions given in its description. For example, if an ingredient is listed in a recipe as

garbanzo beans, canned,
drained, rinsed with water 5 lb drained

the amount required in the recipe is 5 pounds of canned, drained garbanzo beans. *After* the garbanzo beans are weighed, they should be rinsed with water.

Dry ingredients are listed by weight in ounces and pounds unless the amount is less than one ounce, and liquid ingredients are listed by volume measures, teaspoons, tablespoons, cups, pints, quarts, and gallons. Weights of dry ingredients should be measured with a scale, preferably an electronic scale, and volumes of liquid ingredients should be measured with the appropriate measuring containers. Ingredients listed by weight often do not weigh and measure the same. For example, 8 ounces of bread flour by weight measures 2 cups (16 fluid ounces), not 1 cup (8 fluid ounces).

In recipes where an ingredient is required more than one time, it is generally listed only once in the ingredient list followed by (divided). For example, in a fresh corn soup, if the ingredient list calls for

corn, kernels, fresh or frozen
(divided) 4 lb

it might specify in the recipe's directions to puree 8 ounces of the corn kernels in step 1 and in a later step to simmer the remaining $3\frac{1}{2}$ pounds of corn kernels in broth with vegetables and seasoning agents.

Abbreviations

The following abbreviations are used in this book.

alc	alcohol
C	centrigrade
c	cup
cal	calories
carb	carbohydrate
chol	cholesterol
F	fahrenheit
fib	fiber (dietary)
fl oz	fluid ounce
gal	gallon
g	gram

in.	inch
lb	pound
mg	milligram
prot	protein
oz	ounce
%	percent
pt	pint
qt	quart
sat fat	saturated fat
T	tablespoon
t	teaspoon

Ingredient Specifications

Unless specified, herbs and produce are fresh and of high quality and spices should be freshly ground. If dried herbs are substituted for fresh, about one-third the fresh amount can be used, but for best results, dishes should be tasted and seasonings added accordingly. When freshly ground spices are replaced with commercially ground ones, they should be purchased within the previous 6 months and stored in tightly covered containers in a cool, dry environment.

Likewise, bread crumbs are fresh unless specified otherwise. To prepare bread crumbs, process bread with its crusts in a food processor or blender until fine crumbs are formed.

No artificial sweeteners and limited ingredients which have been modified in fat, calories, sugar, and fiber are used in the recipes in this book. These products vary greatly between manufacturers. Modified ingredients which are widely accepted by health-conscious diners and readily available such as nonfat and low-fat dairy products, including milk and yogurt and some cheeses, are used in the recipes.

Lower grade cuts of meat contain less fat than higher grade ones. The dishes in this book are prepared with choice grade meats. The fat, cholesterol, and calories in dishes can be reduced further by replacing the choice grade cuts with lower grade ones, such as select grade beef. Similarly, substituting higher grade (prime) meats for the choice grade meats will increase the fat, cholesterol, and calories in dishes.

When lean beef is specified in a recipe, select a cut with less than 8 grams of fat and 180 calories per 3-ounce trimmed, cooked portion. Six cuts of beef that meet these criteria are: eye of round, top round, tenderloin, round tip, top loin, and sirloin.

In recipes that call for lean pork cuts, select those that contain less than 9 grams of fat and 190 calories per 3-ounce trimmed, cooked portion. Eight cuts of pork that meet these criteria are: tenderloin, boneless sirloin chop, rib chop, center loin chop, boneless loin roast, boneless top loin chop, sirloin roast, and boneless rib roast.

When a recipe specifies lean lamb, select a cut with less than 200 calories per 3-ounce trimmed, cooked portion. Six cuts of lamb that meet these criteria are: shank half leg roast, sirloin roast, loin chops, blade chops, foreshank, and rack (back).

When the type of fish specified in a recipe is not available, the chart opposite will help identify possible substitutions.

The following are tart or slightly acidic apple varieties which may be used in baked dishes like pies or stewed and pureed dishes such as applesauce when the specified tart apple variety is not available or simply calls for a tart apple: Cortland (red), Gravenstein (yellow-green with red stripes), Granny Smith (green), Grimes Golden (gold), Jonathan (brilliant red), McIntosh (red to green), Newton Pippin (green), Northern Spy (red), Rhode Island Greening (green), Stayman (red), Winesap (red), and York Imperial (red).

The following are varieties of chilies commonly marketed in the United States, including their level of heat and most available purchase forms: Anaheim (mild; fresh); ancho (slightly hot to hot; dried); habanero (extremely hot; fresh); hontaka (very pungent; dried); jalapeno (hot; in cans, jars, and sometimes fresh); pasilla (moderately hot; dried); pequin—also called tepin, chiltecpin, chiltepin, bird pepper, or chili bravo (very hot to extremely hot; dried and in bottles); poblano (usually mild, occasionally hot; fresh and in cans); serrano (hot; fresh and in cans); yellow wax—also called Hungarian wax (mildly piquant to very pungent; usually fresh in fall). If the type of chili recommended in a recipe is not available, replace with a similar flavored one.

Nutrient Needs

The new food labels identify these amounts as daily goals for the following nutrients.

Cholesterol	less than 300 milligrams
Fat	less than 65 grams per 2000 calories
Carbohydrate	300 grams per 2000 calories
Fiber	25 grams per 2000 calories
Sodium	less than 2,400 milligrams

In percentage form, nutritionists recommend less than 30% of calories from fat, 12–15% from protein, and 55–60% from carbohydrates. Alcohol is recommended only in moderation. These recommendations can be used as guidelines when planning healthy menu selections.

TABLE I

Common Fresh Fish*

Fish	Water	Fat†	Texture/Flavor
Abalone	Salt	Lean	Rubbery, sweet
Bass, Black	Fresh	Lean	Firm, mild
Bass, Striped	Salt	Moderately fatty	Medium firm, mild
Black Sea Bass	Salt	Moderately fatty	Firm, mild
Catfish	Fresh	Moderately fatty	Medium firm, sweet
Cod	Salt	Lean	Firm white flesh, delicate, mild, sweet
Flounder	Salt	Lean	Firm, mild
Grouper	Salt	Lean	Firm, mild
Haddock	Salt	Lean	Softer flesh than Atlantic cod, mild, sweet
Halibut	Salt	Lean	Medium firm, mild, sweet
Mackerel	Salt	Fatty	Flaky, flesh varies from white to red depending on species, strong
Mahimahi	Salt	Lean	Firm white flesh, mild
Monkfish (also called cotte or anglerfish)	Salt	Lean	Very firm, succulent, lobster-like, sweet
Ocean Perch	Salt	Lean	Somewhat flaky, delicate
Orange Roughy	Salt	Lean	Medium firm, very mild
Pike	Fresh	Lean	Medium firm, flaky, sweet
Pompano	Salt	Fatty	Fine-texture, mild, delicate
Red Snapper	Salt	Lean	Medium firm, mild, sweet
Salmon	Salt	Fatty	Firm, distinctive
Scrod (Small cod—see cod)			
Shark	Salt	Lean	Firm, mild-flavored
Sole	Salt	Lean	Firm, sweet
Swordfish	Salt	Moderately fatty	Firm, mild
Trout, Rainbow	Fresh	Moderately fatty	Flaky, delicate
Tuna, Bluefin	Salt	Moderately fatty	Firm, distinctive
Tuna, Yellowfin	Salt	Moderately fatty	Firm, mildly distinctive
Whitefish	Fresh	Fatty	Firm white flesh, delicate, sweet, nutty
Yellowtail Snapper	Salt	Lean	Medium firm, fine texture, sweet

*Adapted from J. Rosso and S. Lukins, *The New Basics Cookbook*. New York: Workman Publishing, 1989.
†Fish are categorized in this chart as lean (under 2% fat), moderately fatty (2–6% fat), or fatty (over 6% fat).

Calorie Needs

A quick estimate of calorie needs can be made by multiplying weight by the factor 15. For example, a 200-pound person would require about 3,000 calories per day to maintain his/her current weight.

$$200 \text{ lbs} \times 15 = 3,000 \text{ calories}$$

How Recipes Fulfill Nutrient Recommendations

Not all the recipes in this book match the recommended nutrient guidelines. It is assumed that a combination of dishes and foods will be eaten in the course of a day. The goal is to achieve the recommended balance of nutrients from all the meals and snacks consumed throughout the day.

When recipes do not meet the recommended guidelines, the dishes in meals should be combined with foods which help to achieve this goal. For example, while a main course meat dish may exceed the 30% fat recommendation and contain cholesterol, by serving it with low-fat, cholesterol-free vegetable and grain side dishes, the percentages of fat and cholesterol in the combination drop to acceptable levels.

Recipe Nutrient Analysis

Each recipe has been analyzed for calories, grams of protein, fat, carbohydrates, dietary fiber, and alcohol, and milligrams of cholesterol and sodium per serving. The percentages of fat, carbohydrates, protein, and alcohol per serving are also listed.

The calorie and nutrient breakdown of each recipe is derived from computer analysis (The Food Processor R Plus; Version 5.0; ESHA Research, P.O. Box 13028, Salem, OR 97309). The program gathered its information primarily from the U.S. Department of Agriculture.

The calorie and nutrient values are as accurate as possible. The following assumptions were made:

♦ Dishes were prepared with only the ingredients itemized in the ingredient lists. In the event more or less of a listed ingredient is used or an ingredient has been eliminated from or added to a recipe, the nutrition analysis for the dish will not reflect these adjustments.

- Calories and nutrient values are listed per serving.
- The serving size was designed to reflect the way a health-conscious person eats, common portion size, or in some cases, the amount of product resulting when the recipe is evenly divided by 24.
- Since a percentage of alcohol calories evaporates when heated, this reduction is estimated in the nutrient analysis.
- When products are marinated, their nutrient analysis reflects the amount estimated to have been absorbed.
- Garnishes and optional ingredients are not included in the nutrient analysis.
- When a dash denotes an ingredient's amount, for example, vegetable cooking spray, it is not included in the nutrient analysis.
- When there is a range listed in the amount of an ingredient (e.g., 6–8 oz flour), the lesser amount is calculated in the nutrient analysis.
- When more than one ingredient is listed as an option, the nutrient analysis is conducted on the first ingredient listed.
- When the amount of an ingredient such as salt or pepper is listed as "To taste," the ingredient is not included in the nutrient analysis.
- In recipes containing raw meat, fish, or poultry, the nutritional analysis is conducted on either the raw weight or estimated cooked weight of the item.

Converting Recipes*

Unless you are working in an operation that uses only its own standardized recipes, you will very frequently be required to convert recipes to different amounts. For example, you may have a recipe for 24 portions of grilled chicken breast, but you need only 12 portions.

Converting recipes is a very important technique. It is a skill you will probably need to use many times in this book. There is no "best" yield to write recipes for, since every operation, every school, and every individual has different needs. (Please note, however, that when recipes are converted to different yields, the nutrient analyses will vary from those provided in this book.)

Nearly everyone instinctively can double a recipe or cut it in half. It seems more complicated, though, to change a recipe from 10 to 18 portions, say, or from 50 to 35. Actually, the principle is exactly the same: you multiply each ingredient by a number called a conversion factor, as follows:

*Adapted with permission from Wayne Gisslen, *Professional Cooking*, third edition, New York: John Wiley & Sons, Inc., 1995.

Procedure for Converting Total Yield

1. Divide the desired yield by the recipe yield:

$$\frac{\text{new yield}}{\text{old yield}} = \text{conversion factor}$$

2. Multiply each ingredient quantity by the conversion factor:

$$\text{conversion factor} \times \text{old quantity} = \text{new quantity}$$

In order to do this, you will usually have to convert all weights to ounces and all volumes to fluid ounces.

Example: You have a recipe for 10 portions of broccoli topped with low-fat cheese sauce requiring 3 lb broccoli and $2\frac{1}{2}$ c low-fat cheese sauce. Convert to 15 portions.

$$\frac{\text{new yield}}{\text{old yield}} = \frac{15}{10} = 1.5$$

Broccoli: 3 lb = 48 oz
$$48 \text{ oz} \times 1.5 = 72 \text{ oz} = 4\tfrac{1}{2} \text{ lb}$$
Sauce: $2\frac{1}{2}$ c = 20 fl oz
$$20 \text{ oz} \times 1.5 = 30 \text{ oz} = 3\tfrac{3}{4} \text{ c}$$

Procedure for Changing Portion Sizes

If your recipe yields, let's say, 24 4-oz portions, and you need 30 5-oz portions, you must add a few extra steps to the conversion process.

1. Determine total yield of the recipe by multiplying the number of portions by the portion size:

$$\text{portions} \times \text{portion size} = \text{total yield (old)}$$

2. Determine the total yield you desire by multiplying the desired number of portions by the desired portion size:

$$\text{desired portions} \times \text{desired portion size} = \text{total yield (new)}$$

3. Divide desired yield by recipe yield to get the conversion factor:

$$\frac{\text{total yield (new)}}{\text{total yield (old)}} = \text{conversion factor}$$

4. Multiply each ingredient by the conversion factor:

$$\text{conversion factor} \times \text{old quantity} = \text{new quantity}$$

Note: The conversion factor may sometimes turn out to be 1. In these cases the total yield is obviously the same, and the recipe does not need to be changed.

In order to make these procedures clearer, let's work through the conversion of a full recipe to give you practice with the equations.

In the first column that follows is a list of ingredients for a beef dish. As you can see, the quantities given in the second column are enough to make 24 portions at 8 oz each.

Beef tenderloin strips in stroganoff-style sauce
Portions: 24
Portion size: 8 oz

Beef tenderloin	6 lb
Mustard powder	1½ t
Pepper	To taste
Mushrooms	4 lb
Onions	2 lb
Garlic	1½ T
Veal stock	1¼ qt
Tomatoes	1 lb
White wine	½ c
Cornstarch	4 oz
Yogurt	1¼ qt
Nutmeg	¾ t
Salt	To taste

Let's say we need 54 portions instead of 24. To find the conversion factor, we divide the new yield by the old yield:

$$\frac{\text{new yield}}{\text{old yield}} = \frac{54}{24} = 2.25$$

To convert the recipe to 54 portions, we simply multiply each ingredient quantity by this conversion factor of 2.25.

First, to make this easier, we should change pounds to ounces, cups, pints, and quarts to fluid ounces. For example, to change the measurement for beef tenderloin to ounces, multiply 6 (the weight in pounds) by 16 (the number of ounces in a pound) to get 96 oz.

The equivalents we need for this recipe are as follows:

6 lb equals 96 oz
4 lb equals 64 oz
2 lb equals 32 oz
1 lb equals 16 oz
$1\frac{1}{4}$ qt equals 40 fl oz
$\frac{1}{2}$ c equals 4 fl oz

In Example 1, below, we have substituted these equivalent quantities. Then we have multiplied all the ingredient quantities by the conversion factor to get the quantities that we need for 54 portions. Check through all the calculations to make sure you follow them. The quantities for salt and pepper will still, of course, be indicated as "To taste."

Now let's suppose we want to find the quantities needed to give us 120 6-oz portions. Because the portion size changes, we must use the second procedure explained previously. First, to find the total yield of the old recipe, we multiply the number of portions by the portion size:

$$24 \text{ (portions)} \times 8 \text{ oz equals } 192 \text{ oz}$$

Do the same calculation for the desired yield:

$$120 \text{ (portions)} \times 6 \text{ oz equals } 720 \text{ oz}$$

EXAMPLE 1

Ingredient	Quantity	Times	Conversion Factor	Equals	New Quantity
Beef tenderloin	96 oz	×	2.25	=	216 oz or $13\frac{1}{2}$ lb
Mustard powder	$1\frac{1}{2}$ t	×	2.25	=	$3\frac{3}{8}$ t
Pepper	To taste	×	2.25	=	To taste
Mushrooms	64 oz	×	2.25	=	144 oz or 9 lb
Onions	32 oz	×	2.25	=	72 oz or $4\frac{1}{2}$ lb
Garlic	$1\frac{1}{2}$ T	×	2.25	=	$3\frac{3}{8}$ T
Veal stock	40 fl oz	×	2.25	=	90 fl oz or 2 qt + $3\frac{1}{4}$ c
Tomatoes	16 oz	×	2.25	=	36 oz or $2\frac{1}{4}$ lb
White wine	4 fl oz	×	2.25	=	9 fl oz or $1\frac{1}{8}$ c
Cornstarch	4 oz	×	2.25	=	9 oz
Yogurt	40 fl oz	×	2.25	=	90 fl oz or 2 qt + $3\frac{1}{4}$ c
Nutmeg	$\frac{3}{4}$ t	×	2.25	=	$1\frac{5}{8}$ t
Salt	To taste	×	2.25	=	To taste

When we divide the new yield by the old yield (720 divided by 192), we arrive at a conversion factor of 3.75. In Example 2, we have done the conversions, using the new factor of 3.75.

EXAMPLE 2

Ingredient	Quantity	Times	Conversion Factor	Equals	New Quantity
Beef tenderloin	96 oz	×	3.75	=	360 oz or $22\frac{1}{2}$ lb
Mustard powder	$1\frac{1}{2}$ t	×	3.75	=	$5\frac{5}{8}$ t
Pepper	To taste	×	3.75	=	To taste
Mushrooms	64 oz	×	3.75	=	240 oz or 15 lb
Onions	32 oz	×	3.75	=	120 oz or $7\frac{1}{2}$ lb
Garlic	$1\frac{1}{2}$ T	×	3.75	=	$5\frac{5}{8}$ T
Veal stock	40 fl oz	×	3.75	=	150 fl oz or 1 gal + $2\frac{3}{4}$ c
Tomatoes	16 oz	×	3.75	=	60 oz or $3\frac{3}{4}$ lb
White wine	4 fl oz	×	3.75	=	15 fl oz or $1\frac{7}{8}$ c
Cornstarch	4 oz	×	3.75	=	15 oz
Yogurt	40 fl oz	×	3.75	=	150 fl oz or 1 gal + $2\frac{3}{4}$ c
Nutmeg	$\frac{3}{4}$ t	×	3.75	=	$2\frac{4}{5}$ t
Salt	To taste	×	3.75	=	To taste

RECIPES

1

Stocks and Soups

STOCKS

Flavorful Vegetable Stock

A vegetable stock will only be as good as the vegetables from which it is made. For a flavorful stock, select high-quality vegetables at their freshest. The best vegetables to use when producing a vegetable stock are carrots, onions, celery, potatoes, parsnips, sweet potatoes, and winter squashes. Strongly flavored vegetables from the cabbage family like broccoli, cauliflower, turnips, and rutabagas should be used with discretion. Green peppers, eggplant, and the dark outer leaves of celery should be avoided. They can make the stock bitter. A small amount of fresh sweet pear is added to this particular recipe to balance the flavor of the stock.

Servings: 24   *Serving Size: ¾ c*
Yield: 1⅛ gal

Celery, washed, trimmed, coarsely chopped	6 oz	Tomato, coarsely chopped	4 oz
Parsnips, washed, trimmed, coarsely chopped	6 oz	Water, cold (divided)	1¼ gal
Carrots, washed, trimmed, coarsely chopped	4 oz	Sachet:	
		Bay leaf	1
Onions, peeled, coarsely chopped	4 oz	Thyme, sprigs or dried	4 or ¼ t
		Peppercorns	¼ t
Leeks, green and white parts, coarsely chopped	4 oz	Parsley stems	8
		Cloves, whole	2
Pear, washed, cored, coarsely chopped	4 oz	Fennel seeds	½ t

1. In a stock pot, place the celery and next 6 ingredients. Place over medium-high heat; braise-deglaze with 1 c of water, or as needed until tender.
2. Add the remaining water and sachet. Heat to a boil; reduce the heat to low; simmer for 45 minutes. Skim the froth as needed.
3. Strain through a china cap lined with several layers of cheese cloth or a fine mesh strainer. Discard the solids.
4. Cool, vented in a cold-water bath. Store refrigerated. Prior to using, skim any impurities from the stock's surface. Use as a base for soups such as brown lentil soup seasoned

with oregano (see page 10) or thick vegetarian minestrone soup (see page 30), sauces, braised dishes, and stews, and as a cooking medium for grains and vegetables such as pinto beans simmered in vegetable broth (see page 181).

The following nutrition analysis is based on the ingredients used in this recipe. It does not account for the pulp that is strained from the stock before using. As a result, the calories and nutrients likely are much less than the listed figures.

Servings	Calories	Protein (g) (%)	Fat (g) (%)	Cholesterol (mg)	Carbohydrates (g) (%)	Fiber (g)	Sodium (mg)
1	18	0.4 (8%)	0.1 (6%)	0	4.1 (86%)	1	16.3

Rich Brown Veal Stock

Veal bones are a must for this stock. They are high in connective tissue called collagen, which breaks down to form gelatin when simmered in water. Gelatin gives body to the stock. The bones should be cut into small pieces for maximum extraction of nutrients and flavor. When compared to a standard brown stock recipe, the quantity of bones, vegetables, and seasonings in rich brown veal stock is high in relation to the amount of water. Since the object is to create a stock that is full-bodied, tastes and smells good, and will contribute complex, well-rounded flavor without fat to sauces and soups, the higher proportions of flavoring ingredients are recommended.

Servings: 24   *Serving Size: $\frac{3}{4}$ c*
Yield: 1$\frac{1}{8}$ gal

Veal bones, 3-in. pieces, trimmed of fat	12 lb	Tomatoes, coarsely chopped	1 lb
Water, cold	1$\frac{3}{4}$ gal	Sachet:	
Onions, peeled, 1-in. pieces	1 lb	Bay leaf	1
Carrots, washed, trimmed, 1-in. pieces	8 oz	Thyme, sprigs or dried	4 or $\frac{1}{4}$ t
		Peppercorns	$\frac{1}{4}$ t
Celery, washed, trimmed, 1-in. pieces	8 oz	Parsley stems	8
		Cloves, whole	2

1. Place the bones in a roasting pan. Roast in a 400°F (205°C) oven, turning occasionally until well browned, or about 1 hour.
2. Place the bones in a stock pot. Cover with the cold water. Heat to a boil. Reduce the heat to low; simmer for 6 to 8 hours, skimming the froth as required. Add water if needed to keep the bones covered during simmering.
3. Drain the fat from the roasting pan; reserve. Place the roasting pan over moderate heat. Add about 1 c of the cooking stock to the pan; stirring, scrape the browned bits of food from the bottom. Add to the stock pot.
4. Lightly coat the bottom of the roasting pan with the reserved fat. Add the onions, carrots, and celery. Return to the 400°F (205°C) oven. Cook, turning occasionally, until well browned, or about 45 minutes.
5. Add the browned vegetables, tomatoes, and sachet to the stock pot halfway through cooking.
6. Continue simmering, skimming as required. Strain through a fine mesh china cap or one lined with several layers of cheesecloth. Discard the solids.
7. Cool, vented in a cold-water bath. Cover and refrigerate for up to 2 days. Prior to using, skim any fat from the stock's surface.

8. Use as a base for soups such as mushroom, beef, and barley soup (see page 25), sauces, stews, and braised dishes such as beef round roast and vegetables braised in red wine broth (see page 67), and as a cooking medium for grains and vegetables.

Note: It was not possible to calculate the nutritional value of this recipe. It is nearly free of all fat because it is skimmed before using and contains only the sodium in the water and that absorbed from the bones, vegetables, herbs, and spices simmered in it. Calories are negligible.

Rich Fish Fumet

Rich fish fumet requires only 45 minutes cooking for full extraction of body and flavor from the fish bones. In comparison, the recommended cooking time for rich white chicken stock is 4 hours, and for rich brown veal stock is 6 to 8 hours. With prolonged cooking, fish bones and shellfish shells may take on unacceptable flavors.

Servings: 24   *Serving Size: $\frac{3}{4}$ c*
Yield: $1\frac{1}{8}$ gal

Vegetable cooking spray	—	Parchment paper	—
Mushrooms and/or trimmings, chopped	10 oz	Water, cold	$1\frac{1}{4}$ gal
Onion, chopped fine	8 oz	Wine, white, dry	1 qt
Celery, washed, trimmed, chopped fine	4 oz	Sachet:	
		Bay leaf	1
Parsnip, washed, trimmed, chopped fine	4 oz	Peppercorns	$\frac{1}{4}$ t
		Parsley stems	8
Bones and heads of firm white fish, washed of blood, 2-in. pieces	11 lb	Cloves, whole	2

1. Coat the bottom of a stock pot with the cooking spray. Place the vegetables in the bottom of the pot. Lay the bones over the vegetables. Cover loosely with a round of parchment paper.
2. Place over low heat and cook slowly until the bones are opaque and begin to exude some juice and the vegetables are tender.
3. Remove the parchment paper. Add the water, wine, and sachet. Heat to a boil; reduce the heat to low; skim the froth. Simmer for 45 minutes, skimming as needed. Add water if needed to keep the bones covered throughout cooking.
4. Strain through a fine mesh china cap or one lined with several layers of cheesecloth. Discard the solids.
5. Cool, vented in a cold-water bath. Refrigerate for up to 2 days. Prior to using, skim any fat from the stock's surface. Use as a base for soups, sauces, and as a cooking medium for grains or poaching fish.

Note: It was not possible to calculate the nutritional value of this recipe. The stock is nearly free of all fat because it is skimmed before using and contains only the sodium in the water and that absorbed from the bones, vegetables, herbs, and spices simmered in it. Calories are negligible.

Rich White Chicken Stock

Some chefs blanch the chicken bones prior to using them for stock to eliminate the blood and some of the other impurities that may cause the stock to become cloudy. In rich white chicken stock, the chicken bones are not blanched prior to using. This enhances retention of valuable flavors in the bones that might be lost in the blanching process.

Servings: 24 *Service Size:* ¾ c
Yield: 1⅛ gal

		Sachet:	
Chicken bones, trimmed of fat and skin, 3-in. pieces	12 lb	Bay leaf	1
Water, cold	1¼ gal	Thyme, sprigs or dried	4 or ¼ t
Onion, peeled, 1-in. pieces	1 lb	Peppercorns	¼ t
Carrots, trimmed, washed, 1-in. pieces	8 oz	Parsley stems	8
Celery, washed, trimmed, 1-in. pieces	8 oz	Cloves, whole	2

1. Place the bones in a stock pot. Cover with the cold water. Heat to a boil. Reduce the heat to low; simmer for 4 hours, skimming the froth as needed. Add water if necessary to keep the bones covered.
2. After simmering 2 hours, add the vegetables and sachet. Simmer for another 2 hours, skimming as required.
3. Strain through a china cap lined with several layers of cheesecloth or a fine mesh strainer. Discard the solids.
4. Cool, vented in a cold-water bath. Cover and refrigerate for up to 2 days. Prior to using, skim any fat from the stock's surface.
5. Use as a base for soups such as black mushroom and pearl barley soup (see page 9) or butternut squash bisque garnished with a dollop of chunky apple yogurt (see page 11), sauces, braised dishes such as chicken breast cubes simmered in creamy coconut sauce (see page 124), stews, and as a cooking medium for grains and vegetables.

Note: It was not possible to calculate the nutritional value of this recipe. It is nearly free of all fat because the fat is skimmed from the stock before using and contains only the sodium in the water and that absorbed from the bones, vegetables, herbs, and spices simmered in it. Calories are negligible.

Shrimp Broth

The primary ingredient in shrimp broth is one that is typically discarded—the shells of boiled shrimp. The juice may serve as a base for soups or sauces or as a cooking medium in fish and other dishes.

Servings: 24   *Service Size: $1\frac{1}{3}$ T*
Yield: 1 pt

Shells from poached or simmered shrimp	1 lb	*Shrimp cooking liquid, reserved after poaching or simmering raw shrimp	$1\frac{3}{4}$ c

1. In a blender or food processor, blend the shrimp shells and cooking liquid until well crushed.
2. Using cheesecloth, squeeze the juice from the shells into a small container. Use as an ingredient in dishes such as Philippine-style spring rolls filled with beef, tofu, and shrimp (see page 76).

*Shrimp broth is designed to serve as a base for soups, sauces, and salad dressings containing poached or simmered shrimp.

Note: it was not possible to calculate the nutritional value for this recipe.

SOUPS

Black Mushroom and Pearl Barley Soup

While the dried Chinese mushrooms in this soup are pale buff to brown in color, they are commonly called black mushrooms. For best results, select light-colored ones with plump caps. Because their flavor intensifies on drying, they are always sold in dried form.

Servings: 24   *Serving Size: ¾ c*
Yield: 1⅛ gal

Mushrooms, dried, black	3 oz	Worcestershire sauce, very	
Barley, pearl	5 oz	low sodium	1 T
Onions, minced	6 oz	Hot pepper sauce	To taste
Carrots, small dice	6 oz	Salt	To taste
Celery, small dice	3 oz	Pepper, freshly ground	To taste
Rich white chicken stock (see			
page 7) (divided)	3 qt		

1. Soak the mushrooms in several changes of water until totally clean. Drain. In a saucepan, simmer in unsalted water until tender, or about 25 minutes. Strain, reserving the cooking liquid for another use. Remove the tough mushroom stems; discard. Chop the caps fine; set aside.
2. In a clean saucepan, boil the barley in unsalted water until tender, or about 35 to 40 minutes. Drain; refresh in cold water; drain; set aside.
3. Place the onions, carrots, celery, and ½ c of the stock in a sauce pot. Braise-deglaze the vegetables over medium-high heat, adding more stock if needed, until tender without browning.
4. Add the remaining stock, reserved mushrooms, and barley. Heat to a boil; reduce the heat to low; simmer until heated through.
5. Reduce the soup or add stock to adjust the consistency or taste. Season with the Worcestershire and pepper sauces and salt and pepper to taste. Serve a cup as an appetizer course, or a bowl along with a sandwich or salad as a main course offering.

Servings	Calories	Protein (g) (%)	Fat (g) (%)	Cholesterol (mg)	Carbohydrates (g) (%)	Fiber (g)	Sodium (mg)
1	51	3.2 (24%)	0.8 (14%)	0	8.1 (61%)	1.5	51.7

Brown Lentil Soup Seasoned with Oregano

During the cold winter months, this thick and hearty soup is ideal for warming the body. It is prepared by simmering tiny, round, dried brown lentils with vegetables and spices.

Servings: 24   Serving Size: $1\frac{1}{3}$ c
Yield: 2 gal

Lentils, brown	$2\frac{1}{4}$ lb	Bay leaf	1
Onions, minced	2 lb	Oregano, minced or dried	3 T or
Carrots, washed, small dice	12 oz		1 T
Celery, small dice	10 oz	Tomatoes, peeled, coarsely	
Garlic, minced	2 T	chopped, or pureed	8 oz
Flavorful vegetable stock (see		Parsley, minced	$\frac{1}{2}$ c
page 2) or rich white		Salt	To taste
chicken stock (see page 7)		Pepper, freshly ground	To taste
(divided)	$1\frac{1}{2}$ gal		

1. Wash the lentils; soak in 2 gal of cold water for about 30 minutes; discard any lentils that float to the surface; drain and rinse with cold water.
2. In a sauce pot, place the onions, carrots, celery, garlic, and 1 pt of the stock, or as needed; simmer, stirring, until the vegetables are partially tender.
3. Add the lentils, bay leaf, remaining stock, and oregano if dried; simmer until the lentils are partially tender, or about 45 minutes.
4. Add the tomatoes and continue simmering until the lentils and vegetables are tender, or about 20 minutes. To adjust the consistency of the soup, thicken by reducing or thin with additional stock or water.
5. Add the oregano if fresh, parsley, and salt and pepper to taste. Simmer a few minutes longer. Remove the bay leaf; serve in heated soup cups or bowls along with whole wheat tortillas prepared without lard.

Servings	Calories	Protein (g) (%)	Fat (g) (%)	Cholesterol (mg)	Carbohydrates (g) (%)	Fiber (g)	Sodium (mg)
1	214	17.8 (32%)	2.1 (9%)	0	32.3 (59%)	7.1	96.1

Butternut Squash Bisque* Garnished with a Dollop of Chunky Apple Yogurt

While classic recipes for cream soups are often thickened with a butter-flour roux and call for enrichment with cream, more butter, or egg yolks, this soup is sensational, yet contains none of these. Rather, it is thickened and flavored with a puree of butternut squash. It attains its creamy taste and texture by blending with evaporated skim milk.

Servings: 24   *Serving Size:* $\frac{3}{4}$ c
Yield: 1 gal + $1\frac{1}{2}$ *pt*

Vegetable cooking spray, butter-flavored	—	Milk, evaporated, skim	$1\frac{1}{2}$ pt
Onions, minced	1 lb	Nutmeg, freshly ground	$\frac{1}{2}$ t
Gingerroot, minced	2 oz	Salt	To taste
†Squash, butternut, peeled, seeded, thin slices	4 lb ($4\frac{3}{4}$ lb as purchased)	Pepper, freshly ground	To taste
		Yogurt, nonfat, plain	$\frac{1}{2}$ c
Rich white chicken stock (see page 7) or flavorful vegetable stock (see page 2)	$2\frac{1}{2}$ qt	Apple, Granny Smith or other tart apple, peeled, small dice	3 oz

1. Coat a saucepan with cooking spray. Place over medium heat until hot. Add the onions and ginger. Cook until tender.
2. Add the squash and chicken stock. Heat the mixture to a boil. Reduce the heat to low; cover and simmer until the squash is tender, or about 15 minutes.
3. In a blender, puree the mixture until smooth. Transfer to a sauce pot.
4. Add the evaporated milk and nutmeg. Heat to a boil. Reduce the heat to low and heat through. To adjust the consistency, thicken the soup by reducing or thin by adding more evaporated skim milk or stock. Stir in the salt and pepper to taste.

5. Mix the apple into the yogurt in a bowl. Serve the soup garnished with a dollop (2 t) of the yogurt-apple topping.

*Technically, this soup does not meet the criteria for a bisque. However, because the term bisque sounds nice, soups with the creamy texture associated with a bisque have come to be called by this term.

†Substitute sweet potatoes or yams for the squash if not available.

Servings	Calories	Protein (g) (%)	Fat (g) (%)	Cholesterol (mg)	Carbohydrates (g) (%)	Fiber (g)	Sodium (mg)
1	84	5.9 (27%)	0.8 (8%)	1.2	14.5 (65%)	2.5	72.9

Chicken Brown Rice and Vegetable Soup Flavored with Curry

When planning your "weight watchers" specials, begin with a cup of this or other light soup. Studies show that a cup of soup before a meal slows the rate of eating and fills the stomach.

Servings: 24 *Service Size: 1⅓ c*
Yield: 2 gal

Chicken breasts, with bone, skinless	3 lb	Garlic, minced	1½ t
Sachet:		Curry powder	2 T
Bay leaf	1	Red pepper, ground	To taste or ⅛ t
Thyme, sprigs or dried	4 or ¼ t	Carrots, washed, small dice	12 oz
Peppercorns	⅛ t	Peas, fresh, shelled, or frozen	12 oz
Parsley stems	6	*Brown rice, long grain, cooked without salt	7 oz as purchased
Cloves, whole	2		
Rich white chicken stock (see page 7)	1½ gal	Milk, evaporated, skim	1 qt
Onions, coarsely chopped	8 oz	Lemon juice, freshly squeezed	2 t
Carrots, coarsely chopped	4 oz	Salt	To taste
Celery, coarsely chopped	4 oz	Pepper, freshly ground	To taste
Vegetable cooking spray	—		
Onions, minced	1½ lb		

1. Place the chicken, sachet, stock, and coarsely chopped onions, carrots, and celery in a sauce pot. Heat to a boil. Reduce the heat to low; simmer until the chicken is cooked through, or about 25 minutes. Skim the froth as needed.
2. Remove the chicken from the stock. When cool enough to handle, remove the bones from the chicken; discard. Cut into medium dice; set aside briefly or refrigerate.
3. Strain the stock. Discard the sachet. Skim the fat from the stock. Puree the vegetables in a blender until smooth. Return to the stock.
4. Coat a nonstick skillet with cooking spray. Place over medium heat until hot. Add the minced onions and garlic; cook until tender without browning. Add the curry powder and red pepper; cook a few minutes longer.
5. Add the onion mixture to the broth. Simmer until tender and the flavor is mellowed, or about 15 minutes.
6. Add the diced carrots and peas (if fresh); simmer until tender, or about 10 minutes.
7. Stir in the chicken, brown rice, peas (if frozen), and evaporated milk. Heat through.

To adjust the soup's consistency, thin with more stock or water and thicken by reducing.

8. Blend in the lemon juice and salt and pepper to taste. Serve as an appetizer or main course offering with low-fat whole grain biscuits, tortillas, or bread sticks.

*To cook the 7 oz of brown rice: wash the rice; place in a sauce pan with 2⅓ c of water; heat to a boil; reduce the heat to low; stir; cover. Simmer the rice until tender and the water is absorbed, or about 45–50 minutes. Do not remove the cover during cooking. Remove from the heat; stand covered about 10 minutes; fluff.

Servings	Calories	Protein (g) (%)	Fat (g) (%)	Cholesterol (mg)	Carbohydrates (g) (%)	Fiber (g)	Sodium (mg)
1	178	22.2 (51%)	2.5 (12%)	32.8	15.8 (37%)	2.4	169

Chilled Fresh Tomato, Bell Pepper, and Cucumber Gazpacho

Gazpacho is one of the most popular chilled soups throughout the world. It is prepared by blending fresh, ripe tomatoes, green bell peppers, cucumbers, onions, and seasonings. Traditionally, the puree also contained bread and olive oil. These ingredients have been eliminated in this recipe to cut calories and fat. The end result is a refreshing, light, and healthy version of this famous soup. At service, diced vegetables are passed to sprinkle over the soup.

Servings: 24 *Serving Size: 1 c*
Yield: 1½ gal

Tomatoes, coarsely chopped	2¼ lb	Tarragon, minced or dried	2 t or ¾ t
Cucumber, peeled, coarsely chopped	1 lb	Salt	To taste
		Pepper, freshly ground	To taste
Bell pepper, green, coarsely chopped	14 oz	*Onions, sweet, minced	1 lb
		Cucumbers, peeled, small dice	1 lb
Onion, coarsely chopped	6 oz	Bell pepper, green and yellow, small dice	10 oz each
Garlic, minced	2 T		
Vinegar, red wine	½ c		
Freshly prepared spicy tomato cocktail (see page 361) or tomato juice, no salt added	2 qt		

1. In a blender, add the first eight ingredients. Process until relatively smooth.
2. Refrigerate until well chilled, or several hours. Season with salt and pepper to taste.
3. Place the minced onions and diced cucumbers and bell peppers in small bowls. Serve the soup in chilled soup bowls on saucers lined with doilies. Pass the garnishes separately. Serve with whole wheat, low-fat tortillas, fresh corn bread, or whole grain bread sticks.

*Examples of sweet onion varieties are the Walla Walla, Maui, and Granex.

Servings	Calories	Protein (g) (%)	Fat (g) (%)	Cholesterol (mg)	Carbohydrates (g) (%)	Fiber (g)	Sodium (mg)
1	51	2.0 (13%)	0.4 (6%)	0	12 (81%)	2.7	14.6

Chilled Peach Soup Flavored with Cinnamon and Clove

There are two basic types of peaches—freestone and clingstone. As the names imply, the pits of freestone peaches separate easily, while those of the clingstone adhere. Freestone peaches, the juicier of the two and the type most frequently marketed fresh are preferred for this chilled peach soup.

Servings: 24   Serving Size: almost ½ c (7⅓ T)
Yield: 2¾ qt

Water	1¾ pt	*Peaches, peeled, fresh or	
Wine, dry, white	1¾ pt	frozen without sugar,	
White grape juice concentrate,		cubes or slices	2 lb
unsweetened	1¼ c	Yogurt, nonfat, plain (divided)	1½ c
Cloves, whole	¼ t	Cinnamon, freshly ground	1 t
Cinnamon, sticks	1		

1. In a saucepan, combine the first five ingredients. Heat to a boil; reduce the heat to low; simmer until reduced in half, or about 30 minutes. Strain through a china cap lined with cheesecloth. Discard the whole spices. Set the broth aside to cool or chill in an ice bath.
2. In a blender, puree the peaches with a small amount of the broth until smooth.
3. In a mixing bowl, mix the peach puree with the cooled reduction and half (¾ c) of the yogurt until well blended. Refrigerate in a covered storage container until well chilled. Serve in 24 chilled goblets on decorative plate liners. Garnish with a dollop (½ T) of the remaining yogurt and a sprinkle of cinnamon.

*To peel the peaches, blanch in boiling water for 10–20 seconds. Drain. Refresh in ice water. Drain. The skins should slip off easily.

Servings	Calories	Protein (g) (%)	Fat (g) (%)	Cholesterol (mg)	Carbohydrates (g) (%)	Fiber (g)	Sodium (mg)
1	62	1.3 (10%)	0.1 (2%)	0.3	11.9 (88%)	0.7	20.9

Corn Chowder Garnished with Roasted Red Bell Pepper

People love the taste of corn. For a real treat, offer the sweet kernels in a bowl of hearty chowder along with cubes of new potatoes, carrots, and celery. To keep fat and calories at a minimum, replace the cream with evaporated skim milk, replace the ham with lean turkey ham, and thicken with a puree of vegetables rather than a butter-rich roux. A sprinkle of roasted, diced, red bell pepper on top is the perfect finishing touch.

Servings: 24 *Serving Size: 1⅓ c*
Yield: 2 gal

Vegetable cooking spray, butter-flavored	—	Rich white chicken stock (see page 7)	2¼ qt
Onions, medium dice	12 oz	Corn kernels, fresh or frozen	4½ lb
Celery and carrots, washed, medium dice	6 oz each	Turkey, ham, medium dice	12 oz
		Milk, evaporated, skim	1½ qt
Potatoes, new, peeled, medium dice	2¼ lb	Salt	To taste
		Pepper, freshly ground	To taste
Bay leaf	1	*Pepper, red, bell, roasted, peeled, small dice	8 oz
Thyme, dried	2 t		

1. Coat a sauce pot with cooking spray. Place over medium heat until hot. Add the onions, celery, and carrots. Cook until tender without browning.
2. Add the potatoes, bay leaf, thyme, and stock. Heat to a boil. Reduce the heat to low; simmer, covered, until the potatoes are partially cooked, or about 15 minutes.
3. Stir in the corn; simmer, covered, until the potatoes are cooked through and the remaining vegetables are tender, or about 10 minutes. Remove the bay leaf.
4. Transfer one-third of the solids with a slotted spoon to a blender; puree until smooth.
5. Add the pureed vegetables, diced turkey ham, and evaporated milk to the chowder. Heat through. To adjust the consistency, add stock or water to thin and reduce to thicken. Season with salt and pepper to taste. Serve in heated cups or bowls garnished with the diced, roasted, bell pepper.

*To roast and peel bell peppers:
1. Char over a burner, on a grill, or under a broiler until the skins are blackened.
2. Wrap in plastic wrap or place in a plastic bag for about 15 minutes. The steam produced will help loosen the skins.

3. Rub off the skin; rinse under cold water, removing all the blackened skin.
4. Cut in half. Remove the core, seeds, and membranes. Cut into small dice.

Servings	Calories	Protein (g) (%)	Fat (g) (%)	Cholesterol (mg)	Carbohydrates (g) (%)	Fiber (g)	Sodium (mg)
1	203	13.2 (25%)	2.5 (11%)	10.2	34.7 (65%)	4.5	266

Cream of Mushroom Soup Finished with Sherry

While classic recipes for cream soups often require thickening with a butter and flour roux and enrichment with cream, more butter, or egg yolks, this cream of mushroom soup is sensational, yet it contains none of these. Rather, it is thickened with a cornstarch slurry and enriched with evaporated skim milk. Additionally, in the case of vegetable cream soups, the vegetables are generally pureed, strained out, and discarded. Not here; instead, this creamy broth is served filled with the high-fiber and low-calorie onions and mushrooms.

Servings: 24   *Serving size: 1 c*
Yield: 1⅝ gal (1½ gal + 1 pt)

Vegetable cooking spray, butter-flavored	—	Milk, evaporated, skim	2 qt
		Cornstarch	6 oz
Mushrooms, thin slices	3½ lb	Sherry, dry	1 c
Onions, minced	1 lb	Nutmeg, freshly ground	¼ t
Rich white chicken stock (see page 7)	1 gal + 1 pt	Salt	To taste
		Pepper, freshly ground	To taste

1. Coat a sauce pot with cooking spray. Place over medium heat until hot. Add the mushrooms and onions; cook until tender without browning.
2. Add the stock; heat to a boil; reduce the heat to low; simmer until the vegetables are very tender.
3. In a small bowl, whisk a small amount of the evaporated milk into the cornstarch to form a smooth paste. Stir into the remaining evaporated milk.
4. Add the evaporated milk to the soup, beating. Heat to a boil; reduce the heat to low. Simmer until the soup thickens, or a few minutes.
5. Stir in the sherry. Simmer a few additional minutes. To adjust the consistency, thicken by reducing or by adding more cornstarch slurry and thin by adding evaporated skim milk or stock. Season with the nutmeg and salt and pepper to taste. Serve in heated soup bowls accompanied by a basket filled with freshly baked, whole grain breads.

Servings	Calories	Protein (g) (%)	Fat (g) (%)	Cholesterol (mg)	Carbohydrates (g) (%)	Fiber (g)	Sodium (mg)	Alcohol (g) (%)
1	151	11.7 (30%)	1.5 (9%)	3.1	21.6 (57%)	1.3	156	0.6 (4%)

Cream of Tomato and Sweet Red Bell Pepper Soup

This soup obtains its sweet flavor and creamy thickness from a puree of tomatoes, bell peppers, and onions simmered in broth. Rather than using cream, it is finished with evaporated skim milk. When garnished with a dollop of nonfat yogurt and sprinkle of freshly minced chives, it is a delicious, nutritious way to start a meal.

Servings: 24 *Serving Size: 1 c*
Yield: 1½ gal

Vegetable cooking spray	—	Paprika, Hungarian, sweet	2½ T
Onions, minced	1¼ lb	Basil, minced or dried	⅓ c or 1¾ T
Tomatoes, fresh or canned, peeled, coarsely chopped	3 lb	Oregano, minced or dried	2½ T or 2½ t
Peppers, red, bell, coarsely chopped	12 oz	Milk, evaporated, skim, hot	1 pt + 1¾ c
Apple juice concentrate, unsweetened	2 t	Cornstarch	2 oz
Flavorful vegetable stock (see page 2) or rich white chicken stock (see page 7)	1 gal + 1½ qt	Salt	To taste
		Pepper, freshly ground	To taste
		Yogurt, nonfat, plain	¾ c
		Chives, minced	2 oz
Sachet:			
Bay leaf	1		
Peppercorns	10		
Cloves	3		
Parsley stems	5		

1. Coat a nonstick sauce pot with cooking spray. Place over medium heat until hot. Add the onions; cook until tender.
2. Add the tomatoes, bell peppers, and apple juice concentrate. Reduce the heat to low; cook, stirring occasionally until the tomatoes are pulpy and the bell peppers tender, or about 15 minutes.
3. Add the stock, sachet, paprika, and basil and oregano if dried. Heat to a boil. Reduce the heat to low; simmer, stirring occasionally, until the vegetables are very tender and the flavors mellowed, or about 1 hour.
4. Remove the sachet; discard. In a blender, puree until smooth. Return to a clean sauce pot. Stir in the evaporated skim milk and basil and oregano if fresh.
5. In a small bowl, mix the cornstarch with a small amount of cold water until it forms a smooth paste. Stir the slurry into the soup. Heat the soup a few minutes until thick-

ened. To adjust the consistency, thin with additional stock or evaporated skim milk, and thicken by reducing or by adding more cornstarch slurry. Season with salt and pepper to taste. Add more apple juice concentrate if needed to balance the flavors. Serve in heated soup cups topped with a dollop ($\frac{1}{2}$ T) of yogurt and a sprinkle of chives.

Servings	Calories	Protein (g) (%)	Fat (g) (%)	Cholesterol (mg)	Carbohydrates (g) (%)	Fiber (g)	Sodium (mg)
1	94	5.0 (20%)	0.6 (6%)	1.6	18.7 (74%)	3.0	78.4

Fresh Corn Soup in Light Creamy Broth Accented with Cumin

Offer a bowl of this corn soup with a basket of hearty breads or a cup with a salad or half sandwich as a daily special. This healthy version is prepared by simmering fresh corn kernels, tomatoes, and onions in a rich chicken stock, seasoning with cumin, and finishing with evaporated skim milk, and low-fat Monterey Jack cheese.

Servings: 24   *Serving Size: 1 c*
Yield: 1½ gal

Vegetable cooking spray, butter-flavored	—	Cumin, freshly ground	1 t
*Corn kernels, fresh (divided)	4 lb	Milk, evaporated, skim	1 pt
Tomatoes, fresh or canned, peeled, coarsely chopped	2 lb	Monterey Jack cheese, shredded, low-fat, low-sodium	4 oz
Onions, minced	12 oz	Salt	To taste
Rich white chicken stock (see page 7) (divided)	3½ qt	Pepper, freshly ground	To taste

1. Coat a nonstick sauce pot with cooking spray. Place over medium-high heat until hot. Add 1 lb of the corn, the tomatoes, onions, and 1 c of the stock, or as needed; cook until tender, stirring.
2. In a blender, puree the vegetable mixture until smooth. Add more stock if needed to puree.
3. Return the pureed vegetables with the remaining corn, stock, and cumin to the sauce pot. Heat to a boil; reduce the heat to low; simmer until the corn is tender, or about 15 minutes.
4. Stir in the evaporated milk. To adjust the consistency, thicken by reducing or thin with additional stock or water. Add the cheese; cook over low heat until melted; do not boil. Season with salt and pepper to taste. Serve in heated soup cups or bowls along with whole wheat tortillas prepared without lard.

*Use frozen corn to prepare this soup when fresh is not available. Delete the term "fresh" from its name.

Servings	Calories	Protein (g) (%)	Fat (g) (%)	Cholesterol (mg)	Carbohydrates (g) (%)	Fiber (g)	Sodium (mg)
1	126	8.5 (25%)	2.3 (15%)	1.8	20.4 (60%)	3.2	82.8

Gingered Creamy Carrot Bisque

Bisques are classically defined as thickened soups made from shellfish, often finished with cream. In practice, the term is used more liberally, often describing soups such as this gingered creamy carrot bisque which contains neither shellfish nor cream but has the rich flavor and creamlike consistency associated with bisques.

Servings: 24   *Serving Size: 1⅛ c*
Yield: 1¾ gal

Onions, minced	1¼ lb	Rich white chicken stock (see	
Gingerroot, minced	6 oz	page 7)	3¾ qt
Wine, white, dry	1¼ pt	Milk, evaporated, skim	1¼ qt
Carrots, washed, small dice	5 lb	Salt	To taste
Potatoes, all-purpose (chef's), washed (unpeeled), small dice	1¼ lb	Pepper, freshly ground	To taste

1. Add the onions, ginger, and white wine to a nonstick sauce pot. Sweat the onions over medium heat until tender without browning and the wine is reduced by half.
2. Add the carrots, potatoes, and chicken stock. Heat to a boil. Reduce the heat to low; simmer until the potatoes and carrots are tender.
3. Puree the soup in a blender until smooth. Return the puree to a clean sauce pot.
4. Add the evaporated milk to the puree. Heat the soup through. To adjust consistency, thin with additional stock or evaporated skim milk and thicken by reducing. Season with salt and pepper to taste. Serve in heated soup cups as an appetizer course or along with a half sandwich or salad as a main course offering.

Servings	Calories	Protein (g) (%)	Fat (g) (%)	Cholesterol (mg)	Carbohydrates (g) (%)	Fiber (g)	Sodium (mg)
1	143	8.9 (25%)	1.3 (8%)	1.9	23.7 (67%)	3.9	143

No alcohol is listed in the nutrition analysis. It is assumed to be cooked off by reducing the wine in half.

Lean Turkey Ball Soup with Garbanzo Beans and Vegetables

In this filling soup, lean turkey balls are seasoned with a pinch of cinnamon and nutmeg, combined with vegetables and garbanzo beans, and simmered in a broth of rich chicken stock and vegetable juice.

Servings: 24   *Serving Size: $\frac{5}{8}$ c*
Yield: $1\frac{3}{4}$ gal

Turkey, ground, raw, skinless, light and dark meat	$1\frac{1}{2}$ lb	Rich white chicken stock (see page 7)	$1\frac{1}{4}$ gal
Bread crumbs, whole wheat, fresh	3 oz	Vegetable juice, no salt added	1 qt
Egg whites, large, lightly beaten	3 ($3\frac{3}{4}$ oz)	Garbanzo beans, canned with 50% less salt, drained, rinsed in water	1 lb drained
Parsley, minced (divided)	$\frac{1}{2}$ c	Onions, minced	1 lb
Salt	To taste	Carrots, $\frac{1}{8}$-in. thick circles	14 oz
Pepper, freshly ground	To taste	Green beans, 1-in. pieces	14 oz
Cinnamon, freshly ground	$\frac{1}{4}$ t	Coriander, freshly ground	$\frac{3}{4}$ t
Nutmeg, freshly ground	$\frac{1}{4}$ t		

1. Place the turkey, bread crumbs, egg whites, one-third (2 T + 2 t) of the parsley, and next four seasoning ingredients in a bowl; mix until well blended. Using a small (2 t) dipper, shape the turkey mixture into 48 turkey balls. Set aside briefly or refrigerate.
2. In a sauce pot, place the chicken stock, next six ingredients, and remaining parsley. Heat the mixture to a boil. Add the turkey balls; reduce the heat to low; simmer until the vegetables are tender and the turkey balls cooked through, or about 10 minutes. To adjust the consistency, thin with additional stock or water and thicken by reducing. Season with salt and pepper to taste. Serve a bowl with a half sandwich for a light meal or a cup as an appetizer course in a more substantial meal.

Servings	Calories	Protein (g) (%)	Fat (g) (%)	Cholesterol (mg)	Carbohydrates (g) (%)	Fiber (g)	Sodium (mg)
1	152	13.3 (35%)	4.8 (28%)	21.7	14.1 (37%)	3.1	128

Mushroom, Beef, and Barley Soup

This hearty, homestyle soup makes a one-dish meal along with crusty, whole grain bread and a green salad.

Servings: 24   *Serving Size: $\frac{4}{5}$ c*
Yield: $1\frac{1}{4}$ gal

Barley, pearl	5 oz	Thyme, dried	2 t
Vegetable cooking spray	—	Marjoram, dried	2 t
Beef stew meat, very lean,		Bay leaf	1
trimmed of fat and		Mushrooms, thin slices	$1\frac{3}{4}$ lb
silverskin, small dice	12 oz	Salt	To taste
Shallots or onions, minced	5 oz	Pepper, freshly ground	To taste
Tomatoes, fresh or canned,		Parsley, minced	$\frac{1}{4}$ c
peeled, small dice	1 lb		
Wine, dry, red	1 c		
Rich brown veal stock (see			
page 4) or very low			
sodium beef stock	$1\frac{3}{4}$ qt		

1. In a saucepan, cook the barley in unsalted boiling water (about $1\frac{1}{2}$ pt) until tender, or 35–40 minutes. Add water if needed during cooking to keep the barley well covered. Drain; refresh in cold water; drain. Set aside.
2. Coat a sauce pot with cooking spray. Place over medium heat until hot. Add the stew meat and cook until brown. Add the shallots; cook until tender and light brown.
3. Add the tomatoes; cook until pulpy, or about 5 minutes. Add the wine; simmer until reduced by half. Stir in the stock and next three ingredients. Cover; simmer until the meat is tender, or about 1 hour. Skim the froth as needed.
6. Add the mushrooms; simmer until the mushrooms are tender, or about 30 minutes. Add the barley. To adjust the consistency, thicken by reducing and thin with additional stock or water. Remove the bay leaf. Season with salt and pepper to taste. Serve in heated soup bowls or cups sprinkled with parsley.

Servings	Calories	Protein (g) (%)	Fat (g) (%)	Cholesterol (mg)	Carbohydrates (g) (%)	Fiber (g)	Sodium (mg)	Alcohol (g) (%)
1	74	7.1 (37%)	2.0 (24%)	13.6	5.7 (30%)	1.2	33.1	0.9 (8%)

Oriental-Style Vegetable Egg Drop Soup

Unlike most egg drop soups, this one contains only egg whites. While the recipe calls for the egg whites to be at room temperature, this does not mean to store the eggs outside of the refrigerator until they reach room temperature. Rather, when ready to prepare the soup, place the eggs in their shells under warm running water or in a warm water bath until they are no longer cold to the touch.

Servings: 24   *Serving Size: ¾ c broth + vegetables*
Yield: 1⅛ gal broth + vegetables

Rich white chicken stock (see page 7)	1 gal	Wine, rice	¼ c
Mushrooms, thin slices	1 lb	Snow peas, trimmed, strings removed, ½-in. pieces cut diagonally	1¼ lb
Gingerroot, minced	1½ T		
Garlic, minced	1 T	Bean sprouts	12 oz
Soy sauce, low-sodium	3 T	Green onions, thin slices, white and green	4 oz
Red pepper, ground	To taste or ⅛ t		
Pepper, freshly ground	To taste		
Egg whites, large, room temperature, lightly beaten	16 (1 lb + 4 oz)		

1. In a sauce pot, heat the stock to a boil. Add the next six ingredients. Reduce the heat to low; simmer until the flavors are mellowed, or about 30 minutes. Increase the heat until boiling lightly.
2. With one hand, slowly pour the egg whites in a fine stream into the broth. With a whip in the other hand, make wide circles on the surface of the broth, catching the whites as they hit and drawing them out into thin, long strands.
3. Stir in the rice wine. To adjust the consistency, thin with more stock or water and thicken by reducing.
4. Divide the snow peas, sprouts, and green onions evenly among 24 soup cups. Ladle the hot broth over. Serve immediately to maintain the crisp texture of the vegetables.

Servings	Calories	Protein (g) (%)	Fat (g) (%)	Cholesterol (mg)	Carbohydrates (g) (%)	Fiber (g)	Sodium (mg)	Alcohol (g) (%)
1	74	8.7 (45%)	2.0 (24%)	0	5.7 (29%)	1.3	218	0.2 (2%)

Shrimp Ball Soup with Vegetables

This delectable soup is a sophisticated starter for any meal. Toasted sesame seed coated shrimp balls laced with crisp, chopped water chestnuts, fresh minced ginger, and soy sauce are served in a clear broth along with broccoli florets and shredded napa cabbage.

Servings: 24
Yield: 1¾ gal
Serving Size: 1⅛ c soup with 2 shrimp balls

Sesame seeds	2 oz	Rich white chicken stock (see page 7)	1½ gal
Shrimp, raw, shelled, deveined, tiny	1 lb	Broccoli florets; stems reserved for another use	1 lb
Egg whites, large	2 (2½ oz)	Napa cabbage, shredded	1 lb
Soy sauce, low-sodium (divided)	½ c + 1½ T	Green onions, thin slices, white and green	6 oz
Hot pepper sauce	To taste or ⅛ t	Sherry, dry	½ c
Gingerroot, minced	2 T		
Water chestnuts, canned, drained, rinsed with water, chopped	3 oz drained		

1. In a small nonstick skillet, toast the sesame seeds over low heat until brown. Set aside.
2. Blend the shrimp in a blender or food processor until finely ground. Add the egg whites, 1½ T of the soy sauce, hot pepper sauce, and ginger. Whirl until blended. Mix in the water chestnuts.
3. Using a melon ball scoop, shape the shrimp mixture into 48 (2 t) balls. Roll in the sesame seeds. The seeds will only sparsely coat the shrimp balls.
4. In a sauce pot, heat the stock to a boil. Add the shrimp balls. Return to a boil; reduce the heat to a simmer. Remove the shrimp balls with a slotted spoon as they rise to the surface. Refrigerate until service. Chill the stock in a cold-water bath. Refrigerate until service.
5. For service, return the broth to a boil. Add the shrimp balls, broccoli, cabbage, and ½ c soy sauce. Simmer until the vegetables are crisp-tender and the shrimp balls are heated through, or a few minutes.

6. Add the green onions and sherry. Serve *immediately* in heated soup bowls. For extended service, add the shrimp balls and vegetables to the stock as ordered.

Servings	Calories	Protein (g) (%)	Fat (g) (%)	Cholesterol (mg)	Carbohydrates (g) (%)	Fiber (g)	Sodium (mg)	Alcohol (g) (%)
1	96	11.1 (46%)	3.2 (30%)	28.8	5.1 (21%)	1.3	306	0.4 (3%)

Split Pea Soup Laced with Spinach

There's no need for ham in this creamy split pea soup. Rather, it's filled with vegetables and seasoned with fresh herbs.

Servings: 24   *Serving Size: ¾ c*
Yield: 1⅛ gal

Split peas, sorted, washed	1½ lb as purchased	Rosemary, fresh, minced or dried	1 T or 1 t
Rich white chicken stock (see page 7)	1¼ gal	Pepper, freshly ground	To taste or 1 t
Onion, coarsely chopped	6 oz	Milk, nonfat, hot	1½ c
Carrot, washed, coarsely chopped	4 oz	Spinach, fresh or frozen, leaves, washed, chopped	6 oz fresh
Celery, coarsely chopped	4 oz		
Mushrooms, coarsely chopped	4 oz	or frozen	or 4 oz frozen
Garlic, minced	½ T		
Bay leaves	2	Salt	To taste
Thyme, fresh, minced or dried	1 T or 1 t	Yogurt, nonfat, plain	½ c
		Paprika, sweet, Hungarian	1½ t

1. Place the peas and chicken stock in a sauce pot. Place over high heat. Boil for 2 minutes. Turn off the heat. Cover; let stand for 1 hour.
2. Add the onion and next eight ingredients to the peas. Heat to a boil. Reduce the heat to low; simmer uncovered until the peas are tender, or about 1 hour, stirring occasionally. Add more stock or water if needed.
3. Remove the bay leaves. In a blender, in batches if needed, puree the pea mixture with the milk until smooth.
4. Return the soup to a clean sauce pot. Heat to a boil; add the spinach if fresh; reduce the heat to medium; simmer until the spinach leaves are wilted. If using frozen spinach, add to the soup and simmer until the soup is heated through. Season with salt to taste.
5. To adjust the soup's consistency, reduce to thicken the soup and thin with more stock or water. Serve with a dollop (1 t) of yogurt and a sprinkle of paprika.

Servings	Calories	Protein (g) (%)	Fat (g) (%)	Cholesterol (mg)	Carbohydrates (g) (%)	Fiber (g)	Sodium (mg)
1	146	12.3 (13%)	1.7 (10%)	0.4	20.9 (56%)	4.7	87.9

Thick Vegetarian Minestrone Soup

One way to add fiber and lots of vitamins and minerals to the menu without mounting up the calories is by serving a clear soup filled with vegetables like this thick vegetarian minestrone soup. Because it's prepared from a flavorful vegetable stock, egg-free macaroni, and a medley of tender, garden-fresh vegetables, all types of diners and especially those avoiding animal foods will appreciate it. Offer a cup as a low-calorie introduction to a meal or as a main course selection along with a half sandwich.

Servings:24   *Serving Size: $\frac{9}{10}$ c*
Yield: 1 gal + 1½ qt

Vegetable cooking spray, olive-flavored	—	Small macaroni, without eggs, cooked without salt	4 oz as purchased
Onions, very thin slices	8 oz		
Carrots, washed, small dice	4 oz	White beans, cooked without salt or canned, drained, rinsed with cold water	1 lb cooked or canned, drained
Celery, small dice	4 oz		
Zucchini, small dice	4 oz		
Red cabbage, shredded	4 oz		
Tomatoes, fresh or canned, peeled, coarsely chopped	10 oz		
Flavorful vegetable stock (see page 2) or *rich white chicken stock (see page 7)	3½ qt	Parsley, minced	¼ c + 2 T
Basil leaves, minced or dried	1½ T or 1½ t	Garlic, minced	1 T
		Salt	To taste
Oregano, minced or dried	½ T or ½ t	Pepper, freshly ground	To taste

1. Coat a sauce pot with cooking spray. Place over medium heat until hot. Add the onions, carrots, and celery. Saute until almost tender without browning.
2. Add the zucchini and cabbage. Cook partially, or another 5 minutes.
3. Add the tomatoes, stock, and basil and oregano if dried. Heat to a boil. Reduce the heat to low; simmer until the vegetables are almost cooked.
4. Add the pasta and beans; heat through. Stir in the basil and oregano if fresh, and add remaining four ingredients immediately before service.

5. Serve in heated soup bowls. Offer freshly grated part-skim milk parmesan cheese on the side if desired.

*Omit vegetarian from this soup's name if chicken stock replaces the vegetable stock.

Servings	Calories	Protein (g) (%)	Fat (g) (%)	Cholesterol (mg)	Carbohydrates (g) (%)	Fiber (g)	Sodium (mg)
1	69	3.2 (18%)	0.3 (4%)	0	14.2 (78%)	2.2	22.5

Whole Wheat Chicken Noodle Soup with Vegetables

To produce chicken noodle soup with a clear, flavorful broth, tender, whole wheat noodles, and vibrant, al dente vegetables, boil the high-starch noodles separately and allow the vegetables to simmer in the broth only until tender-crisp. It certainly beats cloudy chicken soup with mushy noodles and overcooked vegetables.

Servings: 24   *Serving Size: $1\frac{1}{3}$ c*
Yield: 2 gal

Noodles, whole wheat, medium wide	10 oz	Wine, dry, white	1 c
		Bay leaf	1
Chicken, breasts, skinless, trimmed of fat (with bone)	3 lb	Carrots, washed, small dice	$1\frac{1}{2}$ lb
		Celery, small dice	12 oz
		Peas, fresh, shelled or frozen	10 oz
rich white chicken stock (see page 7)	$1\frac{1}{2}$ gal + 1 pt	Salt	To taste
		Pepper, freshly ground	To taste
		Parsley, minced	$\frac{1}{4}$ c

1. In a saucepan, boil the noodles in unsalted water until tender, or about 8 minutes. Drain. Rinse in cold water. Set aside.
2. Place the chicken breasts, stock, white wine, and bay leaf in a sauce pot. Heat to a boil; reduce the heat to low; simmer until the chicken is no longer pink, or about 25 minutes. Skim the froth as needed.
3. Remove the stock from the heat. Remove the chicken breasts from the stock with a slotted spoon. When cool enough to handle, remove the bones; dice small.
4. Add the carrots, celery, and peas, if fresh, to the stock. Boil until tender.
5. Add the peas if frozen, diced chicken, and noodles to the stock. Heat through.
6. Remove the bay leaf. Skim any fat from the surface. To adjust the soup's consistency, thicken by removing the extra broth or reducing the broth separately from the cooked ingredients and thin by adding stock or water. Season with salt and pepper to taste. Serve in heated bowls, garnished with parsley.

Servings	Calories	Protein (g) (%)	Fat (g) (%)	Cholesterol (mg)	Carbohydrates (g) (%)	Fiber (g)	Sodium (mg)
1	144	20 (57%)	2.5 (16%)	32.9	9.4 (27%)	2.2	151

No alcohol is listed in the nutrition analysis. It is assumed to be cooked off from the wine during simmering.

2

Sauces

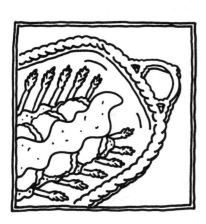

HOT (WARM) SAUCES

Chicken Gravy Thickened with Blended Vegetables

While this gravy doesn't contain the fat that Grandma's gravy did, it tastes mighty good.

Servings: 24   *Serving Size: ⅓ c*
Yield: 2 qt

Flour, cake or all-purpose, unbleached	1 oz	Cloves, freshly ground	⅛ t
Onions, coarsely chopped	8 oz	Rich white chicken stock (see page 7)	1½ qt
Corn kernels, fresh or frozen	6 oz	Milk, evaporated, skim	1 c
Carrots, washed, coarsely grated	4 oz	Salt	To taste
		Pepper, freshly ground	To taste

1. In a saucepan, add the flour; cook over low heat, stirring continuously until lightly browned, or about 5 minutes. Transfer to a small bowl. When cool, mix with enough cold water to form a smooth paste. Set aside.
2. Rinse out the saucepan. Add the onions and next four ingredients. Heat to a boil. Reduce the heat to low; simmer until the vegetables are tender, or about 10 minutes. In a blender, process the vegetables and broth until smooth.
3. Return to the saucepan. Whisk in the flour paste. Heat the sauce to a boil. Reduce the heat to low; simmer until thickening occurs and the mixture is sauce consistency, or about 5 min.
4. Add the evaporated milk; simmer until heated through. If the sauce is too thick, add stock or evaporated skim milk. If the sauce is too thin, thicken by reducing or by adding a cornstarch slurry. Season with salt and pepper to taste. Serve with baked or roasted poultry selections such as crispy baked mustard chicken breast (see page 134) or chicken thighs in crispy cinnamon crust (see page 131), or over hot, sliced, poultry-filled sandwiches or mashed potato dishes like mashed golden buttermilk potatoes (see page 223).

Servings	Calories	Protein (g) (%)	Fat (g) (%)	Cholesterol (mg)	Carbohydrates (g) (%)	Fiber (g)	Sodium (mg)
1	33	2.4 (29%)	0.6 (16%)	0.4	4.6 (55%)	0.5	36.1

Italian-Style Tomato Sauce

This oil-free, meatless Italian-style tomato sauce has a host of uses in a variety of dishes. It might top pizzas or pastas, be baked with chicken or beef, accent steamed vegetables, replace the mayonnaise on sandwiches, season fish or shellfish, or act as a dip with roasted potatoes.

Servings: 24   *Serving Size: $\frac{2}{3}$ c*
Yield: 1 gal

Vegetable cooking spray, olive-flavored	—	Basil, dried	2 T
Onion, minced	1 lb	Oregano, dried	1 T
Garlic, minced	2 t	Thyme, dried	2 t
*Tomatoes, roma or canned, peeled, coarsely chopped	8 lb	Fennel seeds	1 t
		Salt	To taste
Carrots, washed, grated fine	5 oz	Pepper, freshly ground	To taste
Parsley, minced	$\frac{1}{2}$ c	Apple or fruit juice concentrate, unsweetened	Optional
Bay leaves	2		

1. Coat a sauce pot with cooking spray. Place over medium heat until hot. Add the onions and garlic; cook until tender, without browning.
2. Add the tomatoes and next seven ingredients. Heat to boil; reduce the heat to low; simmer until the flavors are mellowed and the liquid is reduced to sauce consistency, or about 45 minutes.
3. Remove the bay leaves. Season with salt and pepper to taste. Add juice concentrate if needed to balance the flavor. Serve over cooked vegetables, meat, or poultry selections or use with pasta dishes such as spinach almond lasagne (see page 263) or manicotti tubes filled with spinach, mushrooms, and cheeses, covered with tomato sauce (see page 259).

*The thick meaty texture and few seeds of the egg-shaped roma tomato make it excellent for sauces. It is also known as the plum tomato, Italian tomato, and paste tomato. When not available, replace with ripe, flavorful, slicing tomatoes.

Servings	Calories	Protein (g) (%)	Fat (g) (%)	Cholesterol (mg)	Carbohydrates (g) (%)	Fiber (g)	Sodium (mg)
1	48	1.8 (13%)	0.7 (11%)	0	10.8 (76%)	3.4	17.5

Low-Fat White Sauce (Medium Consistency)

Low-fat white sauce is made much the same as a standard white sauce. To lighten it up, this sauce is prepared with nonfat milk rather than whole; higher starch cake flour replaces the traditional bread flour and cholesterol-free margarine replaces the butter. Typically, the butter is clarified in a white sauce to prevent lump formation. In this sauce, the fat of choice, margarine, is not clarified so it retains its flavorful milk solid.

Servings: 24   *Serving Size: 2 T + 2 t*
Yield: 1 qt

Margarine, unsalted, corn oil	2 oz	Clove, whole	1
Flour, cake or all-purpose,		Nutmeg, freshly ground	To taste
unbleached	2 oz	Salt	To taste
Milk, nonfat, hot	1¼ qt	Pepper, black or white, freshly	
Onion, very small, peeled	1	ground	To taste
Bay leaf	1		

1. Melt the margarine in a sauce pot over low heat. Stir in the flour, mixing thoroughly with the margarine. Cook over very low heat, stirring constantly until chalky and frothy in appearance, or 2 to 3 minutes. Cool the roux slightly.
2. Gradually add the hot milk to the roux, beating constantly. Heat to a boil, stirring constantly. Reduce the heat to low.
3. Stick the bay leaf to the onion with the clove. Add to the sauce. Simmer until the starchy taste of the flour has cooked out, or at least 10 minutes, stirring occasionally.
4. If necessary to adjust the consistency, add more nonfat milk to thin and reduce to thicken. Season to taste with nutmeg, salt, and pepper.
5. Strain the sauce through a china cap lined with cheesecloth. Cover to prevent skin formation. Keep hot in a bain marie or cool in a cold-water bath for later use. Use this sauce to top steamed vegetables such as broccoli or asparagus, or use as an ingredient in other dishes such as penne pasta baked in a creamy cheddar and Swiss cheese sauce (see page 262) and spinach mushroom souffle (see page 325).

Variations

Low-Fat White Sauce (light consistency): Use 3 oz roux—1½ oz margarine and 1½ oz flour.

Low-Fat White Sauce (heavy consistency): Use 6 oz roux—3 oz margarine and 3 oz flour.

Small Sauces

For each of the following sauces, enhance 1 recipe of the low-fat white sauce (medium consistency) as indicated.

Low-Fat Cheddar Cheese Sauce: Add 8 oz low-fat, low-cholesterol, and low-sodium shredded cheddar cheese, ¼ t dry mustard, and 2 t very low sodium Worcestershire sauce to the sauce.

Low-Fat Creamy Onion Sauce: Simmer 1 lb minced onions in ½ c rich white chicken stock (see page 7) until tender and the stock is evaporated. Simmer the cooked onions in low-fat white sauce for 15 minutes. Strain the sauce in a fine mesh strainer, pressing the onions to extract their flavor; discard.

Low-Fat Creamy Shrimp Sauce: Simmer 6 oz shrimp, cooked without fat or salt and ground very fine, in low-fat white sauce until the flavors are blended, or about 5 minutes.

Low-Fat Mustard Sauce: Add 2½ T prepared mustard or as desired to the sauce.

Low-Fat Swiss Cheese Sauce: Add 8 oz low-fat, low-cholesterol, and low-sodium shredded Swiss cheese to the sauce.

Servings	Calories	Protein (g) (%)	Fat (g) (%)	Cholesterol (mg)	Carbohydrates (g) (%)	Fiber (g)	Sodium (mg)
1	43	1.9 (17%)	2.3 (47%)	1.0	3.8 (35%)	< 0.1	34

Mushroom Sauce Thickened with Pureed Vegetables

A puree of sauteed minced mushrooms and onions serves as both the primary thickening and flavoring agent in this mushroom sauce. To complete the low-fat sauce, the puree is blended with evaporated skim milk and finished with a pinch of freshly ground nutmeg.

Servings: 24   *Serving Size: 1⅓ T*
Yield: 1 pt

Margarine, corn oil, unsalted	1 oz	Wine, white, dry	¼ c
Mushrooms, minced	12 oz	Nutmeg, freshly ground	⅛ t
Onions, minced	8 oz	Pepper, freshly ground	To taste
Flour, cake or all-purpose,			or ¼ t
unbleached	1 oz	Salt	To taste
Milk, evaporated, skim, hot	1¼ pt		

1. Melt the margarine in a nonstick saucepan over low heat. Add the mushrooms and onions; cook until tender.
2. Blend in the flour; cook, stirring for 3–5 minutes. Do not brown.
3. Add the hot milk slowly, stirring. Heat the sauce to a boil; reduce the heat to low; simmer until it reaches sauce consistency and the mushrooms are cooked into the sauce, or about 30 minutes, stirring occasionally.
4. In a blender, puree the mixture until smooth. Return to a clean saucepan; simmer over low heat until reduced by 2 tablespoons. Place the white wine in a small saucepan; heat until reduced to 2 tablespoons. Stir the wine and seasonings into the sauce. To adjust the sauce's consistency, thin with additional evaporated skim milk and thicken by reducing or with a cornstarch slurry.
5. Serve over pasta, with poultry selections, or use as an ingredient in dishes such as macaroni layered with ground turkey in red wine mushroom sauce (see page 257) or zucchini slices layered with ground lamb and cheese sauce (see page 91).

Servings	Calories	Protein (g) (%)	Fat (g) (%)	Cholesterol (mg)	Carbohydrates (g) (%)	Fiber (g)	Sodium (mg)
1	41	2.5 (24%)	1.2 (27%)	1.0	5.2 (50%)	0.3	35.3

No alcohol is listed in the nutrition analysis. It is assumed to be cooked off during the simmering of the wine.

Tomato Coulis Seasoned with Garlic and Basil

This light tomato coulis is prepared from a puree of tomatoes, shallots, and garlic simmered with red wine and apple juice concentrate and seasoned with slivers of fresh basil. A dollop of margarine is melted in the sauce at the end of cooking to maximize its effect on flavor.

Servings: 24   *Serving Size: 2⅓ T*
Yield: 3½ c

Vegetable cooking spray, butter-flavored	—	Apple juice concentrate, unsweetened	¼ c
Shallots, minced	2 T	Pepper, freshly ground	To taste
Garlic, minced	2 T	Margarine, corn oil, unsalted	1 oz
Tomatoes, peeled, coarsely chopped	1½ lb	Basil leaves, thin 1-in. slivers	½ c (½ oz)
Wine, red, dry	¾ c	Salt	To taste

1. Place a saucepan coated with cooking spray over medium-high heat until hot. Add the shallots and garlic; saute until tender.
2. Add the tomatoes, red wine, juice concentrate, and pepper. Heat to a boil; reduce the heat to low; simmer until the pulp is tender and the flavors blended, or about 15 minutes.
3. In a blender, process the mixture until smooth. To adjust the sauce's consistency, thin with water and reduce to thicken. Reheat if needed. Stir in the margarine, basil, and salt to taste. Serve with vegetable or egg dishes such as broccoli timbales enhanced with Swiss cheese (see page 322).

Servings	Calories	Protein (g) (%)	Fat (g) (%)	Cholesterol (mg)	Carbohydrates (g) (%)	Fiber (g)	Sodium (mg)
1	23	0.4 (6%)	1.1 (41%)	0	3.1 (53%)	0.4	3.9

No alcohol is listed in the nutrition analysis. It is assumed to be cooked off during the simmering of the wine.

Vegetable-Thickened Vodka Sauce

A mixture of pureed corn, tomatoes, and onions simmered in rich chicken stock provides the thickening agent for this sauce. They add flavor without fat and enhance the nutritional value of the sauce as well. Rather than cream, the sauce is finished with evaporated skim milk.

Servings: 24   *Serving Size: 2⅓ T*
Yield: 1½ pt + ½ c

Tomato, coarsely chopped	12 oz	Vodka	1 qt + ½ c
Corn kernels, fresh or frozen	8 oz	Milk, evaporated, skim	¾ c
Onion, coarsely chopped	6 oz	Salt	To taste
Rich white chicken stock (see page 7)	1½ pt	Pepper, freshly ground	To taste

1. In a saucepan, heat the first five ingredients to a boil; reduce the heat to low; simmer until the vegetables are tender, or about 15 minutes.
2. In a blender, puree the mixture until smooth. Return to a clean saucepan; cook over medium-high heat until the mixture is sauce consistency. If reduced to 2¾ c and still very thin, thicken with a cornstarch slurry.
3. Stir in the evaporated milk; reduce the heat to low; heat through. Season with salt and pepper to taste. Serve with roasted or grilled white meat selections such as roasted veal sirloin (see page 105).

Servings	Calories	Protein (g) (%)	Fat (g) (%)	Cholesterol (mg)	Carbohydrates (g) (%)	Fiber (g)	Sodium (mg)	Alcohol (g) (%)
1	51	1.7 (13%)	0.4 (7%)	0.3	4.1 (32%)	0.6	21.5	3.5 (48%)

CONDIMENT SAUCES, SALSAS, RELISHES, CHUTNEYS, AND SPREADS

African-Style Spicy Hot Sauce

Hot sauce typically is made from oil and chilies. This version is much healthier, prepared from hot chilies, of course, a small amount of peanut oil, and chicken stock, and seasoned with freshly minced herbs and toasted spices.

Servings: 24
Yield: 1 qt

Serving Size: $2\frac{2}{3}$ T

Cumin seeds	$2 T + 2\frac{1}{4} t$	Rich white chicken stock	
Coriander seeds	$1 T + 2\frac{1}{2} t$	(see page 7) or flavorful	
Oil, peanut	$\frac{1}{2}$ c	vegetable stock (see	
Cilantro, leaves	$1\frac{1}{2}$ oz	page 2)	$1 pt + \frac{3}{4}$ c
Garlic, cloves, peeled	$1\frac{1}{3}$ oz	Salt	To taste
Hot chilies, dried, crushed	$1 T + 2 t$		

1. In a nonstick skillet, toast the cumin and coriander seeds, stirring, until brown.
2. Add the toasted seeds, oil, cilantro, garlic, and chilies to a blender or food processor; puree until chunky consistency. Blend in the stock and salt to taste. The consistency will be thin.
3. Serve as a condiment with meat dishes such as African-inspired lamb stew with vegetables and couscous (see page 82), fish, or poultry selections. Refrigerate for later use.

Servings	Calories	Protein (g) (%)	Fat (g) (%)	Cholesterol (mg)	Carbohydrates (g) (%)	Fiber (g)	Sodium (mg)
1	51	0.9 (7%)	4.9 (84%)	0	1.2 (9%)	0.4	10.3

Cranberry Pineapple Relish

Keep your menu up-to-date with accompaniments beyond ketchup and mustard, like cranberry pineapple relish. Everyone profits, both diners and the bottom line.

Servings: 24   *Serving Size: 3½ T*
Yield: 1¼ qt + ¼ c

Cranberries, fresh or frozen, unsweetened	12 oz	*Pineapple, small dice, fresh or canned without sugar, drained	1½ lb
Pineapple juice concentrate, unsweetened	½ c	Carrots, washed, coarsely grated	6 oz
Orange juice concentrate, unsweetened	¼ c		

1. Heat the first three ingredients to a boil in a saucepan. Cook until most of the berries have popped, or about 5 minutes.
2. Remove the cranberries from the heat. When cool, stir in the pineapple and carrots. Refrigerate until chilled. Serve as a condiment with poultry selections such as roasted turkey or grilled chicken breasts.

*See page 492 for fresh pineapple peeling and dicing directions.

Servings	Calories	Protein (g) (%)	Fat (g) (%)	Cholesterol (mg)	Carbohydrates (g) (%)	Fiber (g)	Sodium (mg)
1	39	0.4 (4%)	0.2 (4%)	0	9.8 (93%)	1.2	3.2

Fresh Mint and Cilantro Chutney

I fell in love with this chutney while living in India. There, it is used as a condiment the way we use ketchup and mustard here. Offer it in a similar fashion with grilled or roasted meat, fish, and poultry selections, as a dip with low-fat chips and vegetables, or on top of sandwiches. One of my favorite ways to enjoy this chutney is as an alternative to butter along with whole grain flat breads, hot out of the oven.

Servings: 24　　　*Serving Size: 2 T*
Yield: 1½ pt

Onion, coarsely chopped	4 oz	Mint leaves	2 oz
Gingerroot, peeled, sliced	1 oz	Red pepper, ground	To taste
Garlic cloves, medium-sized,			or ¼ t
peeled	2	Salt	To taste
Yogurt, nonfat, plain	1½ c	Pepper, freshly ground	To taste
Lemon juice, freshly squeezed	2 t		
Cilantro, washed, stems			
removed	4 oz		

1. In a blender, puree the onion, ginger, and garlic with a small amount of the yogurt until smooth.
2. Add all the remaining ingredients; blend until smooth.
3. Refrigerate until chilled and the flavors are mellowed. Serve as a condiment with meat, seafood, and poultry selections such as grilled chicken drumsticks tandoori-style (see page 135), or offer with bread in lieu of butter or on vegetable sandwiches like cucumber (see page 340).

Servings	Calories	Protein (g) (%)	Fat (g) (%)	Cholesterol (mg)	Carbohydrates (g) (%)	Fiber (g)	Sodium (mg)
1	13	1.1 (33%)	0.1 (6%)	0.3	2.1 (61%)	0.2	14

Fresh Tomato Salsa Seasoned with Cilantro and Chilies

Like salt and pepper on the American dining table, in Mexico, a bowl of fresh tomato or green sauce is essential. This fresh tomato salsa can be prepared in advance but for a fresh, crisp flavor, it's best if prepared no more than a few hours prior to service.

Servings: 24 **Serving Size: 2 T + 2 t**
Yield: 1 qt

Tomatoes, ripe, small dice	1 lb + 3 oz	Lemon juice, freshly squeezed	2 T
Onions, minced	6 oz	Salt	To taste
Cilantro, minced	3 T		
Chili, serrano or any fresh hot, green chili, membranes and seeds removed, minced	1 or to taste		

1. Combine all the ingredients in a bowl; mix well.
2. Serve at room temperature or chilled with raw vegetables, roasted corn tortilla chips (see page 346) or meat, fish, poultry, and vegetarian dishes, such as bean- and cheese-filled whole wheat tortillas (see page 327).

Servings	Calories	Protein (g) (%)	Fat (g) (%)	Cholesterol (mg)	Carbohydrates (g) (%)	Fiber (g)	Sodium (mg)
1	8	0.3 (13%)	0.1 (8%)	0	1.9 (79%)	0.4	2.4

Homestyle Chunky Peanut Butter

This American favorite was concocted in 1890 by a physician as a health food. Today, it is estimated Americans eat about 700 million pounds of peanut butter each year. To prepare a healthy version of Americans' most popular sandwich,* peanut butter and jelly, spread homestyle chunky peanut butter and fruit-sweetened fruit spread on whole grain bread. Serve open-faced or top with another slice of whole grain bread.

Servings: 96   *Serving Size: 1 T*
Yield: 1½ qt

Peanuts, fresh roasted, unsalted	3 lb + 12 oz	Oil, peanut or canola	¼ c + 2 T
		Salt	To taste

1. In a large blender or in batches, add the nuts and about 3 T of the oil; process until the nuts are finely chopped, scraping the sides of the container occasionally. Remove about ¼ of the nuts. Set aside.
2. Add the remaining oil; process the remaining nuts until smooth.
3. Mix in the chopped nuts.
4. Use as an ingredient in dishes such as peanut butter cookies, Oriental noodles with peanut sauce, or ants on a log (celery sticks stuffed with peanut butter and topped with raisins), or serve as a dip. The sandwich possibilities are also unlimited. Homestyle chunky peanut butter might be spread on whole grain bread and featured in solo form or topped with a variety of other ingredients such as sliced bananas, lettuce leaves, fruit-sweetened fruit spread, honey, marshmallows, roasted Idaho potato chips (see page 347), raisins, or a combination of these options. Sandwiches can be presented open-face or covered with another slice of whole grain bread and cut into triangles, squares, or other shapes.

The peanut butter can be stored refrigerated in a covered container for up to 10 days.

*It is estimated that the average American child will eat 1,500 peanut butter sandwiches before graduating from high school.

Servings	Calories	Protein (g) (%)	Fat (g) (%)	Cholesterol (mg)	Carbohydrates (g) (%)	Fiber (g)	Sodium (mg)
1	95	3.6 (14%)	8.3 (73%)	0	3.3 (13%)	1.2	0.9

Hot Red Chili Sauce

In the event that hot red chili sauce is too pungent for your diners' palates, dissolve a tablespoon of unsweetened juice concentrate or honey into 2 tablespoons of cold water mixed with 1 tablespoon of vinegar and blend it into the simmering sauce.

Servings: 24   *Serving Size: 1½ T*
Yield: 1⅛ pt

Chilies, Ancho, dried	4	Garlic, clove	1
Water, hot	½ c + 2 T	Parsley, minced	2 t
		Apple or fruit juice	
Tomatoes, peeled, coarsely		concentrate, unsweetened	2 t
chopped	10 oz	Salt	To taste
Onions, coarsely chopped	6 oz	Vinegar, cider	1 t

1. In a nonstick skillet, cook the chilies over medium-high heat, turning constantly, until lightly toasted, or about 3 minutes. When cool, remove the stems, seeds, and membranes; discard.
2. Place the chilies and hot water in a small bowl. Set aside to soak for 1 hour.
3. In a blender, combine the chilies and soaking broth, tomatoes, onions, and garlic. Puree until smooth.
4. Add the tomato puree to a saucepan; simmer over medium heat, stirring constantly until it reaches sauce consistency and the flavors are mellowed, or about 5 minutes. Stir in the parsley, juice concentrate, and salt. When cool, stir in the vinegar. Serve as a condiment with dishes such as bean- and cheese-filled whole wheat tortillas (see page 327) or offer as a dip with items like roasted corn tortilla chips (see page 346).

Servings	Calories	Protein (g) (%)	Fat (g) (%)	Cholesterol (mg)	Carbohydrates (g) (%)	Fiber (g)	Sodium (mg)
1	9	0.3 (13%)	0.1 (6%)	0	2.1 (81%)	0.4	2.2

Lime Ginger-Garlic Sauce

The cuisine in many of the best contemporary American restaurants has definite Asian overtones to it. Call it Pacific Rim, Pacific New Wave, East-West Fusion Cuisine, or any of a number of variations. Like this lime ginger-garlic sauce, its light and refreshing attributes are being enthusiastically received by diners.

Servings: 24　　　　　*Serving Size: $1\frac{2}{5}$ T*
Yield: 1 pt + 2 T

Gingerroot, peeled, small chunks	$\frac{1}{2}$ oz	Rich white chicken stock (see page 7)	$\frac{3}{4}$ c
Garlic cloves, peeled	2 oz	Soy sauce, low-sodium	$\frac{1}{2}$ c
Chilies, fresh, serrano or other hot, seeds and membranes removed	2	*Fish sauce	2 T
Lime juice, freshly squeezed	$\frac{3}{4}$ c	White grape or fruit juice concentrate, unsweetened	$\frac{1}{2}$ T

1. In a blender, place all the ingredients. Blend until the ingredients are coarsely chopped. Serve with Asian-style steamed squid on a bed of shredded lettuce (see page 165).

*Fish sauce is a strongly flavored, pungent seasoning sauce used in the cuisine of Southeast Asian countries such as Thailand, Vietnam, and Cambodia. For more information, see page 503.

Servings	Calories	Protein (g) (%)	Fat (g) (%)	Cholesterol (mg)	Carbohydrates (g) (%)	Fiber (g)	Sodium (mg)
1	14	1.1 (29%)	0.1 (5%)	0.9	2.6 (66%)	0.3	175

Papaya Mango Salsa

Popular eateries across the nation are now offering tantalizing salsas. Cubes of buttery soft papaya and juicey, peach sweet mango are combined with minced red onions and jalapeno chilies in this terrific salsa. It pairs well with grilled or roasted fish, poultry, and pork selections.

Servings: 24   *Serving Size: 2 T*
Yield: 1½ pt

Papaya, ripe, peeled, seeded, very small dice	12 oz	Cilantro, minced	¼ c
		Lime juice, freshly squeezed	¼ c
*Mango, ripe, peeled, pitted, very small dice	4 oz	Apple juice concentrate, unsweetened	¼ c
Pepper, red and green, bell, very small dice	2 oz each	Vinegar, red wine	1 T
		Salt	To taste
Red onion, minced	2 oz	Pepper, freshly ground	To taste
Chili, jalapeno or other hot, fresh, seeds and membranes removed, minced	1 T		

1. Combine all the ingredients in a storage container; mix. Refrigerate until chilled. Serve along with broiled or grilled poultry or fish selections such as marinated broiled shark fillets (see page 153).

*To dice a mango see page 493.

Servings	Calories	Protein (g) (%)	Fat (g) (%)	Cholesterol (mg)	Carbohydrates (g) (%)	Fiber (g)	Sodium (mg)
1	16	0.2 (5%)	0.1 (3%)	0	4.2 (92%)	0.6	6.6

Spicy Red Pepper Tomato Sauce

Crushed red pepper adds spice to this vegetable-thickened Tomato Sauce. It's the ideal complement to grilled, roasted, or sauteed lean beef selections.

Servings: 24   *Serving Size: 1⅓ T*
Yield: 1 pt

Tomatoes, coarsely chopped	11 oz	Red pepper, crushed	To taste
Water	½ c		or ¾ t
Onions, minced	3 oz	Salt	To taste
Carrots, washed, small dice	2 oz	Pepper, freshly ground	To taste
Garlic, minced	¾ t		

1. Place all the ingredients in a saucepan. Heat to a boil; reduce the heat to low; simmer until the vegetables are tender, or about 15 minutes.
2. In a blender, puree the mixture until smooth. Adjust the consistency by adding water to thin and reducing to thicken. Season with salt and pepper to taste. Serve warm, at room temperature, or chilled as a condiment with meat selections such as sauteed beef sirloin steak (see page 80).

Servings	Calories	Protein (g) (%)	Fat (g) (%)	Cholesterol (mg)	Carbohydrates (g) (%)	Fiber (g)	Sodium (mg)
1	5	0.2 (12%)	0.1 (8%)	0	1.2 (80%)	0.3	2.1

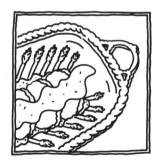

Sweet Spring Roll Sauce

This soy-flavored, fruit, and honey-sweetened sauce with hints of garlic is a pleasing contrast to spicy, hot Asian-style selections.

Servings: 24   *Serving Size: 1 T*
Yield: 1½ c

Rich brown veal stock (see page 4) or very low sodium beef stock	1¼ c	Soy sauce, low-sodium	2 T
		Honey, clover	1 T
		Garlic, minced	1 T
Apple or fruit juice concentrate, unsweetened	3 T	Cornstarch	2 t
		Lemon juice, freshly squeezed	1 T

1. In a saucepan, add the stock and next four ingredients. Heat to a boil; reduce the heat to low. Simmer until the garlic is soft and its flavor mellowed, or about 5 minutes.
2. In a small bowl, stir a small amount of cold water or as needed into the cornstarch to form a smooth paste.
3. Whip the slurry into the stock; cook until thickened, or about 1 minute. To adjust the consistency, thicken the sauce by reducing and thin it by adding stock.
4. Stir in the lemon juice. Pass through a fine mesh strainer to remove the garlic. Set aside to cool. Serve with Asian-style dishes such as Philippine-style spring rolls filled with beef, tofu, and shrimp (see page 76).

Servings	Calories	Protein (g) (%)	Fat (g) (%)	Cholesterol (mg)	Carbohydrates (g) (%)	Fiber (g)	Sodium (mg)
1	11	0.4 (14%)	0.1 (7%)	0	2.2 (79%)	< 0.1	44.3

Tomato Bell Pepper Salsa

The uses for this nearly fat-free and cholesterol-free, fresh salsa are numerous. These are a few:

1. Offer with grilled vegetables, perhaps grilled zucchini, summer squash, or eggplant.

2. Use to dress cold pasta or vegetable salads such as those prepared with short corkscrew pastas like rotelle.

3. Serve as an accompaniment to raw vegetables or chips such as roasted or baked corn or whole wheat tortillas.

4. Use to enhance tacos and burritos filled with lean meat, fish, poultry, or simmered dried beans, low-fat cheeses, and shredded or chopped vegetables.

Servings: 24   *Serving Size: ¼ c*
Yield: 1½ qt

Tomatoes, ripe, small dice	2 lb	Cilantro, minced	¼ c
Onions, minced	6 oz	Garlic, minced	1 T
Peppers, bell, green and		Hot pepper sauce	1 t or
yellow, small dice	3 oz		to taste
	each	Salt	To taste
Lemon juice, freshly squeezed	¼ c	Pepper, freshly ground	To taste

1. Combine all the ingredients in a bowl; mix well. Refrigerate until the flavors are mellowed, or at least 4 hours.
2. Serve at room temperature or chilled as a dip or topping with items such as bean- and cheese-filled whole wheat tortillas (see page 327) or roasted corn tortilla chips (see page 346).

Servings	Calories	Protein (g) (%)	Fat (g) (%)	Cholesterol (mg)	Carbohydrates (g) (%)	Fiber (g)	Sodium (mg)
1	14	0.5 (13%)	0.2 (9%)	0	3.2 (79%)	0.8	3.9

Tomato Cucumber Relish*

Replace mayonnaise, butter, and other high-fat spreads on sandwiches with savory salsas, chunky relishes, and flavorful chutneys like this tomato cucumber relish. Fruit and vegetable sauces add a little something extra to sandwiches. The effect is that the whole sandwich seems greater than the sum of its parts.

Servings: 24   *Serving Size: $3\frac{1}{8}$ T*
Yield: $1\frac{1}{4}$ qt

Tomatoes, ripe, small dice	1 lb + 6 oz	Cilantro, minced	3 T
		Lemon juice, freshly squeezed	3 T
Cucumbers, peeled, small dice	12 oz	Salt	To taste
Red onions, minced	4 oz	Pepper, freshly ground	To taste

1. Combine all the ingredients in a container; mix well.
2. Cover and refrigerate until chilled, or about 1 hour. Serve as a condiment with meat, fish, and poultry dishes or sandwiches such as cajun turkey-tofu burgers (see page 110).

*Adapted from a recipe by Byron Takeuchi.

Servings	Calories	Protein (g) (%)	Fat (g) (%)	Cholesterol (mg)	Carbohydrates (g) (%)	Fiber (g)	Sodium (mg)
1	9	0.4 (14%)	0.1 (10%)	0	2.1 (76%)	0.6	2.8

Tomato Relish Embellished with Fresh Basil and Garlic

Add romance to main course meat, fish, and poultry selections with low-fat, low-calorie chutneys, salsas, and relishes such as this tangy tomato relish flavored with minced garlic and fresh basil.

Servings: 24   *Serving Size: 2⅔ T*
Yield: 1 qt

Tomatoes, ripe, small dice	1½ lb	Basil, fresh, minced or dried	2 T or
Onions, minced	5 oz		2 t
Vinegar, malt	3 T	Worcestershire sauce, very	
Parsley, minced	2 T	low sodium	1 t
Apple or fruit juice		Salt	To taste
concentrate, unsweetened	2 t	Pepper, freshly ground	To taste
Garlic, minced	2 t		

1. Combine all the ingredients in a container; stir until well mixed; cover.
2. Refrigerate until the flavors are blended, or at least 2 hours. Serve with fish, poultry, and lean meat selections such as cajun-style roast tenderloin of beef (see page 68).

Note: If dried basil is used, drop fresh from the name.

Servings	Calories	Protein (g) (%)	Fat (g) (%)	Cholesterol (mg)	Carbohydrates (g) (%)	Fiber (g)	Sodium (mg)
1	10	0.4 (12%)	0.1 (9%)	0	2.3 (79%)	0.5	3.9

Vietnamese-Style Dipping Sauce

Fish sauce, a dominant ingredient in this recipe, is available in Asian markets. It is called *nuoc mam* (NEE-UK MUM) in Vietnam and *nam pla* in Thailand. It is made by layering fish and salt in large jars or barrels and allowing the fish to ferment for three or more months before the accumulated liquid is siphoned off, filtered, and bottled. As a result, while this sauce is low in fat and calories, it is a source of sodium.

Servings: 24   *Serving Size: 2⅔ T*
Yield: 1 qt

Water	1 pt	Chili peppers, fresh, serrano	
*Fish sauce	¾ c	or other small hot, seeds	
White grape or fruit juice		and membranes removed,	
concentrate, unsweetened	¾ c	finely shredded	3
Lime juice, freshly squeezed	½ c	Cilantro leaves	2 T
Carrot, washed, finely		Green onions, white and	
shredded	3 oz	green, thin slices	2 T

1. In a storage container, add all the ingredients; mix to blend. Serve fresh for best flavor. Sprinkle over soups and stir-fries, use as a dip with grilled meats and poultry, such as Asian-inspired broiled Cornish game hen (see page 141), vegetables, egg rolls, or blend with rice to enhance its flavor.

*For more information, see page 503.

Servings	Calories	Protein (g) (%)	Fat (g) (%)	Cholesterol (mg)	Carbohydrates (g) (%)	Fiber (g)	Sodium (mg)
1	29	2.0 (27%)	0.2 (5%)	5.2	5.0 (68%)	0.3	81

Whipped Creamy Cranberry Spread

Reduce the fat and total calories when serving margarine, butter, or cream cheese by whipping and then blending with fruits, fresh herbs, freshly ground spices, minced garlic or green onions, and other flavoring agents. Offer whipped creamy cranberry spread during the Christmas season, whipped strawberry margarine for July Fourth, and whipped honey margarine when the menu calls for a year-round favorite.

Servings: 24   *Serving Size: 1 T + $\frac{1}{2}$ t*
Yield: 1$\frac{3}{4}$ c

Cranberries, fresh or frozen without sugar	5 oz	Orange zest, finely grated	$\frac{1}{2}$ T
Sugar, confectioners'	3 oz	Margarine, unsalted, corn oil	$\frac{1}{2}$ lb

1. In a food processor or blender, place the cranberries and sugar. Using the on-off button, coarsely chop. Mix in the orange zest. Whip the margarine until nearly doubled in volume. Blend the chopped cranberry mixture with the margarine until well mixed. Serve with whole grain breads, waffles, or pancakes.

Servings	Calories	Protein (g) (%)	Fat (g) (%)	Cholesterol (mg)	Carbohydrates (g) (%)	Fiber (g)	Sodium (mg)
1	84	0.1 (< 1%)	7.6 (79%)	0	4.3 (20%)	0.3	0.3

Zesty Freshly Grated Horseradish and Yogurt Sauce with Dillweed

As its name suggests, this sauce is a real "kicker." While most restaurant operators choose prepared horseradish for convenience, the sharpness of creamy, fresh, white horseradish root blended with cool, tart yogurt is what makes this a wonderful sauce for roasted meats. For best results, use fresh horseradish within one week. As it ages, it browns and loses potency.

Servings: 24   *Serving Size: 1 T*
Yield: 1½ c

Yogurt, nonfat, plain	1 c	Dillweed, fresh, minced	1½ T for garnish
Apple, Granny Smith or other tart apple, peeled, coarsely grated	2 oz	Lemon zest, finely grated	1½ t for garnish
Horseradish, fresh, peeled, finely grated	2 oz		

1. Combine the first three ingredients in a storage container.* Stir until well mixed. Cover; refrigerate until the flavors are blended, or at least 2 hours.
2. Serve with meat selections such as Cajun-style roast tenderloin of beef (see page 68). Garnish with dillweed and lemon zest.

*Horseradish tarnishes silver; keep this in mind when selecting storage and serving containers for this sauce.

Servings	Calories	Protein (g) (%)	Fat (g) (%)	Cholesterol (mg)	Carbohydrates (g) (%)	Fiber (g)	Sodium (mg)
1	8	0.6 (27%)	< 0.1 (4%)	0.2	1.5 (69%)	0.1	8.1

RUBS, MARINADES, GLAZES, AND SPICE BLENDS

All-American Barbecue Sauce for Fowl

Barbecued food, as most Americans know it, is basted with a highly seasoned sauce as it cooks. The same sauce is served as an accompaniment to the food after it's cooked. This barbecue sauce, like the version most Americans know, is made with ketchup, vinegar, brown sugar, mustard, and onion.

Servings: 24   *Serving Size: 1⅓ T*
Yield: 1 pt

Onion, minced	4 oz	Worcestershire sauce, very	
Garlic, minced	1 t	low sodium	¼ c
Ketchup, no salt added	1½ c	Vinegar, cider	3 T
Water	1½ c	Mustard powder	½ T
Celery, very small dice	3 oz	Lemon juice, freshly squeezed	¼ c
Sugar, light brown	2 oz	Salt	To taste

1. Add the onion and garlic to a nonreactive saucepan. Braise-deglaze over medium high heat, adding water as needed until tender without browning.
2. Add the ketchup, 1½ c water, and next five ingredients. Heat to a boil; reduce the heat to low; simmer until the flavors are blended and it achieves the consistency to coat a spoon, or about 30 minutes.
3. Stir in the lemon juice and salt to taste. Let the sauce cool before using as a marinade or glaze for grilled or broiled chicken (see All-American barbecue-style chicken, page 122), Cornish game hen, squab, quail, pheasant, or other fowl.

Servings	Calories	Protein (g) (%)	Fat (g) (%)	Cholesterol (mg)	Carbohydrates (g) (%)	Fiber (g)	Sodium (mg)
1	30	0.4 (4%)	0.3 (8%)	0	7.8 (88%)	0.4	17.2

Indian-Inspired Spice Blend

This seasoning agent is a blend of several aromatic spices with a peppery bite. It is a variation of the east Indian seasoning mixture called *garam masala*. Commercial blends are available but often contain unnecessary ingredients, are stale, and prepared from spices that have not been roasted. For best results, prepare your own. Indian-inspired spice blend will keep fresh up to three months stored in an airtight container in a dark, cool, dry place.

Servings: 144   *Serving Size: 1 t*
Yield: 1½ pt or 7⅔ oz

Cardamom pods	½ oz (¼ c)	Cumin seeds	4 oz (1 c)
Cinnamon, 3-in. sticks	¼ oz (6)	Peppercorns	1⅓ oz (½ c)
Coriander seeds	1⅓ oz (1 c)	Cloves, whole	¼ oz (2 T)

1. Break open the cardamom pods. Remove the seeds; discard the skins.
2. Break the cinnamon sticks into small pieces with a kitchen mallet or rolling pin.
3. Add all the spices to a nonstick or heavy skillet. Roast over high heat, stirring, until the spices begin to burst. Set aside until cool.
4. In a coffee grinder, spice mill, or blender, grind the spices to a fine powder. Store in an airtight covered container in a cool, dry, dark place for up to three months.
5. Use to season meat, fish, poultry, dried bean and lentil dishes such as pink lentils seasoned with a roasted blend of spices (see page 180) or vegetable selections such as green peas and fresh cheese in tomato sauce (see page 332).

Servings	Calories	Protein (g) (%)	Fat (g) (%)	Cholesterol (mg)	Carbohydrates (g) (%)	Fiber (g)	Sodium (mg)
1	6	0.2 (12%)	0.3 (30%)	0	1.1 (58%)	0.6	1.6

Orange-Rosemary Mustard Rub*

Add flavor to lean cuts of meat by rubbing their surfaces with seasoned pastes before cooking. While Dijon-style mustard adds moisture to orange-rosemary mustard rub, other low-fat, liquid flavoring agents such as nonfat yogurt, fruit and vegetable juices, soy sauce, or vinegar might be blended with herbs, spices, and other seasoning ingredients to form aromatic, flavorful seasoned pastes.

Servings: 24　　　　*Serving Size: 2 T*
Yield: 1½ pt

Mustard, Dijon-style	1 pt	Rosemary, minced	1⅓ oz (¾ c)
Parsley, minced	1½ oz	Pepper, freshly ground, coarse	1 oz (¼ c)
Orange or lemon zest, finely grated, dried	1½ oz		

1. In a small bowl, combine all the ingredients; mix to blend. Spread or pat on lean cuts of beef, pork, veal, or venison just before cooking, or up to 5 hours in advance. Store refrigerated when not in use.

*Adapted from "Flavorful Rubs and Marinades for Beef" (1992), Beef Board and Beef Industry Council, 444 North Michigan Ave., Chicago, IL 60611.

Servings	Calories	Protein (g) (%)	Fat (g) (%)	Cholesterol (mg)	Carbohydrates (g) (%)	Fiber (g)	Sodium (mg)
1	23	1.2 (18%)	1.1 (37%)	0	3.0 (44%)	1.2	263

Pineapple Yogurt Pepper Sauce*

Yogurt has many uses in light and healthy cooking. In this recipe, it serves as a base for a marinade. While oil is an important ingredient in most marinades, that's not the case here. Because of yogurt's creamy consistency, it readily adheres to ingredients, thereby eliminating the need for oil. It can be complemented by a variety of flavors. In this pineapple yogurt pepper sauce, yogurt is flavored with pineapple juice concentrate, sherry, freshly minced cilantro, and a sprinkle of red pepper.

Servings: 24   *Serving Size: 3⅓ T*
Yield: 1¼ qt

Yogurt, nonfat, plain	1 qt	Cilantro, minced	1 oz
Pineapple juice concentrate,		Mustard, dry	1 T
unsweetened	½ c	Red pepper, ground	To taste
Sherry, dry	¼ c		or ⅛ t

1. In a bowl, mix all the ingredients. Cover and chill to mellow the flavors for at least 12 hours. Use as a marinade with grilled fish and vegetable selections such as shark and vegetable kabob (see page 157).

*Adapted from a recipe by Paul Findly and Rajeev Maini.

Servings	Calories	Protein (g) (%)	Fat (g) (%)	Cholesterol (mg)	Carbohydrates (g) (%)	Fiber (g)	Sodium (mg)	Alcohol (g) (%)
1	36	2.5 (27%)	0.1 (3%)	0.7	5.9 (65%)	0.1	40	0.2 (4%)

Red Wine Marinade for Game

Wine marinades traditionally have been used to marinate venison and other game. For this reason, much of the gamy flavor associated with venison and other game is due to the marinade rather than the meat's natural flavor. For example, domestic meat such as beef will taste somewhat like game after it is marinated and cooked in this particular marinade.

Servings: 24
Yield: 2¼ qt

Serving Size: ⅜ c

Onion, minced	8 oz	Basil, dried	1 T
Celery, small dice	4 oz	Cloves, whole	1 T
Carrot, small dice	4 oz	Allspice, whole	1 T
Parsley, minced	1½ oz	Peppercorns	1 T
Bay leaves	2	Wine, red, dry	2 qt
Thyme, dried	1 T	Vinegar, red, wine	1 c

1. Place all the ingredients in a nonreactive saucepan. Heat to a boil; reduce the heat to low; simmer until the vegetables are tender, or about 20 minutes. Cool. Use as a marinade for game or red meat in dishes such as roasted farm-raised venison napped with mushroom-filled sauce (see page 146).

Servings	Calories	Protein (g) (%)	Fat (g) (%)	Cholesterol (mg)	Carbohydrates (g) (%)	Fiber (g)	Sodium (mg)
1	33	0.6 (10%)	0.2 (9%)	0	4.9 (82%)	1.2	12.9

No alcohol is listed in the nutrition analysis. It is assumed to be cooked off during the simmering of the marinade and later during cooking of the product.

Spicy Cajun-Style Seasoning Blend

Bring Cajun-style flavor to dishes with this seasoning blend. Because it's made from finely ground spices, it might be offered in shakers on dining tables as an alternative to salt.

Servings: 24 **Serving Size: 1 T**
Yield: 1½ c

Onion powder	¼ c + 1 T	Chili powder	2 T
Garlic powder	¼ c + 1 T	Curry powder	2 T
		White pepper, ground	2 T
Paprika, Hungarian, sweet	2 T	Black pepper, ground	2 T
Cumin, ground	2 T	Red pepper, ground	2 T
		Salt	To taste

1. In a small container, combine all the ingredients; mix well. Use to season meat, fish, poultry, egg, vegetable, or potato dishes such as roasted Idaho potato chips (see page 347).
2. To store, place in a tightly sealed container in a cool, dry, dark place.

Servings	Calories	Protein (g) (%)	Fat (g) (%)	Cholesterol (mg)	Carbohydrates (g) (%)	Fiber (g)	Sodium (mg)
1	22	0.9 (14%)	0.5 (17%)	0	4.6 (69%)	1.4	9.2

3

Meat

BEEF

Beef Cubes Braised in Mustard Beer Sauce

This specialty beef dish of Flemish origin was too good to remain exclusive to Belgium. Like its traditional counterpart, in this modified version, the beef's braising broth is thickened with pumpernickel bread. The dark rye crumbs add flavor without fat.

Servings: 24   *Serving Size: 3 oz cooked meat + sauce*
Yield: 1¼ gal (4½ lb cooked meat + sauce)

Vegetable cooking spray	—	Parsley, minced	¼ c + 2 T
Onions, thin slices	2 lb		
Garlic, minced	2 t	Bay leaves	2
Beef, stew cubes, lean, trimmed of fat and silverskin, patted dry	6 lb	Thyme, dried	2 t
		Pepper, freshly ground	To taste or 2 t
Beer, dark	2½ qt	Pumpernickel bread, crusts removed	8 oz
Rich brown veal stock (see page 4) or very low sodium beef stock	2 qt	Mustard, Dijon-style	2 T
		Salt	To taste
Vinegar, red wine	¼ c		
Apple or fruit juice concentrate, unsweetened	¼ c		

1. Coat a brazier with cooking spray. Place over medium heat until hot. Add the onions and garlic; cook until tender, or about 4 minutes. Remove from the pan; set aside.

2. Recoat the brazier with cooking spray. Increase the heat to medium-high. When hot, add the beef cubes; saute until dark brown, or about 5 minutes. Drain any fat from the beef. Add the beer, next seven ingredients, and onion-garlic mixture. Heat to a boil; reduce the heat to very low; cover; simmer until the beef is partially cooked, or about 1 hour.

3. Spread the bread with the mustard. Cut into cubes. Add to the braising liquid. Cover and cook another hour or until the beef is very tender and the bread has disintegrated and thickened the sauce. Stir occasionally to break the bread.

4. To thicken the sauce further, reduce it or add more bread cubes, and to thin the sauce, add water or additional stock. Remove the bay leaves. Season with salt to taste and additional pepper as desired. Serve with boiled, baby new potatoes.

Servings	Calories	Protein (g) (%)	Fat (g) (%)	Cholesterol (mg)	Carbohydrates (g) (%)	Fiber (g)	Sodium (mg)
1	251	28 (45%)	5.8 (21%)	58.7	14.4 (23%)	2.5	164

Beef Patties Studded with Pickled Beets and Capers

You wouldn't normally expect to find pickled beets and capers in a burger, but the combination works well. To eliminate any concern about contamination with *E. coli* bacteria, cook to an internal temperature of 155°F (68°C) unless requested otherwise.

Servings: 24   *Serving Size: 1 beef patty*
Yield: 24 beef patties

Beef, ground, extra-lean	4 lb	Capers, drained, rinsed in	
Mashed potatoes, cooked		water, minced	1½ oz
without salt or fat	1½ lb		(¼ c)
Egg whites, large	4 (5 oz)	Vegetable cooking spray	—
Salt	To taste	Rich brown veal stock (see	
Pepper, freshly ground	To taste	page 4) or very low	
*Pickled beets, minced	1 lb	sodium beef stock	1½ pt
Onions, minced	1 lb		

1. In a mixing bowl, combine the beef, potatoes, egg whites, and salt and pepper to taste. Mix together well.
2. Carefully blend in the beets, onions, and capers; distribute evenly throughout the meat. Shape into 24 ½-in. thick patties.
3. Coat a nonstick skillet with cooking spray. Place over medium heat until hot. Add the patties in batches; cook until deep brown on the exterior and 155°F (68°C) in the center, or about 6 minutes on each side. Be aware, the beets may give the meat a pink color even when it is cooked through. Remove the patties to a serving container. Keep warm.
4. Skim any fat from the skillet. Add the stock; while heating, stir to remove any brown particles from the skillet's bottom. Pour the pan juices over the patties.
5. Serve immediately accompanied by a vegetable and potato dish, perhaps mashed golden buttermilk potatoes (see page 223).

*Red beets pickled German-style (see page 286) are excellent in these patties.

Servings	Calories	Protein (g) (%)	Fat (g) (%)	Cholesterol (mg)	Carbohydrates (g) (%)	Fiber (g)	Sodium (mg)
1	202	18.3 (37%)	9.2 (42%)	56.1	10.6 (21%)	1.0	117

Beef Round Roast and Vegetables Braised in Red Wine Broth

Today, with both parents or caretakers working outside the home, home-cooked meals are becoming fewer and farther between for many families. Yet, older diners who grew up on meals made from less expensive meat cuts like beef round roast are still likely to love them as much as they did in their younger years. This recipe for beef round roast will help more mature diners recall the days of Mom's fork-tender pot roast and offer the unfamiliar a taste of what those good memories are all about.

Servings: 24   Serving Size: 3 oz cooked meat, 3 potatoes + 3 carrots
Yield: 4½ lb cooked meat, 72 carrots + 72 potatoes

Beef, lean, bottom round roast, boneless, trimmed of fat and silverskin	6 lb	Tomato juice, no salt added	1 c
Vegetable cooking spray	—	Carrots, washed, baby or small, cut into 3-in. pieces	6 lb
Wine, red, dry	1 pt	New potatoes, baby, very small, washed	6 lb
Rich brown veal stock (see page 4) or very low sodium beef stock	1 pt	Water	1½ pt
		Salt	To taste
		Pepper, freshly ground	To taste

1. Pat the meat dry so that it will brown more easily.
2. Coat a brazier with cooking spray. Place over medium-high heat until hot. Add the beef; cook, turning until brown on all sides, or about 15 minutes. Drain the fat from the pan; discard.
3. Add the red wine, stock, and tomato juice to the brazier. Cover; place in a 350°F (175°C) oven; bake, turning occasionally for 1 hour.
4. Add the carrots, potatoes, and 1½ pt water or as needed to the brazier; continue cooking, turning the meat and vegetables occasionally, until the meat and vegetables are tender, or about 2 hours.
5. Remove the meat and vegetables from the brazier; skim the fat from the pan juices. Slice the meat across the grain; serve garnished with the vegetables and moistened with the pan juices. Sprinkle with salt and pepper to taste.

Servings	Calories	Protein (g) (%)	Fat (g) (%)	Cholesterol (mg)	Carbohydrates (g) (%)	Fiber (g)	Sodium (mg)
1	320	30.7 (39%)	7.8 (22%)	81.6	30.5 (39%)	5.6	99

No alcohol is listed in the nutrition analysis. It is assumed to be cooked off during the extended braising period.

Cajun-Style Roast Tenderloin of Beef

A blend of Cajun seasonings adds a dash of subtle heat to this roast tenderloin of beef. It is a hit, sliced thin, fanned out on the plate, and garnished with horseradish sauce and tomato relish.

Servings: 24   *Serving Size: 3 oz cooked beef*
Yield: 4½ lb cooked beef

Beef, tenderloin, lean, trimmed of fat and silverskin	6 lb	Red pepper, ground	1 T
		Nutmeg, freshly ground	½ t
		Mustard powder	½ t
Pepper, freshly ground	To taste or 2 T	Onion powder	½ t
		Garlic powder	½ t
Fennel seeds, crushed	1½ T	Salt	To taste

1. Fold the narrow end of the fillets back onto themselves and tie with twine.
2. In a small bowl, combine all the seasonings; mix well. Rub the seasoning mix over all sides of the meat.
3. Place on a rack in a shallow roasting pan; roast uncovered in a 375°F (190°C) oven until desired doneness.* Turn 2–3 times throughout cooking for even browning.
4. Remove from the oven; let stand in a warm place for 10 minutes.
5. Remove the trussing twine. Carve the beef crosswise into thin slices. Arrange on heated serving plates. Accompany with zesty freshly grated horseradish and yogurt sauce with dillweed (see page 56) and tomato relish embellished with fresh basil and garlic (see page 53).

*The internal temperature of the meat should be about 130°F (55°C) for rare and 140°F (60°C) for medium, or about 10 degrees less than desired to allow for carryover cooking.

Servings	Calories	Protein (g) (%)	Fat (g) (%)	Cholesterol (mg)	Carbohydrates (g) (%)	Fiber (g)	Sodium (mg)
1	182	24.2 (55%)	8.6 (44%)	71.4	0.5 (1%)	0.2	54

Extra-Lean Ground Beef Burgers with Onions, Bell Peppers, and Worcestershire

According to the Oxford English Dictionary, the word "hamburger" made its American media debut in 1889. Since then, Americans' appetites for burgers have flourished. To reduce the fat without the flavor of this American favorite, this burger is prepared from extra-lean ground beef, extended with whole wheat bread crumbs and diced vegetables, and seasoned with fresh herbs and spices.

Servings: 24   *Serving Size: 1 patty*
Yield: 24 patties

Bread crumbs, whole wheat, fresh	4 oz	Worcestershire sauce, very low sodium	2 T
Milk, nonfat	¾ c	Egg whites, large	6 (7½ oz)
Beef, ground, extra-lean	5 lb		
Onions, red, minced	12 oz	Salt	To taste
Pepper, green, bell, minced	8 oz	Pepper, freshly ground	To taste
Parsley, minced	6 T		

1. Combine the bread crumbs and milk in a small bowl. Set aside to soak.
2. In a mixing container, combine the remaining ingredients and soaked bread crumbs. Mix well. Shape into 24 ¾-in. thick patties.
3. Place the burgers on the heated rack of a grill or broiler coated with oil. Because the burgers are low in fat, they will stick and fall apart if the grill or broiler rack is not well oiled. Cook over medium heat until 155°F (68°C) or the desired doneness, turning once. The burgers can also be cooked in a nonstick skillet coated with cooking spray or baked on a sheet pan coated with cooking spray.
4. Serve on toasted whole wheat buns garnished with sliced tomatoes, onions, and lettuce leaves.

Servings	Calories	Protein (g) (%)	Fat (g) (%)	Cholesterol (mg)	Carbohydrates (g) (%)	Fiber (g)	Sodium (mg)
1	216	22.2 (42%)	11.4 (49%)	70.4	4.8 (9%)	0.5	106

Flank Steak Topped with Mushrooms and Green Onions

Current dietary recommendations encourage Americans to consume 5 to 7 ounces of cooked meat, fish, or poultry per day, much less than many are accustomed to eating. While the portion size for this flank steak is only 3 ounces of cooked meat, it is topped with a browned mushroom and whole wheat crumb mixture, sliced thin, and fanned out on the plate to appear like more.

Servings: 24   Serving Size: 3 oz cooked steak + topping
Yield: 4½ lb cooked beef + topping

Flank or skirt steak, lean, trimmed of fat and silverskin	6 lb	Vegetable cooking spray, olive-flavored	—
Tomatoes, coarsely chopped	2 lb	Green onions, white and 1-in. green, minced	12 oz
Onions, coarsely chopped	10 oz	Mushrooms, minced	10 oz
Rich brown veal stock (see page 4) or very low sodium beef stock	3 qt	Bread crumbs, whole wheat, fresh	6 oz
Peppercorns, whole	⅛ t	Salt	To taste
Parsley sprigs	6	Pepper, freshly ground	To taste or 1 t
Garlic, cloves, peeled	1 oz	Cornstarch	1 oz
Bay leaves	2		

1. Place the steak and next seven ingredients in a brazier. Heat to a boil; reduce the heat to low; simmer, covered, until the steak is tender, or about 2 hours.
2. Coat a nonstick skillet with cooking spray. Place over medium-high heat until hot. Add the green onions and mushrooms. Cook until tender.
3. Add the bread crumbs and seasonings; mix. Set aside.
4. Remove the steak from the brazier; place on a sheet pan. Set aside in a warm place.
5. Skim any fat from the cooking liquid; remove the bay leaves; discard; puree the pan juices and vegetables in a blender until smooth. Place in a saucepan. Mix the cornstarch with a small amount of cold water to form a smooth paste. Stir into the sauce. Heat to a boil; reduce the heat to a simmer; cook, stirring until thickened, or a few minutes. Season with salt and pepper to taste. Adjust to sauce consistency by adding stock to thin and reducing or adding more cornstarch slurry to thicken.
6. Spread the bread crumb mixture over the steaks. Place the steaks under the broiler

until the topping is golden brown. Slice into thin diagonal slices, cutting across the grain. To serve, fan out on the plate. Pass the sauce separately.

Servings	Calories	Protein (g) (%)	Fat (g) (%)	Cholesterol (mg)	Carbohydrates (g) (%)	Fiber (g)	Sodium (mg)
1	242	27.3 (45%)	10.0 (37%)	57.2	10.5 (17%)	2.4	151

Homestyle Beef Stew Laden with Chunky Winter Vegetables

How could a diner resist this homestyle beef stew when it's described as tender cubes of sauteed beef simmered in a chunky, tomato-based gravy with baby red-skinned potato halves, kelly green peas, and cubes of cream-colored turnip, bright orange carrot, and lime green celery?

These are a few of the secrets to this stew's nutritional success. Rather than thickening with a fat and flour roux, (1) it's thickened with finely chopped onions and tomatoes and a cornstarch slurry; (2) the skins are retained on the potatoes and carrots for added fiber, color, and texture; (3) the vegetables are cooked separately and added at the end of cooking to maintain their flavor and texture; and (4) the need for salt is reduced by flavoring with fresh herbs and freshly ground spices.

Servings: 24   *Serving Size: $\frac{2}{3}$ c*
Yield: 1 gal

Vegetable cooking spray	—	Bay leaves	2
Beef, stew cubes, lean, trimmed of fat and silverskin, patted dry	3 lb	Cloves, freshly ground	$\frac{1}{8}$ t
		Potatoes, new, red, baby, very small, washed, halves	$1\frac{1}{2}$ lb
Onions, minced	$1\frac{1}{2}$ lb	Carrots, washed, 1-in. cubes	$1\frac{1}{2}$ lb
Garlic, minced	1 oz	Celery, 1-in. cubes	1 lb
Tomatoes, finely chopped	3 lb	Turnips, peeled, 1-in. cubes	1 lb
Rich brown veal stock (see page 4) or very low sodium beef stock	$1\frac{1}{2}$ pt	Peas, fresh, shelled, or frozen	12 oz
		Cornstarch	1 oz
		Salt	To taste
Wine, dry, white	$1\frac{1}{2}$ c	Pepper, freshly ground	To taste
Parsley, minced	$\frac{1}{2}$ c		

1. Coat a sauce pot with cooking spray. Place over medium-high heat until hot. Add the beef cubes; saute until brown. Add the onions and garlic. Continue cooking until light brown.
2. Stir in the tomatoes, stock, wine, parsley, bay leaves, and cloves. Heat to a boil. Reduce the heat to low; simmer the meat, covered, until tender, or about $1\frac{1}{2}$ hours. Skim off any fat.
3. Cook the potatoes, carrots, celery, turnips, and peas if fresh separately in unsalted boiling water until almost tender. Drain. Add to the tender beef cubes. Stir in the peas if frozen. Cook until heated through, or about 5 minutes.

4. Mix the cornstarch with a small amount of cold water to form a smooth slurry. Stir into the stew. Heat to a boil. Reduce the heat to low; simmer until thickening occurs, or a few minutes. To adjust the consistency, thicken with more cornstarch slurry and thin with additional stock or water.
5. Remove the bay leaves. Season with salt and pepper to taste. Serve with chunks of hearty, whole grain peasant bread or low-fat mashed potatoes.

Servings	Calories	Protein (g) (%)	Fat (g) (%)	Cholesterol (mg)	Carbohydrates (g) (%)	Fiber (g)	Sodium (mg)
1	194	16.8 (34%)	5.5 (25%)	43.1	19.6 (40%)	4.7	185

Marinated Spicy Pot Roast with Gingersnap Gravy

To achieve its tangy flavor and fork tenderness, this pot roast is marinated for 3 to 4 days in a broth flavored with red wine vinegar, vegetables, herbs, and spices and then simmered in its marinating broth along with red wine, fruit juice sweetener, and tomato product. At service, slices of the juicy, spicy roast are napped with a low-fat, hearty gravy thickened with softened, crushed gingersnaps and a puree of simmered vegetables. The combination tastes like a match made in heaven.

Servings: 24   *Serving Size: 3 oz cooked meat + 7 T sauce*
Yield: 4½ lb cooked meat + 2½ qt + ½ c sauce

Vinegar, red wine	1½ pt	Beef, top round, lean, trimmed	
Water	1½ pt	of fat and silverskin	6 lb
Onions, coarsely chopped	1 lb	Vegetable cooking spray	—
Carrots, washed, ½-in. thick		Wine, red	1 pt
slices	10 oz	Apple or fruit juice	
Celery, ½-in. thick slices	10 oz	concentrate, unsweetened	¼ c
Garlic, minced	2 t	Gingersnaps, crushed	3 oz
Sachet:		Tomato paste, no salt added	¼ c
Bay leaves	2	Salt	To taste
Peppercorns	1 t	Pepper, freshly ground	To taste
Cloves, whole	1 t		
Thyme, dried	¼ t		

1. Heat the wine vinegar, water, onions, carrots, celery, garlic, and the sachet in a saucepan to a boil. Set aside to cool.
2. Place the beef in a nonreactive container. Pour the marinade over. The meat should be completely covered by marinade. If it is not, add water until it is.
3. Cover; refrigerate for 3–4 days, turning occasionally. The longer the meat marinates, the more piquant it will be, so adjust the time to suit your taste.
4. Remove the beef from the marinade. Pat dry. Discard the sachet.
5. Coat a brazier with cooking spray. Place over medium-high heat until hot. Add the beef; cook, turning, until browned on all sides.
6. Add the marinade, red wine, juice concentrate, gingersnaps, and tomato paste. Heat to a boil. Reduce the heat to very low; cover; simmer until the meat is very tender, or about 3 hours.
7. Remove the meat; set aside in a warm place.

8. Skim the fat from the pan juices. In a blender, puree the sauce until smooth. Adjust the consistency by adding stock for a thinner sauce and by reducing or adding more finely ground gingersnap crumbs for a thicker sauce. Season with salt and pepper to taste.
9. Carve the meat across the grain. Serve accompanied by the sauce.

Servings	Calories	Protein (g) (%)	Fat (g) (%)	Cholesterol (mg)	Carbohydrates (g) (%)	Fiber (g)	Sodium (mg)	Alcohol (g) (%)
1	198	27.7 (56%)	4.6 (21%)	71.4	9.8 (20%)	1.0	94.7	0.4 (2%)

Philippine-Style Spring Rolls Filled with Beef, Tofu, and Shrimp

These spring rolls are created by wrapping a tasty, cooked filling of lean beef, diced shrimp, firm tofu, and stir-fried vegetables in a lettuce-lined, paper thin, crepe-like wrapper and finishing with a sweet garlic and soy-flavored sauce.

Servings: 24   **Serving Size: 1 spring roll**
Yield: 24 spring rolls

Ingredient	Amount	Ingredient	Amount
Vegetable cooking spray	—	Pepper, freshly ground	To taste
Onions, green, thin slices, white and 1-in. green	12 oz	Tofu, firm, small dice	1 lb
Gingerroot, minced	1½ oz	Shrimp, peeled, poached or simmered with shells in unsalted water, reserving cooking liquid for shrimp broth (see page 8), small dice	
Garlic, minced	2 T		
Beef, sirloin, lean, trimmed of fat and silverskin, medium dice, patted dry	1 lb		
Green beans, thin diagonal slices	10 oz		1 lb cooked
Cabbage, green, shredded	8 oz	Lettuce leaves, red leafy	1 lb (24)
Shrimp broth (see page 8) or rich white chicken stock (see page 7)	½ c	*Spring roll wrappers (see page 418)	24
Soy sauce, low-sodium	2 T	Sweet spring roll sauce (see page 50)	1 recipe (1½ c)

1. Coat a large nonstick skillet with cooking spray or cook in batches. Place over medium heat until hot. Add the green onions, ginger, and garlic. Cook until tender.
2. Add the beef and cook until no longer pink on the exterior, or about 3 minutes.
3. Add the green beans and next four ingredients; cover and cook until the vegetables are crisp-tender, or about 5 minutes.
4. Add the tofu and shrimp; heat through. Remove from the heat.
5. Place one lettuce leaf on each wrapper with the ruffled edge protruding over the end. Place 7 T (about ½ c) of the filling in the center of the wrapper. Drizzle with 1 T of sweet spring roll sauce.

6. Fold the spring roll wrapper around the filling like an egg roll. Tuck in the end opposite the lettuce leaf. Allow the lettuce leaf to peep out the other end.

*Substitute commercially prepared spring roll or egg roll wrappers for freshly prepared spring roll wrappers. Adjust the amount of filling per wrapper according to the wrapper's size. Revise the nutrition information accordingly.

Servings	Calories	Protein (g) (%)	Fat (g) (%)	Cholesterol (mg)	Carbohydrates (g) (%)	Fiber (g)	Sodium (mg)
1	191	14.6 (30%)	3.4 (16%)	49.5	25.7 (53%)	1.8	137

Sauteed Beef Tenderloin Strips in Stroganoff-Style Sauce

According to one story, count Pavel, Stroganov's French chef, created the recipe for beef stroganoff by simply adding Russian sour cream to a basic French mustard sauce. The finished product was spectacular. He named the dish *Bef-Stroganov* after his employer. The rest is history. Unlike the authentic recipe, mushrooms and tomato product appear in this version of *Bef-Stroganov*.

Servings: 24   *Serving Size: 1⅕ c with 3 oz cooked beef*
Yield: 1¾ gal + 1 c with 4½ lb cooked beef

Vegetable cooking spray	—	Rich brown veal stock (see	
Beef, tenderloin tips, lean,		page 4) or very low	
trimmed of fat and		sodium beef stock	1¼ qt
silverskin, 2 × ½ × ¼-in.		Tomatoes, peeled, pureed in a	
strips, patted dry	6 lb	blender	1½ lb
Mustard powder	1½ t	Wine, white	½ c
Pepper, freshly ground	To taste	Cornstarch (divided)	4 oz
Mushrooms, thin slices	4 lb	Yogurt, plain, nonfat	1¼ qt
Onions, minced	2 lb	Nutmeg, freshly ground	¾ t
Garlic, minced	1½ T	Salt	To taste

1. Coat a large nonstick skillet with cooking spray or cook in batches. Place over medium-high heat until hot. Add the beef; saute until medium rare or desired doneness. Sprinkle with the mustard powder and pepper to taste. Toss to coat. Remove the meat from the pan; set aside.
2. Drain any fat from the skillet; return to the heat. Recoat with cooking spray if needed. Add the mushrooms, onions, and garlic; cook until tender.
3. Add the next three ingredients; heat to a boil; reduce the heat to low; simmer until the flavors are mellowed, or about 10 minutes.
4. Mix half, or 2 ounces, of the cornstarch with enough cold water to form a smooth, thin paste. Add to the sauce, stirring with a whip. Cook a few additional minutes until thickened.
5. Mix the remaining cornstarch with the yogurt until smooth. Mix in the nutmeg.
6. Gradually stir a small amount of the pan liquids into the yogurt to temper it. Slowly add the yogurt mixture to the skillet while stirring. Cook, stirring, over low heat until thickened. Do not boil as the yogurt may curdle. Adjust to sauce consistency by thinning with stock or thickening with more cornstarch slurry.
7. Return the beef to the skillet. Heat through.

8. Season with salt and pepper to taste. Serve immediately over whole wheat pasta or boiled brown basmati rice (see page 235) or along with whole wheat French bread (see page 383) to sop up the sauce.

Servings	Calories	Protein (g) (%)	Fat (g) (%)	Cholesterol (mg)	Carbohydrates (g) (%)	Fiber (g)	Sodium (mg)
1	274	30.3 (45%)	9.4 (31%)	72.3	16.4 (24%)	2.0	114

No alcohol is listed in the nutrition analysis. It is assumed to be cooked off during preparation.

Sauteed Beef Sirloin Steak Napped with Spicy Red Pepper Tomato Sauce

It is estimated that nearly 4 out of 10 beef meals eaten away from home are steak of some sort. Offer sauteed beef sirloin steak for customers who prefer a lean beef menu option.

Servings: 24   *Serving Size: 3 oz cooked beef*
Yield: 4½ lb cooked beef

Vegetable cooking spray, butter-flavored	—	Salt	To taste
Beef, sirloin steaks, lean, 2 in. thick, trimmed of fat and silverskin, patted dry	6 lb (3 2-lb steaks)	Pepper, freshly ground	To taste or ¾ t

1. Coat a nonstick skillet with cooking spray. Place over medium-high heat until hot. In batches, add the steaks; cook until brown and the desired doneness, turning once, or about 8 minutes per side for rare meat.
2. Slice the steak across the grain into ½-in. thick slices. Sprinkle with salt and pepper to taste; serve immediately accompanied by spicy red pepper tomato sauce (see page 49).

Servings	Calories	Protein (g) (%)	Fat (g) (%)	Cholesterol (mg)	Carbohydrates (g) (%)	Fiber (g)	Sodium (mg)
1	171	25.8 (63%)	6.8 (37%)	75.8	0 (0%)	0	56.2

Stir-Fried Strips of Beef Tenderloin in Soy Glaze*

Stir-fried strips of pungent, marinated beef tenderloin are delicious served on a bed of shredded lettuce, Chinese cabbage, brown rice, or whole wheat pasta.

Servings: 24   Serving Size: 3 oz cooked beef
Yield: 4½ lb cooked beef

Soy sauce, low-sodium	1½ c	†Beef, tenderloin, lean,	
Sherry, dry	1 c	trimmed of fat and	
White grape juice concentrate,		silverskin, thin strips	6 lb
unsweetened	¾ c	Vegetable cooking spray	—
Cornstarch	2 oz		
Gingerroot, minced	1 oz		

1. In a nonreactive container large enough to marinate the meat, combine the soy sauce and next four ingredients. Mix until smooth.
2. Add the beef strips to the marinade; coat well. Set aside to marinate for about 30 minutes. Drain the meat from the marinade; reserve the marinade.
3. Place a wok or nonstick skillet coated with cooking spray over medium-high heat until hot. In batches, add the meat; stir-fry until browned, or briefly. Add the reserved marinade. Cook the mixture until the sauce is lightly thickened and the meat is the desired doneness.
4. Serve on a bed of shredded lettuce or Chinese cabbage garnished with springs of watercress or parsley and a radish or cherry tomato, or on a bed of boiled brown basmati rice (see page 235).

*Adapted from a recipe by Tim Allison.
†Sirloin is a less expensive, quite tender, and lean cut of beef that is also well suited to this recipe.

Variation

Substitute tuna or salmon fillets cut into ¾-in. cubes, or thin strips of skinless chicken breast meat, for the beef.

Servings	Calories	Protein (g) (%)	Fat (g) (%)	Cholesterol (mg)	Carbohydrates (g) (%)	Fiber (g)	Sodium (mg)	Alcohol (g) (%)
1	217	25.4 (48%)	8.5 (37%)	71.4	6.5 (12%)	0.1	535	0.9 (3%)

LAMB

African-Inspired Lamb Stew with Vegetables and Couscous

Couscous is almost the national dish of all North African countries. It is an elaborate, hearty stew named for the mound of semolina cereal over which it is served. Traditionally, the meat and vegetables are cooked in the bottom of a couscousiere while the couscous grains steam over it. The process is simplified in this Algerian-inspired couscous recipe by preparing the main ingredients in one pan and the precooked couscous grains in another.

Servings: 24   Serving Size: 1½ oz cooked lamb + vegetables + ½ c couscous
Yield: 2¼ lb cooked meat + vegetables + 3 qt couscous

Vegetable cooking spray	—	Carrots, washed, ¼-in. thick circular slices	1½ lb
Lamb, lean, 1-in. cubes, trimmed of fat and silverskin, patted dry	3 lb	Zucchini, ¼-in. thick circular slices	1½ lb
Onions, thin slices	1¼ lb	Garbanzo beans, canned with 50% less salt, drained, rinsed with water	1¼ lb drained
Leeks, thin slices	6 oz		
Garlic, minced	2 T		
Rich white chicken stock (see page 7)	1½ qt	Mint, minced	3 T
Tomato paste, no salt added	¼ c + 2 T	*Couscous (instant or precooked), cooked without salt or fat	1 lb + 14 oz as purchased
Parsley, minced	¼ c		
Bay leaves	3		
Paprika, Hungarian, sweet	1 T		
Cumin, freshly ground	1 T	Salt	To taste
Thyme, dried	1 T	Pepper, freshly ground	To taste
Basil, dried	1 T		
Potatoes, red-skinned, washed, ¼-in. thick circular slices	1¾ lb		

1. Coat a sauce pot with cooking spray. Place over medium-high heat until hot. Add the lamb cubes; saute until brown; remove; set aside.
2. Add the onions, leeks, and garlic; saute until tender.

3. Add the chicken stock and next seven ingredients. Heat to a boil. Reduce the heat to low; cover; simmer until the meat is almost tender, or about 1 hour. Add water or additional stock as needed. Skim the fat and froth from the cooking broth.
4. Add the potatoes and carrots. Cook until almost tender, or about 20 minutes.
5. Add the zucchini and garbanzo beans; cook until tender, or about 10 minutes longer. Skim the fat and froth from the cooking broth.
6. Add the mint in the last 5 minutes of cooking. Season with salt and pepper to taste.
7. To serve, moisten the cooked couscous with some of the broth and top with stew.

*To cook the 1 lb + 14 oz couscous, place $1\frac{1}{2}$ qt + $\frac{3}{4}$ c of water in a saucepan; heat to a boil; stir in the couscous; cover. Remove from the heat; let stand until the water is absorbed and the couscous softened, or about 5 minutes. Fluff to break up any lumps.

Servings	Calories	Protein (g) (%)	Fat (g) (%)	Cholesterol (mg)	Carbohydrates (g) (%)	Fiber (g)	Sodium (mg)
1	293	20.8 (28%)	4.8 (15%)	37.9	41.9 (57%)	7.0	71.8

Broiled Herb-Marinated Leg of Lamb

According to the American Lamb Council, more restaurants are offering lamb entrees than ever before. Broiled herb-marinated leg of lamb makes a mouth-watering main course selection but is equally good served on a bed of greens, layered between slices of hearty whole grain bread, or tossed with fresh pasta.

Servings: 24   *Serving Size: 3 oz cooked lamb*
Yield: 4½ lb cooked lamb

Lamb, lean, boneless, butterflied legs, trimmed of silverskin and fat, patted dry	6 lb	Thyme, and rosemary, minced or dried	¼ c each or 1½ T each
Wine, white, dry	1 c	Oregano, minced or dried	2 T or 2 t
Lime juice, freshly squeezed	1 c		
Garlic, minced	1½ T	Salt	To taste
Mint, minced or dried	1 T or 1 t	Pepper, freshly ground	To taste

1. Prick the lamb on both sides with the tip of a knife.
2. Mix the remaining nine ingredients in a nonreactive marinating container large enough to hold the lamb. Add the lamb; coat with the marinating mixture. Cover and refrigerate to marinate for 24 hours, turning occasionally.
3. Remove the lamb from the marinade. Place on a hot oiled broiler rack. Brush with the remaining marinade while cooking.
4. Broil the lamb, turning once until the desired degree of doneness, 130°F (55°C) (rare), 140°F (60°C) (medium), and 150°F (65°C) (well done), or about 10 degrees less than desired to allow for carryover cooking.
5. Transfer the lamb to a cutting board. Let rest in a warm place for about 10 minutes. Slice the lamb across the grain into thin slices. Serve with a vegetable and starch accompaniment such as oven-roasted potato wedges seasoned with rosemary (see page 227).

Servings	Calories	Protein (g) (%)	Fat (g) (%)	Cholesterol (mg)	Carbohydrates (g) (%)	Fiber (g)	Sodium (mg)
1	169	24.3 (59%)	6.7 (37%)	75.7	1.5 (4%)	0.3	58.7

Grilled Lamb Kebabs in Apricot Glaze

These grilled lamb kebabs are easy to prepare but require at least 12 hours of marinating before cooking.

Servings: 24　　　*Serving Size: 3 oz cooked lamb*
Yield: 4½ lb cooked lamb

Lamb, boneless, lean, trimmed of fat and silverskin	6 lb	Curry powder	1 T
Garlic cloves, peeled, cut in half	1 oz	Cumin, freshly ground	¾ t
		Red pepper, ground	To taste
		Water	1½ pt
Salt	To taste	Apricot spread, fruit-sweetened	1¼ c
Pepper, freshly ground	To taste or 2 t	Lemon juice, freshly squeezed	3 T
Vegetable cooking spray	—	Bay leaves	4
Onions, minced	2¼ lb	Skewers, wooden, soaked in cold water	24
Coriander, freshly ground	1 T		

1. Rub the lamb with the cut edges of the garlic. Discard garlic.
2. Cut the meat into bite-size cubes. Place in a nonreactive container; sprinkle with the salt and pepper to taste. Set aside.
3. Coat a nonstick skillet with cooking spray. Place over medium heat until hot. Add the onions; cook until golden.
4. Stir in the coriander, curry powder, cumin, and red pepper; cook to blend the flavors, or about 3 minutes.
5. Add the water and next two ingredients. Heat to a boil, stirring; remove from heat.
6. Once cooled, add the bay leaves; pour over the meat.
7. Refrigerate covered, turning occasionally, for at least 12 hours.
8. Thread the meat on the skewers; cook on an oiled grill or broiler rack, turning to brown, until the desired doneness. For medium rare meat, cook about 8 minutes.
9. While the meat is cooking, transfer the marinade to a saucepan. Heat to a boil; reduce the heat to medium and simmer until it is sauce consistency. Remove the bay leaves.
10. Serve the lamb kebabs hot off the grill with skewers of grilled vegetables and a grain pilaf. Pass the sauce separately to pour over the meat.

Servings	Calories	Protein (g) (%)	Fat (g) (%)	Cholesterol (mg)	Carbohydrates (g) (%)	Fiber (g)	Sodium (mg)
1	204	24.2 (48%)	6.3 (28%)	85.1	12.4 (24%)	2.2	44.4

Roasted Leg of Lamb Seasoned with Ginger, Mint, and Lemon

This is an elegant, yet easy, dish to make. The lamb is simply marinated in an herb and spice flavored, fat-free broth and then roasted. It's hard to beat when roasted over a wood or charcoal fire, but good results can be achieved in the oven too.

Servings: 24   Serving Size: 3 oz cooked lamb
Yield: 4½ lb cooked lamb

Marinade:		Lemon juice, freshly squeezed	3 T
Mint, minced or dried	3 T or 1 T	**Meat:**	
Garlic, minced	1½ T	Lamb, leg, boneless, lean,	
Gingerroot, minced	1½ T	butterflied, trimmed of fat	
Cumin, freshly ground	2 t	and silverskin	6 lb
Paprika, Hungarian, sweet	1 t	**Garnish:**	
Red pepper, ground	1 t	Mint leaves	Optional
Clove, freshly ground	¾ t		
Salt	To taste		
Rich white chicken stock (see page 7)	¾ c		

1. In a small bowl, combine all the marinade ingredients; mix well.
2. Place the lamb in a nonreactive shallow container. Pour the marinade over the lamb, coating it well. Cover; refrigerate at least 4 hours and up to 48 hours, turning several times.
3. Remove the lamb from the marinade, scraping any spices from the surface to prevent burning.
4. Place the lamb on a rack in a roasting pan. Place in a 450°F (230°C) oven; roast, turning once, until brown on both sides. Reduce the heat to 325°F (165°C). Continue roasting the lamb, turning once or twice, until it reaches an internal temperature of 130°F (55°C) for rare, 140°F (60°C) for medium, and 150°F (65°C) for well-done meat, or about 10 degrees less than desired to allow for carryover cooking.

5. Remove the lamb from the oven. Let rest in a warm place about 15 minutes. Slice the meat against the grain. Serve on heated plates garnished with fresh mint leaves.

Servings	Calories	Protein (g) (%)	Fat (g) (%)	Cholesterol (mg)	Carbohydrates (g) (%)	Fiber (g)	Sodium (mg)
1	164	24.2 (61%)	6.6 (38%)	75.7	0.3 (1%)	0.1	59.3

Rolled Leg of Lamb Roasted with Mint

In this recipe, leg of lamb is stuffed with a complementary mixture of fresh herbs, spices, and minced turkey ham, and roasted. The aromatic seasoned stuffing eliminates any need to ladle a rich, high-fat sauce over the meat.

Servings: 24   *Serving Size: 3 oz cooked lamb*
Yield: 4½ lb cooked lamb

Turkey ham, minced	4 oz	Pepper, freshly ground	To taste
Parsley, minced	1 oz		or ½ t
Mint, minced	1 oz	Salt	To taste
Garlic, minced	2 T	Leg of lamb, lean, boneless,	
Vinegar, red wine	2 T	trimmed of fat and	
Paprika, Hungarian, sweet	2 t	silverskin	6 lb

1. Mix the first eight ingredients in a small bowl.
2. With a sharp knife, open the leg of lamb flat by cutting lengthwise through the thinnest side of the cavity. With the point of the knife, cut ¼- to ½-in. down into the thicker areas so that the lamb lays even flatter.
3. Lay the leg out flat, outer side down; spread the herb mixture evenly over the meat. Roll into a tight cylinder; tie securely with cotton twine. Cover; refrigerate at least 12 hours.
4. Place the meat on a rack in a shallow roasting pan; cook uncovered in a 450°F (230°C) oven, turning once, until brown on both sides, or about 15 minutes.
5. Reduce the heat to 325°F (165°C); continue roasting, turning once or twice, until it registers an internal temperature of 130°F (55°C) (rare), 140°F (60°C) (medium), or 150°F (65°C) (well done), or about 10 degrees less than desired to allow for carryover cooking.
6. Let stand 10 minutes. Remove the cotton twine; carve crosswise into slices. To serve, arrange slices slightly overlapping on heated plates.

Servings	Calories	Protein (g) (%)	Fat (g) (%)	Cholesterol (mg)	Carbohydrates (g) (%)	Fiber (g)	Sodium (mg)
1	170	25.1 (61%)	6.9 (38%)	78.4	0.5 (1%)	0.2	106

Spicy Lamb Stew with Potatoes and Spinach in Tomato Broth

The American Heart Association (AHA) recommends the average adult reduce his/her meat consumption to 6–7 ounces per day. At the same time, the AHA recommends we increase our consumption of starch and vegetables or fruits. Smaller portions of meat and larger ones of vegetables and starches will hardly be noticed when flavorful combinations like this spicy lamb stew are added to the menu.

Servings: 24   Service Size: 1 c with 3 oz cooked lamb
Yield: 1½ gal with 4½ lb cooked lamb

Lamb, boneless, leg, lean, trimmed of fat and silverskin, 1-in. cubes	6 lb	Tomato, fresh or canned, coarsely chopped	2¾ lb
Vegetable cooking spray	—	Rich brown veal stock (see page 4) or very low sodium beef stock	3 qt
Onions, minced	3 lb		
Gingerroot, minced	2 oz	Potatoes, new, red-skinned, washed, 1-in. cubes	2½ lb
Garlic, minced	2 T		
Cumin, freshly ground	2 T	Spinach leaves, washed and chopped	2 lb
Coriander, freshly ground	2 T		
Red pepper, ground	To taste or ¾ t	Cornstarch	3 oz
		Salt	To taste
Pepper, freshly ground	To taste or ¾ t		

1. Pat the lamb cubes dry so they will brown more easily.
2. Coat a brazier with cooking spray. Place over medium-high heat until hot. Add the lamb cubes; cook until brown. Remove from the brazier with a slotted spoon; set aside temporarily.
3. Drain any fat from the brazier; wipe clean with paper towels; place over medium heat until hot. Add the onions, ginger, garlic, and about ¼ c water; braise-deglaze adding water as needed until tender, or about 5 minutes.
4. Add the cumin and next three seasonings; cook 3 minutes longer.
5. Return the lamb to the brazier; add the tomatoes and stock; heat to a boil; reduce the heat to low; simmer covered until the lamb is quite tender, or about 1½ hours.
6. Add the potatoes; cook until almost soft, or about 20 minutes.
7. Stir in the spinach, cook until tender, or about 5 minutes.
8. Combine the cornstarch with enough cold water to form a smooth paste. Whip the cornstarch slurry into the cooking broth. Simmer until the broth is a thin sauce

consistency, or about 4 minutes. Adjust the sauce's consistency by thinning with stock or thickening by adding more cornstarch slurry or reducing.

9. Season with salt to taste. Serve with thick chunks of rye or other whole grain bread.

Servings	Calories	Protein (g) (%)	Fat (g) (%)	Cholesterol (mg)	Carbohydrates (g) (%)	Fiber (g)	Sodium (mg)
1	278	29.9 (43%)	7.9 (26%)	75.7	21.7 (31%)	3.6	134

Zucchini Slices Layered with Ground Lamb and Cheese Sauce Moussaka-Style

In this healthy main course dish, stir-fried zucchini slices are layered with seasoned, lean ground lamb, nonfat cottage and part-skim milk parmesan cheeses, and a mushroom-thickened sauce enriched with egg whites. It can be prepared in advance and baked off shortly before service.

Servings: 24   *Serving Size: 3 × 3⅓-in. piece*
Yield: 12 × 20 × 2-in. counter pan

Vegetable cooking spray, olive-flavored	—	Salt	To taste
		Pepper, freshly ground	To taste or 2 t
Zucchini, ⅓-in. thick lengthwise slices	6 lb	Bread crumbs, whole wheat, fresh	4 oz
Lamb, lean, ground sirloin	2½ lb	Egg whites (divided)	6 (7½ oz)
Tomatoes, fresh or canned, coarsely chopped	2 lb	Mushroom sauce thickened with pureed vegetables (see page 38)	1¾ qt
Onion, minced	1½ lb		
Garlic, minced	1 T	Cottage cheese, nonfat	1¼ lb
Wine, red, dry	1 c	Parmesan cheese, part-skim milk, freshly grated	12 oz
Parsley, minced	½ c		
Cinnamon, freshly ground	½ t		

1. Coat a large nonstick skillet with cooking spray or cook in batches. Place over high heat until hot. Add the zucchini; saute until brown on each side but still crisp. Remove from the skillet. Set aside.
2. Add the lamb. Cook until brown. Drain the meat in a strainer to remove any fat. Return to the pan.
3. Add the tomatoes and next seven ingredients; reduce the heat to low; cook until the flavors are blended and the liquid evaporated, or about 40 minutes. Remove any fat that may have accumulated.
4. Remove from the heat; let cool; add the bread crumbs and half (3) of the egg whites; mix.
5. Combine the mushroom sauce with the remaining (3) egg whites and the cottage and parmesan cheeses.
6. Coat a 12 × 20 × 2-in. counter pan with cooking spray. Layer ⅓ of the zucchini, ⅓ of the meat mixture, and ⅓ of the cheese and mushroom sauce. Repeat twice.

7. Bake in a 350°F (175°C) oven until golden brown. Remove; let rest to firm up for about 15–20 minutes in a warm place. Cut the pan 4 × 6 into 3 × 3⅓-in. pieces. Serve with hearty whole grain bread.

Servings	Calories	Protein (g) (%)	Fat (g) (%)	Cholesterol (mg)	Carbohydrates (g) (%)	Fiber (g)	Sodium (mg)
1	274	23.4 (34%)	12.7 (41%)	46.3	17.6 (25%)	3.2	435

PORK

Braised Pork Cubes Seasoned with Paprika Finished with Yogurt Goulash-Style

My Mom's goulash was a casserole containing hamburger, egg noodles, celery, onions, and tomatoes. My Dad loved it so, it was on the menu frequently. This dish is nothing like the goulash of my childhood. Rather, more like the Hungarian version, pork cubes seasoned with paprika are braised in a rich, fat-free veal stock. The cooking juices are finished with nonfat yogurt rather than the sour cream of the traditional *gulyas*. The result is tender, moist pieces of lean pork coated in a delicious creamy sauce.

Servings: 24   *Serving Size: 3 oz cooked meat + sauce*
Yield: 4½ lb cooked meat + sauce

Vegetable cooking spray	—	Salt	To taste
Pork tenderloin, lean, 1-in. cubes, trimmed of fat and silverskin, patted dry	6 lb	Pepper, freshly ground	To taste
		Rich brown veal stock (see page 4) or very low sodium beef stock	3 qt
Onion, minced	1½ lb		
Pepper, green, bell, small dice	1 lb	Cornstarch	1½ oz
Paprika, Hungarian, sweet	3 T	Yogurt, nonfat, plain	1 pt

1. Coat a saucepan with cooking spray. Place over medium-high heat until hot. Add the pork cubes; cook until the cubes are brown, or about 8 minutes.
2. Add the onion and bell pepper; continue cooking until the vegetables are tender. Sprinkle the meat and vegetables with paprika to coat and salt and pepper to taste.
3. Add the stock. Heat to a boil; reduce the heat to low; cover. Simmer until the meat is tender, or about 1½ hours.
4. In a small bowl, mix the cornstarch with the yogurt until smooth. Reduce the heat to very low. Temper the yogurt mixture by stirring some of the hot cooking juices into it. Whisk the yogurt mixture into the cooking juices; cook until heated through and of thin sauce consistency. Do not boil or the sauce may curdle. To adjust the consistency,

thicken with an arrowroot or cornstarch slurry (do not boil) and thin with more stock. Serve over boiled brown basmati rice (see page 235) or whole wheat noodles.

Servings	Calories	Protein (g) (%)	Fat (g) (%)	Cholesterol (mg)	Carbohydrates (g) (%)	Fiber (g)	Sodium (mg)
1	195	28.1 (59%)	5.0 (24%)	67.6	7.8 (17%)	1.1	101

Breaded Pork Cutlets with Mozzarella Cheese Filling

In this simple recipe, a surprise slice of mozzarella cheese is pressed into a medallion of pork tenderloin before it is coated with wheat flake crumbs and baked until golden brown.

Servings: 24   *Serving Size: 1 pork cutlet with cheese*
Yield: 24 pork cutlets with cheese

Parchment paper	—	Pepper, freshly ground	To taste or 1 t
Pork tenderloin medallions, lean, trimmed of fat and silverskin	4 lb (24 slices)	Mozzarella cheese, part-skim milk, thin slices	1 lb (24 ⅔-oz slices)
Egg whites, large	8 (10 oz)		
Wheat flake cereal, crushed	10 oz	Vegetable cooking spray, butter-flavored	
Cinnamon, freshly ground	1 t		—
Salt	To taste		

1. Place the pork between two pieces of parchment paper. Using a meat mallet, pound the pork slices until about ⅜-in. thick. Set aside.
2. Place the egg whites in a shallow container. Beat lightly.
3. Mix the crushed wheat flakes, cinnamon, salt and pepper to taste in another shallow container.
4. Pat one slice of cheese firmly into each slice of pork. Dip each in egg white, then seasoned wheat crumbs. Press the crumbs evenly into the meat.
5. Coat a shallow baking pan with cooking spray. Arrange the pork slices, cheese side up, without touching one another.
6. Bake in a 350°F (175°C) oven until the meat is medium done, browned, and the cheese melted, or about 15 minutes. Serve on heated plates with vegetables such as zucchini sauteed with tomatoes and herbs (see page 216) or fresh cream-style grilled corn (see page 201).

Servings	Calories	Protein (g) (%)	Fat (g) (%)	Cholesterol (mg)	Carbohydrates (g) (%)	Fiber (g)	Sodium (mg)
1	194	23.6 (49%)	6.2 (29%)	55	10.1 (21%)	1.3	267

Citrus-Flavored Pan Broiled Pork Chops

It's no wonder meat is once again taking the leading role on America's restaurant menus. Leaner, healthier cuts are now available. In the case of pork, the National Pork Producers Council reports 9 out of 10 fresh pork cuts are all under 200 calories per serving.

Servings: 24   *Serving Size: 3-oz chop + 6 T sauce*
Yield: 24 chops + 2¼ qt sauce

Pork chops, sirloin, boneless, ½-in. thick, trimmed of fat, patted dry	6 lb (24 4-oz chops)	Carrot, washed, small dice	1 lb
		Garlic, minced	1 T
		Orange juice, freshly squeezed	1 qt
		Lemon juice, freshly squeezed	½ c
		Parsley, minced	1 oz
Mustard powder	1½ T	Thyme, minced or dried	1½ T or 1¼ t
Salt	To taste		
Pepper, freshly ground	To taste	Oregano, minced or dried	1½ T or
Vegetable cooking spray	—		1½ t
Onion, minced	1½ lb		

1. Sprinkle the pork chops with the dry mustard and salt and pepper to taste.
2. Coat a large nonstick skillet with cooking spray or cook in batches. Place over medium-high heat until hot. Add the chops; cook until browned, or about 3 minutes per side. Place the chops in a baking pan. Drain any fat that accumulates in the skillet.
3. Add the onions and next four ingredients to the large skillet or a saucepan; heat to a boil. Reduce the heat to low; simmer until the vegetables are tender, or about 15 minutes.
4. In a blender, puree the juice and vegetable mixture until smooth. Mix in the parsley, thyme, and oregano. Season with salt and pepper to taste. Pour the sauce over the chops; cover. Place in a 350°F (175°C) oven; cook until tender, or about 30 minutes. Skim any fat from the citrus sauce. To adjust the sauce's consistency, thin with orange juice or stock and thicken by reducing. Spoon over the chops to serve. Accompany with a vegetable such as grilled corn on the cob (see page 200) and starch such as steamed new red potatoes.

Servings	Calories	Protein (g) (%)	Fat (g) (%)	Cholesterol (mg)	Carbohydrates (g) (%)	Fiber (g)	Sodium (mg)
1	227	25.6 (46%)	9.1 (37%)	73.1	9.6 (17%)	1.3	62.3

Lemon-Scented Grilled Pork Chops Seasoned with Sage

The aroma and flavor of the fresh sage and freshly squeezed lemon juice mixture brushed on these grilled pork chops make them a joy to eat. Another plus is that they are quick and easy to prepare.

Servings: 24   *Serving Size: 1 pork chop*
Yield: 24 pork chops

Lemon juice, freshly squeezed	1½ c	Pepper, freshly ground	To taste
Garlic, minced	1⅓ oz (¼ c)	Pork chops, sirloin, trimmed	
Sage leaves, minced or dried	¼ c or	of fat, ½-in. thick, boneless	6 lb (or
	1 T + 1 t		24 4-oz
Salt	To taste		chops)

1. Mix the first five ingredients in a bowl. Set aside.
2. Place the pork chops in a shallow, nonreactive container; pour the lemon mixture over. Cover and marinate at least 2 hours refrigerated, turning occasionally.
3. Place the chops on an oiled grill over medium heat. Cook until medium done, or about 6 minutes on each side. Cook longer for well-done chops. Baste frequently with the remaining marinade.
4. Serve accompanied by two vegetables such as toasted sesame green beans (see page 213) and sweet chunky corn cakes (see page 211) or a vegetable and grain selection, perhaps sliced gingered orange beets (see page 205) and barley risotto garnished with exotic mushrooms and spinach (see page 233).

Servings	Calories	Protein (g) (%)	Fat (g) (%)	Cholesterol (mg)	Carbohydrates (g) (%)	Fiber (g)	Sodium (mg)
1	187	24.6 (54%)	8.8 (44%)	73.1	1.0 (2%)	0.1	53.8

Oriental-Inspired Roasted Pork Tenderloin

Contrary to popular belief, it is not necessary to cook pork until well done to kill the parasite which causes trichinosis. If the parasite is present, it is killed at 137°F (58°C). When cooked to 155°F (68°C) or medium doneness, the pork will be juicy, tender, and slightly pink. Although this is slightly lower than the 160°F (70°C) recommended by the National Pork Producers Council, it is well above the temperature considered safe.

Servings: 24   *Serving Size: 3 oz cooked pork*
Yield: 4½ lb cooked pork

Vegetable juice, no salt added	1 c	Pork tenderloins, lean,	
Gingerroot, minced	4 oz	trimmed of fat and	
Soy sauce, low-sodium	½ c	silverskin	6 lb
Apple juice concentrate,		Salt	To taste
unsweetened	½ c	Pepper, freshly ground	To taste
Lemon juice, freshly squeezed	½ c		
Garlic, minced	1⅓ oz (¼ c)		

1. Combine the first six ingredients in a nonreactive container large enough to marinate the pork; mix well. Add the pork; coat with the marinade. Cover; marinate refrigerated for 12 hours, turning occasionally.
2. Place the pork on a rack in a roasting pan; add a small amount of hot water to the pan to prevent the dripping marinade from burning during roasting; reserve the remaining marinade. Roast in a 350°F (175°C) oven, turning once or twice, until desired degree of doneness,* or 150°F (65°C), allowing for carryover cooking. Baste the pork with the reserved marinade during all but the last 10 minutes of roasting.
3. Remove the pork from the pan. Let rest in a warm place about 10 minutes. Carve the pork diagonally into thin slices. Season with salt and pepper to taste. Serve with papaya mango salsa (see page 48).

*Cook the pork to 150–155°F (65–68°C) for medium to medium well doneness. For well done, cook to 160–170°F (70–75°C). Keep in mind, it is not necessary to cook to 185°F (85°C) as earlier guidelines recommended. The pork will be overcooked and dry.

Servings	Calories	Protein (g) (%)	Fat (g) (%)	Cholesterol (mg)	Carbohydrates (g) (%)	Fiber (g)	Sodium (mg)
1	151	24.2 (67%)	4.1 (26%)	67.2	2.5 (7%)	0.2	130

Pork Tenderloin Cubes in Soy and Sherry Glaze with Green Onions

When lean cuts of pork or those from the loin or tenderloin are cooked without added fat, pork in moderation is perfectly acceptable. In this recipe, lean cubes of pork tenderloin are marinated in a ginger and garlic flavored broth, browned, and then simmered in a soy and sherry broth with green onions. Served on a bed of brown rice, the tender, glazed chunks of pork make a delicious low-fat main course selection.

Servings: 24   *Serving Size: 3 oz cooked pork + sauce*
Yield: 4½ lb cooked pork + sauce

Pork, tenderloin, lean, trimmed of fat and silverskin	6 lb	Apple juice concentrate, unsweetened	¼ c + 2 T
Soy sauce, low-sodium (divided)	¾ c	Cornstarch	2 T
Sherry, dry	½ c	Pepper, freshly ground	To taste
Gingerroot, minced	2½ T	Vegetable cooking spray	—
Garlic, minced	1½ T	Onions, green, 1-in. sections, white only	1½ lb
Rich white chicken stock (see page 7)	1½ c		

1. Cut the meat into 1½-in. cubes.
2. Combine half (¼ c + 2 T) of the soy sauce and all of the sherry, ginger, and garlic in a nonreactive marinating container.
3. Add the pork cubes; toss to mix. Let stand 30 minutes, turning the meat occasionally. Drain and discard the marinade.
4. In a small bowl, combine the remaining soy sauce, stock, juice concentrate, cornstarch, and pepper in a bowl; mix until smooth.
5. Coat a large nonstick skillet or wok with cooking spray or cook in batches. Place over medium-high heat until hot. Add the pork cubes; stir-fry until brown.
6. Add the green onions; stir-fry a few times. Stir in the soy mixture. Heat to a boil, reduce the heat to very low; cover and simmer until tender, or about 30 minutes. To adjust the sauce's consistency, thin with stock or thicken with a cornstarch slurry. Serve over boiled brown basmati rice (see page 235) with vegetables like a medley of

stir-fried vegetables (see page 202). Another option is to stir-fry vegetables such as bell peppers and mushrooms with the pork, adding them with the green onions.

Servings	Calories	Protein (g) (%)	Fat (g) (%)	Cholesterol (mg)	Carbohydrates (g) (%)	Fiber (g)	Sodium (mg)
1	171	25 (62%)	4.2 (24%)	67.2	5.9 (15%)	0.8	235

Pork Tenderloin Stuffed with Raisin and Ripe Olive Studded Brown Rice

One way to reduce the portion size of meat on the plate and increase that of grains is by stuffing with rice, millet, quinoa, barley, wheat berries, or other grain. In this recipe, pork tenderloin is stuffed with high-fiber, tomato-flavored brown rice, seasoned with chili powder and mixed with raisins and ripe olive bits.

Servings: 24   *Serving Size: 3 oz cooked pork + stuffing + sauce*
Yield: 4½ lb cooked pork + stuffing + sauce

Pork tenderloins, lean, trimmed of fat and silverskin	6 lb	Salt	To taste
Vegetable cooking spray	—	Pepper, freshly ground	To taste
Onion, minced	2½ lb	Wine, white, dry	1 c
Garlic, minced	1 oz	Rich brown veal stock (see page 4) or very low sodium beef stock	1 pt
Tomatoes, coarsely chopped	4½ lb		
Chili powder	2 T		
Olives, ripe, chopped	4 oz		
Raisins, seedless	4 oz		
Rice, brown, long grain, boiled without salt (see page 117 for cooking directions)	2½ lb (14 oz as purchased)		

1. Cut a deep slit in the pork tenderloins lengthwise to make pockets for the stuffing.
2. Coat a nonstick skillet with cooking spray. Place over medium heat until hot. Add the onion and garlic. Cook until tender, or about 5 minutes.
3. Add the tomatoes and chili powder; reduce the heat to low; cook until the flavors are blended and the liquid evaporated, or about 10 minutes. Add the olives and raisins. Remove half of the mixture to another container; set aside.
4. Combine the rice with the remaining half of the tomato mixture. Season with salt and pepper to taste. Stuff the pork pockets with the rice mixture; tie the meat together at 2-inch intervals with cotton twine. Place any remaining stuffing in a baking pan coated with cooking spray. Cover and bake with the tenderloins until heated through.
5. Place the pork tenderloins in a roasting pan on a rack. Roast uncovered in a 325°F (165°C) oven, turning once until they reach an internal temperature of 150°F (65°C)

for medium, allowing for carryover cooking, or until they reach the desired doneness (see page 98).

6. Remove the meat from the pan to a warm place. Let the meat stand for about 10 minutes to firm up.

7. Skim any fat from the pan. Add the wine to deglaze the pan. Add the stock and remaining tomato mixture. Simmer until chunky sauce consistency. Season with salt and pepper to taste.

8. Remove the twine from the meat; slice. Serve accompanied by the chunky sauce.

Servings	Calories	Protein (g) (%)	Fat (g) (%)	Cholesterol (mg)	Carbohydrates (g) (%)	Fiber (g)	Sodium (mg)
1	256	27.1 (43%)	5.6 (20%)	67.2	23.8 (37%)	3.3	103

No alcohol is listed in the nutrition analysis. It is assumed to be cooked off during preparation.

Roasted Tenderloin of Pork Seasoned with Crushed Fennel Seeds

The licorice flavor of fennel seeds mingles well with the hints of red wine in the tomato-vegetable marinade/sauce on this roasted tenderloin of pork.

Servings: 24   *Serving Size: 3 oz cooked pork + ¼ c sauce*
Yield: 4½ lb cooked pork + 1½ qt sauce

Tomatoes, peeled, coarsely chopped	2 lb + 10 oz	Garlic, minced	1 T
		Fennel seeds, crushed	1 T
		Pepper, freshly ground	To taste or 1½ t
Rich brown veal stock (see page 4) or very low sodium beef stock	1½ qt	Salt	To taste
Apple or fruit juice concentrate, unsweetened	1½ c	Pork tenderloins, lean, trimmed of fat and silverskin	6 lb (12 tenderloins)
Wine, red, dry	1½ c		
Carrot, washed, small dice	8 oz		
Onions, minced	6 oz		

1. In a saucepan, combine the first nine ingredients. Heat the mixture to a boil, reduce the heat to low; simmer until the vegetables are tender, or about 15 minutes.
2. Place the mixture in a blender; process until smooth. Season with salt to taste. Remove 1½ qt of the sauce. Reserve to serve as an accompaniment sauce.
3. Once cool, marinate the tenderloins with the remaining sauce refrigerated for 8 hours. Turn occasionally.
4. Place the tenderloins on a rack in a shallow roasting pan; reserve the marinade. Pour a small amount of water in the bottom of the pan to prevent the dripping marinade from burning in the pan. Roast in a 350°F (175°C) oven, turning once or twice, until the meat reaches an internal temperature of 150°F (65°C) for medium, allowing for carry-over cooking, or until the desired degree of doneness (see page 98).
5. Baste the tenderloins every 10 minutes with the sauce remaining from marinating.
6. Remove the tenderloins from the oven; allow to rest in a warm place for 10 minutes. Meanwhile, reheat the reserved 1½ qt of sauce. To adjust the consistency of the sauce, thicken by reducing or thin with stock.

7. Carve the meat crosswise into thin slices; serve 3 oz of meat napped with ¼ c of the sauce.

Servings	Calories	Protein (g) (%)	Fat (g) (%)	Cholesterol (mg)	Carbohydrates (g) (%)	Fiber (g)	Sodium (mg)
1	200	25.9 (54%)	4.7 (22%)	67.2	11.8 (24%)	1.2	79

No alcohol is listed in the nutrition analysis. It is assumed to be cooked off during preparation.

VEAL

Roasted Veal Sirloin Napped with Vegetable-Thickened Vodka Sauce

In this selection, roasted, delicate, mild-flavored veal is married with a light, creamy vegetable-thickened sauce enhanced with vodka. They make a charming pair.

Servings: 24　　　　*Serving Size: 3 oz cooked veal + 2⅓ T sauce*
Yield: 4½ lb cooked veal + 1½ pt + ½ c sauce

*Veal, boneless, sirloin roast, trimmed of fat and silverskin	6 lb	Salt	To taste
		Pepper, freshly ground	To taste
Vodka	¼ c	Vegetable-thickened vodka sauce (see page 40)	1 recipe

1. Sprinkle the roast with the vodka.
2. Place the meat on a rack in a shallow roasting pan. Bake at 425°F (220°C) uncovered, for about 30 minutes, turning once. Reduce the heat to 325°F (165°C); cover the roast loosely with foil. Continue cooking until the center of the roast registers the desired temperature of doneness, about 150°F (65°C) for medium and 160°F (70°C) for well done, or about 10 degrees less than desired to allow for carryover cooking.
3. Let rest in a warm place about 10 minutes; carve into ½-inch thick slices; season with salt and pepper to taste. Serve with vegetable-thickened vodka sauce.

*For a more economical approach, substitute pork for the veal.

Servings	Calories	Protein (g) (%)	Fat (g) (%)	Cholesterol (mg)	Carbohydrates (g) (%)	Fiber (g)	Sodium (mg)	Alcohol (g) (%)
1	190	24.2 (50%)	5.7 (27%)	88.8	4.1 (8%)	0.6	94	3.7 (13%)

Veal Shanks Braised in Mediterranean-Style Tomato Sauce

This delicate stew is a variation of the Milanese dish osso buco. It is prepared by braising the osso buco or shanks of meaty veal until fork tender. Like its traditional counterpart, veal shanks braised in Mediterranean tomato sauce is finished with a gremolata—a spicy mixture of finely grated citrus zest, minced garlic, and parsley.

Servings: 24 *Serving Size: 2-in. shank + sauce*
Yield: 24 shanks + sauce

Vegetable cooking spray, olive-flavored	—	Rosemary, minced or dried	2 T + 2 t or 2¾ t
Veal shanks, sawed crosswise into 2-in. pieces, trimmed of fat and silverskin, patted dry	12 lb	Rich brown veal stock (see page 4) or very low sodium beef stock	1½ pt
Salt	To taste	Sherry, cream	1 c
Pepper, freshly ground	To taste	Brandy	¾ c
Onions, minced	1 lb		
Carrots, washed, small dice	6 oz	Gremolata:	
Celery, small dice	4 oz	Parsley, minced	3 T
Garlic, minced	1 T	Garlic, minced	1 T
Mushrooms, small dice	1 lb	Orange and lemon zest,	
Tomatoes, coarsely chopped	1 lb + 10 oz	finely grated	½ t each

1. Coat a large nonstick skillet with cooking spray or cook in batches. Place over medium-high heat until hot. Add the veal shanks; cook until well browned on all sides. Season with salt and pepper to taste. Transfer the shanks to a roasting pan. Drain any fat from the skillet.
2. Return the skillet to medium heat until hot. Add the onions, carrots, celery, garlic, and about ¼ c water to the skillet. Braise-deglaze, adding water as needed, until the onions are golden and the other vegetables tender.
3. Add the mushrooms; cook 5 additional minutes. Add the tomatoes and rosemary. Cook 10 additional minutes. Add the stock, cream sherry, and brandy.
4. Pour the sauce over the veal. Cover; place in a 325°F (165°C) oven; cook until the meat is fork tender, or about 2½ hours. Remove the shanks from the roasting pan; set aside in a warm place.
5. Skim the fat from the cooking broth. In a blender, puree until smooth. To adjust the

consistency, thin with stock or thicken by reducing. Season with salt and pepper to taste.

6. Pour the sauce over the veal shanks. In a small bowl, combine the gremolata ingredients. To serve, sprinkle over the veal shanks.

Servings	Calories	Protein (g) (%)	Fat (g) (%)	Cholesterol (mg)	Carbohydrates (g) (%)	Fiber (g)	Sodium (mg)	Alcohol (g) (%)
1	203	29.4 (58%)	5.9 (26%)	134	5.4 (11%)	1.4	107	0.8 (3%)

4

Poultry

T U R K E Y

*Cajun Turkey-Tofu Burgers**

The hamburger may be more American than apple pie. While apple pie was brought to America by the colonists from England, it is believed the hamburger was born in 1898 in an American restaurant kitchen. Whose kitchen is still being disputed.

Cajun turkey-tofu burgers are a low-fat variation of this century-old favorite. Rather than ground beef, these burgers are prepared with ground turkey. Since turkey lacks the fat and meaty taste of beef, the burgers are kept moist and flavorful by blending the ground turkey with roasted bell peppers, soft tofu, and sauteed onions and garlic, coating with ground spices, and pan broiling over medium to low heat.

Servings: 24   *Serving Size: 1 patty*
Yield: 24 patties

Vegetable cooking spray	—	White pepper, freshly ground	1 T
Onions, minced	2 oz	Pepper, freshly ground	To taste or 1 T
Garlic, minced	1½ T		
Turkey, raw, ground, skinless, dark and light meat	3 lb	Red pepper, ground	To taste or 2 t
Tofu, soft	1½ lb	Salt	To taste
Pepper, red, bell, roasted,† peeled, minced	1¼ lb	Hamburger buns, whole wheat, toasted	2¼ lb (24)
Paprika, sweet, Hungarian	¼ c + 2 T	Tomato cucumber relish (see page 52)	1½ pt
Onion powder	1½ T	Lettuce, leaves, red leaf	1 lb (24)

1. Coat a nonstick skillet with cooking spray. Place over medium heat until hot; add the onions and garlic. Cook until tender. Set aside to cool.
2. Mix together the turkey, tofu, bell pepper, and sauteed onions and garlic. Shape into 24 patties.
3. In a small bowl, mix the paprika with the next five seasonings. Coat each turkey-tofu patty with the seasoning blend.
4. Coat a nonstick skillet with cooking spray. Place over medium-low heat until hot. Add the burgers in batches and cook until the turkey is no longer pink, or about 3 minutes

per side. The burgers can also be baked in a 350°F (175°C) oven on a baking sheet coated with cooking spray, turning once until cooked through. Do not overcook the burgers or they will become dry.

5. Serve the burgers open-face. Place the patties on the hamburger bun bottoms. Spoon 2 T of the relish over each patty. Accompany with lettuce leaf-covered bun tops.

*Adapted from a recipe by Byron Takeuchi.

†See page 493 for bell pepper roasting directions.

Servings	Calories	Protein (g) (%)	Fat (g) (%)	Cholesterol (mg)	Carbohydrates (g) (%)	Fiber (g)	Sodium (mg)
1	234	18.5 (32%)	5.5 (21%)	32.2	27.5 (47%)	2.6	275

Mini Turkey Balls with Hints of Allspice

Unlike most meatballs, these mini turkey balls are blended with mashed potatoes. The potatoes can be credited with the turkey balls' light and delicate consistency. Served plain and melon ball–sized, mini turkey balls are ideal as hors d'oeuvres; and when offered in larger sizes simmered au jus or in pan gravy, they are appropriate as main course selections.

Servings: 24   Serving Size: 6 mini turkey balls
Yield: 144 mini turkey balls

Vegetable cooking spray	—	Milk, evaporated, skim	1 c
Onions, minced	1 lb	Egg whites, large	8
Turkey, raw, ground, skinless,			(10 oz)
dark and light meat	4 lb	Parsley, minced	¼ c
Potatoes, mashed, cooked		Allspice, freshly ground	1 t
without salt or fat	2 lb	Salt	To taste
	(1 qt)	Pepper, freshly ground	To taste
	mashed		
Bread crumbs, whole wheat,			
dry, fine	3 oz		

1. Coat a nonstick skillet with cooking spray. Place over medium heat until hot. Add the onions; cook until tender. Set aside to cool.
2. In a mixing bowl, combine all the remaining ingredients and the onions. Mix until smooth.
3. Using a very small or melon ball scoop, shape into 144 very small turkey balls or ones with about a ½-in. diameter. Place the turkey balls in a baking pan coated with cooking spray.
4. Bake in a 350°F (175°C) oven, turning once or as needed until brown on the outside and showing no trace of pink on the inside. Do not overcook or the turkey balls will become dry. Serve on wooden picks as hor d'oeuvres or in a serving dish as part of a buffet or smorgasbord.

Servings	Calories	Protein (g) (%)	Fat (g) (%)	Cholesterol (mg)	Carbohydrates (g) (%)	Fiber (g)	Sodium (mg)
1	159	19.9 (51%)	3.1 (18%)	43.3	12.2 (31%)	1.2	92.4

Variation

Turkey Balls with Hints of Allspice Braised in Pan Gravy

1. To serve the turkey balls as a main course, shape the turkey mixture into 48 balls. Place in a baking pan coated with vegetable cooking spray.
2. Bake in a 400°F (205°C) oven until brown on the outside and light pink on the inside. Remove the turkey balls to another baking pan. Set aside, keeping warm.
3. Skim any fat from the original baking pan.
4. Reduce 1 qt of rich brown veal stock (see page 4) or rich white chicken stock (see page 7) to 1 pt. Place the original baking pan over medium-high heat. Add the stock to the pan, stirring to remove any brown bits of food. Stir in 1 pt of evaporated skim milk.
5. Mix 2 oz of cake or all-purpose flour, browned without fat (or unbrowned cornstarch), with cold water as needed to form a smooth paste. Whip the slurry into the sauce. Cook until thickened to a creamy consistency and the starchy taste is gone, or about 15 minutes if using a flour slurry and only a few minutes if using a cornstarch slurry. To adjust the consistency of the sauce, thicken with more browned flour slurry or cornstarch slurry, and thin with stock.
6. Pour the sauce over the turkey balls. Cover. Bake in a 350°F (175°C) oven until the turkey balls are no longer pink. Season with salt and pepper to taste. Serve with mashed golden buttermilk potatoes (see page 223) or whole wheat noodles.

Sliced Moist Turkey Breast Napped with Creamy Cranberry-Enriched Sauce

Turkey and cranberries are made for each other. For a fresh approach, in this recipe, skinless turkey breast meat is poached in flavorful chicken stock. To complement the tender, juicy turkey white meat, its cooking broth is thickened with a puree of vegetables and flavored with concentrated fruit juices and balsamic vinegar. For the finishing touch, fresh, ruby red cranberries are simmered in the sauce with a tad of creme de cassis (black currant liqueur). In one word, the thin slices of moist turkey lightly coated with the creamy, tangy cranberry sauce might be described as "heavenly."

Servings: 24   *Serving Size: 3 oz cooked turkey + 6 T sauce*
Yield: 4½ lb cooked turkey + 2¼ qt sauce

Turkey, breast, bone in, skinless, trimmed of fat	7 lb	Apple or fruit juice concentrate, unsweetened	¾ c
Onions, coarsely chopped	1¼ lb	Orange juice concentrate, unsweetened	3 T
Carrots, washed, coarsely chopped	8 oz	Cranberries, fresh or frozen without sugar	12 oz
Sachet:		Creme de cassis	¼ c +
Parsley sprigs	6		2 T
Bay leaves	2	Salt	To taste
Peppercorns	8	Pepper, freshly ground	To taste
Cloves, whole	4	Watercress, sprigs	1 oz
Rich white chicken stock (see page 7)	3½ qt		(24)
Balsamic vinegar	¾ c		

1. Place the turkey breast in a brazier, breast side up. Surround with the onions, carrots, and sachet.
2. Combine the chicken stock, vinegar, and juice concentrates. Pour over the turkey breast. It should barely cover. Add additional stock or water if needed to cover initially and during cooking.
3. Cover the turkey with a round of parchment or wax paper. Place the brazier over low heat. Simmer until the turkey's internal temperature registers 160°F (70°C), or about 1½ hours.
4. Remove the pan from the heat. Let the turkey finish cooking in its hot broth until its temperature reaches 180°F (82°C), or about 30 minutes. Remove the breast from the broth to a warm place; cover.

5. Remove the sachet. Skim any fat from the broth. Place over high heat; reduce the liquid to 3 qt.
6. Puree the poaching broth and vegetables in a blender until smooth. Return to the pan. Heat to a boil. Add the cranberries and creme de cassis.
7. Reduce the heat to low; simmer until the cranberries have popped, or about 5 minutes.* Add stock or water to thin the sauce and reduce to thicken. Season with salt and pepper to taste.
8. To slice the turkey, carefully remove each side of the breast from the carcass in one piece.
9. Cut the meat at a slant, crosswise against the grain into thin slices.
10. Overlap two turkey slices on each heated plate. Nap with the sauce. Garnish with a watercress sprig.

*For a smoother sauce but one lower in fiber, strain out the cranberry skins.

Servings	Calories	Protein (g) (%)	Fat (g) (%)	Cholesterol (mg)	Carbohydrates (g) (%)	Fiber (g)	Sodium (mg)	Alcohol (g) (%)
1	196	29 (61%)	1.9 (9%)	72.9	12 (25%)	1.3	96.8	1.2 (5%)

Stuffed Bell Peppers Layered with Ground Turkey, Brown Rice, and Mozzarella Cheese*

One way to get more vegetables in the diet is by stuffing them with tasty grain and lean meat or low-fat poultry mixtures. For a sure sell, top them with golden brown, melted cheese, like these stuffed bell peppers.

Servings: 24   *Serving Size: 1 small stuffed bell pepper*
Yield: 24 small stuffed bell peppers

Bell peppers, small, washed	6 lb (24)	Basil, minced or dried	1 T or
Vegetable cooking spray	—		1 t
Turkey, ground, raw, skinless,		Salt	To taste
dark and light meat	2 lb	Pepper, freshly ground	To taste
Onions, minced	4 oz	†Brown rice, long grain,	
Garlic, minced	½ oz	cooked without salt	12 oz as
Tomatoes, fresh or canned,			purchased
peeled, small dice	2 lb	Mozzarella cheese, part-skim	
Oregano, minced or dried	1½ T or	milk, shredded	12 oz
	1½ t	Paprika, sweet, Hungarian	½ t
Rosemary, minced or dried	1 T or		
	1 t		

1. Cut a thin slice from the stem end of the peppers. Reserve for another use. Remove the seeds and membranes. Steam or parboil until crisp-tender, or 3 to 5 minutes. Shock in cold water to stop the cooking; drain. Place in baking pans coated with cooking spray.
2. Coat a nonstick skillet with cooking spray. Place over medium heat until hot. Add the turkey, onions, and garlic. Saute until the turkey is no longer pink. Do not overcook or the turkey will become dry. Drain any fat from the mixture, likely none.
3. Add the tomatoes and next three seasonings. Reduce the heat to low. Cook until the turkey and tomatoes are cooked together and the flavors are mellowed, or about 15 minutes. Season with salt and pepper to taste.
4. Layer one-third each of the rice, turkey, and cheese in the bell peppers. Repeat twice. Sprinkle with paprika.
5. Cover the stuffed peppers loosely with foil. If covered tightly, the cheese will stick to the foil as it melts during cooking. Place in a 350°F (175°C) oven until the peppers are tender, the filling is heated through, and the cheese is melted, or about 20 minutes. Place under a salamander to brown the cheese. Serve on heated plates as an appetizer

or vegetable course. Feature as a main course on a buffet, tapas-style menu, or when using family style service.

*Adapted from a recipe by Alicia Rowan.

†Directions to cook 12 ounces of brown rice: Wash the rice; place in a saucepan with $3\frac{1}{2}$ cups of water. Heat to a boil; reduce the heat to a simmer; stir; cover tightly. Do not uncover during cooking. Simmer until the grains are tender and the water is absorbed, or 45–50 minutes. Remove from the heat; let stand without stirring for 10 minutes. Fluff the rice with a fork. It's ready to use.

Servings	Calories	Protein (g) (%)	Fat (g) (%)	Cholesterol (mg)	Carbohydrates (g) (%)	Fiber (g)	Sodium (mg)
1	178	14.3 (32%)	4.4 (22%)	29.6	21 (46%)	3.0	92.7

Tamale Casserole with Cornmeal Crust and Ground Turkey Filling

This tamale casserole is an updated version of a Mexican-style favorite. A spicy, ground turkey filling is baked between layers of cornmeal crust prepared without egg yolks or fat.

Servings: 24   *Serving Size: 3 × 3⅓-in. piece*
Yield: 12 × 20 × 2-in. counter pan

Filling:		Oregano, dried	2 T
Turkey, raw, ground, skinless, dark and light meat	3 lb	Salt	To taste
		Pepper, freshly ground	To taste
Tomatoes, fresh or canned, coarsely chopped	4 lb	Red pepper, ground	To taste
		Crust:	
Onions, minced	1½ lb	Cornmeal, yellow, stone-ground	2 lb
Pepper, bell, green, very small dice	1 lb	Water (divided)	1 gal + 1 pt (4½ qt)
Chilies, green, canned, seeds and membranes removed, rinsed with water, minced	4½ oz or to taste	Salt	To taste or 1½ t
Chili powder	¼ c	Egg whites, large, beaten until foamy	8 (10 oz)
Cumin, freshly ground	2 T	Vegetable cooking spray	—

1. In a nonstick skillet, cook the ground turkey over medium heat until no longer pink, stirring to crumble. Do not overcook or the turkey will become dry. Drain any fat from the turkey, likely none.
2. Add the tomatoes and next six filling ingredients. Reduce the heat to low; cook, stirring occasionally until the flavors are mellowed and the liquid cooked from the mixture, or about 20 minutes. Season with salt, pepper, and red pepper to taste.
3. In a bowl, mix the cornmeal with 1½ qt of the cold water.
4. In a sauce pot, heat the remaining 3 qt of water and salt to taste to a boil. Gradually stir in the cornmeal; continue stirring until the mixture is very thick.
5. Remove from the heat. Set aside until cool. Stir in the egg whites. The egg whites will coagulate (scramble) if added while the polenta is still hot.
6. Coat a 12 × 20 × 2-in. counter pan with cooking spray. Spread half of the cornmeal mixture in a thin layer over the bottom of the pan. Add the turkey filling; smooth it out to evenly cover the cornmeal. Spread the remaining cornmeal mixture thinly over the turkey.

7. Bake in a 350°F (175°C) oven until the cornmeal topping is golden and has a cake-like texture, or about 30 minutes. To serve, cut the pan 4 by 6 into 24 3 × 3⅓-in. pieces.

Servings	Calories	Protein (g) (%)	Fat (g) (%)	Cholesterol (mg)	Carbohydrates (g) (%)	Fiber (g)	Sodium (mg)
1	255	18.3 (28%)	4.2 (14%)	32.2	38 (58%)	6.6	86.4

Turkey Tacos with Low-Fat Cheese and Fresh Tomato Bell Pepper Salsa

When it comes to menu trends, Mexican entrees are definitely in the picture. Reports estimate that consumption by food service diners has nearly doubled in the last 10 years. For health-conscious diners with a yearning for some south of the border cuisine, serve these soft tacos—whole wheat tortillas filled with ground turkey, low-fat cheddar cheese, shredded lettuce, and freshly prepared chunky tomato salsa.

Servings: 24　　　*Serving Size: 1 taco*
Yield: 24 tacos

Turkey, raw, ground, skinless, light and dark meat	$3\frac{1}{2}$ lb	Chili powder	$2\frac{1}{2}$ T
Onions, minced	$\frac{1}{2}$ lb	Cumin, freshly ground	2 t
Garlic, minced	$1\frac{1}{2}$ T	Salt	To taste
Rich white chicken stock (see page 7)	$1\frac{1}{2}$ c	Pepper, freshly ground	To taste or 1 t
Green chilies, canned, seeds and membranes removed, rinsed in water, minced	6 oz or to taste	Whole wheat tortillas, prepared without lard, 8-in.	24
Oregano, minced or dried	$\frac{1}{4}$ c or $1\frac{1}{2}$ T	Cheddar cheese, shredded, low-fat and low-sodium	$1\frac{1}{2}$ lb
		Lettuce, iceberg, shredded	1 lb
Rosemary, minced or dried	$\frac{1}{4}$ c or $1\frac{1}{2}$ T	Tomato bell pepper salsa (see page 51)	1 recipe ($1\frac{1}{2}$ qt)

1. Place a nonstick skillet over medium heat until hot. Add the turkey, onions, and garlic; cook until the turkey loses its pink color, stirring to crumble. Add a little of the chicken stock if the turkey begins to stick to the skillet. Do not overcook or the turkey will become dry.
2. Mix in the remaining chicken stock and next seven ingredients. Cook until the flavors are blended, or about 10 minutes. Add more chicken stock or water if needed during cooking.
3. Wrap the tortillas tightly in foil; place in a 350°F (175°C) oven until heated through, or about 10 minutes.
4. Spoon equal portions of the following ingredients, in the order listed, over the center

of the tortillas: turkey (2½ oz), cheese (1 oz), lettuce (¼ c/⅔ oz), and salsa (¼ c). To serve, fold in half.

Servings	Calories	Protein (g) (%)	Fat (g) (%)	Cholesterol (mg)	Carbohydrates (g) (%)	Fiber (g)	Sodium (mg)
1	238	25.9 (40%)	5.5 (19%)	43.5	27 (41%)	3.6	231

CHICKEN

All-American Barbecue-Style Chicken

All-American barbecue-style chicken is moist and juicy with a spicy, sweet tomato glaze. To cut the fat without sacrificing the traditional barbecue flavor, skinless breasts are partially cooked by poaching and then finished on the grill, basting with sauce.

Servings: 24   *Serving Size: 1 skinless chicken breast half*
Yield: 24 chicken breast halves

Chicken breast halves, skinless, boneless, trimmed of fat	6 lb (24 4-oz pieces)	Rich white chicken stock (see page 7)	2 qt
		All-American barbecue sauce for fowl (see page 57)	1 qt

1. Place the chicken breasts in a 12 × 20 × 2-in. counter pan presentation side (side with skin originally on) up.
2. Add the chicken stock to barely cover the chicken. Cover the chicken with a piece of parchment paper.
3. Heat to a simmer on the stove top. Reduce the heat to very low; poach until the chicken is no longer pink on the exterior, or 5–10 minutes.
4. Remove the chicken from the cooking broth to another counter pan. Reserve the broth for another purpose.
5. Brush both sides of the chicken generously with the barbecue sauce. Place presentation side down on a grill or broiler rack coated with oil.
6. Grill over or broil under medium-high heat, turning once until the chicken is glazed on the outside and no longer pink on the inside, or about 5 minutes. Baste with the barbecue sauce frequently.
7. Serve with oven-roasted garlic-seasoned potato wedges (see page 227) and vegetable slaw coated in ranch-style dressing (see page 290) for an all-American-style meal.

Servings	Calories	Protein (g) (%)	Fat (g) (%)	Cholesterol (mg)	Carbohydrates (g) (%)	Fiber (g)	Sodium (mg)
1	136	26.4 (80%)	1.5 (10%)	65.7	3.1 (9%)	0.2	87.7

Chicken Breasts Braised in Tomato Port Wine Sauce

The distinct flavor of port, a wine fortified with brandy, makes this simple chicken dish far from dull.

Servings: 24   *Serving Size: 1 skinless chicken breast half + sauce*
Yield: 24 chicken breast halves + sauce

Vegetable cooking spray, olive-flavored	—	Garlic, minced	1 T
		Port wine, dry	1½ pt
Chicken breast halves, skinless, trimmed of fat	7½ lb (24 5-oz pieces)	Rich white chicken stock (see page 7)	1½ pt
		Parsley, minced	¼ c + 2 T
Onions, minced	2 lb	Cornstarch	2 oz
Tomatoes, peeled, coarsely chopped	2½ lb	Salt	To taste
		Pepper, freshly ground	To taste

1. Coat a nonstick skillet with cooking spray. Place over medium heat until hot. Add the chicken in batches and cook, turning once, until no longer pink, or about 8 minutes. Transfer the chicken from the skillet to a counter pan; keep warm.
2. Recoat the skillet with cooking spray. In batches, or using a saucepan, add the onions and garlic; cook until tender.
3. Add the tomatoes and next three ingredients; heat to a boil; reduce the heat to low; simmer until the sauce is pulpy, or about 10 minutes. Pour over the chicken. Bake in a 350°F (175°C) oven until tender, or about 30 minutes. Remove the chicken from the pan. Hold in a warm place.
4. In a small bowl, mix the cornstarch with cold water as needed to form a smooth paste. Whip the cornstarch slurry into the cooking sauce. Simmer until the sauce is thickened, or a few minutes. To adjust the sauce's consistency, thicken by adding more cornstarch slurry or thin by adding stock. Season with salt and pepper to taste. Serve the chicken breasts with the sauce ladled over.

Servings	Calories	Protein (g) (%)	Fat (g) (%)	Cholesterol (mg)	Carbohydrates (g) (%)	Fiber (g)	Sodium (mg)
1	185	28 (63%)	3.4 (18%)	72.3	8.4 (19%)	1.3	79.6

No alcohol is listed in the nutrition analysis. It is assumed to be cooked off during preparation.

Chicken Breast Cubes Simmered in Creamy Coconut Sauce

While it is true that coconut is high in fat, the creamy coconut sauce coating these skinless chicken breast cubes is not. It is prepared from a mixture of reduced, fat-free chicken broth and rice vinegar and finished with evaporated, skim milk flavored with coconut extract. It's amazing how good it tastes.

Servings: 24   *Serving Size: 3 oz cooked chicken + sauce*
Yield: 1¼ gal (4½ lb cooked chicken + sauce)

Chicken, breast meat, skinless, boneless, 2-in. cubes	6 lb	Pepper, freshly ground	2 T
		Bay leaves	2
Rich white chicken stock (see page 7)	1½ pt	Cornstarch	2 oz
		Milk, evaporated, skim, hot	1 qt
Vinegar, rice	1½ pt	Coconut extract	2 T
Garlic cloves, peeled	5 oz	Salt	To taste

1. In a sauce pot, add the chicken and next five ingredients. Heat to a boil; reduce the heat to low; simmer until the chicken is no longer pink and tender, or about 25 minutes.
2. Add the evaporated milk to the chicken; heat to a boil; reduce the heat to low.
3. In a small bowl, mix the cornstarch with enough cold water to form a smooth paste. Stir into the sauce; simmer until sauce consistency. For further thickening, stir in more cornstarch slurry, and to thin, add stock or evaporated skim milk.
4. Remove the bay leaves. Stir in the coconut extract and salt to taste. Serve over boiled brown basmati rice (see page 235).

Servings	Calories	Protein (g) (%)	Fat (g) (%)	Cholesterol (mg)	Carbohydrates (g) (%)	Fiber (g)	Sodium (mg)
1	208	30.7 (59%)	3.4 (14%)	73.8	12.4 (24%)	1.2	122.7

Chicken Breasts Seasoned with Paprika, Braised Hungarian-Style

In the more traditional form of this Hungarian dish, chicken paprikash, chicken pieces are browned in bacon drippings, then braised in chicken stock, and served with the cooking liquids mixed with sour cream. In this version, skinless chicken breasts are cooked in a nonstick skillet coated with cooking spray until no longer pink, then braised in rich chicken stock, and served with the cooking liquids finished with yogurt. This lighter form of chicken paprikash has the same appeal as its counterpart without the fat and calories.

Servings: 24　　　*Serving Size: 1 skinless breast half*
Yield: 24 skinless breast halves

Vegetable cooking spray	—	Pepper, freshly ground	To taste
Chicken, breast halves, boneless, skinless, trimmed of fat	6 lb (24 4-oz pieces)	Onions, minced	12 oz
		Rich white chicken stock (see page 7)	2 qt
		Cornstarch	5 oz
Paprika, Hungarian, sweet	1 oz	Yogurt, nonfat, plain	1½ pt
Salt	To taste		

1. Coat a nonstick skillet with cooking spray. Place over medium heat until hot. Add the chicken in batches; cook until no longer pink, or about 5 minutes on each side. Sprinkle both sides with paprika and salt and pepper to taste. Place in a counter pan.
2. Add the onions to the skillet. Saute until tender. Sprinkle the onions and pour the stock over the chicken, cover. Braise in a 350°F (175°C) oven until cooked through and tender, or about 1 hour. Remove the chicken from the pan; keep warm. Skim any fat from the cooking juices.
3. In a small bowl, mix the cornstarch with the yogurt until smooth. Temper the yogurt by mixing some of the hot cooking juices into it.
4. Whip the yogurt mixture into the chicken juices. Cook over low heat, stirring until thickened. Do not boil or the yogurt may curdle. To adjust the sauce's consistency, thin with stock and thicken with a cornstarch slurry. Season with salt and pepper to

taste. Serve the chicken on a bed of boiled brown basmati rice (see page 235) or whole wheat noodles with the sauce poured over.

Servings	Calories	Protein (g) (%)	Fat (g) (%)	Cholesterol (mg)	Carbohydrates (g) (%)	Fiber (g)	Sodium (mg)
1	185	29.9 (67%)	2.1 (11%)	66.3	9.9 (22%)	0.8	122

Chicken Breasts and Celery Seasoned with Fresh Herbs, Slowly Braised with Garlic Cloves

In this recipe, whole cloves of garlic are slowly braised with skinless chicken breasts until the chicken is tender and the garlic mellowed in flavor and softened to a buttery consistency. To eat, the garlic cloves are squeezed from their paper hulls and spread onto slices of crisply grilled, whole grain French bread.

Servings: 24   *Serving Size: 1 skinless chicken breast half + ¼ c vegetables + ¼ c sauce*

Yield: 24 skinless chicken breast halves + 1½ qt vegetables + 1½ qt sauce

Celery, 2-in. segments	1½ lb	Vermouth, dry	1 pt
Onion, coarsely chopped	1½ lb	Nutmeg, freshly ground	¼ t
Parsley, minced	½ c	Pepper, freshly ground	To taste
Herbs, mixed, minced (thyme, oregano, savory) or dried	¼ c or 1 T + 1 t	Garlic heads, broken into cloves, cleared of loose hulls, unpeeled	12
Bay leaves	2	Rich white chicken stock (see page 7)	1 qt
Chicken, breast halves, skinless, boneless, trimmed of fat	6 lb (24 4-oz pieces)	Cornstarch	1½ oz
		Salt	To taste

1. Cover the bottom of a baking pan with the celery, onion, parsley, mixed herbs, and bay leaves.
2. Place the chicken breasts over the vegetables. Pour the vermouth over the chicken. Sprinkle with the nutmeg and pepper to taste. Tuck the garlic cloves around and between the chicken pieces.
3. Cover with aluminum foil, securing the edges tightly. Bake in a 350°F (175°C) oven until the chicken and vegetables are tender, or about 1¾ hours.
4. Remove the chicken, garlic, vegetables, and bay leaves from the pan. Set the garlic aside. Keep the chicken and vegetables warm. Discard the bay leaves. Skim any fat from the cooking juices; reduce over heat to 1 pt. Add the chicken stock to the juices.
5. Mix the cornstarch with cold water as needed to form a smooth paste. Stir the cornstarch slurry into the broth; simmer until thickened, or a few minutes. To adjust the consistency of the sauce, thicken with more cornstarch slurry and thin with stock or water.

6. Season the sauce, chicken, and vegetables with salt and pepper to taste. Serve the chicken on a bed of the vegetables with the sauce ladled over. Press the garlic between the thumb and index finger to release it from its skin; discard the skin. Accompany with slices of grilled or toasted whole wheat French bread (see page 383).

Servings	Calories	Protein (g) (%)	Fat (g) (%)	Cholesterol (mg)	Carbohydrates (g) (%)	Fiber (g)	Sodium (mg)
1	175	28.4 (68%)	1.8 (10%)	65.7	9.5 (23%)	1.8	115

No alcohol is listed in the nutrition analysis. It is assumed to be cooked off during the simmering of the broth.

Chicken Croquettes Topped with Mushroom-Filled Sauce

These delicate, low-fat croquettes are prepared from ground chicken breast meat but would be delicious made from ground turkey or veal as well. After being sauteed, the croquettes are briefly simmered and served in a light, chicken-flavored mushroom sauce which calls for no butter, egg yolks, or cream.

Servings: 24 *Serving Size: 1 croquette + ½ c mushroom-filled sauce*
Yield: 24 croquettes + 3 qt mushroom-filled sauce

Flour, cake or all-purpose, unbleached	4 oz	Salt	To taste
Chicken, breast meat, ground	4½ lb	Pepper, freshly ground	To taste
Onions, minced	12 oz	Vegetable cooking spray	—
Bread crumbs, whole wheat, fresh	8 oz	Mushrooms, thin slices	3 lb
Parsley, minced	1 oz	Rich white chicken stock (see page 7)	1½ qt
Nutmeg, freshly ground	½ t	Sherry, dry	¼ c

1. In a nonstick skillet, add the flour; cook, stirring, over low heat until golden brown, or about 5 minutes. Cool. Add cold water as needed to mix into a smooth paste. Set the slurry aside.
2. In a bowl, mix the chicken with the next six ingredients. Shape into 24 chop-like patties.
3. Coat a large nonstick skillet with cooking spray or cook in batches. Place over medium heat until hot. Add the patties; cook until golden brown and the centers are no longer pink, or about 5 minutes on each side. Do not overcook or they will become dry. Transfer to a counter pan; keep warm.
4. In a saucepan, add the mushrooms and stock. Heat to a boil; reduce the heat to medium; simmer until the mushrooms are tender.
5. Stir in the flour and water slurry; simmer until the sauce has a thin consistency and the starchy taste of the flour has cooked out, or about 10 minutes. To adjust the sauce's consistency, thicken with a cornstarch slurry or thin with stock. Add the sherry. Heat through. Pour over the croquettes.
6. Simmer the croquettes in the sauce on the range or in the oven briefly to heat through

if needed. Season with salt and pepper to taste. Serve the chops with the mushrooms and sauce spooned over.

Servings	Calories	Protein (g) (%)	Fat (g) (%)	Cholesterol (mg)	Carbohydrates (g) (%)	Fiber (g)	Sodium (mg)	Alcohol (g) (%)
1	156	19 (49%)	2 (12%)	36.9	14.7 (38%)	1.5	145	0.2 (1%)

Chicken Thighs in Crispy Cinnamon Crust

Fried chicken is an all-American favorite. Give customers crispy crusted chicken without the fat in fried chicken by coating skinless chicken pieces in seasoned, shredded cereal crumbs and baking in the oven. Once diners have tried these moist and juicy chicken thighs with a hint of cinnamon, they'll wonder why they ever sacrificed their health and wasted their calories on fried chicken.

Servings: 24   Serving Size: 1 skinless chicken thigh
Yield: 24 skinless chicken thighs

Bran cereal, shredded, crumbs (All Bran)	12 oz	Chicken, thighs, skinless, trimmed of fat	7½ lbs
Cinnamon, freshly ground	1½ t		(24 5-oz
Salt	To taste		pieces)
Pepper, freshly ground	To taste or 1½ t	Vegetable cooking spray, butter-flavored	—

1. In a shallow container, mix the first four ingredients. Dip the chicken thighs into the seasoned crumbs, turning to coat. Shake off the excess crumbs.
2. Coat a shallow baking pan with cooking spray. Add the chicken. Cook uncovered in a 350°F (175°C) oven, turning once, until cooked through and evenly browned, or about 50 minutes. Serve with mashed golden buttermilk potatoes (see page 223) or grilled corn on the cob (see page 200), choice of steamed vegetables, and a crisp green salad.

Servings	Calories	Protein (g) (%)	Fat (g) (%)	Cholesterol (mg)	Carbohydrates (g) (%)	Fiber (g)	Sodium (mg)
1	137	18.8 (50%)	3.6 (22%)	70.6	10.6 (28%)	5.1	233

Chicken Thighs Simmered in Chunky Tomato Sauce with Mushrooms and Bell Peppers

When your guests are hungry for pizza but want something lighter, these chicken thighs are an excellent suggestion. Sauteed skinless chicken thighs are braised in a tomato sauce seasoned with fresh oregano and basil and filled with sliced mushrooms and bell pepper and onion strips. The combination is pleasing to both the eye and the palate.

Servings: 24   *Serving Size: 1 skinless thigh + sauce*
Yield: 24 skinless thighs + sauce

Vegetable cooking spray, olive-flavored	—	Wine, white, dry	1 c
		Oregano, minced or dried	¼ c or
Chicken, thighs, skinless, trimmed of fat	7½ lb		1 T +
			1 t
	(24 5-oz pieces)	Basil, minced or dried	¼ c or
			1 T +
Garlic, minced	1½ T		1 t
Tomatoes, fresh or canned, pureed to chunky or		Thyme, minced or dried	2 T or
			2 t
coarsely chopped	3½ lb	Flour, cake or all-purpose,	
Onions, thin slices	1½ lb	unbleached, browned	
Mushrooms, thin slices	1 lb	without fat	2 oz
Peppers, bell, green,		Salt	To taste
matchstick strips	14 oz	Pepper, freshly ground	To taste
Carrots, washed, finely grated	4 oz	Parsley, minced	¼ c

1. Coat a nonstick skillet with cooking spray. Place over medium heat until hot. Add the chicken thighs in batches. Cook, turning occasionally, until no longer pink on the surface, or about 5 minutes. Transfer the thighs to a baking pan coated with cooking spray.
2. Coat a saucepan with cooking spray; add the garlic; braise-deglaze adding water as needed over medium-high heat until tender.
3. Add the tomatoes and next eight ingredients; heat the mixture to a boil. Pour the mixture over the chicken; cover and bake in a 350°F (175°C) oven until the chicken is cooked through and tender.
4. Remove the chicken to another pan. Cover; set aside in a warm place.
5. Stir cold water as needed into the flour to form a smooth paste.
6. Skim the fat from the cooking mixture. Whip the flour-water slurry into the sauce.

Heat to a boil; reduce the heat to low; simmer until the sauce is thickened and the starchy taste of the flour has cooked out, or about 10 minutes. To adjust the sauce's consistency, thin by adding stock and thicken by adding more browned flour slurry or a cornstarch slurry.

7. Season with salt and pepper to taste. Pour the sauce over the chicken; sprinkle with the parsley. Serve on a bed of whole wheat pasta or in a bowl with chunky whole grain bread to sop up the sauce, and accompany with a salad such as green salad tossed with vegetables and dressed with saffron and basil orange vinaigrette (see page 280). For an easier to eat dish with a more upscale appeal, replace the chicken thighs with skinless, boneless chicken breasts.

Servings	Calories	Protein (g) (%)	Fat (g) (%)	Cholesterol (mg)	Carbohydrates (g) (%)	Fiber (g)	Sodium (mg)
1	150	18.5 (49%)	4.0 (24%)	70.7	9.8 (26%)	2.2	91.4

No alcohol is listed in the nutrition analysis. It is assumed to be cooked off during preparation.

Crispy Baked Mustard Chicken Breast

Diners need not fear. There are healthy alternatives to fried chicken like this crispy baked mustard chicken breast. It is prepared by dipping skinless breasts of chicken in a garlic and onion-flavored mustard-yogurt mixture and then coating with crunchy, high fiber, wheat flake cereal crumbs. Rather than deep frying the chicken breast in oil, they are baked without added fat in the oven. The finished product is crispy-crusted, moist, and juicy breasts of chicken.

Servings: 24   *Serving Size: 1 skinless chicken breast half*
Yield: 24 skinless breast halves

Wheat flake cereal	1¼ lb	Yogurt, nonfat, plain	1 c
Paprika, Hungarian, sweet	1 T	Mustard, Dijon-style	½ c
Garlic powder	1½ t	Chicken, breast halves,	
Onion powder	1½ t	boneless, skinless,	
Tarragon, ground	1½ t	trimmed of fat	6 lb (24
Pepper, freshly ground	To taste		4-oz pieces)
	or 1 t	Vegetable cooking spray,	
Salt	To taste	butter-flavored	—

1. Crush the wheat flakes into coarse crumbs with a rolling pin. Place in a container with the paprika and next five seasonings; mix well.
2. In another container, mix the yogurt and mustard together until well blended.
3. Dip the chicken breasts in the yogurt-mustard mixture. Dredge in the wheat flake crumbs. Place in a baking pan coated with vegetable cooking spray.
4. Bake uncovered in a 350°F (175°C) oven presentation side up until the chicken flesh is no longer pink and the coating is crisp and brown, or about 30 minutes. Serve accompanied by a potato and vegetable selection, perhaps cheesy mashed potatoes with green onions (see page 219) and sliced gingered orange beets (see page 205).

Servings	Calories	Protein (g) (%)	Fat (g) (%)	Cholesterol (mg)	Carbohydrates (g) (%)	Fiber (g)	Sodium (mg)
1	218	29.4 (54%)	2.1 (9%)	65.9	20.4 (37%)	2.8	372

Grilled Chicken Drumsticks Tandoori-Style

Restaurateurs are responding to a marked change in the American palate by adding more ethnic selections to their menus. Rather than serving American-style barbecue chicken, one way to diversify the menu is by offering grilled chicken drumsticks tandoori-style, an adaptation of a traditionally light Indian favorite. While normally cooked in a tandoor (clay oven that blasts meat with very intense heat), similar results can be produced on a regular grill.

Servings: 24   Serving Size: 2 skinless chicken drumsticks
Yield: 48 skinless chicken drumsticks

Paprika, Hungarian, sweet	3 T	Garlic cloves, peeled	1 oz
Salt	To taste	Yogurt, nonfat, plain	1½ pt
Cardamom pods, skins		Lemon juice, freshly squeezed	3 T
removed	6	Coriander, freshly ground	3 T
Cloves, whole	6	Cumin, freshly ground	2 T
Cinnamon bark, ¼-in. chips	3	*Chicken drumsticks, skinless,	
Peppercorns	9	trimmed of fat	8 lb (48
Cumin seeds	¼ t		pieces)
Coriander seeds	¼ t	Limes, cut into eighths	1 lb (6
Gingerroot, peeled, coarsely			pieces)
chopped	1 oz		

1. In a small bowl, mix the paprika and salt to taste. Set aside.
2. In a nonstick skillet, saute the cardamom and next five spices over medium-high heat until lightly browned without popping. Grind the spices to a powder in a spice grinder or blender.
3. Blend the ginger and garlic in a blender until it forms a paste. Mix in a small amount of the yogurt if necessary to blend. Mix in the remaining yogurt, lemon juice, freshly ground coriander and cumin, and browned spice mixture until well blended.
4. Score the chicken legs at 1-in. intervals, cutting through the meat. Rub the legs with the paprika mixture until well coated and inserted into the cuts.
5. Rub the yogurt paste on the legs, inserting into the cuts. Cover and marinate refrigerated for 24 hours.
6. Remove the excess paste from the legs; discard. Place the legs on an oiled grill rack. Grill at moderately low heat until the chicken is half cooked.
7. Turn the chicken over using tongs. Continue grilling until the chicken is cooked

through, turning as needed. Remove from the grill. Serve the legs garnished with the limes. Accompany with fresh mint and cilantro chutney (see page 43).

*This recipe is equally good prepared with chicken thighs, breasts, or wings and other types of poultry like turkey, cornish game hen, pheasant, squab, or quail.

Servings	Calories	Protein (g) (%)	Fat (g) (%)	Cholesterol (mg)	Carbohydrates (g) (%)	Fiber (g)	Sodium (mg)
1	145	22.4 (64%)	2.9 (28%)	70.5	2.9 (8%)	0.5	84.2

Oregano Seasoned Chicken Breasts Topped with Melted Mozzarella Cheese

This recipe demonstrates how a dish can be simple to prepare and at the same time "oh, so good." Skinless chicken breasts are merely sauteed in a nonstick skillet lightly coated with cooking spray and then baked, sprinkled with freshly minced oregano and part-skim milk mozzarella cheese. The finished product is moist and juicy chicken breast meat hinting of oregano, covered with golden brown melted cheese.

The chicken breasts might be featured on the dinner menu with a brightly colored steamed vegetable and whole grain pilaf, or sliced thin and fanned out on a bed of pasta tossed in a light marinara sauce. They are equally good on the lunch menu. The chicken breasts might be presented in sandwich form on toasted whole grain buns garnished with shredded raw vegetables or promoted in the salad of the day tossed with baby greens and garden vegetables, all coated in a light balsamic vinaigrette.

Servings: 24   *Serving Size: 1 skinless chicken breast half with cheese*
Yield: 24 skinless chicken breast halves with cheese

Vegetable cooking spray, olive-flavored	—	Oregano, minced or dried	$\frac{1}{4}$ c or 1 T + 1 t
Chicken, breast halves, skinless, boneless, trimmed of fat, lightly flattened	6 lb (24 4-oz pieces)	Salt	To taste
		Pepper, freshly ground	To taste or 1 t
		Mozzarella cheese, part-skim milk, shredded	12 oz

1. Coat a nonstick skillet with cooking spray. Place over medium heat until hot. Add the chicken in batches and cook until no longer pink on the exterior, turning once. Place the chicken in a baking pan coated with cooking spray.
2. Sprinkle with the seasonings and cheese. Cover loosely. This will prevent the cheese from sticking as it melts during cooking. Bake in a 350°F (175°C) oven until the chicken is cooked through and the cheese melted, or about 15 minutes. To brown the cheese, place the chicken breasts under the salamander. Serve with a vegetable such as zucchini sauteed with tomatoes and herbs (see page 216) or toasted sesame green beans

(see page 213), and starch, perhaps oven-roasted garlic-seasoned potato wedges (see page 227).

Servings	Calories	Protein (g) (%)	Fat (g) (%)	Cholesterol (mg)	Carbohydrates (g) (%)	Fiber (g)	Sodium (mg)
1	176	29.9 (68%)	5.3 (27%)	80.5	0.6 (1%)	0.1	129

Spit-Roasted Chicken on the Rotisserie

A study was published in the *New England Journal of Medicine* which showed that very little fat migrates from poultry's skin to its flesh during cooking. This spit-roasted chicken applies this principle. At service, the skin is removed from the whole roasted chicken and discarded. The end result is moist, roasted, skinless chicken, an ideal dish for health-conscious diners watching their fat and cholesterol intakes.

Servings: 24
Yield: 4 chickens

Serving Size: 1 skinless chicken thigh, breast half, or leg + wing

Chickens, whole	10 lb (4 2½-lb chickens)	Parsley, washed	1 bunch for stuffing
		Salt	To taste
		Pepper, freshly ground	To taste

1. Distribute the parsley among the chickens' cavities. Truss the chickens.
2. Place the chickens head to tail on a spit rod. Leave an inch or two between the chickens to allow the heat to circulate between. Fasten in place tightly with holding forks. Install the spit rod on a rotisserie unit. Follow the manufacturers' directions for roasting.
3. Cook until the juices run clear, the hip bone is loose when jiggled, the thigh meat reaches 180–185°F (82–85°C), or about 45 minutes.
4. Cut each chicken into 8 pieces—2 legs, 2 thighs, 2 wings, and 2 breast halves. Remove the skin from the chicken pieces; discard. Season with salt and pepper to taste. Serve the chicken with colorful vegetable dishes like baby carrots in fruit glaze (see page 190) and grilled corn on the cob (see page 200). Pass all-American barbecue sauce for fowl (see page 57).

Servings	Calories	Protein (g) (%)	Fat (g) (%)	Cholesterol (mg)	Carbohydrates (g) (%)	Fiber (g)	Sodium (mg)
1	129	19.7 (63%)	5.0 (37%)	60.3	0 (0%)	0	58.3

Variation

Oven-Roasted Chicken: Follow step 1. Omit step 2. Place in a 325°F (165°C) oven, breast sides down on a rack in a shallow roasting pan. After 1 hour, turn the chickens breast side up. Roast according to step 3, allowing about 1¼–1½ hours cooking time. Finish with step 4. Replace the barbecue sauce with chicken gravy thickened with blended vegetables (see page 34).

Replace the whole chicken with turkey, cornish game hen, quail, pheasant, guinea hen, or other poultry. Adjust the cooking time according to size.

OTHER POULTRY AND GAME

Asian-Inspired Broiled Cornish Game Hens

Rock cornish hens are a cross-breed between cornish game cocks and Plymouth rock hens. The plump little birds contain only white meat. A fragrant blend of cassia bark, Sichuan peppercorns, cloves, and wild fennel seeds enhances the mild gamy flavor of the birds in this recipe.

Servings: 24   *Serving Size: 1 skinless game hen*
Yield: 24 skinless game hens

Garlic cloves, peeled	2 oz	Pepper, freshly ground	To taste
Onions, green, white only	2 oz	†Cornish game hens, split	12 lb
Soy sauce, low-sodium	¼ c		(24 8-oz
Apple or fruit juice			hens)
concentrate, unsweetened	2 T	Vegetable cooking spray	—
Wine, rice	2 T	Lettuce, iceberg, shredded	2 lb
*Five spice powder	1 T		
Salt	To taste		

1. In a blender, puree the garlic and green onions. Add the soy sauce and juice concentrate if needed to puree. Add the remaining soy sauce, juice concentrate, rice wine, five spice powder, and salt and pepper to taste; mix to blend.
2. Separate the skin of the game hens from the meat by using the index finger and/or thumb or inserting an inverted teaspoon between the skin and meat starting at the breast bone and working to the thigh and back; leave the skin attached ¼ in. on the back bone side.
3. Spoon the five spice marinade under the skin all the way to the thigh. Massage the skin to disperse the mixture evenly.
4. Marinate refrigerated for 6 hours.
5. Place skin side down on a heated broiler rack or grill,‡ coated with oil. Broil or grill at moderately low heat until the hens are half cooked and well browned on one side. Turn the hens over using tongs. Continue cooking until the hens are done, the juices run clear, or the hip bone is loose when jiggled. If limited by grill space, using moderate heat, cook the hens on the grill only until grill marks are formed and the hens have taken on a light smoky flavor, or about 5 minutes. Place in counter pans and bake, skin side up, in a 325°F (165°C) oven until cooked through.

6. At service, remove the skin; discard. Cut each hen into 4 pieces. Season with salt and pepper to taste. Serve on a bed of crisp shredded lettuce. Accompany with Vietnamese-style dipping sauce (see page 54).

*Five spice is an aromatic Chinese spice powder with a unique flavor.

†To split the hens for broiling:
1. Hold by the tail. Cut through the bones to one side of the back bone all the way to the neck.
2. Split the hen open.
3. Cut off the back bone.
4. Pull out the breast bone. This helps the hens to lie flat and cook evenly.

‡Change the recipe's name to Asian-inspired grilled cornish game hens if grilling rather than broiling the hens.

Servings	Calories	Protein (g) (%)	Fat (g) (%)	Cholesterol (mg)	Carbohydrates (g) (%)	Fiber (g)	Sodium (mg)	Alcohol (g) (%)
1	224	33.2 (62%)	8.4 (35%)	100	1.7 (3%)	0.4	403	0.1 (<1%)

Rabbit Braised in Chunky Tomato Wine Sauce Seasoned with Fresh Rosemary

This braised rabbit is a healthy variation of a Spanish dish called Conejo (rabbit) a la Navarra. In Spain, where the geography and climate are well suited to the proliferation of game, rabbit is more readily available than chicken.

Servings: 24 *Serving Size: 2 pieces skinless rabbit + ½ c potatoes + sauce*
Yield: 48 pieces skinless rabbit + 3 qt potatoes + sauce

Vegetable cooking spray, olive-flavored	—	Bay leaves	2
		Parsley, minced	¼ c
Rabbit, skin removed, trimmed of fat, each cut into 12 pieces	10 lb (4)	Rosemary, minced, or dried	¼ c or 1 T + 1 t
		Pepper, freshly ground	To taste
Onions, minced	1½ lb		
Garlic, minced	1 oz	Potatoes, new, red-skinned, washed, ¼-in. thick slices	5 lb
Tomatoes, coarsely chopped	4 lb	Salt	To taste
Wine, dry, white	1 pt	Parsley for garnish	2 bunches

1. Coat a nonstick skillet with cooking spray. Place over medium heat until hot. Add the rabbit in batches; cook until no longer pink. Place in a counter pan.
2. Using a saucepan or in batches, add the onions and garlic to the skillet; saute until tender, or about 5 minutes. Add the tomatoes, wine, bay leaves, parsley, rosemary, and pepper. Cook for a few minutes.
3. Pour the chunky sauce over the rabbit; cover. Bake in a 325°F (165°C) oven until the rabbit is almost tender, or about 1½ hours.
4. Add the potatoes. Continue cooking until both the rabbit and potatoes are tender, or about 45 minutes longer.
5. Remove the bay leaves. Season with salt and pepper to taste. Serve on heated plates garnished with fresh parsley.

Servings	Calories	Protein (g) (%)	Fat (g) (%)	Cholesterol (mg)	Carbohydrates (g) (%)	Fiber (g)	Sodium (mg)
1	241	22.8 (38%)	5.9 (22%)	55.8	23.6 (40%)	3.1	46.8

No alcohol is listed in the nutrition analysis. It is assumed to be cooked off during preparation.

Roasted Breast of Guinea Hen Infused with Madeira

Guinea hen's impressive nutritional attributes along with its pleasant chicken-like flavor will catch the eye of diners. The percentage of fat in its meat is comparable to chicken breast meat. At the same time, unlike many other game meats, it is exceptionally moist, tender, and dense.

Servings: 24   *Serving Size: 1 skinless guinea hen breast half*
Yield: 24 skinless guinea hen breast halves

Vegetable cooking spray, olive-flavored	—	Paprika, Hungarian, sweet	2½ t
		Salt	To taste
Shiitake mushrooms, caps only,* minced	3½ lb	Pepper, freshly ground, coarse	To taste
		†Guinea hen, breast halves, boneless	10½ lb
Shallots, minced	14 oz		(24 7-oz
Garlic, minced	1 T + 2 t		pieces)
Wine, madeira (divided)	1¼ pt		
Parsley, minced (divided)	½ c + 2 T	Rich white chicken stock (see page 7)	1½ c
Thyme leaves, minced or dried	3½ T or 1 T + ½ t		

1. Coat a nonstick skillet with cooking spray. Place over medium heat until hot. Add the shiitake mushrooms, shallots, and garlic. Saute until almost tender, or about 3 minutes.
2. Add ¾ c of the madeira wine; continue cooking until au sec (dry).
3. Add ¼ c + 2 T of the parsley, all the thyme and paprika, and salt and pepper to taste; mix well. Set aside momentarily.
4. Rinse the guinea hen breasts well; pat dry. Using your index finger and thumb or an inverted teaspoon, separate the skin from the breasts, leaving attached about ¼ in. on 3 sides. Spoon the mushroom mixture under the skin, massaging to disperse evenly. Cover any parts of the breast tops not covered by skin with the mushroom mixture to prevent drying during baking.
5. Coat baking pans with cooking spray. Pour the remaining 1¾ c madeira into the pans. Place the hen breasts in the pans skin side up. Bake in a 350°F (175°C) oven until cooked through, or about 30 minutes. Remove the breasts from the pans. Keep warm.
6. Carefully skim the fat from the pan juices. Add the chicken stock. Place over medium-high heat; reduce the juices to a flavorful broth, stirring to remove cooked particles

from the pans' bottoms. At service, remove the skin from the guinea breasts; discard. Place the breasts on heated dinner plates; sprinkle with the remaining parsley ($\frac{1}{4}$ c). Accompany with the pan juices.

*Note: Reserve the shiitake stems for stock making or other use.

†If whole guinea hens are purchased, the legs and thighs might be served tandoori-style (see page 135) and the wings flavored with ginger and coated with sesame seeds (see page 342). Chicken and cornish game hen breasts are delicious alternatives to the guinea hen breasts when they are not available or their price is prohibitive.

Servings	Calories	Protein (g) (%)	Fat (g) (%)	Cholesterol (mg)	Carbohydrates (g) (%)	Fiber (g)	Sodium (mg)
1	254	38.7 (62%)	4.6 (17%)	113	13.2 (21%)	3.0	131

No alcohol is listed in the nutrition analysis. It is assumed to be cooked off during preparation.

Roasted Farm-Raised Venison Napped with Mushroom-Filled Sauce

In this dish, farm-raised venison is marinated in a red wine broth for 24 hours, roasted, and served napped with a creamy sauce filled with wild and domestic mushrooms. The sauce is prepared by simmering spicy, apricot-flavored chanterelle and mild earthy-flavored button mushrooms in rich brown stock, thickening with a cornstarch slurry, and finishing with nonfat sour cream.

Servings: 24   Serving Size: 3 oz cooked venison + 6⅔ T mushroom-filled sauce
Yield: 4½ lb cooked venison + 2½ qt mushroom-filled sauce

Venison, saddle, trimmed of fat and silverskin	6 lb (2- to 3-lb saddles)	Mushrooms, chanterelle (see page 501), sliced	1 lb
		Mushrooms, button, sliced	1 lb
		Cornstarch	1½ oz (4½ T)
Red wine marinade for game (see page 61)	3 qt	Sour cream, nonfat	1½ c
Rich brown veal stock (see page 4) or very low sodium beef stock	1½ qt + ½ c	Parsley, minced	2 T
		Salt	To taste
		Pepper, freshly ground	To taste

1. Place the venison in a nonreactive marinating container. Pour the marinade over, turning to coat. Marinate refrigerated for 24 hours, turning to coat occasionally.
2. Drain the venison from the marinade; pat dry. Discard the marinade.
3. Place the venison on a rack in a roasting pan. Roast in a 400°F (205°C) oven until 130°F (55°C) (rare) allowing for carryover cooking (about 45–55 minutes), or to the desired degree of doneness.
4. Remove the meat from the pan; let stand in a warm place to firm up for 15 minutes. Carve into thin slices.
5. Skim any fat from the pan juices. Place over medium-high heat. Add the brown stock; stir to deglaze the pan. Add the mushrooms. Reduce the heat to medium. Cook until the pan juices are reduced to 1 pt and the mushrooms are tender.
6. In a small bowl, mix the cornstarch with water as needed to form a smooth paste. Stir into the cooking liquids. Simmer until thickened, or a few minutes. Reduce the heat to very low.
7. Temper the sour cream with a small amount of the pan juices. Stir the sour cream into the broth. Do not boil or the sour cream may curdle. Cook until heated through.

Season with parsley and salt and pepper to taste. Serve the sliced venison napped with the mushroom-filled sauce.

Servings	Calories	Protein (g) (%)	Fat (g) (%)	Cholesterol (mg)	Carbohydrates (g) (%)	Fiber (g)	Sodium (mg)
1	173	28.9 (69%)	3.3 (18%)	95.3	5.6 (13%)	0.6	78.4

No alcohol is listed in the nutrition analysis. It is assumed to be cooked off during preparation.

5

Fish and Shellfish

FISH

Crispy Crusted Orange-Scented Sole Fillets

Feature fish 'n' chips as your healthy menu special of the day. Serve crispy crusted orange-scented sole fillets for the "fish" and oven-roasted potato wedges seasoned with rosemary for the "chips" (see page 227). For an authentic touch, present with a cruet of vinegar.

Servings: 24   *Serving Size: 3½ oz cooked sole*
Yield: 5¼ lb cooked sole

Corn flakes, crumbs	12 oz	Pepper, freshly ground	To taste
Tarragon, minced or dried	2 T or	Egg whites, large	4 (5 oz)
	2 t	*Fillets, sole	6 lb (24
Orange zest, finely grated	1 T		4-oz pieces)
Garlic powder	2 t		
Onion powder	2 t	Vegetable cooking spray,	
Salt	To taste	butter-flavored	—

1. In a shallow dredging container, mix the corn flake crumbs and next six ingredients.
2. Place the egg whites in a shallow container; beat lightly. Dip the fillets in the egg whites; coat both sides with the corn flake mixture. Place on a sheet pan coated with cooking spray. Bake in a 450°F (230°C) oven until the fillets are crisp and nearly flake, or about 10 minutes. Serve with shredded cabbage with corn and bell pepper tossed in pineapple tofu dressing (see page 287) and roasted potatoes.

*Replace the sole fillets with other lean, white fish fillets like perch, pike, bass, flounder, or haddock.

Servings	Calories	Protein (g) (%)	Fat (g) (%)	Cholesterol (mg)	Carbohydrates (g) (%)	Fiber (g)	Sodium (mg)
1	173	25.3 (60%)	1.5 (8%)	59.5	12.8 (30%)	0.7	245

Mackerel in Soy-Ginger Glaze Baked en Papillote

Mackerel is naturally a high-fat fish, but the type of fat is called omega-3s. Like other polyunsaturated fats, the omega-3s can help reduce cholesterol when they are substituted for saturated fats in the diet. In addition, omega-3s have anti-clotting abilities. As a result, they may prevent heart attacks and possibly high blood pressure. Further, they may help control inflammatory reactions in the body that cause conditions such as arthritis and psoriasis.

By coating the mackerel in a soy-ginger glaze and baking in parchment paper, the need for additional fat is eliminated. To minimize the need for salt as well, the fish is coated with low-sodium soy sauce, freshly grated ginger, sliced green onions, minced fresh cilantro, and slices of lime prior to baking. When the lightly browned mackerel parchment packages are opened tableside, the wonderful aromas released are sure to delight diners.

Servings: 24 or 1   Serving Size: 3½ oz cooked mackerel
Yield: 5¼ lb cooked mackerel

	24 servings	1 serving
Green onion, white and 1-in. green, thin slices	2¼ lb	1½ oz
Cilantro, minced	1½ oz	2¼ t
Gingerroot, grated	2 T	¼ t
Soy sauce, low-sodium	¾ c	1½ t
White pepper, freshly ground	1½ t	Pinch
Parchment paper	—	—
Mackerel, fillet	6 lb (24 4-oz pieces)	4 oz
Lime, thin slices	1½ lb (72)	3
Vegetable cooking spray	—	—

1. In a bowl, mix the green onion, cilantro, ginger, soy sauce, and white pepper together. Set aside.
2. Cut the parchment paper into 24 heart shapes large enough to hold a fillet and still have room for crimping the edges.
3. Place a fillet on one side of each heart. Spoon the green onion mixture over; lay 3 lime slices on top.
4. Fold the empty half of the parchment paper over each fillet and crimp the edges to seal tightly. For more information on how to crimp the package's edges, see page 492.
5. Spray the parchment packages with vegetable cooking spray.
6. Place the packets on a sheet pan; bake in a 450°F (230°C) oven until the parchment is puffed and brown, or about 5–8 minutes.

7. Place on heated serving plates. At service, cut about $\frac{3}{4}$ of the paper on the curved edges next to the fold to release the aroma and display the attractively garnished fillets. Accompany with a grain and vegetable side dish.

Servings	Calories	Protein (g) (%)	Fat (g) (%)	Cholesterol (mg)	Carbohydrates (g) (%)	Fiber (g)	Sodium (mg)
1	208	24.4 (47%)	9.1 (39%)	53.4	7.0 (14%)	1.7	345

Marinated Broiled Shark Fillets Garnished with Papaya Mango Salsa

A garlic-lemon marinade adds flavor to these broiled shark fillets without fat. Garnished with papaya mango salsa, speckled with red and green bell peppers, and seasoned with fresh chilies, these shark fillets are a "winner."

Servings: 24   *Serving Size: 3½ oz cooked shark + 2 T salsa*
Yield: 5¼ lb cooked shark + 1½ pt salsa

Lemon juice, freshly squeezed	2 T	Shark fillets, skinless, boneless	6 lb (24 4-oz pieces)
Green onions, white only, minced	2 oz	Vegetable cooking spray	—
Garlic, minced	2 T	Salt	To taste
Paprika, Hungarian, sweet	2 T	Papaya mango salsa (see page 48)	1 recipe
Pepper, freshly ground	To taste or 2 t		

1. Combine the first five ingredients in a small bowl.
2. Cover a sheet pan with parchment paper; place the shark fillets on it. Brush the marinade on the fillets, turning to coat both sides evenly. Cover; marinate refrigerated for 2 hours.
3. Broil on sheet pans coated with cooking spray or grill in oiled hand racks, turning once, until they reach the desired doneness. Season with salt to taste.
4. Serve on heated plates accompanied by the salsa.

Servings	Calories	Protein (g) (%)	Fat (g) (%)	Cholesterol (mg)	Carbohydrates (g) (%)	Fiber (g)	Sodium (mg)
1	180	25.5 (57%)	5.3 (26%)	49.6	6.4 (14%)	1.1	124

Red Snapper Simmered in Tomato Sauce Veracruz-Style

In this recipe, red snapper fillets are sauteed and then simmered in a delicious, low-fat tomato sauce peppered with sliced onions, minced green olives, and capers and seasoned with freshly ground cinnamon and cloves.

Servings: 24   *Serving Size: 3½ oz cooked red snapper + ¼ c sauce*
Yield: 5¼ lb cooked red snapper + 1½ qt sauce

Red snapper or other lean fish, fillets	6 lb (24 4-oz pieces)	Capers, drained, rinsed in water	1½ oz (¼ c) drained
Vegetable cooking spray	—	Parsley, minced	1 oz
Onions, thin slices	2 lb	Bay leaves	3
Garlic, minced	2 T	Cinnamon, freshly ground	¼ t
Tomatoes, peeled, coarsely chopped	4 lb	Cloves, freshly ground	¼ t
Green olives with pimentos, coarsely chopped	3 oz	Salt	To taste
		Pepper, freshly ground	To taste
Jalapeno peppers, canned, drained, seeds and membranes removed, thin strips, rinsed in water	3 oz	Limes, thin slices	1 lb

1. Cut the fish fillets into serving pieces if needed.
2. Coat a nonstick skillet with cooking spray. Place over medium heat until hot. Add the fish in batches; cook until no longer translucent, or about 3 minutes on each side. Remove from the skillet to a counter pan coated with cooking spray. Keep warm.
3. Add the onions and garlic to the skillet. Cook over medium heat until tender, or about 5 minutes. Add the tomatoes and next seven ingredients. Reduce the heat to low; simmer the mixture until it reaches sauce consistency and the flavors are mellowed, or about 10 minutes. Season with salt and pepper to taste.
4. Spoon the sauce over the fillets. Cover; place in a 350°F (175°C) oven; cook until the fillets are almost flaky, or about 5 minutes. Remove the bay leaves. Arrange the fish on heated plates. Spoon the sauce over to serve. Garnish with the lime slices.

Servings	Calories	Protein (g) (%)	Fat (g) (%)	Cholesterol (mg)	Carbohydrates (g) (%)	Fiber (g)	Sodium (mg)
1	167	27.4 (66%)	2.5 (14%)	46.6	8.4 (20%)	2.1	202

Salmon Baked in Parchment on a Bed of Vegetables with Fresh Tarragon

Cooking in parchment concentrates the flavors and aromas of ingredients without adding fat. When serving salmon baked in parchment, cut open the parchment packages in front of diners to release delicate aromas and display attractively garnished fillets of salmon on beds of vegetables. Aluminum foil can be used but is not as pretty as parchment paper.

Servings: 24 or 1   Serving Size: 3½ oz cooked salmon + ½ c vegetables
Yield: 3½ oz or 5¼ lb cooked salmon + ½ c or 3 qt vegetables

	24 servings	1 serving
Vegetable cooking spray, butter-flavored	—	—
Carrots, washed, coarsely grated	2½ lb	1⅔ oz
Onions, thin slices	2½ lb	1⅔ oz
Mushrooms, thin slices	12 oz	½ oz
Salt	To taste	To taste
Pepper, freshly ground	To taste	To taste
Tarragon, minced	2 T	¼ t
Parchment paper	—	—
Salmon, pink, fillets, boneless	6 lb (24 4-oz pieces)	4 oz
Shallots, minced	4 oz	¾ t
Tarragon leaves	6 doz	3
Wine, white, dry	1½ pt	2 T

1. Coat a saucepan with cooking spray. Add the carrots and onions. Cook over medium heat until almost tender.
2. Add the mushrooms; cook until all the vegetables are tender.
3. Season with salt and pepper to taste and the minced tarragon.
4. Cut out 24 heart-shaped pieces of parchment paper. One half of each heart should be large enough to hold a salmon fillet plus ½ c of vegetables and still allow room to crimp the edges.
5. To cut, fold the parchment in half and cut half of a heart from the folded side.
6. Place ½ c of vegetables in the center of one side of each heart. Lay a salmon fillet over the vegetables and sprinkle with ¾ t of the minced shallots and salt and pepper to taste.
7. Place 3 tarragon leaves on top of each salmon fillet. Add 2 tablespoons of wine to each package.
8. To seal the papillotes, fold the empty half of the parchment paper over the mixture. Then starting at the top of the fold, make a small crimp in the edge. Continue

crimping around the edge. Each crimp should hold the previous one in place. When you reach the bottom of the heart, fold the point under to hold it in. Spray the packages with cooking spray.

9. Place the packages on a sheet pan. Bake in a 450°F (230°C) oven until the parchment is puffed and browned, or about 5–8 minutes.

10. Serve on heated plates. In front of diners, cut about ¾ of the paper on the curved edge next to the fold to release the aromas and display the fish and vegetables.

Servings	Calories	Protein (g) (%)	Fat (g) (%)	Cholesterol (mg)	Carbohydrates (g) (%)	Fiber (g)	Sodium (mg)
1	182	24 (55%)	4.2 (21%)	59	10.5 (24%)	2.5	96.7

No alcohol is listed in the nutrition analysis. It is assumed to be cooked off during preparation.

Shark and Vegetable Kabob Broiled with Pineapple Yogurt Pepper Sauce*

The combination of mild-flavored shark and fresh bell peppers, mushrooms, and pineapple cubes glazed in pineapple yogurt sauce works well together on these broiled kabobs.

Servings: 24 *Serving Size: 2 skewers with 3½ oz cooked shark + vegetables*
Yield: 5¼ lb cooked shark + vegetables

Shark steak, skinless, boneless, 1-in. cubes (½ oz each)	6 lb	Bell peppers, green and red, 1-in. cubes (⅛ oz each)	1¼ lb each
†Pineapple, fresh or canned without sugar, 1-in. cubes (¼ oz each)	3 lb	Bell peppers, yellow, 1-in. cubes (⅛ oz each)	10 oz
Mushroom caps, small	2 lb (96)	Pineapple yogurt pepper sauce (see page 60)	1 recipe
		Skewers, wooden, soaked in cold water	48

1. Marinate the shark, pineapple, and each of the vegetables with the pineapple yogurt sauce for 3 hours refrigerated, spooning the sauce over occasionally.
2. Thread on each skewer a colorful arrangement of 2 red, 2 green, and 1 yellow bell pepper cube, 4 shark cubes, 4 pineapple cubes, and 2 mushroom caps.
3. Place the kabobs on a sheet pan. Broil the kabobs about 4 inches from the flame, turning, until desired doneness. Brush the remaining pineapple yogurt sauce over the kabobs as they cook. Remove the fish, vegetables, and fruit from their skewers in front of diners tableside. Serve on a bed of boiled brown basmati rice (see page 60).

*Adapted from a recipe by Paul Findly and Rajeev Maini.
†See page 492 for fresh pineapple peeling and cubing directions.

Servings	Calories	Protein (g) (%)	Fat (g) (%)	Cholesterol (mg)	Carbohydrates (g) (%)	Fiber (g)	Sodium (mg)	Alcohol (g) (%)
1	205	25 (4%)	5.1 (22%)	44.5	14.8 (29%)	2.0	123	0.1 (<1%)

Spicy Catfish with Garlic and Cilantro Corn Bread Topping

Diners are continuing to select more fish and seafood dishes than ever before. This spicy catfish is a healthy alternative to red meat and lighter than fried fish.

Servings: 24   *Serving size: 3½ oz cooked fish + topping*
Yield: 5¼ lb cooked fish + topping

Celery seeds	2 t	Vegetable cooking spray	—
Peppercorns	2 t	*Catfish, fillets	6 lb (24
Cloves, whole	8		4-oz pieces)
Cardamom pods, skins		Mustard, Dijon-style	½ c
removed	4	Garlic, minced	1 T
Bay leaves	2	Buckwheat stone-ground	
Lemon zest, finely grated	1 T	yellow corn bread	
Paprika, sweet, Hungarian	1 t	(see page 371), or other	
Mace, ground	⅛ t	corn bread, crumbled	12 oz
Red pepper, ground	To taste	Cilantro, minced	1 oz
Salt	To taste		

1. In a spice grinder or blender, grind the celery seeds, peppercorns, cloves, cardamom, and bay leaves. Combine with the lemon zest, paprika, mace, and red pepper, and salt to taste.
2. Place the fillets on a sheet pan coated with cooking spray. Brush the mustard on both sides of the fillets. Sprinkle both sides of the fillets with the spice blend.
3. Coat a nonstick skillet with cooking spray. Place over medium heat until hot. Add the garlic; saute until tender. Mix in the corn bread crumbs. Raise the heat to medium-high. Cook, stirring until the crumbs are golden and crisp. Remove from the heat. Mix in the cilantro.
4. Spoon the seasoned crumbs over the catfish; cover. Place in a 350°F (175°C) oven for 15 minutes. Uncover and continue baking until the fish is nearly flaky and the topping brown and crisp. Place under the salamander for final browning if needed. Serve on heated dinner plates with a vegetable such as citrus-glazed carrots sprinkled with

minced parsley (see page 195) and starch, perhaps brown rice simmered in tomato broth (see page 236).

*Substitute monkfish, cod, perch, or any firm white fish fillets for the catfish. Adjust the dish's name and nutritional analysis accordingly.

Servings	Calories	Protein (g) (%)	Fat (g) (%)	Cholesterol (mg)	Carbohydrates (g) (%)	Fiber (g)	Sodium (mg)
1	143	20 (57%)	4.2 (27%)	65.8	5.8 (16%)	0.8	147

Steamed Whole Sea Bass with Black Bean Sauce

The Chinese believe a fish without a head or tail is incomplete and not aesthetic. From a culinary standpoint, there are also advantages for cooking fish whole. The juices are better retained, resulting in more tender and moist fish meat. Keep in mind, when steaming whole sea bass, it will continue to cook in its covered container after the heat is turned off. Remove from the steaming vessel immediately to prevent over-cooking.

Servings: 4 or 24   Serving Size: 3½ oz cooked edible sea bass + sauce
Yield: 14 oz or 5¼ lb cooked edible sea bass + sauce

	4 servings	24 servings
Black or rock sea bass, halibut, pike, snapper, or swordfish, whole, scaled, and cleaned (drawn*)	1½ lb (1)	9 lb (6)
†Black beans, fermented	1 T	¼ c + 2 T
Green onions, thin slices, green stems included (divided)	¼ c	8½ oz
Gingerroot, minced	2 t	¼ c
Garlic, minced	2 t	¼ c
Sherry, dry	2 T	¾ c
Soy sauce, low-sodium	2 T	¾ c

1. Place each fish in a serving dish suitable for steaming if using a steaming vessel such as a bamboo steamer and in counter pans if using a commercial steamer.
2. Mash the black beans in a bowl; add ⅓ of the green onions (1⅓ T for 4 servings and 2.8 oz for 24 servings) and all the ginger and garlic; mix. Spread evenly over each fish.
3. Sprinkle the sherry and soy sauce over each fish.
4. Place the fish in a commercial steamer or steaming vessels over boiling water. Steam until the fish are almost opaque and 90% cooked, or about 15 minutes in a bamboo steamer. Remove from the steaming containers immediately.
5. Serve the whole fish garnished with the remaining green onions. Portion onto dinner plates tableside.

*Drawn means with the entrails removed.

†Fermented black beans are small black soybeans with a pungent salty flavor. This salt-preserved Chinese

specialty is available packed in cans or plastic bags at Asian grocery stores. The dried, cooked, salted, and fermented soybeans are also known as black beans, dried black beans, and preserved black beans.

Servings	Calories	Protein (g) (%)	Fat (g) (%)	Cholesterol (mg)	Carbohydrates (g) (%)	Fiber (g)	Sodium (mg)
1	141	24.6 (73%)	2.8 (19%)	36.3	2.6 (8%)	0.4	344

No alcohol is listed in the nutrition analysis. It is assumed to be cooked off during preparation.

Swordfish Steaks in Chunky Tomato Sauce

Chunky tomato sauce seasoned with garlic and rosemary makes an excellent match for these mild-flavored, moderately oily, firm, dense, and meat-like fleshed swordfish steaks. It's no wonder they are one of the most popular fish in the United States.

Servings: 24   *Serving Size: 3½ oz cooked steak + 5⅓ T sauce*
Yield: 5¼ lb cooked swordfish + 2 qt sauce

Vegetable cooking spray	—	Salt	To taste
Swordfish, steaks, skinless,		Pepper, freshly ground	To taste
boneless, washed, patted		Tomatoes, peeled, chopped	4 lb
dry	6 lb (24	Garlic, minced	1⅓ oz (¼ c)
	4-oz pieces)	Onions, minced	2 lb
Mustard powder	1 T	Parsley, minced	¼ c
Rosemary, minced or dried	2 T or 2 t		

1. Coat a nonstick skillet with cooking spray. Place over medium-high heat until hot. Add the fish steaks in batches; cook until brown, turning once, or about 5 minutes on each side.
2. Transfer the fish to a counter pan coated with cooking spray. Rub each side with the mustard powder; sprinkle with the rosemary and salt and pepper to taste; keep warm.
3. Place the tomatoes and garlic in a large nonstick skillet or saucepan; simmer until pulpy, or about 5 minutes. Add the onions and parsley; simmer until the onions are tender and the mixture reduced to sauce consistency, stirring occasionally, or about 15 minutes. If there is excess liquid in the tomato mixture, increase the heat to medium high and cook, stirring, until reduced. Season with salt and pepper to taste. Spoon over the fish.
4. Cover; place in a 350°F (175°C) oven; cook until the fish is nearly flaky, or about 5 minutes. Serve immediately with the sauce spooned over.

Servings	Calories	Protein (g) (%)	Fat (g) (%)	Cholesterol (mg)	Carbohydrates (g) (%)	Fiber (g)	Sodium (mg)
1	173	23.8 (56%)	5.0 (26%)	44.2	7.6 (18%)	1.8	110

❤ Butternut Squash Bisque Garnished with a Dollop of Chunky Apple Yogurt

Recipe appears on page 11

❦ Cajun-Style Roast Tenderloin of Beef

Recipe appears on page 68

Turkey Tacos with Low-Fat Cheese and Fresh Tomato Bell Pepper Salsa

Recipe appears on page 120

❦ Mediterranean-Inspired Shrimp

Recipe appears on page 170

❦ Black Bean Patties Topped with Tomato Bell Pepper Salsa

Recipe appears on page 172

Oriental Chicken Salad with Orange-Pineapple Soy Dressing

Recipe appears on page 274

Malaysian-Inspired Tropical Fruit and Crisp Vegetable Salad

Recipe appears on page 294

Peach Meringue Mousse Cake

Recipe appears on page 380

Yellowfin Tuna Burgers Coated with Teriyaki Ginger Glaze

Two ingredients that may look unfamiliar in this recipe are mirin and sake. Mirin is a low-alcohol, sweet golden wine used in Japanese cooking. It is also referred to simply as rice wine. If not available, replace it with a well-flavored sweet sherry. Sake, the national alcoholic drink of Japan, is a yellowish, slightly sweet low-alcohol (12–15%) beverage made from fermented rice.

Servings: 24   Serving Size: 1 tuna patty + 2 t glaze
Yield: 24 tuna patties + 1 c glaze

Burgers:			Glaze:		
Tuna, yellowfin, fillets, skin and bones removed, chopped fine	6 lb		Rich white chicken stock (see page 7)	1 pt	
*Rice, brown, cooked without salt	5 oz as purchased		Sake or rice wine	½ c + 2 T	
			Mirin or sweet sherry	½ c + 2 T	
			Soy sauce, low-sodium	½ c + 2 T	
†Peppers, bell, yellow and red, roasted, skin removed, small dice	8 oz each		Honey, clover	½ c	
			Mustard, Dijon-style	½ c	
			Vinegar, champagne	½ c	
			Gingerroot, minced	2 T	
			Garlic, minced	1 T	
Green onions, minced	6 oz				
Garlic, minced	2 T		To serve:		
Mustard, Dijon-style	2 T		Hamburger buns, whole		
Red pepper, ground	To taste or 1 T		wheat, toasted	Optional (24 buns)	
Salt	To taste		Lettuce, red leaf, leaves	Optional (24—1 lb)	
Pepper, freshly ground	To taste				
Egg whites, large	4 (5 oz)				

Burgers:
1. In a mixing bowl, combine all the burger ingredients; mix well. Shape into 24 patties.
2. Coat a nonstick skillet with cooking spray. Place over medium heat until hot. Add the tuna patties in batches; cook until just cooked through, turning once, or about 5 minutes per side. Be careful not to overcook or the patties will dry out. The tuna patties can also be cooked in the oven on a sheet pan coated with cooking spray, turning once.

3. Place on the bottoms of toasted whole wheat buns. Spread the bun tops evenly with the glaze. Cover with a lettuce leaf. Serve open face on dinner plates.

Glaze:

1. In a saucepan, combine all the ingredients. Place over moderate heat. Cook, stirring occasionally until the mixture coats a spoon, or about 30 minutes. Strain through a fine mesh strainer. Set aside until service.

*Directions to cook the 5 oz of brown rice: Wash the rice; place in a saucepan with 1½ c of water; heat to a boil; reduce the heat to very low; stir; cover. Simmer the rice until tender and the water is absorbed, or about 45–50 minutes. Do not remove the cover during cooking. Remove from the heat; stand covered about 10 minutes; fluff with a fork.

†See page 493 for pepper roasting directions.

Servings	Calories	Protein (g) (%)	Fat (g) (%)	Cholesterol (mg)	Carbohydrates (g) (%)	Fiber (g)	Sodium (mg)
1	252	32.4 (52%)	6.9 (25%)	48.7	14 (23%)	1.1	349

No alcohol is listed in the nutrition analysis. It is assumed to be cooked off during preparation.

SHELLFISH

Asian-Style Steamed Squid on a Bed of Shredded Lettuce

In this East meets West combination, firm chewy squid rings are mounded on a bed of shredded, crisp iceberg lettuce, sprinkled with lots of freshly minced cilantro and garnished with lime wedges. The mild, somewhat sweet flavor of the steamed squid rings is accented by a light marinade hinting of soy, lime, and garlic.

Servings: 24   *Serving Size: 3½ oz cooked squid + 2 oz lettuce*
Yield: 5¼ lb cooked squid + 3 lb lettuce

Garlic, minced	1½ oz	Squid, small, cleaned, bodies	
Lime juice, freshly squeezed	¼ c +	sliced into ⅛-in. rings	6 lb
	2 T	Lettuce, iceberg, shredded	3 lb
*Fish sauce	3 T	Cilantro, minced	2 oz
Soy sauce, low-sodium	3 T	Lime wedges	12 oz
Pepper, freshly ground	To taste	Salt	To taste

1. In a nonreactive container large enough to hold the squid, combine the garlic and next four ingredients. Mix well. Add the squid; turn to coat well. Cover; marinate refrigerated 2–3 hours.
2. Steam the squid in a compartment steamer or preferably on platters in steamer vessels, tightly covered, until tender, or about 15 minutes. Remove from the covered steaming vessels immediately to prevent overcooking. If cooking in a compartment steamer, place in a solid pan to retain the juices and watch the cooking time very carefully to avoid overcooking. Avoid pressure steaming if possible; its high temperature will toughen the squid's protein very quickly and cause it to become rubbery.
3. To serve, place a bed of shredded lettuce on each dinner plate. Mound the squid in the center. Sprinkle with cilantro. Scatter the lime wedges over to garnish. Accompany

with lime ginger-garlic sauce (see page 47). Offer as an appetizer, salad, or main course selection.

*Fish sauce is a strongly flavored, pungent seasoning sauce used in the cuisine of Southeast Asian countries such as Thailand, Vietnam, and Cambodia. It is available at Asian grocery stores.

Servings	Calories	Protein (g) (%)	Fat (g) (%)	Cholesterol (mg)	Carbohydrates (g) (%)	Fiber (g)	Sodium (mg)
1	154	20 (53%)	4.8 (29%)	280	6.8 (18%)	0.7	452

Barbecued Spicy Coconut Shrimp

These spicy-hot grilled shrimp derive their flavor from a marinade later served as a sauce. For a coconut flavor, without the fat of coconut milk, the marinade is prepared from evaporated skim milk flavored with coconut extract. Red pepper gives it just the right finishing bite.

Servings: 24   *Serving Size: 6 large shrimp*
Yield: 12 doz large shrimp

Marinade:		Seafood:	
Milk, evaporated, skim	1½ pt	*Shrimp, "jumbo," raw,	
Coconut extract	½ T	in the shell	6 lb (12 doz)
Parsley, minced	¼ c + 2 T	Skewers, wooden, soaked	
Garlic, minced	2 T	in cold water	24
Red pepper, ground	To taste		
	or ½ T		
Salt	To taste		

1. In a container large enough to hold the shrimp, mix all the marinade ingredients. Remove one-half of the marinade to a small container; cover and refrigerate for later use.
2. Peel and devein the shrimp. Discard the shrimp peels or reserve for another use. Add the shrimp to the remaining marinade; turn to coat well. Cover; marinate refrigerated for at least 2 hours, turning occasionally.
3. Place 6 shrimp on each skewer; broil on a sheet pan or grill on an oiled rack, basting frequently with the marinade from the shrimp and turning as needed. Cook until the shrimp have curled and are barely firm when pressed, or about 2 minutes on each side.
4. Heat the reserved refrigerated marinade in a saucepan. Serve the shrimp accompanied by the sauce.

*See page 170 for description of shrimp size.

Servings	Calories	Protein (g) (%)	Fat (g) (%)	Cholesterol (mg)	Carbohydrates (g) (%)	Fiber (g)	Sodium (mg)
1	70	13.1 (79%)	0.6 (9%)	111	2.1 (13%)	0.1	145

Variation

Substitute 24 (4-oz) skinless, boneless chicken breast halves for the shrimp. Grill or broil the chicken breasts until the meat is no longer pink, or about 8 minutes on each side.

Crab Cakes Peppered with Roasted Corn and Bell Peppers

These corn bread-crusted crab cakes, speckled with diced, roasted bell peppers and grilled corn kernels, are a delicious way to eat crab. For a healthy approach, the cakes are baked rather than fried.

Servings: 24   *Serving Size: 2 2½-oz cooked crab cakes*
Yield: 48 cooked crab cakes

Crabmeat, lump, fresh or frozen, cartilage removed	4 lb	Pepper, freshly ground	To taste
Green onion, thin slices, white only	10 oz	Hot pepper sauce	To taste or 2 t
Pepper, bell, green, roasted,* peeled, small dice	10 oz	Egg whites, large, lightly beaten	6 (7½ oz)
Corn, kernels, grilled (see page 201)	8 oz	Buckwheat stone-ground yellow corn bread (see page 371), or other corn bread, crumbs, oven-dried (divided)	1 lb
Parsley, minced	1 oz		
Yogurt, nonfat, plain	¾ c		
Mustard, Dijon-style	1½ T	Vegetable cooking spray	—
Salt	To taste		

1. In a mixing bowl, combine the crabmeat, green onion, bell pepper, corn, and parsley; mix until well blended.
2. In another bowl, combine the yogurt, mustard, and salt, pepper, and pepper sauce to taste. Stir into the crab mixture.
3. Gently fold the egg whites and 6 oz of the corn bread into the crab mixture. Shape the crab mixture into 48 patties. Carefully coat with the remaining crumbs; chill for at least 30 minutes but no longer than 2 hours.
4. Place on a sheet pan coated with cooking spray. Bake in a 500°F (260°C) oven until the cakes are brown on both sides and cooked through, turning once, or about 10 minutes. Serve with a crunchy whole grain pilaf and crisp, steamed vegetable.

*See page 493 for bell pepper roasting directions.

Servings	Calories	Protein (g) (%)	Fat (g) (%)	Cholesterol (mg)	Carbohydrates (g) (%)	Fiber (g)	Sodium (mg)
1	139	18.6 (54%)	2.4 (15%)	75.9	10.8 (31%)	1.4	291

Mediterranean-Inspired Shrimp

These large, sauteed shrimp, coated in a tomato-brandy–flavored sauce can be served as an appetizer or main course selection. Either way, they are sure to please.

Servings: 24   *Serving Size: 4 large shrimp*
Yield: 8 doz large shrimp

*Shrimp, large, raw, in shell	3 lb (96)	Parsley, minced (divided)	½ c
Vegetable cooking spray,		Wine, red, dry	1 T
olive-flavored	—	Brandy or cognac	1 T
Onions, minced	12 oz	Salt	To taste
Garlic, minced	1 T	Pepper, freshly ground	To taste
Tomatoes, peeled, coarsely			
chopped	2 lb		

1. Peel and devein the shrimp; set aside.
2. Coat a large nonstick skillet with cooking spray or cook in batches. Place over medium heat until hot. Add the onions and garlic; cook until tender.
3. Add the tomatoes, ⅔ (5 T) of the parsley, the wine, and brandy; cook until the flavors are blended and the mixture reaches thick chunky sauce consistency. Season with salt and pepper to taste.
4. Add the shrimp. Cook until the shrimp begin to turn bright pink, or a few minutes. Serve sprinkled with the remaining parsley.

*Raw shrimp in their shells are classified according to the number per pound. There are over 70 "tiny," 31–35 "large," 21–25 "jumbo," and 10–15 "colossal" shrimp per pound. Generally, the larger the size of the shrimp, the greater their cost.

Servings	Calories	Protein (g) (%)	Fat (g) (%)	Cholesterol (mg)	Carbohydrates (g) (%)	Fiber (g)	Sodium (mg)	Alcohol (g) (%)
1	44	6.5 (59%)	0.5 (9%)	55.3	3.2 (29%)	0.8	67.9	0.2 (3%)

6

Dried Beans, Peas, Lentils, and Vegetables

DRIED BEANS, PEAS, AND LENTILS

Black Bean Patties Topped with Tomato Bell Pepper Salsa

Because of health, environmental, and ethical concerns, a growing number of Americans are shifting away from meat. For those diners who prefer to patronize establishments offering vegetarian selections, offer items on the menu like black bean patties topped with tomato bell pepper salsa.

Servings: 24   Serving Size: 2 ¼-c patties + ¼ c salsa
Yield: 48 ¼ c patties + 1½ qt salsa

Black beans, dried, sorted, rinsed	2¾ lb as purchased	Salt	To taste
		Pepper, freshly ground	To taste or 1½ t
Onions, minced	2½ lb	Red pepper, ground	To taste or ½ t
Flavorful vegetable stock (see page 2) or rich white chicken stock (see page 7)	1½ gal	Vegetable cooking spray, butter-flavored	—
Parsley, minced	2 oz	Tomato bell pepper salsa (see page 51)	1 recipe

1. In a sauce pot, soak the beans overnight or for 8 hours in enough cold water to cover by 3 inches.* Drain the beans.
2. Add the onions and stock. Heat to a boil; reduce the heat to low; simmer until the beans are tender, or about 1½ hours, adding water as needed to cover.
3. Continue cooking until the beans form a chunky puree and most of the liquid has evaporated, or about 30 minutes. Stir frequently, mashing with a spoon. Set aside to cool.
4. Stir in the parsley and next three seasonings. Shape the mixture into 48 ¼-c balls using a scoop. Place on a sheet pan allowing space to flatten.
5. Flatten into patties.
6. Coat a nonstick skillet with cooking spray. Place over medium heat until hot. Add the bean cakes in batches; cook until brown and heated through, or about 3 minutes per side. The patties can also be cooked in the oven on a sheet pan coated with cooking

spray. Serve the patties topped with salsa as an appetizer course or part of a vegetarian main course.

*If there is not time to soak the black beans for 8 hours, proceed as follows. Place the beans in a sauce pot; cover with cold water; heat to a boil; continue boiling for 1 minute. Turn off the heat; cover; set aside for 1 hour. Drain the beans; discard the broth.

Servings	Calories	Protein (g) (%)	Fat (g) (%)	Cholesterol (mg)	Carbohydrates (g) (%)	Fiber (g)	Sodium (mg)
1	124	15.5 (28%)	2.3 (9%)	0	34.2 (62%)	7.9	79.8

Freshly Fried Pinto Beans Simmered in Broth

Freshly fried pinto beans simmered in broth are more commonly known as refried beans. However, unlike this title suggests, the beans are not fried more than once, but rather well fried. In this recipe, the beans are fried in a nonstick skillet coated with cooking spray and seasoned with a blend of spices, herbs, and vegetables.

Servings: 24   *Serving Size: ½ c + 1 T*
Yield: 3 qt + 1½ c

Pinto beans simmered in vegetable broth (see page 181)	½ recipe	Clove, freshly ground	¼ t
		Salt	To taste
Vegetable cooking spray	—	Pepper, freshly ground	To taste
Onions, minced	1½ lb	*Farmer cheese, skim milk,	
Garlic, minced	1 T	crumbled	Optional
Tomatoes, peeled, fresh, or			(5 oz)
canned, coarsely chopped	1½ lb	Radish roses	Optional
Cilantro, minced	1 oz		(8 oz—24)
Chili powder	1 T	Romaine lettuce leaves,	
Cumin, freshly ground	1½ t	washed	Optional
			(1 lb—24)

1. Strain ¾ c liquid from the pinto beans. In a food processor or blender, process the beans until chunky, paste-like in appearance, adding the strained broth if needed.
2. Add the minced onions and garlic to a large nonstick skillet or cook in batches; braise-deglaze over medium-high heat with the strained bean broth or water as needed until tender. Reduce the heat to medium.
3. Add the tomatoes; cook until pulpy.
4. Add the pureed beans, cilantro, chili powder, cumin, cloves, and salt and pepper to taste. Heat through. To adjust the consistency, add the reserved bean broth or water to thin or reduce to thicken.
5. Serve on a buffet line in a heated serving dish sprinkled with farmer cheese and decorated with radish roses and lettuce leaves. The beans might also be served with

roasted corn tortilla chips (see page 346) as an appetizer or used as an ingredient in bean- and cheese-filled whole wheat tortillas (see page 327).

*Farmer cheese is a fresh, mild, slightly tangy flavored cheese sold in a solid loaf. This dry cheese is similar to cottage cheese with most of its liquid pressed out. If not available, replace with hoop cheese, fresh nonfat milk white cheese (see page 330), or part-skim ricotta cheese.

Servings	Calories	Protein (g) (%)	Fat (g) (%)	Cholesterol (mg)	Carbohydrates (g) (%)	Fiber (g)	Sodium (mg)
1	125	7.4 (23%)	0.6 (4%)	0	23.8 (73%)	7.7	18.1

Garbanzo Beans in Ginger Sauce

One glance at the nutritional composition of this recipe and there's no doubt that it rates high in this respect. But this bean dish and others are healthy to the bottom line as well. Despite huge portions, their price per serving is low.

Servings: 24   *Serving Size: $\frac{2}{3}$ c*
Yield: 1 gal

Vegetable cooking spray	—	Garbanzo beans, cooked from	
Onions, minced	2½ lb	dried without salt or	
Gingerroot, shredded	2½ oz	canned, rinsed with water	5 lb
Garlic, minced	2 T		cooked
Coriander, freshly ground	2 T		or
Cardamom, freshly ground	¾ t		canned,
Red pepper, ground	¼ t		drained
Pepper, freshly ground	To taste	Garbanzo bean cooking liquid	
Tomatoes, fresh or canned,		or flavorful vegetable	
coarsely chopped	1¼ lb	stock (see page 2)	1½ pt
		Lemon juice, freshly squeezed	1½ T
		Salt	To taste

1. Coat a sauce pot with cooking spray. Place over medium-high heat until hot. Add the onions; cook until light brown.
2. Add the ginger and garlic; reduce the heat to medium; cook until tender.
3. Add the coriander and next three ingredients. Mix well.
4. Add the tomatoes; cook, stirring until the mixture is pulpy.
5. Add the garbanzo beans, liquid, and lemon juice. Cook covered until the flavors are blended, or about 10 minutes. Add more bean liquid, stock, or water if needed to thin the mixture or reduce to thicken it. Season with additional pepper and salt to taste.
6. Serve on a bed of boiled brown basmati rice (see page 235) or accompanied by whole wheat tortillas prepared without lard.

Servings	Calories	Protein (g) (%)	Fat (g) (%)	Cholesterol (mg)	Carbohydrates (g) (%)	Fiber (g)	Sodium (mg)
1	182	9.3 (20%)	2.7 (13%)	0	32.1 (68%)	7.2	10.8

Jamaican-Style Brown Rice and Kidney Beans

The light, coconut flavor of this low-fat, high-protein rice and bean dish makes it unique. While traditionally prepared with coconut milk, because of its saturated fat, in this recipe, coconut extract adds plenty of coconut flavor without any fat or cholesterol.

Servings: 24   *Serving Size:* 1⅔ c
Yield: 2½ gal

Kidney beans, dried, sorted, rinsed	2½ lb as purchased	Coconut extract	2 T
		Green onions, white and 1 in. green, minced	1 lb
Garlic, minced	2 oz	Red pepper, crushed	To taste
Water	1½ gal + 1 pt		or 1½ t
		Thyme, dried	2 t
Brown rice, basmati or long grain, soaked	3¼ lb as purchased	Pepper, freshly ground	To taste
		Salt	To taste

1. Soak the kidney beans 8 hours or overnight;* drain.
2. In a saucepan, combine the kidney beans, garlic, and water. Heat to a boil; reduce the heat to low; cover; simmer until partially cooked, or 40 minutes.
3. Add the rice and remaining six ingredients to the beans.
5. Heat to a boil; reduce the heat to low; cover. Simmer, stirring occasionally, until both the rice and beans are tender and the liquid is absorbed, or about 50 minutes to 1 hour longer. Add more water if needed. If excess liquid remains near the end of cooking, remove the lid and cook over medium-high heat, stirring, until evaporated and/or absorbed but do not overcook the rice and beans. Rather, drain excess liquid from the mixture. Adjust the seasonings. Serve as a side or main course dish.

*See page 173 for directions to replace soaking overnight.

Servings	Calories	Protein (g) (%)	Fat (g) (%)	Cholesterol (mg)	Carbohydrates (g) (%)	Fiber (g)	Sodium (mg)
1	400	16.1 (16%)	2.4 (5%)	0	78.5 (79%)	13.1	20.6

Kidney Beans Simmered in Spicy Tomato Broth Garnished with Bell Peppers, Carrots, and Celery

The National Restaurant Association has reported that many American adults are likely or very likely to look for a restaurant that serves vegetarian items. Kidney beans simmered in spicy tomato broth makes a hearty vegetarian main course selection when served on a bed of rice. Both those who eat animal products and those who don't will be pleased to hear that it's also low in fat, cholesterol-free, and rich in complex carbohydrates, vitamins, minerals, and fiber.

Servings: 24   *Serving Size: 1 c*
Yield: 1½ gal + 1 pt

Vegetable cooking spray	—	Allspice, freshly ground	¼ t
Onions, minced	2½ lb	Red pepper, ground	To taste
Garlic, minced	2½ T		or ¼ t
Celery, small dice	2½ lb	Kidney beans, cooked from	
Carrots, washed, small dice	1 lb	dried without salt, or	
Peppers, green, bell, small dice	2 lb	canned, rinsed with water	7 lb
Tomatoes, coarsely chopped	1½ lb		cooked
Wine, red, dry	¾ c		or
Apple or fruit juice			canned,
concentrate, unsweetened	3 T		drained
Mustard, prepared	1 T	Salt	To taste
Oregano, minced or dried	¼ c or 1 T	Pepper, freshly ground	To taste
	+ 1 t		
Thyme, minced or dried	¼ c or 1 T		
	+ 1 t		

1. Coat a large nonstick skillet or a saucepan with cooking spray. Place over medium heat until hot. Add the onions and garlic; saute until tender. Add the celery and carrots; saute until tender. Add the green peppers and tomatoes; saute a few minutes longer.
2. In a small bowl, mix the wine and next six ingredients. Add to the vegetable mixture; mix together.
3. In a sauce pot, combine the drained beans and vegetable mixture. Heat to a boil, reduce the heat to low. Simmer until the flavors are mellowed, or about 30 minutes, stirring frequently. Add stock or water if the mixture becomes too dry. Season with salt

and pepper to taste. Serve on a bed of boiled brown basmati rice (see page 235); top with chopped, peeled cucumbers, tomatoes, and hot sauce if desired.

Servings	Calories	Protein (g) (%)	Fat (g) (%)	Cholesterol (mg)	Carbohydrates (g) (%)	Fiber (g)	Sodium (mg)	Alcohol (g) (%)
1	250	14.7 (23%)	1.0 (3%)	0	47.8 (76%)	15.7	68.7	0.2 (<1%)

Pink Lentils Seasoned with a Roasted Blend of Spices

Vegans, or those vegetarians who eat no foods of animal origin, rely on dried beans and peas of all shapes and kinds to supply them with their necessary protein. The salmon-colored, split pea–like lentils in this dish are unique in that they turn a dull yellow when cooked.

Servings: 24   Serving Size: 1 c
Yield: 1½ gal

*Pink lentils, sorted, rinsed	3 lb 6 oz as purchased	Vegetable cooking spray	—
		Coriander, freshly ground	2 T
Onions, minced (divided)	3 lb	Cumin, freshly ground	2 T
Water	2 gal	Indian-inspired spice blend	
Gingerroot, minced	1 oz	(see page 58)	1 T
Turmeric powder	3 T	Salt	To taste

1. Add the pink lentils, half of the onions (1½ lb), and all the water, ginger, and turmeric to a sauce pot. Heat to a boil, stirring often to prevent lumping. Reduce the heat to very low. Cook partially covered until soft and creamy consistency, or about 30 minutes, stirring occasionally. When ready to serve, the lentils should be like a moderately thick lentil soup. Add water to thin or reduce to thicken.
2. Coat a nonstick skillet with cooking spray. Place over medium-low heat until hot. Add the remaining onions, coriander, cumin, and Indian-inspired spice blend. Cook until the onions are soft and the spices golden brown.
3. Add the onion mixture and salt to taste to the cooked lentils. Serve hot over boiled brown basmati rice (see page 235).

*Pink lentils are available at Indian grocery stores. They are also called *masar dal*.

Servings	Calories	Protein (g) (%)	Fat (g) (%)	Cholesterol (mg)	Carbohydrates (g) (%)	Fiber (g)	Sodium (mg)
1	244	18.8 (30%)	1.0 (4%)	0	42.3 (67%)	8.9	19.1

Pinto Beans Simmered in Vegetable Broth

Pinto beans simmered in vegetable broth are a healthy, simple, soupy bean dish. They make a charming appetizer or main course offering when served in small earthenware-like bowls topped with shredded lettuce, bell peppers, and onions and accompanied by roasted corn tortilla chips (see page 346) or whole wheat tortillas prepared without lard. For best results, let their flavors mellow for a day or so before serving.

Servings: 24   *Serving Size: 1 c*
Yield: 1½ gal

Pinto or pink beans, dried, sorted, rinsed	3 lb as purchased	Onions, coarsely chopped	12 oz
		Salt	To taste
		Pepper, freshly ground	To taste
Flavorful vegetable stock (see page 2)	1 gal		

1. Place the beans, stock, and onions in a large sauce pot. Heat to a boil; reduce the heat to low. Cook covered without stirring until the beans are almost tender, or about 1½ hours. Add water if the beans become dry.
2. Stir in salt and pepper to taste; cook until the beans are soft, thick, and soupy, or about 30 minutes. Use to prepare freshly fried pinto beans simmered in broth (see page 181). If to be served as an appetizer or main course selection, for more flavor, simmer the beans with minced and braise-deglazed onions (1½ lb) and garlic (2 T) and season to taste or with 2 T chili powder, 2 t ground cumin, ¼ t ground cloves, salt, pepper, and 1 oz minced cilantro.

Servings	Calories	Protein (g) (%)	Fat (g) (%)	Cholesterol (mg)	Carbohydrates (g) (%)	Fiber (g)	Sodium (mg)
1	212	13.3 (25%)	0.7 (3%)	0	39.4 (72%)	13.4	21.8

Puerto Rican-Style Black Beans

Even nonvegetarians are eating far less red meat these days. End their search for alternative sources of protein with dishes like these Puerto Rican-style black beans. Served on a bed of brown rice, garnished with freshly minced cilantro and raw onions, they make for a filling meal.

Servings: 24   *Serving Size: 1 c*
Yield: 1½ gal

Black beans, dried, sorted, rinsed	4 lb as purchased	Carrots, washed, finely grated	½ lb
		Bay leaves	4
Vegetable cooking spray, olive-flavored	—	Pepper, freshly ground	To taste or 2 t
Onions, minced (divided)	3 lb	Oregano, dried	1 T
Chili peppers, fresh, mild, seeds and membranes removed, minced	8 oz or to taste	Cumin, freshly ground	1½ t
		Wine, white	1 c
		Vinegar, white	¼ c
		Salt	To taste
Garlic, minced	1⅓ oz (¼ c)	Cilantro, minced	1½ oz

1. Soak the beans in water to cover 8 hours or overnight.* Drain the beans; rinse in cold water; drain again.
2. In a sauce pot, place the soaked beans and 2 qt of water. Heat to a boil; reduce the heat to low; cover; simmer 45 minutes.
3. Coat a nonstick skillet with cooking spray. Place over medium heat until hot. Add 2½ lb of the onions, the chili peppers, and garlic; saute until tender without browning. Set aside.
4. In a blender, puree the carrots with about 1 qt of the boiled black beans. Add the puree, seasoned onions, bay leaves, pepper, oregano, and cumin to the beans. Cover; simmer over very low heat for 1 hour, stirring occasionally. Add water if needed during simmering.
5. Add the wine and vinegar; simmer over low heat for another hour. If excess liquid remains, reduce to remove or drain to avoid overcooking. If dry, add water. Remove

the bay leaves. Season with salt and additional pepper to taste. At service, stir in the cilantro. Serve topped with the remaining ½ lb minced onion.

*See page 173 for directions to replace soaking overnight.

Servings	Calories	Protein (g) (%)	Fat (g) (%)	Cholesterol (mg)	Carbohydrates (g) (%)	Fiber (g)	Sodium (mg)
1	206	12.5 (24%)	0.9 (4%)	0	38.4 (72%)	9.1	8.4

No alcohol is listed in the nutrition analysis. It is assumed to be cooked off during preparation.

Red Kidney Beans with Indian Seasonings

If your diners are watching their meat intake, these kidney beans, seasoned with an aromatic blend of spices and fresh ginger and garlic, will likely be a real treat for them.

Servings: 24   *Serving Size: 1 c*
Yield: 1½ gal

Gingerroot, coarsely chopped	1½ oz	Red kidney beans, dried,	
Red kidney bean cooking		cooked without salt, or	
liquid or flavorful		canned, rinsed in water	7½ lb
vegetable stock (see page			cooked
2) (divided)	1½ qt		or
Garlic, minced	1¼ oz		canned,
Indian-inspired spice blend			drained
(see page 58)	2 T	Lemon juice, freshly squeezed	¼ c
Vegetable cooking spray	—	Parsley, minced	1½ oz
Tomatoes, fresh or canned,		Salt	To taste
coarsely chopped	3½ lb		

1. In a blender, process the ginger with 1 c of the kidney bean liquid or vegetable stock until smooth.
2. Mix in the minced garlic and spice blend. The mixture should have the consistency of cream.
3. Coat a sauce pot with cooking spray. Place over medium heat until hot. Add the spice mixture; cook briefly to slightly mellow the flavors.
4. Add the tomatoes; cook until thick paste consistency, or about 8 minutes.
5. Add the kidney beans with the remaining bean liquid or vegetable broth and lemon juice; simmer over low heat to blend the flavors, or about 15 minutes. Add more bean broth or stock if the mixture becomes too dry. If the quantity of liquid is too great, cook over medium-high heat, stirring, until evaporated or drain off excess to avoid overcooking.
6. Stir in the parsley and salt to taste. Serve on a bed of boiled brown basmati rice (see page 235) or accompany with whole wheat tortillas prepared without lard.

Servings	Calories	Protein (g) (%)	Fat (g) (%)	Cholesterol (mg)	Carbohydrates (g) (%)	Fiber (g)	Sodium (mg)
1	200	13 (25%)	1.0 (4%)	0	36.7 (71%)	13.2	10.6

Smooth Lentil Sandwich Spread Seasoned with Asian Spices

Many American sandwiches contain half (or more) of the total fat most people should eat in a day. Rather than a bologna, salami, meatball, grilled American cheese, or BLT sandwich, often containing more than 25 grams of fat, serve low-fat, high-fiber, open-face vegetarian sandwiches with fillings like this smooth lentil sandwich spread. It is delightful served on whole grain bread topped with shredded lettuce, sliced ripe tomatoes, and a sprinkle of freshly grated ginger.

Servings: 24   *Serving Size: $3\frac{1}{2}$ T*
Yield: $1\frac{1}{3}$ qt

Vegetable cooking spray, butter-flavored	—	Flavorful vegetable stock (see page 2) or rich white chicken stock (see page 7)	$1\frac{1}{2}$ qt
Onions, minced	6 oz	Bay leaves	3
Celery and carrots, washed, small dice	4 oz each	Turmeric powder	$\frac{1}{2}$ t
		Cumin, freshly ground	$\frac{1}{4}$ t
Peppers, green, bell, small dice	2 oz	Coriander, freshly ground	$\frac{1}{4}$ t
Garlic, minced	1 T	Salt	To taste
Gingerroot, minced	$1\frac{1}{2}$ t	Pepper, freshly ground	To taste
*Lentils, sorted, rinsed	14 oz as purchased	Red pepper, ground	To taste or $\frac{1}{8}$ t

1. Coat a saucepan with cooking spray; place over medium heat until hot. Add the onions, celery, carrots, peppers, garlic, and ginger; saute until tender, or about 7 minutes.
2. Add the lentils, stock, and bay leaves. Heat to a boil; reduce the heat to low. Simmer covered, stirring until the lentils are tender and most of the liquid absorbed, or about 45 minutes.
3. Remove the bay leaves. In a blender, puree the mixture until very smooth.
4. Stir in the turmeric and remaining seasonings. Serve on croutons or use as a sandwich filling.
5. For a tasty, healthy open-face sandwich, top a slice of whole wheat bread with $\frac{1}{4}$ c of

shredded lettuce, 2 thin tomato slices, 2 servings (7 T) lentil sandwich spread and a teaspoon of peeled, grated gingerroot.

*While there are many varieties of lentils cultivated throughout the world, only a few are readily available in the United States. Furthermore, these are generally sold without standardized names. In this recipe, those lentils known as green or brown lentils and generally simply labeled "lentils" are used.

Servings	Calories	Protein (g) (%)	Fat (g) (%)	Cholesterol (mg)	Carbohydrates (g) (%)	Fiber (g)	Sodium (mg)
1	37	2.0 (20%)	0.3 (7%)	0	7.4 (74%)	2.5	11.4

Split Mung Beans Laced with Cauliflower and Spinach

In this stew, yellow, split mung beans are combined with sauteed cauliflower and spinach and seasoned with roasted spices and minced cilantro, ginger, and garlic. The results are a nutritious, low-fat, texturally pleasing and colorful vegetarian offering.

Servings: 24   *Serving Size: $\frac{2}{5}$ c ($\frac{1}{4}$ c + 3 T)*
Yield: 2$\frac{1}{2}$ qt + 1 c

*Mung beans, dried, yellow, split, without skins, sorted, rinsed	13 oz as purchased	Cumin seeds	2 t
		Cauliflower florets	1$\frac{3}{4}$ lb
		Turmeric powder	1 t
		Red pepper, ground	To taste or $\frac{1}{8}$ t
Onions, minced (divided)	1 lb		
Gingerroot, minced (divided)	2$\frac{1}{2}$ T	Spinach, leaves, washed, chopped	8 oz
Garlic, minced (divided)	1 T + 2 t		
Bay leaves	2	Salt	To taste
Water	2$\frac{1}{4}$ qt	Cilantro, minced	$\frac{1}{4}$ c

1. Combine the mung beans, $\frac{1}{2}$ each of the onions ($\frac{1}{2}$ lb), ginger (1$\frac{1}{4}$ T), and garlic (2$\frac{1}{2}$ t), the bay leaves, and water. Heat the mixture to a boil; reduce the heat to low. Simmer covered until tender but still firm, or about 10 minutes.
2. Meanwhile, toast the cumin seeds in a nonstick skillet over medium-high heat, stirring constantly, until they turn dark brown and begin to crackle, or about 3 minutes.
3. Reduce the heat to medium. Add the remaining onions, ginger, and garlic and a small amount of water if needed to prevent sticking. Cook until tender.
4. Add the cauliflower, turmeric, and red pepper. Saute briefly to coat the vegetables in the mixture.
5. Add the seasoned vegetables to the beans; continue simmering until almost tender.
6. Add the spinach. Simmer until tender. The mixture should be of soupy consistency. Add water to thin or reduce to thicken. Remove the bay leaves.
7. Mix in the salt to taste and cilantro. Serve on a bed of boiled brown basmati rice (see page 235) or accompanied by whole wheat tortillas prepared without lard.

*Yellow, split mung beans are available at Indian grocery stores. They are also called *moong dal.*

Servings	Calories	Protein (g) (%)	Fat (g) (%)	Cholesterol (mg)	Carbohydrates (g) (%)	Fiber (g)	Sodium (mg)
1	64	4.2 (24%)	0.4 (5%)	0	12.2 (71%)	2.6	21.9

Three Bean, Lentil, and Pea Stew

This hearty, thick stew is prepared from a colorful array of dried beans, peas, and lentils.* The soupy mixture is easy to assemble but does require over 1½ hours to cook. When served with brown rice, it becomes a low-fat, high-fiber, protein, and B vitamin and iron rich vegetarian meal.

Servings: 24   Serving Size: 1⅔ c
Yield: 2⅛ gal

Mung beans, dried, yellow, split without skins (*moong dal*)	12 oz as purchased	Turmeric powder	1½ T
		Coriander, freshly ground	¼ c
		Gingerroot, minced	1½ oz
		Bay leaves	2
Gram beans, white split, dried (*urad dal*)	12 oz as purchased	Spinach, leaves, washed, coarsely chopped	1 lb + 2 oz
Yellow lentils, split, skinless, dried (*toovar dal*)	12 oz as purchased	Oil, canola or vegetable	1 T
		Chilies, fresh, hot, green, seeds and membranes removed, minced	2 oz or to taste
Garbanzo beans, skinless, dried (*chana dal*)	12 oz as purchased		
		Cumin seeds	3 T
Split peas, green, dried	12 oz as purchased	Mustard seeds	1½ t
		Paprika, Hungarian, sweet	1¼ t
Water	1¾ gal + 1 pt	Indian-inspired spice blend (see page 58)	2¼ t
		Cilantro, minced	½ c
		Salt	To taste

1. Sort, rinse, and drain the five dried beans, peas, and lentils.
2. Place in a sauce pot; cover with hot water and soak 4 hours. Drain.
3. Add the 1¾ gal + 1 pt water and next four ingredients. Heat to a boil; reduce the heat to low and cover. Simmer, stirring occasionally, until the beans, peas, and lentils are soft and fully cooked, or about 1½ hours.
4. Stir in the spinach. Cook gently for about 3 minutes.
5. While the lentils are cooking, add the oil to a nonstick skillet. Place over medium-high heat until hot. Add the green chilies and cumin and mustard seeds. Reduce the heat to medium; saute until the seeds turn brown.
6. Add the paprika; saute 1–2 seconds longer. Set aside.

7. Stir the cooked spices and spice blend into the cooked lentils. Remove from the heat; let stand a few minutes.
8. Stir in the cilantro and salt to taste. Serve on a bed of boiled brown basmati rice (see page 235) or accompanied by whole wheat tortillas prepared without lard.

*The dried beans, peas, and lentils used in this recipe are available at Indian grocery stores.

Servings	Calories	Protein (g) (%)	Fat (g) (%)	Cholesterol (mg)	Carbohydrates (g) (%)	Fiber (g)	Sodium (mg)
I	306	22 (28%)	2.7 (8%)	0	51.4 (65%)	12.1	38.6

VEGETABLES

Baby Carrots in Fruit Glaze with Apple Slices

While vegetables and fruits are rarely paired in American cuisine, German chefs combine the two frequently. After you've tried these baby carrots, you'll know why.

Servings: 24   *Serving Size: ½ c*
Yield: 3¼ qt

Carrots, baby, trimmed or matchstick strips, washed	3¾ lb	Carrot cooking broth or flavorful vegetable stock (see page 2)	1½ c
Vegetable cooking spray, butter-flavored	—	Apple or fruit juice concentrate, unsweetened	3 T
Onions, minced	8 oz	Lemon juice, freshly squeezed	1 T
*Apples, firm, sweet, peeled, ½-in. thick slices	1½ lb	Nutmeg, freshly ground	⅛ t
		Salt	To taste
		Pepper, freshly ground	To taste

1. Steam or boil the carrots in unsalted water, covered, until crisp tender, or about 10 minutes. If the carrots are cut into matchstick strips, they can be boiled to al dente in about 8 minutes. Drain, reserving 1½ cups of the carrot broth. Refresh the carrots in ice water to stop the cooking; drain; set aside.
2. Coat a nonstick skillet with cooking spray. Place over medium heat until hot. Add the onions; cook until tender, or about 5 minutes.
3. Add the apple slices and reserved carrot broth or stock. Simmer until the apples are nearly tender.
4. Add the carrots; heat through. Season with the juice concentrate, lemon juice, nutmeg, and salt and pepper to taste. Serve as a side dish along with meat, fish, and poultry items or as an item on a vegetable plate.

*Enzymatic reactions cause apples to turn brown when peeled. This can be prevented by soaking in water or water and lemon juice. However, unless a sufficient amount of salt or sugar is added to the water, the apples will become mushy. This in turn will affect the flavor and nutrient value of the apples. For best results, peel the apples as close to cooking as possible. Also, since the apples in this dish become lightly browned through cooking and from the nutmeg, preliminary browning of the apples will not detract from the appearance of this dish.

Servings	Calories	Protein (g) (%)	Fat (g) (%)	Cholesterol (mg)	Carbohydrates (g) (%)	Fiber (g)	Sodium (mg)
1	51	0.8 (6%)	0.5 (8%)	0	11.8 (86%)	2.9	25.6

Beets Glazed in Orange and Red Wine Vinegar Sauce

A light orange and red wine vinegar sauce make a nice complement to the natural earthy, sweet flavor of these beets. When selecting beets, keep in mind, their most common color is red but they are available in other colors too—orange, yellow, white, and even candy cane style (concentric rings of red and white). Small to medium beets are preferred for their tenderness.

Servings: 24   *Serving Size: ½ c*
Yield: 3 qt

Beets, whole, unpeeled, 1- to 2-in. stem or canned, water packed, sliced, drained, rinsed in water	6 lb or number 10 can	Beet cooking liquid or flavorful vegetable stock (see page 2)	1 pt
Cornstarch	2 T + 2 t	Apple or fruit juice concentrate, unsweetened	½ c
		Vinegar, red wine	½ c
		Orange juice concentrate, unsweetened	¼ c + 2 T
		Salt	To taste
		Pepper, freshly ground	To taste
		Margarine, unsalted, corn oil	1½ oz (3 T)

1. If using fresh beets, wash them with their stems. Steam the fresh beets with their stems or boil in unsalted water, covered, until tender, or about 25 minutes for small beets.
2. Drain; reserve 1 pt of the cooking liquid; refresh in cold water; drain.
3. Remove the stems and skins from the fresh beets. Slice ⅛-in. thick.
4. In a saucepan, combine the cornstarch and the next six ingredients. Whip well.
5. Heat to a boil. Reduce the heat to medium; simmer, stirring constantly, until the mixture is clear and thickened, or about 4 minutes. Remove the pan from the heat.
6. Stir in the margarine. Pour the sauce over the cooked or canned beets. Toss gently. Serve at room temperature or hot as a vegetable side dish. Reheat the cooked fresh or canned beets in the sauce if hot beets are desired.

Servings	Calories	Protein (g) (%)	Fat (g) (%)	Cholesterol (mg)	Carbohydrates (g) (%)	Fiber (g)	Sodium (mg)
1	70	1.5 (8%)	1.6 (20%)	0	13.3 (72%)	2.7	68

Cauliflower Florets Coated with Cilantro and Onions

A tasty coating made from browned eggs, primarily whites, blended with cilantro and onions makes these cauliflower florets unique.

Servings: 24
Yield: 1¼ gal

Serving Size: ⅝ c

Cauliflower, florets	4½ lb	Salt	To taste
Egg whites, large	20 (1 lb + 9 oz)	Pepper, freshly ground	To taste
		Vegetable cooking spray,	
Eggs, whole, large	6 (12 oz)	butter-flavored	—
Cilantro, minced	1¼ oz	Onions, minced	2 lb

1. Steam or boil the cauliflower in unsalted water until crisp-tender, or about 5 minutes. Drain. Refresh in cold water; drain.
2. In a bowl, mix the egg whites, whole eggs, cilantro, and salt and pepper to taste; set aside.
3. Coat a very large nonstick skillet with cooking spray or cook in batches. Place over medium heat until hot. Add the onions; cook until tender, or about 5 minutes.
4. Add the cauliflower to the skillet; cook until tender and heated through, or about 3 minutes. Drain any liquid from the skillet.
5. Stir in the egg mixture; toss to coat; cook until the eggs are set. Serve as a side dish with main course offerings such as chicken croquettes topped with mushroom-filled sauce (see page 129).

Servings	Calories	Protein (g) (%)	Fat (g) (%)	Cholesterol (mg)	Carbohydrates (g) (%)	Fiber (g)	Sodium (mg)
1	69	6.8 (37%)	1.5 (18%)	53	8.2 (45%)	2.7	91.2

Cauliflower Stir-Fried with Tomatoes Accented with Turmeric, Ginger, and Cilantro

This cauliflower dish is a good, year-round vegetable. It will complement a variety of meat dishes but is equally good on a vegetable plate. For a balanced vegetarian meal, it might be served along with other vegetable dishes such as sweet potato patties with hints of orange (see page 212), grilled corn on the cob (see page 200), greens with freshly ground peanuts (see page 199), a cracked wheat, barley, or rice pilaf such as wild rice studded with blueberries and shiitake mushrooms (see page 253), or spicy brown rice pilaf peppered with bell peppers, celery, and onions (see page 245) and a yogurt salad.

Servings: 24   Serving Size: ½ c
Yield: 3 qt

Oil, canola or vegetable	1 T	Tomatoes, coarsely chopped	1¾ lb
Red chilies, small, dried, stems		Water	¾ c
and seeds removed	3 or to	Coriander, freshly ground	2½ t
	taste	Turmeric powder	2 t
Cumin seeds	2 t	Paprika, Hungarian, sweet	1½ t
Gingerroot, minced	2½ T	Salt	To taste
Garlic, minced	1½ T	Pepper, freshly ground	To taste
Cauliflower florets	3¾ lb	Cilantro, minced	½ c

1. Heat the oil in a very large nonstick skillet over medium heat until hot or cook in batches. Add the chilies and cumin seeds. Cook until the red pepper is lightly browned and the cumin seeds pop, or about 2 minutes.
2. Add the ginger and garlic. Cook until tender and golden.
3. Add the cauliflower and cook until lightly browned and crisp-tender.
4. Add the tomatoes and next four ingredients. Reduce the heat to very low. Cover and cook until the cauliflower is tender, or 5 to 7 minutes. Add more water if needed. Remove the chilies for a milder dish. To serve, sprinkle with the salt and pepper to taste and cilantro.

Servings	Calories	Protein (g) (%)	Fat (g) (%)	Cholesterol (mg)	Carbohydrates (g) (%)	Fiber (g)	Sodium (mg)
1	35	1.9 (19%)	0.9 (20%)	0	6.4 (61%)	2.4	25.5

Citrus-Glazed Carrots Sprinkled with Minced Parsley

In classical cuisine, vegetables were often cooked by simmering in butter with little or no additional liquid. In this recipe, carrots are simmered in rich white chicken stock and then coated in a light orange syrup enriched with a tad of margarine. It's a more healthful yet flavorful approach.

Servings: 24   *Serving Size: ½ c*
Yield: 3 qt

Rich white chicken stock (see page 7) or flavorful vegetable stock (see page 2)	1½ c	Orange juice concentrate, unsweetened	¼ c
Carrots, washed, matchstick strips	4 lb	Margarine, unsalted, corn oil	3 T
		Orange zest, finely grated	2 T
		Nutmeg, freshly ground	¼ t
		Parsley, minced	3 T

1. Heat the stock to a boil in a sauce pot. Add the carrots; reduce the heat to low; cover. Simmer, stirring occasionally, until partially cooked, or about 8 minutes.
2. Add the juice concentrate, margarine, orange zest, and nutmeg. Raise the heat to medium-high; cook uncovered until the sauce is a thin syrup and the carrots are crisp-tender. Add more stock if the carrots need further cooking or the sauce needs thinning.
3. Serve garnished with the parsley.

Servings	Calories	Protein (g) (%)	Fat (g) (%)	Cholesterol (mg)	Carbohydrates (g) (%)	Fiber (g)	Sodium (mg)
1	53	1.0 (7%)	1.6 (25%)	0	9.6 (68%)	2.6	51.7

Corn-Stuffed Zucchini with Melted Cheese and Oat Flake Topping

With a little bit of creativity, zucchini can be stuffed with practically anything and turn out good. In this recipe, zucchini shells are filled with high-fiber corn kernels blended with oat flakes and part-skim milk mozzarella cheese.

Servings: 24   Serving Size: 1 stuffed zucchini shell
Yield: 24 stuffed zucchini shells

Zucchini, washed	2¾ lb (12)	Mozzarella cheese, part-skim milk, shredded	2½ oz
Vegetable cooking spray, butter-flavored	—	Thyme, minced or dried	½ T or ½ t
Onions, minced	5 oz	Salt	To taste
Garlic, minced	1½ t	Pepper, freshly ground	To taste
Corn kernels, fresh, blanched or frozen	7 oz	Egg whites, large, lightly beaten	5 (6¼ oz)
Oat flake cereal, coarsely crushed	1 oz		

1. Steam the zucchini or boil in unsalted water until crisp-tender, or about 8 minutes. Trim the ends.
2. Halve the zucchini lengthwise.
3. Scoop out the center pulp. Squeeze out the pulp's moisture and finely chop. Transfer the pulp to a bowl. Set aside.
4. Place the zucchini shells in a counter pan coated with cooking spray. Set aside.
5. Coat a nonstick skillet with cooking spray. Place over medium heat until hot. Add the onions and garlic. Cook until tender, or about 5 minutes. Cool.
6. Add the onions, garlic, and all the remaining ingredients to the chopped zucchini pulp; mix.
7. Spoon the filling into the zucchini shells. Bake in a 350°F (175°C) oven until the filling is golden brown and heated through, or about 20 minutes. Serve as an appetizer course, accompaniment to a meat, fish, or poultry selection, or as a component on a vegetable plate.

Servings	Calories	Protein (g) (%)	Fat (g) (%)	Cholesterol (mg)	Carbohydrates (g) (%)	Fiber (g)	Sodium (mg)
1	32	2.6 (30%)	0.7 (17%)	1.7	4.5 (52%)	1.0	39.3

Crispy Crusted Baked Eggplant*

These golden brown, crispy on the outside and tender on the inside slices of eggplant are reminiscent of their fried counterpart without the fat and calories. Although eggplant is commonly thought of as a vegetable, it is a fruit. Look for fruit with firm, smooth skin which seems heavy for its size. For a change, replace the common pear-shaped eggplant with the very narrow, straight, slightly sweet fleshed Japanese variety.

Servings: 24   *Serving Size: 3 slices*
Yield: 6 doz slices

Eggplant, pear-shaped or Japanese, washed, ends removed	5 lb	Oregano, dried	2 t
		Garlic powder	2 t
Salt	—	Thyme, dried	1 t
Whole wheat bread, cubes	14 oz	Salt	To taste
Sourdough bread, cubes	6 oz	Pepper, freshly ground	To taste or 1 t
Flour, whole wheat, stone-ground	7 oz	Egg whites, large	12 (15 oz)
Parsley, dried	1 T + 1 t	Vegetable cooking spray, olive-flavored	—
Basil, dried	2 t		

1. Slice the eggplant into ⅓-in. thick circles. Sprinkle the eggplant with salt on all cut sides to remove the bitter flavors. Set aside for about 20 minutes.
2. Place the whole wheat and sour dough bread cubes in a food processor or blender. Process until the bread is chopped into fine crumbs. Place in a shallow container.
3. In another shallow container, combine the flour and next seven ingredients. Place the egg whites in a third shallow container; beat lightly.
4. Rinse the salt from the eggplant. Pat dry.
5. Using standard breading procedure, dredge each slice of eggplant through the seasoned flour, egg whites, and bread crumbs. Use more egg whites, seasoned flour, and bread crumbs if needed. (The nutrition analysis will not reflect these additions.)
6. Place the eggplant in a single layer on a sheet pan coated with cooking spray. Bake in a 400°F (205°C) oven for about 5 to 7 minutes. Turn over and bake until crispy and lightly browned on both sides, or another 5 to 7 minutes. If removed from the oven too soon, the eggplant slices will not be crispy. Serve as a vegetable side dish or appetizer course accompanied by Italian-style tomato sauce (see page 35). The crispy eggplant slices can also be transformed into a vegetarian main course by topping with Italian-

style tomato sauce and shredded part-skim milk mozzarella cheese and baking until heated through and the cheese is melted and golden brown.

*Adapted from a recipe by Victoria Mylne.

Servings	Calories	Protein (g) (%)	Fat (g) (%)	Cholesterol (mg)	Carbohydrates (g) (%)	Fiber (g)	Sodium (mg)
1	123	6.3 (19%)	1.1 (8%)	0	23.8 (73%)	4.9	164

Greens with Freshly Ground Peanuts

Topping this dish with freshly ground, roasted, unsalted peanuts adds protein and fiber to the already high-fiber, vitamin- and mineral-rich greens and tomatoes in this dish. Offer it as a side dish or main course selection accompanied by whole wheat tortillas or steamed brown rice. Both meat eaters and vegetarians will find it appealing for its flavor and nutritional value.

Servings: 24 *Serving Size: ½ c*
Yield: 3 qt

Peanuts, roasted, unsalted	2.5 oz (7½ T)	Spinach, kale, or collards, leaves, washed, chopped	3 lb
Vegetable cooking spray	—	Salt	To taste
Tomatoes, peeled, chopped	3½ lb	Pepper, freshly ground	To taste
Onions, minced	1 lb		

1. In a blender grind the peanuts into small bits. Set aside.
2. Coat a sauce pot with cooking spray. Place over medium heat. Add the tomatoes and onions. Cook until the onions are tender, or about 8 minutes.
3. Add the spinach to the sauce pot. Cook, stirring occasionally until the spinach is tender. Season with salt and pepper to taste. Serve garnished with the ground peanuts sprinkled over. Offer as a vegetable side dish or one component on a vegetable plate.

Servings	Calories	Protein (g) (%)	Fat (g) (%)	Cholesterol (mg)	Carbohydrates (g) (%)	Fiber (g)	Sodium (mg)
1	51	3.1 (21%)	1.9 (29%)	0	7.3 (50%)	2.9	51.5

Grilled Corn on the Cob

For the freshest corn, look for bright green, snug-fitting husks, golden brown and shiny silk, and plump, moist kernels, a little bit translucent. If it's not possible to cook the corn immediately, store it refrigerated with the husks on. Remove the husks just before cooking.

Servings: 24 *Serving Size: 1 ear of corn*
Yield: 24 ears of corn

Fresh corn, medium-sized ears	24	Salt	To taste
Limes, cut into quarters	1 lb (6)	Pepper, freshly ground	To taste

1. Peel open the husks and remove the silk from the corn. Rub the kernels with a damp paper towel to remove any remaining silk. Close the husks back over the cobs; soak in cold water for 10 minutes. To secure the corn husks, tie them together at the top of the ear with twine or a narrow piece of the husk. Alternatively, wrap shucked ears in heavy duty aluminum foil.
2. Place on an oiled grill rack and cook turning frequently until tender, or about 15 minutes. The husks will char.
3. Remove the husks; rub with the lime quarters, squeezing until the cobs are coated with lime juice. Sprinkle with salt and freshly ground pepper to taste. Other low-fat seasoning options might be all-American barbecue sauce for fowl (see page 57), fresh mint and cilantro chutney (see page 43), or a fresh herb or freshly ground spice blend. Serve as a meat, fish, or poultry accompaniment. Grilled corn on the cob is a nice side dish with crispy baked mustard chicken breasts (see page 134) or chicken thighs in crispy cinnamon crust (see page 131).

Servings	Calories	Protein (g) (%)	Fat (g) (%)	Cholesterol (mg)	Carbohydrates (g) (%)	Fiber (g)	Sodium (mg)
1	86	2.6 (10%)	1 (9%)	0	20.3 (81%)	4.0	13.3

Variations

Boiled Corn on the Cob

1. Strip the husks away; cut off or break the stem ends and tips; remove the silk.
2. Add to unsalted boiling water to cover. Cover and boil until tender, or about 5 minutes, longer if the corn is mature. Drain.
3. Serve coated with lime juice and salt and pepper to taste.

Steamed Corn on the Cob: Follow step 1 of boiled corn. Steam in a compartment steamer or steaming vessel tightly covered until tender, or about 15 minutes. Proceed to step 3 of boiled corn.

Oven-Steamed Corn on the Cob: Follow step 1 of grilled corn. Place on a sheet pan in a 375°F (190°C) oven. Cook until tender, or about 25 minutes. Proceed to step 3 of grilled corn.

Fresh Grilled, Boiled, Steamed, or Oven-Steamed Cream-Style Corn: To prepare one of these, cook the corn by the appropriate method. With the corn ears standing on end, cut down, removing 3 to 4 rows of corn. Continue until all the kernels are removed; using the dull side of the knife, remove the remaining pulp and richly flavored juice from the cob. Heat in a saucepan. Season with salt and pepper to taste.

Medley of Stir-Fried Vegetables

In this medley, fresh broccoli, green beans, carrots, cabbage, mushrooms, and onions, or vegetables typically found in the kitchen, are stir-fried together. A light coat of low-sodium soy sauce and sauteed fresh minced ginger and garlic flavor the attractive medley. It's a winner.

Servings: 24   *Serving Size: $\frac{5}{8}$ c*
Yield: 1$\frac{1}{4}$ gal

Vegetable cooking spray	—	Cabbage, shredded	12 oz
Onions, thin slices	1$\frac{1}{4}$ lb	Broccoli florets, stems	
Garlic, minced	1 T	reserved for another use	12 oz
Gingerroot, minced	1 T	Rich white chicken stock	
Carrots, washed, thin diagonal		(see page 7) or flavorful	
slices	1$\frac{1}{2}$ lb	vegetable stock (see	
Green beans, 1-in. diagonally		page 2)	1$\frac{1}{2}$ c
cut pieces	1 lb	Soy sauce, low-sodium	3 T
Mushrooms, thin slices	10 oz		

1. Coat a large nonstick skillet or wok with cooking spray or cook in batches. Place over medium-high heat until hot. Add the onions, garlic, and ginger; stir-fry a few times.
2. Add the carrots, green beans, and mushrooms; stir-fry 2 minutes longer.
3. Add the cabbage; stir-fry a few minutes.
4. Add the broccoli; stir-fry another 2 minutes.
5. Add the stock and soy sauce; heat the broth to a boil; reduce the heat to low. Cover and simmer until all the vegetables are crisp-tender. Serve immediately as a side dish with a main course selection such as a grilled pork chop, pan-broiled chicken breast, or broiled fish steak, or as one component on a vegetable plate.

Servings	Calories	Protein (g) (%)	Fat (g) (%)	Cholesterol (mg)	Carbohydrates (g) (%)	Fiber (g)	Sodium (mg)
1	41	2 (17%)	0.3 (5%)	0	9.0 (78%)	2.8	79.9

Sherried Chunky Puree of Green Peas

The unique texture and flavor of this vibrantly colored puree of green peas is persuasive evidence that vegetables need not be boiled and coated with butter to be good.

Servings: 48   *Serving Size: ⅓ c*
Yield: 1 gal

Peas, fresh, blanched, or frozen, thawed	6 lb	Sherry, dry	1½ c
Rich white chicken stock (see page 7) or flavorful vegetable stock (see page 2)	1½ c	Salt	To taste
		Pepper, freshly ground	To taste
		Vegetable cooking spray, butter-flavored	—

1. In a food processor or blender, puree the peas with the next four ingredients until very chunky in consistency. Some of the peas should remain whole.
2. Coat a saucepan with cooking spray; add the peas; cook over low heat stirring, until heated through. Watch closely so that they don't burn. Serve as a side dish with a main course offering, perhaps crispy baked mustard chicken breast (see page 134) or roasted tenderloin of pork seasoned with crushed fennel seeds (see page 103).

Servings	Calories	Protein (g) (%)	Fat (g) (%)	Cholesterol (mg)	Carbohydrates (g) (%)	Fiber (g)	Sodium (mg)	Alcohol (g) (%)
1	104	6.5 (24%)	0.5 (<5%)	0	16.6 (62%)	5.6	10.8	1.4 (9%)

Note: The nutrition analysis does not account for any of the alcohol being lost during the cooking of this dish. Likely some is, and calories per serving are less.

Shredded Green Cabbage and Apples Accented with Cinnamon

Overcooked cabbage can taste outrageously bad, but as this recipe illustrates, cooked properly, it can be delicious.

Servings: 24   *Serving Size: ½ c*
Yield: 3 qt

Cabbage, green, shredded	3 lb	Cinnamon, freshly ground	1¼ t
Vegetable cooking spray,		Salt	To taste
butter-flavored	—	Pepper, freshly ground	To taste
Onions, minced	8 oz		
Apples, firm, sweet, peeled,			
1-in. cubes	12 oz		

1. Steam or boil the cabbage in unsalted water until crisp-tender. Drain. Refresh in cold water. Drain; set aside.
2. Coat a large nonstick skillet with cooking spray or cook in batches. Place over medium heat until hot. Add the onions; cook until almost tender.
3. Add the apple; cook until tender. Sprinkle with the cinnamon.
4. Add the cabbage; heat through. Season with salt and pepper to taste. Serve immediately.

Servings	Calories	Protein (g) (%)	Fat (g) (%)	Cholesterol (mg)	Carbohydrates (g) (%)	Fiber (g)	Sodium (mg)
1	26	1.0 (13%)	0.2 (6%)	0	6.1 (81%)	1.4	10.5

Sliced Gingered Orange Beets

Beets will retain their color, flavor, and nutritional value best if cooked with their peels on, long root ends, and some stem attached to their bulbs. After cooking, plunge the beets in cold water and their skins will slip off easily. The remaining stems and roots can be cut off.

To remove red beet stains from hands and nonporous surfaces, rub with table salt. It is difficult to remove beets' ruby stains from porous materials such as fabric or wood. For best results, avoid contact with these materials.

Servings: 24   *Serving Size: ½ c*
Yield: 3 qt

Beets, whole unpeeled, 1- to 2-in. stem attached	6 lb	Orange juice, freshly squeezed	1 pt + ¼ c

Vegetable cooking spray,
    butter-flavored
	—	White grape juice concentrate,
		    unsweetened
			1½ c

Gingerroot, minced	1½ T	Vinegar, red wine	¼ c
		Salt	To taste
		Pepper, freshly ground	To taste

1. Wash the beets. Steam or boil the beets with their stems in unsalted water, covered, until nearly tender, or about 25 minutes for small beets. Drain. Refresh in cold water. Drain. Remove the skins and stems. Cut into ⅛-in. thick slices. Set aside.
2. Coat a large nonstick skillet or sauce pot with cooking spray. Place over medium heat until hot. Add the ginger; cook until tender. Stir in the orange juice and next two ingredients; heat through.
3. Add the beets to the sauce. Cook until heated through. Season with salt and pepper to taste. Serve as a side dish with meat, fish, and poultry items or include as an item on a vegetable plate.

Servings	Calories	Protein (g) (%)	Fat (g) (%)	Cholesterol (mg)	Carbohydrates (g) (%)	Fiber (g)	Sodium (mg)
1	80	1.7 (8%)	0.2 (3%)	0	18.8 (89%)	3.1	67.8

Smoky Eggplant Puree Seasoned with Green Chilies

Dishes seasoned with chilies are becoming commonplace in the United States. In this recipe, the readily available canned chilies enhance the flavor of smooth, pureed, broiled eggplant. You may have noticed varying spellings for the vitamin C-packed, potent seasoning agents. In Mexico, they are referred to as chile (singular) and chiles (plural) versus the more familiar chili and chilies in the United States.

Servings: 24   *Serving Size: $\frac{3}{5}$ c*
Yield: $3\frac{1}{2}$ qt

Eggplants	7 lb as purchased	Cilantro, minced	$\frac{1}{4}$ c + 2 T
Onions, minced	12 oz	Salt	To taste
Chilies, canned, seeds and membranes removed, rinsed in water, minced	3 oz or to taste	Pepper, freshly ground	To taste
		Egg whites, large, lightly beaten	6 (7$\frac{1}{2}$ oz)
Bread crumbs, whole wheat, fresh	6 oz	Vegetable cooking spray	—

1. Pierce the eggplants with a fork. Place on a sheet pan. Roast in a broiler about 4 inches from the heating element. Cook until charred and soft, or about 20 minutes, turning with tongs every 5 minutes or so. The eggplants can also be roasted on a grill or gas burner.
2. Peel off the charred skin; rinse in cold water, removing the charred skin; squeeze to remove the liquid. Chop coarsely.
3. In a blender, puree the eggplant until smooth.
4. Mix the onions and next six ingredients with the puree until well blended.
5. Coat a baking pan with cooking spray. Add the eggplant mixture. Bake in a 350°F (175°C) oven until heated through, or about 30 minutes. Serve as an accompaniment with meat, such as flank steak topped with mushrooms and green onions (see page 70), fish, such as red snapper simmered in tomato sauce Veracruz style (see page 154), and poultry selections, or as a component of a vegetarian plate.

Servings	Calories	Protein (g) (%)	Fat (g) (%)	Cholesterol (mg)	Carbohydrates (g) (%)	Fiber (g)	Sodium (mg)
1	56	3.0 (20%)	0.4 (6%)	0	12.8 (74%)	3.4	56.8

Snow Peas Stir-Fried with Bamboo Shoots and Shiitake Mushrooms

After stir-frying vegetables, the Chinese often flavor them with soy sauce and a small quantity of refined sugar. For a similar effect, these snow peas are seasoned with vegetable stock, low-sodium soy sauce, and natural fruit juice sweetener.

Servings: 24   Serving Size: $\frac{2}{3}$ c
Yield: 1 gal

Vegetable cooking spray	—	Flavorful vegetable stock (see page 2) or rich white chicken stock (see page 7)	$1\frac{1}{2}$ c
Snow peas, trimmed, strings removed	$1\frac{3}{4}$ lb	Soy sauce, low sodium	1 c
Gingerroot, minced	2 T	Apple or fruit juice concentrate, unsweetened	2 T
Garlic, minced	2 T		
*Mushrooms, shiitake, fresh, quarters, stems reserved for another use	1 lb		
Bamboo shoots, canned, 1 to $1\frac{1}{2}$–in. strips, packed in water, drained, rinsed in water	2 lb		

1. Coat a large wok or nonstick skillet with cooking spray or cook in batches. Place over medium-high heat until hot. Add the snow peas. Stir-fry until bright green, or about 30 seconds. Remove; set aside.
2. Add the ginger and garlic; stir-fry until tender.
3. Add the mushrooms. Cook, stirring another few minutes.
4. Add the bamboo shoots. Stir-fry another few minutes.
5. Mix in the stock, soy sauce, and juice concentrate. Heat to a boil; reduce the heat to medium. Cover; simmer until the vegetables are tender and the flavors blended, or about 3 minutes. The sauce can be thickened if desired with a cornstarch slurry. The carbohydrates and calories in the dish will increase slightly.
6. Return the snow peas; stir-fry to heat through. Serve immediately as an accompaniment to meat, seafood, or poultry selections, or as one component on a vegetable plate.

*Replace the shiitake mushrooms with 6 oz of dried black mushrooms to add an authentic touch to this dish. To prepare the black mushrooms, rinse them with cold water to clean. Soak in warm water 30 to 60 minutes.

Drain. Squeeze the mushrooms dry. Cut off the tough stems; reserve for another use. Cut the caps into quarters.

Dried black mushrooms are also known as winter mushrooms. Before soaking, the brownish-black mushrooms are brittle and hard, ranging in size from ½ to 2 in. in diameter. Large, thick ones with light skins, curled edges, and cracked skins are the most preferred. They are available at stores offering Asian food ingredients.

Servings	Calories	Protein (g) (%)	Fat (g) (%)	Cholesterol (mg)	Carbohydrates (g) (%)	Fiber (g)	Sodium (mg)
1	54	3.2 (21%)	0.4 (5%)	0	11.2 (74%)	2.4	326

Spicy Coconut-Flavored Stir-Fried Vegetables

For a spicy coconut taste without any ingredients rich in saturated fat, cholesterol, or sodium, the vegetables in this colorful stir-fried medley are seasoned with curry powder and coconut extract.

Servings: 24 *Serving Size: $\frac{5}{8}$ c*
Yield: $1\frac{1}{4}$ gal

Vegetable cooking spray, butter-flavored	—	Carrots washed, diagonal thin slices	2 lb
Onions, sliced	1 lb	Green beans, diagonal thin slices	2 lb
Garlic, minced	$1\frac{1}{2}$ T	Green peas, fresh, shelled or frozen	2 lb
Curry powder	$1\frac{1}{2}$ T	Coconut extract	1 T
Flavorful vegetable stock (see page 2) or rich white chicken stock (see page 7)	1 pt	Salt	To taste
Carrot, washed, finely grated	2 oz	Pepper, freshly ground	To taste

1. Coat a large nonstick skillet or wok with cooking spray or cook in batches. Place over medium heat until hot. Add the onions and garlic; cook until tender, or about 5 minutes.
2. Add the curry powder; mix well. Stir in the stock and grated carrots. Cook until the carrots are soft, or about 3 minutes.
3. Add the sliced carrots, beans, and peas if fresh. Cook until crisp-tender, or about 8 minutes. Add the peas if frozen; cook until all the vegetables are heated through.
4. Stir in the coconut extract. Season with salt and pepper to taste. Serve immediately.

Servings	Calories	Protein (g) (%)	Fat (g) (%)	Cholesterol (mg)	Carbohydrates (g) (%)	Fiber (g)	Sodium (mg)
1	72	3.5 (18%)	0.4 (4%)	0	14.9 (77%)	4.9	20.9

Stir-Fried Broccoli with Wine, Soy Sauce, and Ginger

The excellent natural flavor, bright color, and tender-crisp texture of this stir-fried broccoli are enhanced with a fat-free (no oil, margarine, or butter) mixture of low-sodium soy sauce, fruit sweetener, white wine, and freshly minced ginger.

Servings: 24　　　*Serving Size: 1⅛ c*
Yield: 1¾ gal

Soy sauce, low-sodium	¼ c	Salt	To taste
Wine, white	2 T +	Vegetable cooking spray	—
	1 t	Gingerroot, minced	2 T +
Apple or fruit juice			2 t
concentrate, unsweetened	1 T +	*Broccoli florets, stems	
	1 t	reserved for another use	4 lb

1. In a small bowl, mix the soy sauce, wine, juice concentrate, and salt to taste.
2. Coat a large nonstick skillet or wok with cooking spray or cook in batches. Place over medium-high heat until hot. Add the ginger; cook until tender, or about 2 minutes.
3. Add the broccoli; cook, stirring, another minute. Add the wine-soy sauce mixture. Heat to a boil; reduce the heat to medium, cover and cook until crisp-tender, or about 4 minutes. Serve as part of a vegetable plate or as a main course accompaniment.

*Replace the broccoli with Chinese broccoli cut into 2–3-in. diagonal segments for a more authentic Chinese version of this dish. Chinese broccoli is available at stores offering Chinese food ingredients.

Servings	Calories	Protein (g) (%)	Fat (g) (%)	Cholesterol (mg)	Carbohydrates (g) (%)	Fiber (g)	Sodium (mg)
1	25	2.5 (32%)	0.3 (8%)	0	4.7 (60%)	2.1	101

No alcohol is listed in the nutrition analysis. It is assumed to be cooked off during preparation.

Sweet Chunky Corn Cake

This corn cake is a vitamin-rich, high-fiber cake. By preparing with a mixture of stone-ground, yellow cornmeal, coarsely chopped corn kernels, and masa,* the end result is equally tasty and nutritious.

Servings: 24   Serving Size: 3 × 3⅓-in. piece
Yield: 12 × 20 × 2-in. counter pan

Margarine, unsalted, corn oil	8½ oz (1 c + 1 T)	Cornmeal, yellow, stone-ground	6 oz
		Baking powder	1½ t
*Masa	1 lb + 1 oz	Salt	To taste or 1½ t
Apple or fruit juice concentrate, unsweetened	2¼ c	Milk, evaporated, skim	¾ c
Corn, kernels, fresh, blanched or frozen	4 lb	Vegetable cooking spray, butter-flavored	—

1. Whip the margarine in a mixing bowl until fluffy and creamy.
2. Add the masa gradually, mixing until well blended.
3. Gradually mix in the fruit juice concentrate until well blended.
4. In a blender or food processor, coarsely chop the corn kernels.
5. In another mixing bowl, mix the cornmeal, baking powder, salt to taste, and evaporated milk. Add the masa-margarine mixture and the chopped corn; mix just until blended.
6. Pour into a 12 × 20 × 2-in. counter pan coated with cooking spray. Cover with foil; bake in a 350°F (175°C) oven until the cake is firm, or about 50 minutes. Stand in a warm place to set up for about 10 minutes. To serve, cut the cake 6 × 4 into 24 3⅓ × 3-in. pieces, or portion with a scoop.

*Masa is made with sun- or fire-dried corn kernels which have been cooked in limewater. After they have been cooked, then soaked in the limewater overnight, the wet corn is ground into masa (masa harina). Masa is available at stores offering Mexican food ingredients.

Servings	Calories	Protein (g) (%)	Fat (g) (%)	Cholesterol (mg)	Carbohydrates (g) (%)	Fiber (g)	Sodium (mg)
1	285	5.7 (8%)	10.1 (30%)	0.3	46.9 (62%)	6.0	57.8

Sweet Potato Patties with Hints of Orange

Soft on the inside and crisp on the outside, the natural sweetness of these low-fat, beta-carotene (vitamin A)-rich sweet potato patties is accented with hints of orange and nutmeg. Unlike most croquettes, these are coated with wheat flake cereal crumbs and browned in a nonstick skillet or baked on a sheet pan rather than deep fried.

Servings: 24   *Serving Size: 2 patties*
Yield: 48 patties

Sweet potatoes, cooked without salt, peeled, mashed	4 lb mashed	Orange zest, finely grated	2 T
		Nutmeg, freshly ground	2 t
		Salt	To taste
Flour, whole wheat, stone-ground	4 oz	Wheat flake cereal, crumbs	6 oz
Sugar, light brown	4 oz	Vegetable cooking spray, butter-flavored	—

1. In a bowl, mix the sweet potatoes, flour, sugar, orange zest, nutmeg, and salt. Refrigerate until chilled.
2. Shape the sweet potato mixture into 48 small (1½ oz) patties.
3. Place the cereal crumbs in a container for dredging.
4. Dip the patties into the cereal crumbs to coat evenly.
5. Coat a nonstick skillet with cooking spray. Place over medium heat until hot. Add the patties in batches; cook until brown on each side and heated through, or about 4 minutes per side. The patties can also be baked on a nonstick baking pan coated with cooking spray in a 350°F (175°C) oven, turning once, until brown on both sides and heated through. Serve as a vegetable side dish with meat, seafood, or poultry dishes or as an appetizer course.

Servings	Calories	Protein (g) (%)	Fat (g) (%)	Cholesterol (mg)	Carbohydrates (g) (%)	Fiber (g)	Sodium (mg)
1	139	2.6 (7%)	0.5 (3%)	0	32.3 (90%)	3.6	79.4

Toasted Sesame Green Beans

A pinch of minced garlic and ginger, a splash of low-sodium soy sauce, and a sprinkle of toasted sesame seeds elevate everyday green beans to a new level.

Servings: 24   *Serving Size: ¾ c*
Yield: 1⅛ gal

Sesame seeds	2 oz	Gingerroot, minced	1½ T
Green beans, washed, trimmed	6 lb	Soy sauce, low-sodium	½ c
Vegetable cooking spray, butter-flavored	—	Apple or fruit juice concentrate, unsweetened	2 t
Garlic, minced	2 T	Pepper, freshly ground	To taste

1. In a small nonstick skillet, toast the sesame seeds, stirring, until light brown. Set aside.
2. Steam or blanch the beans in unsalted boiling water until partially tender, or about 4 minutes. Drain. Refresh in cold water. Drain. Set aside.
3. Coat a large nonstick skillet with cooking spray or cook in batches. Place over medium heat until hot. Add the garlic and ginger. Saute until tender without browning.
4. Add the green beans, soy sauce, juice concentrate, pepper, and sesame seeds. Mix well. Heat through. Serve as a side dish with meat, fish, or poultry selections or as one component on a vegetable plate.

Servings	Calories	Protein (g) (%)	Fat (g) (%)	Cholesterol (mg)	Carbohydrates (g) (%)	Fiber (g)	Sodium (mg)
1	55	3.1 (20%)	1.4 (21%)	0	9.3 (59%)	3.7	168

Tomatoes Stuffed with Zucchini and Carrots Laced with Cheese

Tomatoes don't need to be stuffed with high-fat, rich ingredients to be good. In this dish, sauteed vegetables are lightly seasoned with very low sodium worcestershire sauce and layered with low-fat cheddar cheese in a tomato shell coated with Dijon-style mustard.

Servings: 24   *Serving Size: 1 stuffed tomato half*
Yield: 24 stuffed tomato halves

Tomatoes, medium-sized	4 lb as purchased (12)	Zucchini, washed, small dice	1 lb
		Worcestershire sauce, very low sodium	1½ t
Mustard, Dijon-style	¼ c	Salt	To taste
Vegetable cooking spray	—	Pepper, freshly ground	To taste
Garlic, minced	1 T	Cheddar cheese, shredded, low-fat and low-sodium (divided)	6 oz
Carrots, washed, small dice	1 lb		

1. Cut the tomatoes in half; hollow out the halves, removing the pulp; coarsely chop the pulp.
2. Spread the insides of the tomato shells with the mustard. Place the shells in a baking pan coated with cooking spray.
3. In a nonstick skillet, place the garlic and tomato pulp. Cook over medium heat until the flavors are mellowed, or about 5 minutes.
4. Add the carrots and zucchini; cook until the vegetables are crisp-tender. Add water if needed to prevent sticking.
5. Mix in the worcestershire sauce, salt and pepper to taste, and half (3 oz) of the cheese. Spoon the vegetable mixture into the shells; top with the remaining cheese.
6. Bake in a 350°F (175°C) oven until the filling is heated through, the tomato shells are tender, and the cheese is melted, or about 15 minutes. Serve as an appetizer selection, accompaniment for a main course, or as one component on a vegetable plate.

Servings	Calories	Protein (g) (%)	Fat (g) (%)	Cholesterol (mg)	Carbohydrates (g) (%)	Fiber (g)	Sodium (mg)
1	42	2.9 (26%)	0.9 (18%)	1.5	6.5 (56%)	1.9	49.3

Zucchini, Bell Peppers, and Tomatoes Stewed with Turkey Ham

This zucchini preparation is a variation of a Spanish dish called Pisto Espagnol. Since water was historically a rare commodity in Spain, natives rarely boiled their vegetables. Rather, they sauteed them in oil or slowly stewed them, relying on juicy vegetables like the tomatoes, zucchini, and bell peppers in this colorful vegetable medley for moisture. The end result is a low-fat, low-calorie, vitamin-rich dish.

Servings: 24   *Serving Size: 1 c*
Yield: 1½ gal + 1 pt

Vegetable cooking spray, olive-flavored	—	Tomatoes, fresh or canned, coarsely chopped	3 lb
Onion, minced	2 lb	Turkey ham, large dice	1 lb
Pepper, bell, green, small dice	2 lb	Salt	To taste
Garlic, minced	1 T	Pepper, freshly ground	To taste
Zucchini, washed, ¼-in. thick circles	5 lb		

1. Coat a large nonstick skillet or sauce pot with cooking spray or cook in batches if using a small skillet. Place over medium heat until hot. Add the onion, bell pepper, and garlic; cook until tender, or about 5 minutes.
2. Add the next three ingredients; cook until all the vegetables are tender, or about 10 minutes. Add water if needed to prevent sticking. Season with salt and pepper to taste. Serve as a main dish accompaniment.

Servings	Calories	Protein (g) (%)	Fat (g) (%)	Cholesterol (mg)	Carbohydrates (g) (%)	Fiber (g)	Sodium (mg)
1	70	5.8 (30%)	1.3 (16%)	10.6	10.4 (54%)	2.9	196

Zucchini Sauteed with Tomatoes and Herbs

The mild flavor of zucchini pleases both children and adults. It's lovely simply sauteed with roma tomatoes, onion, garlic, and fresh herbs.

Servings: 24 **Serving Size:** ¾ c
Yield: 1 gal + 1 pt

Vegetable cooking spray, olive-flavored	—	Zucchini, washed, trimmed, thin disc-like slices	4½ lb
Tomatoes, roma or slicing, small dice	1 lb	Parsley, minced	¼ c
Onion, minced	1 lb	Salt	To taste
Garlic, minced	1 T	Pepper, freshly ground	To taste
Marjoram, minced or dried	1 T or 1 t		

1. Coat a large nonstick skillet with cooking spray or cook in batches if using a small skillet. Place over medium heat until hot. Add the tomatoes, onions, garlic, and marjoram. Cook until tender and the flavors are mellowed, or about 10 minutes.
2. Add the zucchini; cook until tender, or about 5 minutes. Season with parsley and salt and pepper to taste. Serve as part of a vegetable plate or as a main course accompaniment.

Servings	Calories	Protein (g) (%)	Fat (g) (%)	Cholesterol (mg)	Carbohydrates (g) (%)	Fiber (g)	Sodium (mg)
1	28	1.6 (19%)	0.3 (8%)	0	6 (73%)	1.9	6.9

7

Potatoes, Grains, and Pastas

POTATOES

Baked Russet Potatoes

Because of their high-starch and low-sugar and low-moisture content, Russet potatoes are the preferred choice for baking. When baked, the result is a crisp, slightly shriveled skin and a fluffy interior. For a flavorful, low-fat, high-carbohydrate entree, offer baked potatoes topped with veggies and/or other low-fat toppings. They might include diced crisp bell peppers, grilled onion rings, roasted elephant garlic (see page 359), braise-deglazed sliced mushrooms, buttermilk sour cream potato topping (see page 352), red kidney beans with Indian seasonings (see page 184), turkey taco filling (see page 120), shredded, low-fat cheddar cheese, and/or minced, fresh chives.

Servings: 24   Serving Size: 1 baked potato
Yield: 24 baked potatoes

| Potatoes, Russet or Idaho, medium-sized, washed | 8 lb (24) | Salt | To taste |
| Pepper, black or white, freshly ground | | | To taste |

1. Pierce the ends of the potatoes with a skewer or fork so that steam can escape as they bake. Place on a sheet pan.
2. Bake in a 400°F (205°C) oven until the potatoes feel soft when squeezed, or 45–60 minutes. Cut a crisscross in each top with a knife. Press in and up on the ends of each potato. Sprinkle with salt and pepper to taste. Serve with toppings of choice.

Servings	Calories	Protein (g) (%)	Fat (g) (%)	Cholesterol (mg)	Carbohydrates (g) (%)	Fiber (g)	Sodium (mg)
I	165	3.5 (8%)	0.2 (1%)	0	38 (91%)	3.1	12.1

Variation

Baked Sweet Potatoes: Replace the baking potatoes with beta-carotene rich sweet potatoes.

Cheesy Mashed Potatoes with Green Onions

This tempting version of mashed potatoes needs no butter, cream, or gravy. Creamy, smooth, mashed potatoes are blended with low-fat Swiss cheese, warm, evaporated skim milk, and freshly minced green onions.

Servings: 24   *Serving Size: $\frac{5}{6}$ c*
Yield: $1\frac{1}{4}$ gal

Potatoes, all-purpose, peeled, 1-in. cubes	6 lb	Salt	To taste
Milk, evaporated, skim, hot	1 pt + $\frac{1}{2}$ c	Pepper, white or black, freshly ground	To taste
Swiss cheese, shredded, low-fat (divided)	1 lb	Green onions, white and 1-in. green, minced	12 oz

1. Steam or place the potatoes in a sauce pot; cover with cold water. Heat to a boil. Reduce the heat to medium; boil until soft.
2. Drain well in a colander. Let the potatoes steam dry a few minutes in the colander.
3. Pass the potatoes through a food mill or ricer or place in a mixing bowl. Begin mashing the potatoes with a paddle; follow by beating with a whip until smooth. Don't over-whip or they will become pasty.
4. Beat in the evaporated milk, 12 oz of the cheese, and salt and pepper to taste.
5. Heat the mixture over low heat, stirring until the cheese is melted and the potatoes are heated through.
6. Mix in the minced green onions.
7. Sprinkle with the remaining 4 oz of cheese. The heat from the potatoes should melt the cheese. If not, place in a salamander or hot oven until the cheese is melted and light brown. Serve as a side dish with meat, seafood, and poultry selections or as one item on a vegetable plate.

Servings	Calories	Protein (g) (%)	Fat (g) (%)	Cholesterol (mg)	Carbohydrates (g) (%)	Fiber (g)	Sodium (mg)
1	151	9.9 (26%)	1.2 (7%)	7.6	25.4 (67%)	2.2	87.4

Creamy Garlic Sliced Potatoes

Garlic spices up the golden fleshed and butter-tasting Yukon gold potatoes in this dish. A light cover of toasted whole wheat bread crumbs makes them ever so tempting.

Servings: 24   *Serving Size: ½ c*
Yield: 3 qt

Vegetable cooking spray, butter-flavored	—	Garlic, minced	3 T
		Salt	To taste
Potatoes, Yukon golds or other yellow potatoes (yellow Finnish), peeled, ¼-in. thick slices	6 lb as purchased	Pepper, white or black, freshly ground	To taste or ¾ t
		Bread crumbs, whole wheat, fresh	3 oz
Low-fat white sauce (see page 36), medium consistency, hot	1¼ qt	Paprika, Hungarian, sweet	1 t

1. Coat a 12 × 20 × 2-in. counter pan with cooking spray. Add the sliced potatoes.
2. Mix the garlic into the white sauce. Season with salt and pepper to taste. Pour over the potatoes. Mix to coat.
3. In a small bowl, mix the bread crumbs and paprika. Sprinkle over the potatoes. Bake in a 350°F (175°C) oven until the potatoes are soft and the crumbs browned, or about 1 hour. Serve with meat, fish, or poultry items such as sauteed beef sirloin steak napped with spicy red pepper tomato sauce (see page 80).

Servings	Calories	Protein (g) (%)	Fat (g) (%)	Cholesterol (mg)	Carbohydrates (g) (%)	Fiber (g)	Sodium (mg)
1	109	3.2 (11%)	0.8 (6%)	0.2	23.2 (83%)	2.2	32.7

Golden Potato Slices in Cheese Custard

Traditionally, a recipe for potatoes in cheese custard would likely have contained several egg yolks, whole milk, and a good share of butter. That is not the case in this recipe. Rather, the potatoes are simmered in chicken stock and finished in a custard prepared from nonfat milk, a small amount of Swiss cheese, and egg whites and seasoned with nutmeg.

Servings: 24   *Serving Size:* $\frac{1}{2}$ c
Yield: 2 10 × 12 × 2½-in. counter pans

Vegetable cooking spray, butter-flavored	—	Egg whites, large	10 (12½ oz)
Potatoes, yellow (Yukon gold, yellow Finnish) peeled, thick slices	5 lb	Swiss cheese, shredded	3 oz
		Nutmeg, freshly ground	⅛ t
Rich white chicken stock (see page 7), boiling	1¼ qt	Salt	To taste
Milk, nonfat	1¼ pt	Pepper, white or black, freshly ground	To taste

1. Coat two 10 × 12 × 2½-in. counter pans with cooking spray; add the potatoes; pour the boiling chicken stock over. Add more stock or water if needed to cover initially and during cooking. Place on a flat top. Heat to a boil; reduce the heat to very low. Cover and simmer until the potatoes are tender and the broth absorbed. This step may also be done in the oven.
2. In a bowl, mix the milk, egg whites, cheese, nutmeg, and salt and pepper to taste. Pour the mixture over the potatoes. Cover; place in a 350°F (175°C) oven; bake until the custard is firm and the potatoes are soft. This step may also be done on a flat top over very low heat. To brown the top of the potatoes, place under a broiler or salamander, watching closely, until golden brown. Serve immediately.

Servings	Calories	Protein (g) (%)	Fat (g) (%)	Cholesterol (mg)	Carbohydrates (g) (%)	Fiber (g)	Sodium (mg)
1	112	6.4 (23%)	1.4 (11%)	3.7	18.7 (66%)	1.5	67.2

Italian Seasoned Potatoes Baked in Parchment

In this recipe, new potatoes are baked in parchment packages along with freshly minced Italian herbs, garlic, and onions. This method of cooking gently steams the potatoes, producing an enticing, aromatic, and flavorful dish.

Servings: 24   *Serving Size: 1 c*
Yield: 1½ gal

Potatoes, new, washed, 1-in. cubes	8 lb as purchased	Thyme, minced or dried	3 T or 1 T
Onions, minced	1½ lb	Oregano, minced or dried	3 T or 1 T
Garlic, minced	1 T	Salt	To taste
Parsley, minced	¼ c + 2 T	Pepper, freshly ground	To taste
		*Parchment paper	—
Basil, minced or dried	3 T or 1 T	Vegetable cooking spray, butter-flavored	—

1. Place the potatoes in a deep counter pan. Sprinkle with the onions and next seven ingredients. Mix to coat evenly.
2. Cut 24 16 × 24-in. sheets of parchment. Fold each in half lengthwise. Cut each into a half heart shape, so that when each paper is unfolded, there is a full heart.
3. Place one portion (6⅔ oz) of the potato mixture on the left half of the paper heart near the fold. Bring the right side of the paper over to meet the left side; seal the edges by making tight double folds.
4. Place the packets slightly apart on baking sheets. Coat the exterior of each with cooking spray; bake in a 400°F (205°C) oven until the potatoes are soft when poked with a skewer, or about 25 minutes.
5. At service, cut x-shaped slits on top of the paper hearts; tear back the paper and let the guests enjoy.

*Tin foil may be substituted for the parchment paper.

Servings	Calories	Protein (g) (%)	Fat (g) (%)	Cholesterol (mg)	Carbohydrates (g) (%)	Fiber (g)	Sodium (mg)
1	133	3.6 (10%)	0.2 (1%)	0	30.2 (90%)	3.1	10.7

Mashed Golden Buttermilk Potatoes

While these potatoes contain no butter or margarine, you'd never guess by their buttery color and taste. Another nutritional plus for these potatoes is that their high-fiber skins are never removed. To make the potatoes light and fluffy, a tad of baking soda is combined with the nonfat buttermilk, lightly moistening them.

Servings: 24 *Serving Size: $\frac{5}{8}$ c*
Yield: 1$\frac{1}{4}$ gal

Potatoes, yellow (yellow Finnish, Yukon golds), washed	8 lb as purchased	Buttermilk, nonfat	1$\frac{1}{2}$ pt
		Baking soda	2 t
		Salt	To taste
		Pepper, black or white, freshly ground	To taste or 2 t
Onions, peeled, halves	12 oz		
Bay leaves	4	Nutmeg, freshly ground	$\frac{1}{4}$ t

1. In a sauce pot, add the potatoes, onions, bay leaves, and cold water to cover; boil covered until tender, or about 30 minutes. Drain the water; reserve 1$\frac{1}{2}$ pt of the cooking liquid; discard the onions and bay leaves. Cut the unpeeled potatoes into chunks.
2. Mash the potatoes by passing through a food mill or ricer or placing in a mixing bowl, breaking up with a paddle, and beating until pureed with a whip. Don't overwhip or they will become pasty.
3. Place the buttermilk in a double boiler. Heat through, stirring. Mix the baking soda, salt and pepper to taste, and nutmeg into the buttermilk; mix into the potatoes. If creamier potatoes are desired, mix in the cooking liquid. Serve the mashed potatoes as a base for roasted or grilled meat, fish, or poultry selections or as a main course side dish accompanied by whipped margarine or roasted elephant garlic (see page 359).

Servings	Calories	Protein (g) (%)	Fat (g) (%)	Cholesterol (mg)	Carbohydrates (g) (%)	Fiber (g)	Sodium (mg)
1	132	4.1 (12%)	0.4 (3%)	1.1	28.7 (85%)	2.4	110

Mashed Potato Pancakes Accented with Onion and Garlic

Nutritionally, potatoes have a lot going for them. They are loaded with carbohydrates, nearly fat-free, and a significant source of vitamin C, thiamine, and potassium. Mashed, blended with nonfat yogurt, and seasoned with freshly grated onions and minced garlic, they provide the basis for these delightful potato pancakes.

Servings: 24　　　Serving Size: 2 ¼-c (2-oz) pancakes
Yield: 48 ¼-c pancakes

Mashed potatoes, cooked without salt or fat	6 lb (3 qt)	Salt	To taste
		Pepper, white or black, freshly ground	To taste
Onion, grated or finely minced	6 oz	Nutmeg, freshly ground	¼ t
Yogurt, nonfat, plain	½ c	Vegetable cooking spray, butter-flavored	—
Garlic, minced	1 T		

1. In a bowl, combine and thoroughly mix all the ingredients through the nutmeg. Using a scoop, divide into 48 equal (¼ c or 2 oz) ball-shaped portions; flatten into small pancakes.
2. Coat a nonstick skillet with cooking spray. Place over medium-high heat until hot. Add the pancakes in batches; cook, turning once, until brown, or about 3 minutes per side. Reduce the heat to low; cover and cook until heated through, or abut 5 minutes. The pancakes can also be baked in the oven on sheet pans coated with cooking spray. Serve as one item on a vegetarian plate or as a main course starch accompaniment.

Servings	Calories	Protein (g) (%)	Fat (g) (%)	Cholesterol (mg)	Carbohydrates (g) (%)	Fiber (g)	Sodium (mg)
1	104	2.3 (9%)	0.1 (1%)	0.1	23.8 (90%)	1.8	9.8

New Red Potatoes Adorned with Parsley and Chives

Many diners don't consider dinner complete without potatoes. Offer steamed baby, red-skinned ones, sprinkled with parsley and chives for a satisfying low-fat, high-fiber way to round out a meal.

Servings: 24   *Serving Size: 3 very small potatoes*
Yield: 6 doz very small potatoes

Potatoes, new, red, very small, baby, washed	5 lb as purchased	Parsley, minced	$\frac{1}{4}$ c
		Chives, minced	$\frac{1}{4}$ c
		Salt	To taste
*Butter-flavored liquid	Optional	Pepper, white or black, freshly ground	To taste

1. Peel a band around the center of each potato. Cut a small piece off the bottom of each so it will stand upright.
2. Steam or place in a sauce pot; cover with cold water. Heat to a boil; reduce the heat to medium; simmer until soft.
3. Drain the potatoes in a colander. Let stand to steam dry a few minutes.
4. Toss the potatoes gently with the butter-flavored liquid if desired, herbs, and salt and pepper to taste. Serve as part of a vegetarian plate or as a main course accompaniment.

*Commercially, products prepared from natural ingredients are available that can add butter flavor to dishes with only a fraction of the calories, fat, and cholesterol in regular butter. Butter Buds and Molly McButter are two brands of butter substitutes.

Servings	Calories	Protein (g) (%)	Fat (g) (%)	Cholesterol (mg)	Carbohydrates (g) (%)	Fiber (g)	Sodium (mg)
1	97	2.1 (8%)	0.1 (< 1%)	0	22.4 (92%)	1.9	7.5

Onion-Flavored Mashed Potatoes

These potatoes are a variation of a popular Tunisian hors d'oeuvre. Baked in round pans and cut into wedges, they make delicious, high-carbohydrate, low-fat snacks, or main course starch accompaniments.

Servings: 24   *Serving Size: 1 wedge*
Yield: 3 9-in. rounds

Vegetable cooking spray, butter-flavored	—	Egg whites, large, lightly beaten	12 (15 oz)
Onions, minced	1 lb	Parsley, minced	1½ oz
Potatoes, chef's, cooked without salt or fat, peeled after cooking	4½ lb as purchased	Salt	To taste
		Pepper, black or white, freshly ground	To taste or ½ t
		Red pepper, ground	To taste

1. Coat a nonstick skillet with cooking spray. Place over medium heat until hot. Add the onions. Saute until tender. Set aside.
2. Mash the potatoes with a food mill or ricer or place in a mixing bowl. Begin mashing the potatoes with a paddle; follow by beating with a whip until smooth. Do not over-whip or the potatoes will become pasty. Add the remaining ingredients to the mashed potatoes; mix well.
3. Place in three 9-in. round baking pans coated with cooking spray.
4. Bake in a 450°F (230°C) oven until golden and set, or about 20 minutes. When slightly cool, cut each pan into eight wedges to serve.

Servings	Calories	Protein (g) (%)	Fat (g) (%)	Cholesterol (mg)	Carbohydrates (g) (%)	Fiber (g)	Sodium (mg)
1	82	3.4 (17%)	0.1 (1%)	0	17 (82%)	1.5	34.4

Oven-Roasted Potato Wedges Seasoned with Rosemary

In Belgium, fried potatoes are sold from push carts on street corners and eaten right out of the bag. Oven-roasted potato wedges are a low-fat, tasty variation on this favorite snack.

Servings: 24   *Serving Size: 3 potato wedges*
Yield: 6 doz potato wedges

Potatoes, Russets, medium-sized, washed	6 lb as purchased (12)	Rosemary, minced or dried (divided)	2 T or 2 t
		Salt	To taste
Vegetable cooking spray, olive-flavored (divided)	8 3-second sprays	Pepper, white or black, freshly ground	To taste

1. Cut the potatoes into six wedges each. Cover with cold water; let stand about 30 minutes. Drain; pat dry.
2. Place cut side down on a baking sheet coated with cooking spray. Spray exposed surfaces of potatoes lightly with cooking spray, or four 3-second sprays. Sprinkle with half (1 T or 1 t) of the rosemary and salt and pepper to taste.
3. Place in a 400°F (205°C) oven; bake for 20 minutes. Turn over; lightly spray with cooking spray, or four 3-second sprays; sprinkle with the remaining rosemary and salt and pepper to taste. Bake until tender and light brown, or about 25 minutes longer. Serve as a main course accompaniment or an appetizer selection along with malt or balsamic vinegar, tomato bell pepper salsa (see page 51), and/or ranch-style chip dip (see page 358).

Servings	Calories	Protein (g) (%)	Fat (g) (%)	Cholesterol (mg)	Carbohydrates (g) (%)	Fiber (g)	Sodium (mg)
1	116	2.4 (8%)	0.1 (<1%)	0	26.8 (92%)	2.2	8.6

Variation

Oven-Roasted Garlic-Seasoned Potato Wedges: Replace the rosemary with a blend of 1½ t garlic powder, 1½ t onion powder, and 1½ t sweet Hungarian paprika.

Potato Boats Stuffed with Cheesy Buttermilk Mashed Potatoes, Studded with Diced Bell Peppers

Because of the butter, sour cream, cheese, and/or high-fat cream sauces the potato has traditionally been served with, and/or the lard, suet, shortening, or oil it has been fried in, the potato has developed a reputation as a fattening food. It's simply not true. Rather, the potato contains almost no fat. As a result, it is relatively low in calories, about 150 for a medium-sized 5-oz baked potato. For a healthy potato offering, try these potato boats. Fiber-rich potato skins are filled with high-starch mashed potatoes blended with warm nonfat buttermilk, low-fat Swiss cheese, minced chives, and sauteed, diced red, green, and yellow bell peppers.

Servings: 24   Serving Size: 1 stuffed potato shell
Yield: 24 stuffed potato shells

Potatoes, Russet or Idaho, washed	6 lb as purchased (12)	Buttermilk, nonfat	1 c
		Swiss cheese, shredded, low-fat	12 oz
		Chives, minced	1½ oz ($\frac{1}{4}$ c)
Vegetable cooking spray, butter-flavored	—	Salt	To taste
Peppers, bell, green, red, and yellow, small dice	8 oz each	Pepper, black or white, freshly ground	To taste

1. Pierce the potatoes with a skewer or fork. Place on a sheet pan. Bake in a 400°F (205°C) oven until soft, or about 1 hour. Test for doneness by squeezing the potatoes gently.
2. Meanwhile, coat a nonstick skillet with cooking spray. Place over medium heat until hot. Add the bell peppers; cook until tender.
3. When baked, while warm, halve the potatoes lengthwise; scoop out the pulp, leaving the shell as thin as possible. Pass the potatoes through a food mill or ricer or place in a mixing bowl; break up with a paddle; follow by beating with a whip until smooth. Don't overwhip or they will become pasty.
4. Place the buttermilk in a double boiler. Heat through, stirring. Beat the warm buttermilk, cheese, chives, and salt and pepper to taste into the mashed potatoes. Fold in ½ (12 oz) of the bell peppers.
5. Fill the potato shells using a pastry bag or a spoon. Sprinkle with the remaining bell

peppers. Place a sheet of foil lightly over to cover. Return to a 400°F (205°C) oven until heated through, or about 15 minutes.

6. Serve as one component on a vegetarian plate or as an accompaniment to a main course selection.

Servings	Calories	Protein (g) (%)	Fat (g) (%)	Cholesterol (mg)	Carbohydrates (g) (%)	Fiber (g)	Sodium (mg)
1	153	7.1 (18%)	1.0 (5%)	5.3	29.7 (77%)	2.7	56.7

Potato Cubes Sauteed with Ginger, Garlic, and Fennel Seeds

There's no need for butter when potatoes are sauteed with a ginger-garlic paste and toasted fennel seeds. Whether the potatoes are freshly boiled or left over, the end results are equally good.

Servings: 24   *Serving Size: ½ c*
Yield: 3 qt

Potatoes, new, red-skinned, washed, boiled without salt, reserving cooking liquid	5 lb (about 5¼ lb as purchased)	Garlic cloves, peeled	2 oz
		Turmeric powder	2 t
		*Red pepper, ground	To taste or ½ t
		Vegetable cooking spray, butter-flavored	—
		Fennel seeds	1½ T
Gingerroot, minced	2 oz	Salt	To taste

1. Once the potatoes are cool, peel them and cut into 1-in. cubes. Set aside.
2. In a blender, add the ginger, garlic, turmeric, red pepper, and ¼ c of potato broth; puree until paste consistency. Add more potato broth as needed.
3. Coat a large, nonstick skillet with cooking spray or cook in batches. Place over medium heat until hot. Add the fennel seeds. Saute, stirring for a few seconds.
4. Add the ginger-garlic paste. Continue cooking and stirring briefly to mellow the flavors.
5. Add the potatoes. Increase the heat to medium-high. Stir to coat with the seasonings. Cook until heated through. Season with salt to taste. Serve as a side dish with meat, fish, and poultry items such as grilled chicken drumsticks tandoori style (see page 135).

*For a milder flavor, replace the red pepper with sweet Hungarian paprika.

Servings	Calories	Protein (g) (%)	Fat (g) (%)	Cholesterol (mg)	Carbohydrates (g) (%)	Fiber (g)	Sodium (mg)
1	73	1.7 (9%)	0.2 (2%)	0	16.7 (91%)	1.5	4.1

Potatoes Speckled with Turkey Bacon and Seasoned with Rosemary*

Potatoes are often cooked by frying in oil or if cooked without fat—by boiling, steaming, or baking—are finished with butter and/or sour cream. For lots of flavor and little fat, season cubes of boiled new potatoes with the flavors of sliced, crisp green onions, fresh, minced rosemary, and smoky bits of turkey bacon.

Servings: 24   *Serving Size:* ½ c
Yield: 3 qt

Potatoes, new, red-skinned, washed, large dice	5 ¼ lb	Rosemary, minced or dried	¼ c or 1 T + 1 t
Bacon, turkey or Canadian, lean	1 lb	Paprika, Hungarian, sweet	3 T
		Salt	To taste
Onions, green, sliced, white only	12 oz	Pepper, freshly ground	To taste

1. Place the potatoes in a sauce pot. Cover with cold water; heat to a boil. Reduce the heat to low; simmer until tender. Drain and let the potatoes steam dry in a colander for a minute. Turn into a counter pan.
2. In a nonstick skillet, cook the bacon over medium heat, turning once, until cooked through, or about 5 minutes. Remove slices to paper towels. Pat dry. Chop into small dice.
3. Add the bacon and remaining ingredients to the potatoes; toss to mix. Serve as a side dish along with meat, fish, or poultry selections or as part of a (nonvegetarian) vegetable plate.

*Adapted from a recipe by Karen Fitzgerald.

Servings	Calories	Protein (g) (%)	Fat (g) (%)	Cholesterol (mg)	Carbohydrates (g) (%)	Fiber (g)	Sodium (mg)
1	122	5.4 (17%)	0.7 (5%)	6.1	24.6 (78%)	3	163

Sliced Potatoes Layered with Onions

Potatoes can accommodate a wide range of flavors. Here, they are seasoned with freshly minced tarragon, oregano, and thyme and simmered in chicken stock, layered with thinly sliced onions.

Servings: 24   *Serving Size: $\frac{1}{2}$ c*
Yield: 3 qt

Vegetable cooking spray, butter-flavored	—	Pepper, freshly ground	To taste
Onions, thin slices	10 oz	Potatoes, new or all purpose, washed, $\frac{1}{8}$-in. thick slices	5 lb as purchased
Tarragon, minced or dried	2 t or $\frac{3}{4}$ t		
Oregano, minced or dried	2 t or $\frac{3}{4}$ t	Rich white chicken stock (see page 7) or flavorful vegetable stock (see page 2)	
Thyme, minced or dried	2 t or $\frac{3}{4}$ t		1 pt + $\frac{3}{4}$ c
Salt	To taste		

1. Coat a nonstick skillet with cooking spray. Place over medium heat until hot. Add the onions; cook until tender without browning.
2. Mix the tarragon and next four seasonings in a small bowl.
3. Coat a 12 × 20 × 2-in. counter pan with cooking spray. Layer the potatoes, onions, and a sprinkle of the seasoning mixture until all the potatoes are used up.
4. Pour the stock over.
5. Bake in a 350°F (175°C) oven covered until the potatoes are soft, or about 1 hour. Add more stock or water if required during cooking.

Servings	Calories	Protein (g) (%)	Fat (g) (%)	Cholesterol (mg)	Carbohydrates (g) (%)	Fiber (g)	Sodium (mg)
1	105	2.3 (8%)	0.1 (1%)	0	24.3 (90%)	2.2	10.1

GRAINS

Barley Risotto Garnished with Exotic Mushrooms and Spinach

Italian risotto is a classic dish made with special varieties of short-grain rice, most commonly arborio. As the rice simmers, it is constantly stirred so that it gradually absorbs its cooking broth and releases starch. The finished dish is a creamy mixture, wonderful as a first or main course, or as an accompaniment to meat, fish, or poultry entrees. For an innovative touch with a slightly more chewy texture, the traditional rice has been replaced with barley in this recipe.

Servings: 24   *Serving Size: $\frac{2}{3}$ c*
Yield: 1 gal

Vegetable cooking spray, olive-flavored	—	Spinach, leaves, fresh, chopped, washed or frozen	8 oz or 5 oz
Mushrooms, shiitake, fresh, cleaned, stems removed and reserved for another use, sliced	$1\frac{1}{4}$ lb caps	Salt	To taste
		Pepper, freshly ground	To taste
Shallots or onions, minced	4 oz	Parmesan cheese, freshly grated, part-skim milk	Optional (8 oz)
Garlic, minced	$1\frac{1}{2}$ T		
Wine, dry, white	1 c		
Barley, pearl	$1\frac{1}{2}$ lb		
Flavorful vegetable stock (see page 2) or rich white chicken stock (see page 7)	$2\frac{1}{2}$ qt		

1. Coat a sauce pot with cooking spray. Place over medium heat until hot. Add the mushrooms. Saute until light brown, or about 5 minutes. Transfer to a container using a slotted spoon.
2. Add the shallots and garlic to the pot; cook until tender, or about 5 minutes.
3. Add the wine. Increase the heat to a boil; cook until slightly syrupy. Reduce the heat to medium-low; add the barley and mushrooms.
4. Meanwhile, in another saucepan, heat the stock to a boil. Reduce the heat to low; keep at a low simmer while cooking the risotto.

5. Slowly add 1 pt of the hot stock to the barley, stirring constantly. Continue to stir, allowing the barley to simmer. When the stock has been absorbed, slowly add another pint of stock. Simmer, stirring frequently, until all the liquid has been absorbed. Add a third pint of stock following the same procedure.

6. Stir in the spinach if fresh. Continue slowly adding the remaining stock, 1 pt at a time, stirring and cooking until all the liquid is absorbed and the barley is slightly creamy and tender. Add the spinach if frozen only to heat through. If the mixture is too wet in the end, increase the heat slightly and reduce the liquid. If additional liquid is needed, add water or additional stock. Serve as an appetizer or starch accompaniment with a poultry, seafood, or meat selection such as sauteed beef sirloin steak napped with spicy red pepper tomato sauce (see page 80), and a cooked vegetable, perhaps steamed green beans or zucchini sauteed with garlic and seasoned with fresh herbs, or offer as an item on a vegetable plate.

Servings	Calories	Protein (g) (%)	Fat (g) (%)	Cholesterol (mg)	Carbohydrates (g) (%)	Fiber (g)	Sodium (mg)
1	123	3.6 (11%)	0.5 (3%)	0	27 (85%)	5.3	20.5

No alcohol is listed in the nutrition analysis. It is assumed to be cooked off during preparation.

Boiled Brown Basmati Rice

Basmati is an extra long grain rice which grows along the foot hills of the Himalayas in northern India. It is considered to be the best rice in the world. While it costs more than the American long grain variety, it is well worth the price. In this recipe, the higher fiber brown basmati rice is used.

Servings: 24　　　　*Serving Size: ½ c*
Yield: 3 qt

| Rice, brown, basmati or long grain, washed | 1 lb 10 oz as purchased | Water | 2 qt + ¾ c |
| Salt | To taste |

1. Place the rice and water in a sauce pot. Stand to soak ½ hour. Heat the water to a boil. Reduce the heat to low; cover; simmer until tender and the water is absorbed, or about 45 minutes. Do not stir or uncover.
2. Remove from the heat. Let stand 5 minutes. It will remain warm up to 25 minutes if covered. Add salt to taste. Fluff with a fork. Serve with creamy dishes such as split mung beans laced with cauliflower and spinach (see page 187) or those that have a sauce, such as garbanzo beans in ginger sauce (see page 176).

Servings	Calories	Protein (g) (%)	Fat (g) (%)	Cholesterol (mg)	Carbohydrates (g) (%)	Fiber (g)	Sodium (mg)
1	114	2.4 (9%)	0.9 (7%)	0	23.6 (84%)	1.1	4.8

Brown Rice Simmered in Tomato Broth

In this recipe, high-fiber brown rice takes on the red color of the tomato mixture in which it is simmered. By simmering the rice in flavorful chicken stock, seasoning with juicy, ripe tomatoes, and blending with sauteed onions and garlic, the need to coat with butter or a high-fat sauce is eliminated.

Servings: 24   *Serving Size: ½ c*
Yield: 3 qt

Vegetable cooking spray	—	Brown rice, long grain,	
Onions, minced	1 lb	washed, soaked, drained	1½ lb as
Garlic, minced	1 oz		purchased
Tomatoes, peeled, fresh or		Salt	To taste
canned, coarsely chopped	1¼ lb	Pepper, freshly ground	To taste
Rich white chicken stock (see			
page 7) (divided)	2½ qt		

1. Coat a nonstick skillet with cooking spray. Place over medium heat until hot. Add the onions and garlic; saute until tender, or about 5 minutes.
2. In a blender, place the cooked vegetables, tomatoes, and ½ c of the stock; process until smooth.
3. In a saucepan, place the rice, tomato mixture, remaining stock, and salt and pepper to taste. Heat to a boil; reduce the heat to low; cover. Simmer for 50 minutes without removing the cover or stirring. Test and cook longer if needed. Add more stock or water as required during cooking. Remove from the heat; let stand 10 minutes. Uncover; fluff and serve.

Servings	Calories	Protein (g) (%)	Fat (g) (%)	Cholesterol (mg)	Carbohydrates (g) (%)	Fiber (g)	Sodium (mg)
1	135	4.8 (14%)	1.5 (10%)	0	25.3 (75%)	1.7	34.9

Buckwheat Corn Bread, Spinach, and Ham Stuffing

This stuffing has all kinds of nutritional goodies in it. For starters, there's the buckwheat corn bread. It's rich in the complex carbohydrates, starch and fiber, and a good source of low-quality protein, vitamins, and minerals to boot. Spinach, of course, is well known for its iron, vitamin C, and beta-carotene. Flavored with extra-lean, high-protein ham, this stuffing rates dietarily on top. Best of all, it tastes wonderful.

Servings: 24   *Serving Size: 1 c*
Yield: 1½ gal

*Buckwheat stone-ground yellow corn bread (see page 371), 1-in. cubes	4 lb	Parsley, minced	1 oz
		Thyme, minced or dried	3 T or 1 T
Vegetable cooking spray, butter-flavored	—	Sage, minced or dried	2 T or 2 t
Onion, minced	1½ lb		
Celery, small dice	12 oz	Paprika, Hungarian, sweet	1 T
Garlic, minced	1 T	Rich white chicken stock, cold (see page 7)	2 qt
Spinach, leaves, chopped, washed	1¾ lb	Salt	To taste
		Pepper, freshly ground	To taste
Corn kernels, fresh, blanched or frozen	12 oz	Vegetable cooking spray	—
Ham, extra lean, cooked, small dice	8 oz		

1. Spread the corn bread out on a baking sheet. Bake in a 400°F (205°C) oven, stirring occasionally, until dried, or about 10 minutes.
2. Coat a nonstick skillet with cooking spray. Place over medium heat until hot. Add the onion, celery, and garlic. Cook until almost tender without browning. Add the spinach. Cook until the spinach is wilted and the rest of the vegetables are tender. Remove from the heat. Set aside to cool.
3. Add the spinach, onion, celery, and garlic mixture and remaining ingredients through the paprika to the corn bread; toss until well mixed. Add the stock a little at a time until the stuffing is slightly moist but not soggy. Use more or less stock as required. Season with salt and pepper to taste. Use as stuffing for rolled meat, poultry, game, fish, or vegetables or bake in a baking pan coated with cooking spray in a 350°F

(175°C) oven until the center is hot, or about 45 minutes, and serve as a side dish with meat, fish, or poultry such as roasted turkey.

*Replace the buckwheat corn bread with another type of corn bread if desired. Adjust the stuffing's name to reflect the change.

Servings	Calories	Protein (g) (%)	Fat (g) (%)	Cholesterol (mg)	Carbohydrates (g) (%)	Fiber (g)	Sodium (mg)
1	216	10.5 (19%)	5.1 (21%)	4.4	33.9 (61%)	4.6	339

Couscous Seasoned with Fresh Ginger and Soy

The gastronomic possibilities with grains are endless. In this dish, couscous, tiny pellets of moistened and rolled semolina that are popular in North African cuisine, is refreshingly complemented with freshly minced ginger and low-sodium soy sauce.

Servings: 24   *Serving Size: 1⅛ c*
Yield: 1¾ gal

Couscous (instant or precooked)	2 ¾ lb as purchased	Gingerroot, minced	3 oz
Salt	To taste	Carrots, washed, small dice, blanched in unsalted water until crisp-tender	1½ lb raw
Pepper, freshly ground	To taste or 1 ½ t		
Vegetable cooking spray	—	Soy sauce, low-sodium	½ c + 1 T
Green onion, white with 1-in. green, thin slices	9 oz	Parsley, minced	½ c + 1 T

1. In a sauce pot, heat 2 qt + ¾ c of water to a boil. Stir in the couscous, and salt and pepper to taste; let stand 5 minutes. The water should be completely absorbed and the couscous softened. Transfer the couscous to a sheet pan. Break up any lumps; let cool completely. Cover to prevent surface drying if to be held for an extended period.
2. Coat a nonstick skillet with cooking spray. Place over medium heat until hot; add the green onion and ginger; cook until tender, or about 5 minutes. Add the green onion, ginger, carrots, soy sauce, and parsley to the couscous. Stir to mix well. Serve at room temperature as a grain dish with meat, seafood, or poultry dishes, or include on a vegetarian plate.

Servings	Calories	Protein (g) (%)	Fat (g) (%)	Cholesterol (mg)	Carbohydrates (g) (%)	Fiber (g)	Sodium (mg)
1	161	5.7 (14%)	0.3 (2%)	0	33.5 (88%)	4.7	207

Crunchy Triticale Sprinkled with Dried Peaches

One of the new grains gaining popularity is the hybrid, triticale. It is the offspring of wheat and rye. In this recipe, the crunchy grain is pleasantly complemented by freshly minced ginger and dried peaches.

Servings: 24   *Serving Size:* ⅔ c
Yield: 1 gal

*Triticale or wheat berries or rye berries	2 ½ lb	Garlic, minced	1⅓ oz (¼ c)
Vegetable cooking spray	—	Sesame oil, light-colored	2 T
Green onions, minced (reserve green tops for garnish)	8 oz	†Dried peaches, very small dice	12 oz
Gingerroot, minced	1⅓ oz (¼ c)	Salt	To taste

1. In a sauce pot, soak the triticale or wheat berries in 1¼ gal of cold water for 8 hours or overnight. Heat to a boil; reduce the heat to low; cover. Simmer until tender, or 60–70 minutes. Drain any excess water. Stand covered 10 minutes; keep warm.
2. Meanwhile, coat a nonstick skillet with cooking spray. Place over medium heat until hot. Add the green onions, ginger, and garlic. Cook until tender, or about 5 minutes.
3. Mix the onions, ginger, garlic, oil, and dried fruit with the triticale. Season with salt to taste. Slice the green onion tops; sprinkle over the triticale. Serve as part of a vegetarian plate or as a starch accompaniment with meat, fish, or poultry selections.

*Triticale, wheat berries, and rye berries are available at stores offering healthy, gourmet, or specialty food ingredients.

†Replace the dried peaches with dried diced apricots, blueberries, cherries, cranberries, or a mixture of colorful dried fruits.

Servings	Calories	Protein (g) (%)	Fat (g) (%)	Cholesterol (mg)	Carbohydrates (g) (%)	Fiber (g)	Sodium (mg)
1	213	7.0 (12%)	2.3 (9%)	0	44.8 (79%)	10.2	4.5

Fried Brown Rice Beaming with Vegetables

Fried rice is a good way to use up almost any ingredients on hand, both leftover and fresh. When additional rice is boiled or steamed, a light vegetarian entree can be cooked in minutes.

Servings: 24   *Serving Size: $\frac{9}{10}$ c*
Yield: $1\frac{1}{4}$ gal + 1 pt

Vegetable cooking spray	—	Gingerroot, minced	$1\frac{1}{3}$ oz ($\frac{1}{4}$ c)
Egg whites, large, lightly beaten	16 ($1\frac{1}{4}$ lb)	Garlic, minced	2 T
		Cauliflower, florets	2 lb
*Brown rice, long grain, cooked without salt or fat, chilled	1 lb + 2 oz as purchased	Carrots, washed, thin diagonal slices	$1\frac{1}{4}$ lb
		Broccoli, florets and thin diagonal slices of stem	2 lb
		Soy sauce, low-sodium	1 c
Green onions, white only, thin slices, reserve stems for garnish	1 lb	Sherry, dry	$\frac{1}{2}$ c
		Salt	To taste

1. Coat a large nonstick skillet with cooking spray or cook in batches. Place over medium heat until hot. Add the egg whites and cook as a flat omelet. Roll the omelet and cut into long strips.
2. Separate the rice grains.
3. Coat a large wok or nonstick skillet with cooking spray or cook in batches. Place over medium heat until hot. Add the green onions, ginger, and garlic; stir-fry until tender, or about 5 minutes.
4. Add the cauliflower and carrots; stir-fry until crisp-tender or about 8 minutes.
5. Add the broccoli; stir-fry until crisp tender, or about 4 minutes. Add water if the mixture becomes too dry.

6. Add the rice, soy sauce, sherry, salt to taste, and omelet strips; stir fry until heated through, or about 5 minutes. Serve the rice garnished with sliced green onion stems.

*Boiled brown rice: Place 1 lb + 2 oz of long grain brown rice in a saucepan with 1¼ qt of water. Heat to a boil. Stir. Cover and simmer over low heat until done, or 45 minutes. Test and cook a few minutes longer if necessary. Let stand 10 minutes.

Servings	Calories	Protein (g) (%)	Fat (g) (%)	Cholesterol (mg)	Carbohydrates (g) (%)	Fiber (g)	Sodium (mg)
1	146	7.7 (21%)	1.0 (6%)	0	27.4 (73%)	4.6	401

No alcohol is listed in the nutrition analysis. It is assumed to be cooked off during preparation.

Paella-Style Brown Rice Strewn with Chicken, Seafood, and Vegetables

This is a healthy variation of traditional paella. In this version of the famous Spanish rice dish, saffron-coated brown basmati rice is peppered with cubes of monk fish and skinless chicken breast meat, large, steamed shrimp, little neck clams, and rings of baby squid. Tender, green peas and beans, diced tomatoes, julienne strips of yellow and red bell peppers, garbanzo beans, and freshly minced cilantro further enhance the medley of flavors, textures, colors, and shapes comprising this enchanting rice mixture.

Servings: 24   *Serving Size: 4 oz cooked skinless chicken and seafood + $1\frac{1}{6}$ c rice and vegetables*

Yield: 6 lb cooked skinless chicken and seafood + $1\frac{3}{4}$ gal rice and vegetables

Rich white chicken stock (see page 7), (divided)	$2\frac{1}{2}$ qt + $\frac{1}{2}$ c	Baby squid, cleaned, cut into $\frac{1}{8}$-in. thick rings	1 lb
Clams, little neck, well scrubbed	2 doz	Monk or other lean, firm, white fish fillets, 2-in. cubes	2 lb
Shrimp, large, shell on	1 lb	Paprika, Hungarian, sweet	$1\frac{1}{2}$ T
Vegetable cooking spray, olive-flavored	—	Saffron, strands	$1\frac{1}{2}$ t
		Salt	To taste
Onions, red, minced	$1\frac{1}{2}$ lb	Pepper, freshly ground	To taste
Garlic, minced	1 oz	Wine, white, dry	1 c
Chicken breast meat, skinless, trimmed of fat, 2-in. cubes	$2\frac{1}{2}$ lb	Peas, fresh, shelled or frozen	$1\frac{1}{2}$ lb
Brown rice, basmati or long grain, washed, soaked, drained	2 lb as purchased	Green beans, trimmed, 2-in. lengths	$1\frac{1}{2}$ lb
		Bell peppers, red and yellow, matchstick strips	12 oz each
Tomatoes, coarsely chopped	2 lb	Cilantro, minced	1 oz
Garbanzo beans, cooked from dried without salt or canned, rinsed with water	$\frac{1}{2}$ lb cooked or canned, drained		

1. In a saucepan, add enough of the stock to fill to $1\frac{1}{2}$ in. on the bottom. Add the clams; steam until they open, or about 3 minutes. If they don't, discard them. Remove the

clams from the pan, reserving the broth; loosen the meat from the shells; refrigerate the clam meat until use. Discard the shells or reserve for garnish.

2. Heat the broth from the clams to a boil; add the shrimp; reduce the heat; simmer until they turn bright pink, or about 3 minutes. Remove the shrimp from the saucepan, reserving the broth. Refresh the shrimp in cold water to stop the cooking; drain; peel and devein. Refrigerate until use. Strain the broth; set aside.

3. Coat a sauce pot with cooking spray. Place over medium heat until hot. Add the onions and garlic. Cook until tender, or about 5 minutes. Add the chicken; cook until no longer pink, or about 5 minutes. Add the rice, tomatoes, garbanzo beans, squid, and monk fish. Sprinkle with the paprika, saffron, and salt and pepper to taste. Mix gently. Combine the reserved fish broth with enough chicken stock to yield 2 qt. Add to the rice mixture with the wine. Reserve the remaining chicken stock. Heat to a boil. Reduce the heat to low. Stir carefully; cover. Simmer without stirring until the rice grains are tender and the liquid is absorbed, or about 50 minutes. Add stock or water as needed.

4. Meanwhile, blanch the peas if fresh and green beans in unsalted boiling water. Drain. Refresh in cold water. Drain; set aside. Braise-deglaze the bell peppers in the remaining stock or water as needed until nearly tender. Set aside.

5. When the rice is cooked, remove from the heat. Let stand covered 10 minutes. Reheat the beans, peas, and peppers by braise-deglazing in any remaining stock or water as needed. Quickly place the clams and shrimp on top of the rice; cover. Let stand until the clams and shrimp are heated through. Add the vegetables; toss to mix.

6. Serve with a colorful medley of vegetables and shellfish attractively arranged on the rice. Sprinkle with the cilantro to garnish.

Servings	Calories	Protein (g) (%)	Fat (g) (%)	Cholesterol (mg)	Carbohydrates (g) (%)	Fiber (g)	Sodium (mg)
1	365	33.8 (37%)	4.8 (12%)	113	45.6 (50%)	5.9	173

No alcohol is listed in the nutrition analysis. It is assumed to be cooked off during preparation.

Spicy Brown Rice Pilaf Peppered with Bell Peppers, Celery, and Onions

Potatoes may be an American staple, but rice consumption is on the rise. A recent study by the National Restaurant Association showed that rice is gaining popularity at the expense of potatoes. For a rice dish that is high in fiber, low in fat, and filled with flavor, offer spicy brown rice pilaf peppered with bell peppers, celery, and onions.

Technically, a pilaf is rice or grains that have been cooked in fat and then simmered in stock or other liquid, usually with seasonings or other ingredients. While the brown rice in this recipe is not sauteed in oil or butter before simmering in stock, the results are similar to a pilaf, and thus its name.

Servings: 24   *Serving Size: $\frac{2}{5}$ c ($6\frac{2}{3}$ T)*
Yield: $2\frac{1}{2}$ qt

Brown rice, long grain, washed	1 lb + 2 oz as purchased	Mustard, dry	2 t
		Thyme, dried	$1\frac{1}{2}$ t
		Oregano, dried	$1\frac{1}{2}$ t
		Cumin, freshly ground	1 t
Flavorful vegetable stock (see page 2) or rich white chicken stock (see page 7)	$1\frac{1}{2}$ qt	Red pepper, ground	$\frac{1}{4}$ t
		Bay leaves	2
		Salt	To taste
Paprika, Hungarian, sweet	1 T	Vegetable cooking spray	—
Pepper, freshly ground	To taste or 2 t	Onions, celery, and pepper, green, bell, very small dice	12 oz each
		Garlic, minced	2 T

1. Place the rice and stock in a heavy sauce pot. Let stand $\frac{1}{2}$ hour. Add the paprika and next eight ingredients. Heat to a boil, stirring occasionally. Reduce the heat to low; cover; simmer until done, or about 50 minutes, without stirring. Test and cook longer if needed, adding stock or water as required. Let stand 10 minutes.
2. Meanwhile, coat a nonstick skillet with cooking spray. Place over medium heat until hot. Add the remaining ingredients; saute until tender.
3. Turn out the rice into a counter pan. Remove the bay leaves. Fold in the vegetables

and fluff. Season with additional salt and pepper if needed. Serve as a main dish accompaniment or as one item on a vegetable plate.

Servings	Calories	Protein (g) (%)	Fat (g) (%)	Cholesterol (mg)	Carbohydrates (g) (%)	Fiber (g)	Sodium (mg)
1	101	2.4 (10%)	0.9 (8%)	0	21.1 (83%)	2.1	20.5

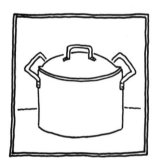

Turmeric-Flavored Brown Rice Simmered with Tomatoes

In this recipe, nutty-flavored, slightly crunchy-textured brown rice is simmered in the oven in vegetable broth along with tomatoes, onions, bell peppers, and low-fat cheddar cheese. A sprinkle of mildly sweet, freshly minced marjoram and bright yellow turmeric makes this carbohydrate-rich dish a winner with both meat and nonmeat eaters.

Servings: 24   *Serving Size: ⅔ c*
Yield: 1 gal

Vegetable cooking spray	—	Flavorful vegetable stock (see page 2) or rich white chicken stock (see page 7), boiling	1 qt
Tomatoes, fresh or canned, peeled, coarsely chopped, with juice	3 ½ lb		
Brown rice, long grain, washed, soaked, drained	1½ lb as purchased	Marjoram, minced or dried	3 T or 1 T
		Bay leaves	3
Cheddar cheese, shredded, low-fat and low-sodium	1 lb	Turmeric powder	2 t
		Salt	To taste
Onions, minced	1 lb	Pepper, freshly ground	To taste or 2 t
Pepper, green, bell, very small dice	12 oz		

1. Coat a 12 × 20 × 2-in. counter pan with cooking spray. Combine all the ingredients in the pan; mix well.
2. Cover; bake in a 350°F (175°C) oven until the rice is tender, or about 1 hour and 35 minutes. If it is not done, return it to the oven for a few minutes longer. Add water or stock as needed throughout cooking. Stand covered for 10 minutes. Remove the bay leaves. Fluff. Offer as a vegetarian selection or starch accompaniment with meat, fish, or poultry dishes.

Servings	Calories	Protein (g) (%)	Fat (g) (%)	Cholesterol (mg)	Carbohydrates (g) (%)	Fiber (g)	Sodium (mg)
1	168	7.9 (19%)	2.5 (13%)	4.0	28.9 (68%)	2.7	16.5

Whole Grain Granola with Sunflower Seeds, Cashews, Almonds, Dried Apricots, and Raisins

Traditionally, granola was laden with fat. Fortunately, this granola recipe is a delicious combination of high-fiber, whole grain cereals, nuts, seeds, and dried fruit which is not only rich in vitamins and minerals but reduced in fat too. Recommend it to diners who want to eat a high-fiber cereal that tastes good too.

Servings: 24   *Serving Size: $\frac{9}{10}$ c*
Yield: $1\frac{3}{8}$ gal (1 gal + 6 c)

Raisins, seedless	6 oz	Sunflower seeds, raw, shelled	2 oz
Rolled oats (long-cooking oatmeal)	2 lb	Almonds, slivered, blanched	2 oz
		Bran, wheat, toasted, cereal	$1\frac{1}{2}$ oz
Rolled wheat (looks similar to rolled oats)	12 oz	White grape or apple juice concentrate, unsweetened	$1\frac{1}{2}$ pt
Cashew pieces, raw	$2\frac{1}{2}$ oz	Apricots, dried, small dice	12 oz

1. Plump the raisins in water. Drain. Set aside.
2. Mix the rolled oats and next five ingredients in a bowl. Gradually add the juice concentrate, stirring to mix.
3. Spoon the mixture evenly over a baking sheet. Bake in a 250°F (120°C) oven until the grains are toasted crisp and somewhat dry, or about $1\frac{1}{4}$ hours. Stir occasionally.
4. Sprinkle the mixture with the apricots and raisins. Let cool. Store in a tightly covered container. Serve for breakfast coated with nonfat milk or freshly squeezed orange juice, or use as a topping or coating on desserts such as frozen banana bonbons (see page 446).

Servings	Calories	Protein (g) (%)	Fat (g) (%)	Cholesterol (mg)	Carbohydrates (g) (%)	Fiber (g)	Sodium (mg)
1	361	10.7 (11%)	6.8 (16%)	0	68.8 (73%)	9.4	7.6

Whole Grain Oat Porridge Flavored with Cinnamon and Cardamom

In Sweden, a rice porridge similar to this whole grain oat porridge traditionally was served on Christmas Eve. Unlike this porridge, however, it contained one blanched almond, the recipient of which was supposed to be wed before the next Christmas. To create some dining fun, recreate this scenario in your operation.

Servings: 24
Yield: 3½ qt

Serving Size: ⅞ c

*Oat groats	1 lb + 10 oz as purchased	Milk, skim, evaporated	1½ qt
		Cinnamon, sticks	2
		Sugar, light brown	1 lb
Water	1¼ qt	Vanilla extract	1 T
Milk, nonfat	3 qt	Cardamom, ground	1½ t
		Salt	To taste

1. In a sauce pot, add the oat groats and water. Heat to a boil; reduce the heat to low. Cover; simmer without stirring or removing the cover until tender and the water is absorbed, or about 45 minutes.
2. Stir in the nonfat milk, evaporated skim milk, and cinnamon sticks. Heat to a boil; reduce the heat to very low; simmer, stirring occasionally, until the oat mixture thickens, or about 3 hours. Stir in additional water or nonfat milk if needed.
3. Blend in the brown sugar, vanilla, cardamom, and salt to taste. Remove the cinnamon sticks.
4. Divide among bowls. Serve with nonfat milk, additional brown sugar or honey, freshly ground cinnamon, and raisins or other dried fruit as desired.

*Oat groats contain both the oat's bran and germ. They are available at stores offering healthy, gourmet, or specialty food ingredients. Replace with medium grain brown rice if not available.

Servings	Calories	Protein (g) (%)	Fat (g) (%)	Cholesterol (mg)	Carbohydrates (g) (%)	Fiber (g)	Sodium (mg)
1	280	11.5 (16%)	1.2 (4%)	4.5	55.4 (80%)	1.1	147

Wild Pecan Rice Speckled with Raisins and Vegetables*

Sweet raisins and a sprinkle of nutmeg and coriander are the ideal match for wild pecan rice, a rice with an aroma and taste reminiscent of pecans. Because this beige colored, long grain rice, grown in the colorful Acadian Country of South Louisiana, retains part of its bran coating, it is higher in fiber and has a firmer texture than white, milled rice.

Servings: 24 **Serving Size:** ⅔ c
Yield: 1 gal

Raisins, seedless	6 oz	Parsley, minced	2 T
Vegetable cooking spray,		Coriander, freshly ground	1 t
butter-flavored	—	Nutmeg, freshly ground	¼ t
Garlic, minced	2 T	Salt	To taste
Onions, red, minced	1½ lb	Flavorful vegetable stock,	
Peppers, red, bell, small dice	1¼ lb	boiling (see page 2)	2 qt
†Rice, wild pecan, washed,			
soaked, drained	1 lb +		
	12 oz as		
	purchased		

1. Plump the raisins in water for about 5 minutes. Drain; set aside.
2. Coat a nonstick skillet with cooking spray. Place over medium heat until hot. Add the garlic, onions, and peppers. Cook, stirring until the vegetables are almost tender, or about 5 minutes.
3. Place in a 12 × 20 × 2-in. counter pan coated with cooking spray. Add the rice, parsley, coriander, nutmeg, salt to taste, and stock; mix to blend. Cover tightly.
4. Place in a 350°F (175°C) oven; bake for 1 hour or until the liquid is absorbed and the rice is tender. Taste the rice; return to the oven if it is not done adding stock or water as needed. Stand covered about 10 minutes. Uncover and fluff the rice. Serve as a grain dish with meat, fish, and poultry items or as one component on a vegetarian plate.

*Adapted from a recipe by Karen Fitzgerald.

†For wild pecan rice suppliers and further information, contact Conrad Rice Mill Inc., P.O. Box 296, 307 Ann St, New Iberia, LA 70560; (318) 364-7242.

Servings	Calories	Protein (g) (%)	Fat (g) (%)	Cholesterol (mg)	Carbohydrates (g) (%)	Fiber (g)	Sodium (mg)
1	169	3.6 (8%)	1.2 (6%)	0	36.7 (85%)	2.9	11.8

Wild Rice Embellished with Exotic Mushrooms and Toasted Almonds

Wild rice has been reported to have more zinc than any other grain. Furthermore, it's rich in B vitamins, magnesium, and fiber. As delicious as wild rice is in its own right, it's even better when enhanced with sauteed porcini and shiitake mushrooms and toasted, slivered almonds.

Servings: 24 *Serving Size: $\frac{5}{8}$ c*
Yield: $3\frac{3}{4}$ qt

Mushrooms, porcini, dry	3 oz	Vegetable cooking spray, butter-flavored	—
Flavorful vegetable stock (see page 2), or rich white chicken stock (see page 7) (divided), hot	$2\frac{1}{2}$ qt	Onions, minced	2 lb
		Parsley, minced	$\frac{1}{2}$ c
		Salt	To taste
Wild rice, long grain	$1\frac{1}{4}$ lb	Pepper, freshly ground	To taste
Almonds, slivered, blanched	3 oz		
Shiitake mushroom caps, fresh, cleaned, stems reserved for another use	$1\frac{1}{2}$ lb caps		

1. Soak the dried porcini mushrooms in $1\frac{1}{4}$ qt of the hot stock until soft, or about 30 minutes. Remove the mushrooms and squeeze them dry over the soaking liquid. Rinse the mushrooms under cool water and pat dry. Chop coarsely and set aside. Combine the mushroom-flavored stock with the remaining stock and enough water to make $2\frac{1}{2}$ qt of broth. Set aside.
2. Wash the wild rice in a strainer with cold water until the water runs clear. Place in a sauce pot. Add the $2\frac{1}{2}$ qt of broth; heat to a boil. Reduce the heat to low; cover. Simmer until the rice is tender and most of the grains have split slightly, or 50–60 minutes. Drain any excess liquid. Let stand covered for 10 minutes.
3. While the rice is cooking, place the almonds in a nonstick skillet. Saute over low heat until brown. Remove from the skillet. Set aside.
4. Slice the shiitake mushroom caps.
5. Coat a nonstick skillet with cooking spray. Place over medium heat until hot. Add the onions; saute until tender without browning. Add the shiitake mushrooms; saute until tender. Add the porcini mushrooms and saute a few minutes longer.
6. Turn the cooked wild rice into a counter pan. Fold in the mushrooms, almonds, parsley, and salt and pepper to taste. Fluff. Serve as a main dish starch accompaniment

with game or poultry items such as spit-roasted chicken on the rotisserie (see page 139) or as one component on a vegetable plate.

Servings	Calories	Protein (g) (%)	Fat (g) (%)	Cholesterol (mg)	Carbohydrates (g) (%)	Fiber (g)	Sodium (mg)
1	127	5.0 (15%)	2.4 (16%)	0	23.3 (69%)	3.8	14.9

Wild Rice Studded with Blueberries and Shiitake Mushrooms

Wild rice is really not a rice at all. Rather, it is the seed of a marsh grass. Its crunchy texture and earthy flavor make it the natural partner to wild game. When purchasing, be aware that wild rice is graded. The most desirable wild rice is called giant (long grain). Medium grain wild rice is rated second, and last place goes to select (short grain). Short grain wild rice is an acceptable ingredient in waffles or soups, while the preferred choice for a pilaf or dish like this one is long grain.

Servings: 24 Serving Size: ½ c
Yield: 3 qt

Wild rice, long grain	1 lb + 2 oz	†Blueberries, dried, unsweetened	4 oz
Water	1½ qt	Rich white chicken stock (see page 7) or flavorful vegetable stock (see page 2)	2½ qt
Vegetable cooking spray, butter-flavored	—		
Green onions, white and 1-in. green, minced	8 oz	Salt	To taste
*Mushrooms, shiitake, caps, fresh, ¼-in. strips	5 oz	Pepper, freshly ground	To taste or ¾ t
Madeira wine	¼ c + 2 T		

1. Wash the wild rice in a colander under cold water until the water runs clear.
2. Place the rice in a saucepan with the 1½ qt of water; heat to a boil. Reduce the heat to low; simmer until the rice has softened but is still hard when you bite into it, or about 10 minutes.
3. Drain and wash the rice again to remove any remaining grit.
4. Meanwhile, coat a nonstick skillet with cooking spray. Place over medium heat. Add the green onions and mushrooms. Saute until the vegetables are tender.
5. Add the madeira wine; simmer until completely evaporated.
6. Add the mushroom mixture and remaining ingredients to the rice. Heat the rice to a boil. Cover and reduce the heat to low. Simmer until the rice is tender with a touch of chewiness, or 40 to 50 minutes.

7. Add more water or stock if needed. Drain any remaining liquid from the rice. Serve as a side dish with game or poultry selections.

*Reserve stems for another use.

†Replace the blueberries with other dried fruits such as cherries or cranberries, changing the name of the dish accordingly.

Servings	Calories	Protein (g) (%)	Fat (g) (%)	Cholesterol (mg)	Carbohydrates (g) (%)	Fiber (g)	Sodium (mg)
1	99	5.2 (21%)	0.9 (8%)	0	18 (71%)	2.3	36.4

Note: alcohol is not listed in the nutrition analysis. It is assumed the alcohol in the madeira wine is cooked off during simmering.

PASTAS

Carrot-Flavored Angel Hair Pasta Pancakes Spotted with Bell Peppers

Pasta pancakes make a unique side dish, appetizer course, or salad garnish. When flavored pastas are seasoned with vegetables and fresh herbs, the absence of high-cholesterol egg yolks and cream goes unnoticed.

Servings: 24   Serving Size: 3 small pasta pancakes
Yield: 6 doz small pasta pancakes

Vegetable cooking spray, olive-flavored	12 2-second sprays	Milk, evaporated, skim	1 c
		Swiss cheese, low-fat, shredded	8 oz
Onions, minced	12 oz	Parsley, minced	$\frac{1}{2}$ c + 3 T ($\frac{3}{4}$ oz)
Peppers, bell, red, small dice	10 oz	Basil, minced	$\frac{1}{2}$ c + 3 T ($\frac{3}{4}$ oz)
Peppers, bell, green, small dice	8 oz		
Garlic, minced	3 oz	Salt	To taste
Egg whites, large	36 (2 lb + 13 oz)	Pepper, freshly ground	To taste
*Angel hair pasta, carrot, cooked without salt or fat, rinsed in cold water, coated in oil if cooked in advance	3 qt cooked (1$\frac{1}{2}$ lb dry)		

1. Coat a nonstick skillet with cooking spray. Place over medium heat until hot. Add the onions, bell peppers, and garlic. Saute until tender. Set aside to cool.
2. In a mixing bowl, place the egg whites, beat lightly. Add the pasta (rinse off the oil if coated), evaporated milk, cheese, herbs, and salt and pepper to taste. Add the cooled bell pepper mixture to the pasta mixture; mix gently to blend. Continue mixing throughout cooking to make sure all the ingredients are evenly blended. The eggs and milk will settle to the bottom of the container.

3. Coat a nonstick skillet with cooking spray; place over medium heat. Cooking in batches, add ⅓ c of the pasta mixture to the skillet; cook until set and golden, turning once. Serve immediately as an appetizer, salad garnish, or main dish accompaniment. Offer with a spicy tomato sauce such as Italian-style tomato sauce (see page 35) if desired.

*Substitute whole wheat, lemon pepper, spinach, tomato, beet, or other whole grain, enriched, or flavored pasta for the carrot angel hair pasta, changing the recipe's name accordingly.

Servings	Calories	Protein (g) (%)	Fat (g) (%)	Cholesterol (mg)	Carbohydrates (g) (%)	Fiber (g)	Sodium (mg)
1	168	13.1 (32%)	1.1 (6%)	3.7	25.9 (63%)	2.0	127

Macaroni Layered with Ground Turkey in Red Wine Mushroom Sauce

This dish is tasty but also low in calories, fat, and cholesterol. It is prepared by layering macaroni with low-fat, low-cholesterol, and low-calorie ground turkey and a mushroom-thickened sauce. Hints of red wine, tomato, oregano, and cinnamon further enhance its unique flavor.

Servings: 24   *Serving Size: 3 × 3⅓-in. piece*
Yield: 12 × 20 × 2-in. counter pan

Filling:		Cinnamon, freshly ground	½ t
Turkey, raw, ground, skinless,		Salt	To taste
dark and light meat	2½ lb		
Onions, minced	1½ lb	**Macaroni:**	
Garlic, minced	1 T	Macaroni, elbow	2 lb
Tomatoes, fresh or canned,			
peeled, coarsely chopped	3½ lb	**Topping:**	
Wine, red, dry	1¼ c	Mushroom sauce (see page 38)	2 qt
Oregano, minced or dried	¼ c or	Mozzarella cheese, part-skim	
	1 T +	milk, shredded (divided)	1 lb
	1 t	Egg whites, large	10
Pepper, freshly ground	To taste		(12½ oz)
	or 2 t	Vegetable cooking spray,	
		olive-flavored	—

1. Saute the turkey, onions, and garlic in a nonstick skillet over medium heat until the meat is no longer pink. Drain any fat from the pan, likely none.
2. Add the remaining filling ingredients; cook until the flavors are blended and the liquid is evaporated, or about 25 minutes. Set aside.
3. Cook the macaroni in unsalted, boiling water (2 gal), stirring occasionally, until almost tender, or about 8 minutes. Slightly undercook the macaroni because it will cook further during baking.
4. Drain in a colander; refresh in cold water; drain; set aside.
5. In a saucepan, heat the mushroom sauce and 14 oz of the mozzarella cheese over low heat until blended.
6. In a small bowl, beat the egg whites; slowly add a small amount of the hot sauce to temper the egg whites. Slowly beat the egg mixture into the sauce. Set aside.
7. Coat a 12 × 20 × 2-in. counter pan with cooking spray. Layer half of the macaroni, half of the meat sauce, and half of the topping; repeat; sprinkle with the remaining cheese.

8. Bake uncovered in a 350°F (175°C) oven until the top is golden brown and the mixture is heated through, or about 25 minutes.
9. Remove from the oven; let stand to firm up about 10 minutes. To serve, cut 4 × 6 into 24 3 × 3⅓-in. pieces.

Servings	Calories	Protein (g) (%)	Fat (g) (%)	Cholesterol (mg)	Carbohydrates (g) (%)	Fiber (g)	Sodium (mg)
1	228	21.1 (38%)	6.0 (24%)	37.3	21.7 (39%)	2.3	168

No alcohol is listed in the nutrition analysis. It is assumed to be cooked off during preparation.

Manicotti Tubes Filled with Spinach, Mushrooms, and Cheeses, Covered with Tomato Sauce

This dish might be called vegetarian manicotti for short. To keep it light and healthy, yet full of flavor, the pasta shells are stuffed with a mixture of nonfat ricotta and part-skim milk mozzarella cheeses, spinach, and mushrooms and baked in a low-fat Italian-style tomato sauce. Sauteed, minced onions, fresh basil, freshly ground pepper, and a pinch of freshly ground nutmeg give the filling its zip. The melted, golden brown cheese-topped manicotti shells look and taste so good, it's hard to believe they are good for you too.

Servings: 24   Serving Size: 1 stuffed tube with sauce
Yield: 24 stuffed tubes with sauce

Manicotti, tubes	14 oz (24)	Salt	To taste
		Pepper, freshly ground	To taste
Spinach, leaves, chopped, fresh	1 lb + 7 oz	Egg whites, large	6 (7½ oz)
		Ricotta cheese, nonfat	12 oz
Vegetable cooking spray, olive-flavored	—	Mozzarella cheese, part-skim milk, shredded (divided)	1½ lb
Mushrooms, finely minced	12 oz	Basil, fresh, minced or dried	1 oz or 2 T
Onions, minced	8 oz		
Nutmeg, freshly ground	½ t	Italian-style tomato sauce (see page 35)	1½ qt

1. Boil the manicotti tubes in unsalted water (3½ qt), stirring occasionally, until barely tender, or about 10 minutes. Drain; refresh in cold water; drain.
2. Blanch the spinach in unsalted boiling water. Refresh in cold water; drain; squeeze dry.
3. Coat a nonstick skillet with cooking spray. Place over medium heat until hot. Add the mushrooms and onions; saute until almost tender, or about 3 minutes. Add the spinach, nutmeg, and salt and pepper to taste. Cook, stirring until the flavors are blended, or a few additional minutes. Drain any liquid that may have accumulated in the mixture. Set aside to cool.
4. Beat the egg whites until light and fluffy. Stir into the cooled spinach mixture. Mix in the ricotta cheese, 1 lb of the mozzarella cheese, and the basil.
5. Stuff the tubes with the filling.
6. Coat a 12 × 20 × 2-in. counter pan with cooking spray. Pour 1 c of the tomato sauce in the bottom of the pan. Arrange the stuffed manicotti tubes over the sauce. Pour the remaining sauce over the tubes. Sprinkle with the remaining mozzarella cheese.
7. Cover loosely to prevent the cheese from sticking as it melts during baking; place in a

350°F (175°C) oven; bake for about 15 minutes. Remove the cover. Continue baking until heated through and the cheese is melted and golden brown, or about 15 additional minutes. For further browning, place under a salamander. Serve with a crisp green salad.

Servings	Calories	Protein (g) (%)	Fat (g) (%)	Cholesterol (mg)	Carbohydrates (g) (%)	Fiber (g)	Sodium (mg)
1	220	15 (27%)	6.9 (27%)	42.5	25.9 (46%)	3.9	199

Orzo Pilaf Flavored with Cloves and Cinnamon

Current dietary recommendations encourage Americans to increase their consumption of complex carbohydrates while reducing their intake of fat. To help diners meet these recommendations, offer low-fat pasta dishes like this orzo (rice-shaped pasta) pilaf flavored with hints of orange, cinnamon, and clove.

Servings: 24   *Serving Size: ½ c*
Yield: 3 qt

Vegetable cooking spray, olive-flavored	—	Bay leaves	2
Onion, red, minced	12 oz	Salt	To taste
Orzo	2 lb + 7 oz	Pepper, freshly ground	To taste
Orange juice, freshly squeezed	1½ c	Rich white chicken stock (see page 7) or flavorful vegetable stock (see page 2), boiling	1½ qt
Cloves, whole	6		
Cinnamon, freshly ground	1½ t	Parsley, minced	3 T

1. Coat a nonstick skillet with cooking spray. Place over medium heat until hot. Add the red onion; cook until tender without browning.
2. Place the orzo, next six ingredients, and onions in a 12 × 20 × 2-in. counter pan coated with cooking spray.
3. Stir in the boiling stock. Cover tightly. Place in a 350°F (175°C) oven; bake until the liquid is absorbed and the orzo is dry and fluffy, or about 20 minutes. Remove the bay leaves. Stir in the parsley. Serve as a main course accompaniment or as one component on a vegetable plate.

Servings	Calories	Protein (g) (%)	Fat (g) (%)	Cholesterol (mg)	Carbohydrates (g) (%)	Fiber (g)	Sodium (mg)
1	118	3.8 (13%)	0.7 (5%)	0	24.4 (82%)	1.9	7.8

Penne Pasta Baked in a Creamy Cheddar and Swiss Cheese Sauce

Give a new twist to macaroni and cheese. Offer it with penne pasta (diagonally cut tubes, smooth or with ridges) coated in a smooth and creamy, reduced-fat cheddar and Swiss cheese sauce. A topping of toasted, whole wheat bread crumbs is a nice finishing touch.

Servings: 24   *Serving Size:* $\frac{5}{8}$ *c*
Yield: $1\frac{1}{4}$ *gal*

Low-fat white sauce, medium consistency, seasoned, hot (see page 36)	2½ qt	Swiss cheese, low-fat, shredded	1 lb
Mustard, dry	1 t	Salt	To taste
Red pepper, ground	¼ t	Pepper, freshly ground	To taste
Penne pasta	2 lb	Vegetable cooking spray, butter-flavored	—
Cheddar cheese, low-fat, low-sodium, shredded	1 lb	Bread, whole wheat, fresh, crumbs	4 oz
		Paprika, Hungarian, sweet	1 t

1. Add the dry mustard and ground red pepper to the white sauce; mix well.
2. Heat 2 gal of unsalted water to a boil. Add the penne pasta. Stir gently to keep it from sticking together and to the bottom.
3. Boil until cooked al dente, or firm to the bite, stirring occasionally. Drain. Refresh in cold water. Drain.
4. Mix the pasta with the 2 cheeses.
5. Combine the pasta with the white sauce. Season with salt and pepper to taste.
6. Coat a 12 × 20 × 2-in. counter pan with the cooking spray. Add the pasta mixture.
7. Mix the bread crumbs and paprika in a small bowl. Sprinkle over the pasta. Place in a 350°F (175°C) oven; bake until heated through and the crumbs are browned, or about 50 minutes. To further brown the crumb topping, place under a salamander or broiler. Serve as a first or main course selection.

Servings	Calories	Protein (g) (%)	Fat (g) (%)	Cholesterol (mg)	Carbohydrates (g) (%)	Fiber (g)	Sodium (mg)
1	241	16.9 (28%)	8.4 (32%)	13.1	23.9 (40%)	0.8	162

Spinach Almond Lasagne with Whole Wheat Noodles

Across the nation, food service operators are experiencing increased demands for vegetarian selections. Both meat and nonmeat eaters will rate this spinach almond lasagne a palate pleaser. Whole wheat noodles are layered with sauteed spinach, toasted slivered almonds, nonfat ricotta cheese, part-skim mozzarella and parmesan cheeses, and chunky Italian-style tomato sauce.

Servings: 24   *Serving Size: 3 × 3⅓-in. piece*
Yield: 12 × 20 × 2-in. counter pan

Lasagne noodles, whole wheat	1½ lb	Ricotta cheese, nonfat	1½ lb
Vegetable cooking spray, olive-flavored	—	Parmesan cheese, part-skim milk, freshly grated	8 oz
Spinach, leaves, chopped, washed	4 lb	Mozzarella cheese, part-skim milk, shredded	1 lb
Almonds, slivered, blanched	8 oz		
Italian-style tomato sauce (see page 35)	3¾ qt		

1. Heat 1½ gal of unsalted water to a boil in a sauce pot. Add the lasagne noodles. Stir gently to keep from sticking together and to the pan bottom. Boil until al dente or firm to the bite, stirring occasionally. Drain. Refresh in cold water. Drain. Set aside.
2. Coat a large nonstick skillet or sauce pot with cooking spray. Place over medium-high heat until hot. Add the spinach; cook until wilted. Place in a colander; press any remaining liquid from it. Set aside.
3. Add the almonds to a small nonstick skillet. Cook over medium heat until brown, stirring. Set aside.
4. Spread 1 pt (2 c) of the tomato sauce in the bottom of a 12 × 20 × 2-in. counter pan.
5. Layer one-fourth of the noodles, one-third each of the spinach, almonds, and ricotta cheese, one-fourth each of the parmesan and mozzarella cheeses and 3½ c of the tomato sauce in the pan. Repeat twice.
6. Top with the remaining noodles, remaining 2½ c of tomato sauce, 2 oz of the parmesan cheese, and 4 oz of the mozzarella cheese.
7. Place in a 350°F (175°C) oven uncovered; bake until heated through and the cheese is melted and lightly browned on top, or about 40 minutes. Let stand until firm, or about

15 minutes in a warm place. Cut 4 × 6 into 24 3 × 3⅓-in. pieces. Serve on heated dinner plates.

Servings	Calories	Protein (g) (%)	Fat (g) (%)	Cholesterol (mg)	Carbohydrates (g) (%)	Fiber (g)	Sodium (mg)
1	341	23 (25%)	12 (29%)	17.3	42.9 (29%)	10.2	379

Translucent Noodles, Beef, and Vegetables in Soy Glaze*

Add pizzazz to this healthy one-pot meal by cooking it at the table and allowing diners to serve themselves from the cooking vessel.

Servings: 24   *Serving Size: 1 pt*
Yield: 2 gal

Sherry, dry	1 pt	Vegetable cooking spray	—
Soy sauce, low-sodium	1½ c	Mushrooms, thin slices	2 lb
Apple or fruit juice		Broccoli florets, reserve stems	
concentrate, unsweetened	¼ c + 2 T	for another use	2½ lb
	(3 fl oz)	Carrots, washed, thin slices,	
Gingerroot, minced	1 oz	diagonally cut	2½ lb
Garlic, minced	2 T	‡Chinese cabbage, ¼-in. thick	
†Beef sirloin, trimmed of fat		strips	2½ lb
and silverskin, matchstick		Leek, white only, thin slices	1 lb
strips	6 lb		
Translucent or cellophane			
vermicelli noodles			
(Japanese noodles called			
shiritaki)	2 lb		

1. Combine the sherry and next four ingredients in a nonreactive container large enough to marinate the beef. Mix well. Add the beef. Coat with the marinade; cover; marinate refrigerated 4–6 hours, turning occasionally.
2. Parboil the noodles in unsalted water, stirring occasionally until soft. Drain. Refresh in cold water. Drain. If cooked in advance, rinse in cold water before using to separate the noodles.
3. Drain the marinade from the meat into a saucepan; place over medium heat. Simmer until reduced to thin syrup consistency; reserve.
4. Coat a nonstick skillet or wok with cooking spray. Place over medium-high heat until hot. In batches, add part of the meat; saute briefly. Push the meat to the edge of the pan.
5. One or two at a time, add comparable portions of the following items to the skillet: mushrooms, broccoli, carrots, cabbage, leeks, noodles, and reserved marinade. Stir-fry briefly before adding the next item. Cook until the vegetables are crisp-tender and all the ingredients heated through, or about 4 minutes.

6. Serve immediately, distributed among heated plates; repeat the cooking and serving process until all the ingredients are finished.

*Adapted from a recipe by Tim Allison.

†Substitute lean pork, trimmed of fat, or skinless turkey breast for the beef.

‡Chinese cabbage is also known as napa cabbage, Chinese celery cabbage, and Peking cabbage.

Servings	Calories	Protein (g) (%)	Fat (g) (%)	Cholesterol (mg)	Carbohydrates (g) (%)	Fiber (g)	Sodium (mg)
1	388	30.9 (32%)	7.4 (17%)	75.8	48.9 (51%)	4.4	600

Note: No alcohol is listed in the nutrition analysis. It is assumed to be cooked off as the sherry simmers.

Whole Wheat Spaghetti Tossed with Lightly Sauteed Vegetables

Eating pasta is an easy way for diners to increase their consumption of complex carbohydrates. For an offering that is high in fiber and low in fat, offer whole grain pasta dishes like this one. Flavored with fresh herbs and a light wine sauce and sprinkled with part-skim milk parmesan cheese, there's no need for a rich cream or butter sauce.

Servings: 24　　　*Serving Size: ⅔ c*
Yield: 1 gal

Spaghetti, whole wheat	1 lb	Garlic, minced	1 T
Olive oil, extra virgin	2 T	Wine, white, dry	¾ c
Onions, very thin slices	1 lb	Parsley, minced	¼ c
Carrots, washed, thin diagonal		Basil, minced	¼ c
slices	1 lb	Salt	To taste
Broccoli, florets, stems		Pepper, freshly ground	To taste
reserved for another use	1 lb	Parmesan cheese, part-skim	
Tomatoes, peeled, small dice	1 lb	milk, freshly grated	3 oz
Mushrooms, slices	8 oz		

1. Heat 1 gal of unsalted water to a boil. Add the spaghetti. Stir gently to keep from sticking together and to the pan bottom. Boil until al dente or firm to the bite, stirring occasionally. Drain. Refresh in cold water; drain. Toss with the olive oil. Set aside.
2. Add the onions and next six ingredients to a large nonstick skillet or cook in batches; cook, stirring, over medium-high heat until tender.
3. Add the spaghetti, parsley, basil, and salt and pepper to taste to the vegetables. Toss to mix. Cover and cook until heated through, or a few minutes. Sprinkle with parmesan cheese to garnish. Serve as a side dish or light lunch main course.

Servings	Calories	Protein (g) (%)	Fat (g) (%)	Cholesterol (mg)	Carbohydrates (g) (%)	Fiber (g)	Sodium (mg)
1	126	5.9 (18%)	2.7 (18%)	2.8	21.3 (64%)	3.8	82.8

Note: No alcohol is listed in the nutrition analysis. It is assumed to be cooked off as the wine simmers.

8

Salads and Dressings

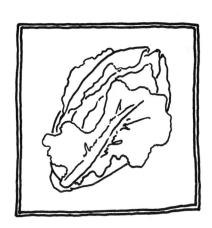

MAIN COURSE SALADS

Beefalo and Shrimp Thai-Style Cellophane Noodle Salad

Beefalo is a cross breed between the buffalo and beef cow. Like buffalo, beefalo is lower in fat and stronger in flavor than beef. When cooking this delicacy with dry heat, serve it rare to medium-rare. Because beefalo is low in fat, excess cooking causes it to become tough, stringy, and dry.

Servings: 24   Serving Size: 1 main course salad
Yield: 24 main course salads

*Noodles, cellophane	3 lb	Rich white chicken stock (see page 7)	2 qt
Vegetable cooking spray	—		
Garlic, minced	2 oz	Shrimp, medium, shelled, deveined	2 lb
Beefalo, buffalo, or beef tenderloin, trimmed of fat and silverskin, matchstick strips	3 lb	Lettuce, green leaf, leaves	4 lb
		Tomatoes, ripe, thin slices	4 lb
Shallots or onions, thin slices, crosswise	1 lb	Asian-inspired lime dressing (see page 305)	4 recipes
†Lemongrass, minced	1 oz	Cilantro, minced	½ oz
Chilies, fresh, serrano or other hot green, seeds and membranes removed, minced	8 or to taste		

1. In a container, soak the cellophane noodles in cold water for 30 minutes. Drain well; cut into 3-in. lengths.
2. Meanwhile, coat a nonstick skillet with cooking spray. Place over medium-high heat. Add the garlic. Stir-fry until light brown.
3. Add the beefalo, shallots, lemongrass, and chilies. Stir-fry until the beefalo is rare to medium-rare. Set aside.
4. Add the stock to a wok or sauce pot; heat to a boil. Add the shrimp; Cook until they turn pink, or about 2 minutes. Add the noodles and beefalo mixture. Cook until the noodles are somewhat soft and the mixture heated through, or about 3 minutes.
5. To serve, layer the lettuce leaves on dinner plates; surround with tomato slices; top

with the noodle mixture; accompany with or pour the dressing over and garnish with the minced cilantro.

*Cellophane noodles, also called transparent vermicelli and bean threads, are translucent threads (not really noodles) made from the starch of green mung beans. Substitute vermicelli noodles if not available. Cellophane noodles are available in food stores offering Chinese and other Asian ingredients.

†Lemongrass is an herb with long thin, gray-green leaves and a green onionlike base used in Thai and Vietnamese cooking. It has a sour lemon flavor and fragrance. Lemongrass is available in food stores offering Southeast Asian ingredients.

Servings	Calories	Protein (g) (%)	Fat (g) (%)	Cholesterol (mg)	Carbohydrates (g) (%)	Fiber (g)	Sodium (mg)
1	505	30.9 (24%)	4.9 (9%)	97.7	85.1 (67%)	3.9	373

Cashew Chicken Salad with Grapes and Water Chestnuts

Americans are making salads their main course choice more often when dining out. For a lighter and certainly delicious version of the long-time favored chicken salad, extend it with green onions, grapes, and water chestnuts and coat it with an oil-free mayonnaise-style dressing, or for an east meets west touch, use a nonfat creamy curry dressing. Garnished with a sprinkle of roasted cashew bits, it's hard to believe healthy dishes can look and taste so good.

Servings: 24   *Serving Size: 1 c*
Yield: 1½ gal + 1 pt

Chicken breast meat, skinless, cooked without salt or fat, large dice	3 lb cooked	Green onions, white only, thin slices	12 oz
Grapes, green, seedless, lengthwise halves	1½ lb	Oil-free mayonnaise-like dressing (see page 311) or nonfat creamy curry dressing (see page 310)	2½ c
Celery, small dice	1 lb	Lettuce, red leaf, leaves	1 lb (24)
Water chestnuts, thin slices, drained, rinsed with water	1 lb drained	Cashews, unsalted, toasted without fat, chopped	5½ oz

1. Mix all the ingredients except the lettuce leaves and cashews in a bowl.
2. Refrigerate until chilled, or about 2 hours. Place the lettuce leaves on chilled plates. Spoon the salad over. Serve garnished with the cashews sprinkled over.

Servings	Calories	Protein (g) (%)	Fat (g) (%)	Cholesterol (mg)	Carbohydrates (g) (%)	Fiber (g)	Sodium (mg)
1	190	20.6 (43%)	6.4 (30%)	72.4	13.5 (28%)	2.2	76.5

Hot Potato, Sausage, and Broccoli Salad

In this salad, bright green, fresh broccoli spears are gently tossed with steamed, new, baby red-skinned potatoes, and mouth-watering, browned, extra-lean, pork sausage balls hinting of sage, thyme, and marjoram. Slightly tart, freshly squeezed lime and vegetable dressing is the ideal finishing touch for this salad.

Servings: 24   *Serving Size: 1⅛ pt*
Yield: 3 gal + 1½ qt

Vegetable cooking spray	—	Potatoes, new, red, very small, baby	6 lb
Ground pork, extra lean	3 lb	Broccoli, florets and stalks cut in julienne strips	6 lb
Sage, marjoram, thyme, dried	½ t each		
Salt	To taste	Freshly squeezed lime and vegetable dressing (see page 309)	1 recipe
Pepper, freshly ground	To taste		
Bread crumbs, whole wheat, fresh	6 oz		
Egg whites, large	6 (7½ oz)		

1. In a mixing bowl, mix the ground pork with the seasonings, bread crumbs, and egg whites; portion into 96 (½-oz) small balls. Place on a sheet pan coated with cooking spray.
2. Place in a 350°F (175°C) oven; bake, turning once or twice for uniform cooking, until light brown on the exterior and no longer pink in the center, or about 10 minutes. Do not overcook or the meatballs will become dry. The meatballs can be sauteed in a nonstick skillet also. When cooked, place on a paper towel with a slotted spoon; pat to remove excess fat, likely none; set aside.
3. Steam the potatoes or cook in unsalted boiling water until soft. Drain; cut each into bite size pieces or four wedges.
4. Steam the broccoli or cook in unsalted, boiling water until crisp-tender. Refresh in cold water. Drain.
5. At service, in a nonstick skillet, reheat the meat balls, potatoes, and broccoli in batches, turning gently, until heated through. Sprinkle with salt and pepper to taste. Serve accompanied by or tossed with freshly squeezed lime and vegetable dressing or low-fat dressing of choice.

Servings	Calories	Protein (g) (%)	Fat (g) (%)	Cholesterol (mg)	Carbohydrates (g) (%)	Fiber (g)	Sodium (mg)
1	313	19.3 (24%)	9.9 (28%)	40.1	39.7 (49%)	7.0	161

Oriental Chicken Salad with Orange-Pineapple Soy Dressing

This refreshing and colorful chicken salad is great during the summer months. Shredded napa cabbage and romaine lettuce are gently tossed with julienne strips of chicken breast meat, carrots, snow peas, red and yellow bell peppers, and enoki mushrooms. The medley is lightly coated with a tasty dressing prepared by seasoning a blend of orange and pineapple juices, low-sodium soy sauce, and a splash of sesame oil with ginger and garlic. Diners will appreciate its exotic charm.

Servings: 24 *Serving Size: 3⅓ c*
Yield: 5 gal

*Napa cabbage	5 lb as purchased (4 heads)	Snow peas, trimmed, strings removed, matchstick strips	1 lb
		Carrots, matchstick strips	1 lb
Chicken breast meat, skinless, cooked without fat or salt, matchstick strips	5 lb cooked	Bell peppers, red and yellow, matchstick strips	1 lb each
		Mushrooms, enoki, washed	½ lb
Lettuce, romaine, matchstick strips	1¼ lb (2 heads)	Orange-pineapple soy salad dressing (see page 312)	2 recipes
		Sesame seeds, toasted without fat	1 oz

1. Select 24 nice leaves from the napa cabbage; set aside. Shred the remaining cabbage.
2. Combine the shredded cabbage and ingredients through the mushrooms with the salad dressing.
3. Arrange the reserved cabbage leaves on chilled dinner plates. Mound the salad in the center. Serve sprinkled with the toasted sesame seeds.

*Napa cabbage is also known as Chinese cabbage, Chinese celery cabbage, and Peking cabbage.

Servings	Calories	Protein (g) (%)	Fat (g) (%)	Cholesterol (mg)	Carbohydrates (g) (%)	Fiber (g)	Sodium (mg)
1	322	34 (41%)	11.4 (31%)	80.3	22.2 (27%)	3.8	417

VEGETABLE AND GRAIN SALADS

Broccoli Marinated in Rice Wine Vinaigrette

One half cup of broccoli has as much vitamin C as a half cup of orange juice and more calcium than a half cup of cottage cheese. At only 24 calories per raw cup, broccoli is also a good source of beta-carotene (vitamin A), iron, and potassium. Marinated in rice wine vinaigrette, it makes a tasty salad.

Servings: 24   *Serving Size: 1 c*
Yield: 1½ gal

Broccoli, florets, stalks		**Sesame seeds**	½ oz
reserved for another use	3 lb		
Rice wine vinaigrette (see page 316)	1 recipe		

1. Steam or blanch the broccoli in boiling water until barely crisp-tender, or about 2–3 minutes. Refresh in cold water; drain; place in a shallow container. This salad can also be made with raw broccoli if desired. The blanching process brightens the color of the broccoli and lightly tenderizes it.
2. Pour the vinaigrette over the broccoli; mix until well coated. Cover; refrigerate; stir to coat, occasionally, for 1–2 hours.
3. Toast the sesame seeds in a small nonstick skillet over medium-low heat, stirring until golden, or about 3 minutes.
4. Serve the broccoli sprinkled with the sesame seeds as a salad or vegetable garnish with a sandwich.

Servings	Calories	Protein (g) (%)	Fat (g) (%)	Cholesterol (mg)	Carbohydrates (g) (%)	Fiber (g)	Sodium (mg)
1	29	2.0 (23%)	1.0 (28%)	0	4.3 (49%)	1.7	75.4

Bulgur Salad Peppered with Garden Vegetables

While bulgur and cracked wheat are often thought to be one and the same, they aren't. Bulgur is wheat that has been steamed, dried, and then crushed into coarse, medium, or fine grinds. Cracked wheat, on the other hand, is uncooked wheat that has been dried and then coarsely milled. Choose medium grind bulgur for cooked side dishes. Coarse grind bulgur with its rice-like texture is well suited for pilafs and stuffings, while fine grind bulgur is preferred for dessert and bread recipes.

Servings: 24   *Serving Size: $\frac{2}{3}$ c*
Yield: 1 gal

Ingredient	Amount	Ingredient	Amount
Bulgur, medium grind	1 lb	Oil, walnut	$\frac{1}{4}$ c
Rich white chicken stock (see page 7), boiling	1½ qt	Pineapple juice concentrate, unsweetened	2 T
Peppers, green, bell, washed	12 oz as purchased	Garlic, minced	3 T
		Mint leaves, coarsely chopped	3 oz
*Tomatoes, plum, medium dice	1¼ lb	Parsley, Italian (flat leaf), coarsely chopped	3 oz
Summer squash, yellow or zucchini, washed, medium dice	12 oz	Salt	To taste
		Pepper, freshly ground	To taste
Cucumbers, young, unwaxed or peeled, medium dice	6 oz	Lettuce, red leaf, leaves	1 lb (24)
Onion, red, minced	6 oz	Nasturtium flowers or leaves or mint leaves	For garnish
Lime juice, freshly squeezed	1 c		

1. Place the bulgur in a heat-proof container. Pour the boiling stock over. Cover and let stand 40 minutes or longer. Strain any excess liquid from the bulgur. For best results, line a colander with cheesecloth. Drain the bulgur; twist the cheesecloth around the bulgur, squeezing to extract any remaining liquid. Place in a mixing/storage container.
2. Roast, grill, or broil the bell peppers.† Rub off the charred skin; rinse under cold water removing any remaining blackened skin. Cut in half; remove the core, membrane, and seeds; cut into medium dice.
3. Add the bell peppers, tomatoes, and ingredients through the black pepper to the bulgur. Toss gently to mix. Adjust the seasonings if necessary. Cover; refrigerate for at

least 2 hours for the flavors to come out. Serve on lettuce liners. Garnish with nasturtium flowers or leaves or mint leaves.

*Plum tomatoes are also known as roma tomatoes, Italian tomatoes, and paste tomatoes. These thick, meaty textured tomatoes with few seeds can be replaced with ripe, flavorful, slicing tomatoes when not available.

†See page 493 for bell pepper roasting directions.

Servings	Calories	Protein (g) (%)	Fat (g) (%)	Cholesterol (mg)	Carbohydrates (g) (%)	Fiber (g)	Sodium (mg)
1	121	4.7 (14%)	3.2 (22%)	0	20.7 (64%)	4.9	28.3

Cucumbers and Onions Marinated in Sweet and Sour Dill Dressing

Typically, refined sugar would provide the sweetness in a salad such as this one. In this recipe, unsweetened apple juice concentrate serves this purpose. At the same time, it rounds out the dressing with a light apple flavor.

Servings: 24   *Serving Size: ½ c salad + ½ oz yogurt*
Yield: 3 qt salad + 12 oz yogurt

Vinegar, cider	1 pt + 1½ c	Cucumbers, young, unwaxed or peeled, thin slices	5 lb
Apple juice concentrate, unsweetened	2¼ c	Onions, thin rings	12 oz
Dillweed, minced or dried	¼ c or 1 T + 1 t	Lettuce, leaves, red leaf	1 lb (24)
		Yogurt, plain, nonfat	12 oz
		Dillweed, sprigs	For
Salt	To taste		garnish
Pepper, freshly ground	To taste		

1. Combine the vinegar, juice concentrate, dill, and salt and pepper to taste in a bowl; mix well.
2. Place the cucumbers and onions in a nonreactive storage container. Pour the marinade over. Mix to coat. Cover; marinate refrigerated for at least 6 hours.
3. Drain the cucumbers and onions in a colander. Discard the marinade.
4. Arrange the lettuce leaves on chilled salad plates. Spoon the cucumber salad over. Garnish with a dollop of yogurt and a sprig of dill.

Servings	Calories	Protein (g) (%)	Fat (g) (%)	Cholesterol (mg)	Carbohydrates (g) (%)	Fiber (g)	Sodium (mg)
1	78	2.0 (9%)	0.3 (3%)	0.3	18.5 (87%)	1.4	21.8

Variation

Toss the drained cucumbers with the yogurt and mix before serving.

Diced Cucumber, Red Onion, and Tomato Salad

This vegetable mixture makes an excellent light and flavorful side salad. Freshly squeezed lemon juice adds zing to the low-calorie medley. Offer it with spicy main course dishes such as grilled chicken drumsticks tandoori-style (see page 135).

Servings: 24　　　*Serving Size: $\frac{2}{3}$ c*
Yield: 1 gal

Cucumbers, peeled, small dice	4 lb	Cilantro, minced	1 oz
Onion, red, minced	1 lb	Paprika, sweet, Hungarian	1 t
Tomatoes, small dice	1 lb	Salt	To taste
Lemon juice, freshly squeezed	$\frac{3}{4}$ c	Pepper, freshly ground	To taste

1. Combine all the ingredients in a bowl or storage container, mix. Refrigerate until chilled.
2. Serve on chilled plates lined with salad leaves.

Servings	Calories	Protein (g) (%)	Fat (g) (%)	Cholesterol (mg)	Carbohydrates (g) (%)	Fiber (g)	Sodium (mg)
1	23	1.0 (15%)	0.2 (8%)	0	5.1 (77%)	1.3	4.0

Green Salad Tossed with Vegetables and Dressed with Saffron and Basil Orange Vinaigrette

In a meal with many courses, the salad may follow the main course, serving as a cleanser before the cheese course or between two wines. In a simpler meal, it may be the introductory course. This green salad is a light and harmonious combination of delicate greens and colorful vegetables, appropriate as a meal starter or an interlude between two courses.

Servings: 24   *Serving Size: 1⅓ c*
Yield: 2 gal lightly packed

Boston lettuce, bite-sized pieces, washed	3 lb (4 heads)	Summer squash, washed, thin slices	1¼ lb
Arugula, bite-sized pieces, washed	1¼ lb	Onion, red, thin slices	1 lb
		Tomato, wedges	2 lb
Bell peppers, green and red, matchstick strips	2 lb each	Saffron and basil orange vinaigrette dressing (see page 317)	2 qt
Zucchini, washed, thin slices	1¼ lb	Parsley, minced	½ c

1. In a storage container, gently mix the ingredients through the red onion.
2. At service, add the tomatoes and gently toss with the dressing. Serve sprinkled with the parsley.

Servings	Calories	Protein (g) (%)	Fat (g) (%)	Cholesterol (mg)	Carbohydrates (g) (%)	Fiber (g)	Sodium (mg)
1	152	4.0 (10%)	6.4 (34%)	0	23.5 (56%)	4.9	32.4

Grilled Summer Vegetable Salad

This colorful summer salad speaks for itself. Fresh, garden vegetables are grilled until tender and drizzled with balsamic-rice vinegar dressing.

Servings: 24   *Serving Size: 1¼ c*
Yield: 1⅞ gal

Balsamic-rice vinegar dressing (see page 306)	1 recipe	Bell pepper, red, quarters	4 lb as purchased (12)
Olive oil, extra-virgin	2 T		
Corn on the cob, husked	12 small ears	Belgian endive, halves	4 lb as purchased (12)
Zucchini, small, lengthwise halves	4 lb as purchased (12)	Summer squash, yellow, small, lengthwise halves	3 lb as purchased (12)
Eggplant, medium, ¼-in. thick rounds	4 lb as purchased (4)	Onions, red, ½-in. thick slices	1 lb

1. In a bowl, mix the vinegar dressing with the olive oil until well blended. Set aside.
2. Place the vegetables cut side down on an oiled grill over medium heat. Cook 5 minutes. Turn the vegetables over; grill until tender, or about 5 minutes longer. Cut each ear of corn into sixths and the onion slices into quarters. Present the vegetables attractively on dinner plates. Serve drizzled with the balsamic-rice vinegar dressing.

Servings	Calories	Protein (g) (%)	Fat (g) (%)	Cholesterol (mg)	Carbohydrates (g) (%)	Fiber (g)	Sodium (mg)
1	135	5.6 (14%)	2 (12%)	0	29.6 (74%)	7.8	32.5

Jicama and Orange Salad Splashed with Freshly Squeezed Lime Juice and a Sprinkle of Chili Powder

Jicama is a root vegetable shaped like a deformed turnip with a thin, patchy, light brown skin; juicy, crisp, sweet, white flesh; and the texture of a raw potato. In this salad, a mixture of oranges, jicama, and other vegetables is flavored with fresh lime juice and chili powder.

Servings: 24 *Serving Size: $\frac{7}{8}$ c*
Yield: $1\frac{1}{4}$ gal + 1 c

*Jicama, peeled, small cubes	$2\frac{1}{2}$ lb	Lime juice, freshly squeezed	1 c
Orange, peeled, small cubes	3 lb	Chili powder	1 T
Cucumber, peeled, thin slices	12 oz	Boston lettuce leaves	12 oz
Peppers, bell, green, small dice	1 lb		(24)
Onions, red, thin slices	1 lb		

1. Combine the first seven ingredients in a bowl; mix together. Cover; refrigerate until chilled.
2. To serve, line chilled salad plates with 1 lettuce leaf each. Top with the salad mixture.

*Jicama is available in stores offering Mexican food ingredients.

Servings	Calories	Protein (g) (%)	Fat (g) (%)	Cholesterol (mg)	Carbohydrates (g) (%)	Fiber (g)	Sodium (mg)
1	66	1.9 (11%)	0.4 (5%)	0	15.4 (85%)	4.1	8.4

Potato, Kidney Bean, and Bell Pepper Salad in Oil-Free Vinaigrette

The varied shapes, contrasting textures, rainbow of colors, and balance of flavors in this potato and kidney bean salad make it a pleasure to the eye and palate. It works well as a separate course salad, sandwich accompaniment, or side dish with meat, fish, or poultry selections.

Servings: 24   **Serving Size: $\frac{5}{8}$ c**
Yield: $1\frac{1}{4}$ gal

Potatoes, new, very small, baby, red-skinned	3 lb	Peppers, bell, red, green, yellow, matchstick strips	8 oz each
Kidney beans, canned with 50% less salt, drained, rinsed with water or dried, cooked without salt	1 lb canned or cooked, drained or 7 oz dried	Onions, thin slices	8 oz
		Vegetable-thickened oil-free vinaigrette (see page 319), hot	1 recipe

1. Steam the potatoes or boil in unsalted water until soft, or about 10–15 minutes. Drain; place on a sheet tray to cool.
2. When cool, cut the potatoes into quarters or bite-sized pieces.
3. In a bowl, combine the potatoes, kidney beans, bell peppers, and sliced onions.
4. Pour the dressing over the vegetables; toss to coat. Serve at room temperature or chilled.

Servings	Calories	Protein (g) (%)	Fat (g) (%)	Cholesterol (mg)	Carbohydrates (g) (%)	Fiber (g)	Sodium (mg)
1	91	3.6 (15%)	0.3 (2%)	0	19.7 (82%)	3.7	10.8

Quinoa Salad Decorated with Pineapple, Mandarin Oranges, and Water Chestnuts

The U.S. Department of Agriculture's Food Guide Pyramid recommends Americans consume 6–11 servings of grains each day. To help diners meet this need, offer selections prepared from long-time favorites as well as less familiar grains at every course of the meal. In this recipe, quinoa (keen-wah), a pale, yellowish, mini grain that looks like a cross between mustard and millet, is transformed into a charming salad by combining it with pineapple cubes, mandarin oranges, and water chestnuts and tossing in a light orange-flavored dressing. Since quinoa has only begun to appear in America recently, look for it at natural food stores or gourmet groceries.

Servings: 24   Serving Size: $\frac{5}{8}$ c
Yield: $1\frac{1}{4}$ gal

Quinoa, rinsed in cold water	$1\frac{1}{2}$ lb as purchased	Water chestnuts, thin slices, canned, drained, rinsed in water	8 oz drained
Flavorful vegetable stock (see page 2) or rich white chicken stock (see page 7), boiling	2 qt	Green onions, white and 2 in. green, thin slices	6 oz
*Pineapple, cubes, fresh or canned, without sugar	1 lb	Orange zest, finely grated	2 T
		Mint leaves, minced	1 oz
Mandarin oranges, sections, fresh or canned, without sugar	1 lb	Orange pineapple soy salad dressing (see page 312)	$1\frac{1}{2}$ pt

1. Place the quinoa in a sauce pot over medium-high heat; stir until it takes on a light golden hue, or 2 to 3 minutes.
2. Add the stock slowly to prevent splashing, stirring; heat to a boil; reduce the heat to low. Simmer covered until the liquid is absorbed and the quinoa looks transparent and is tender, or 12 to 15 minutes.
3. Place the quinoa on a sheet pan to cool.
4. Combine the quinoa with the remaining ingredients in a serving container; toss gently to mix thoroughly. Serve chilled as a salad or at room temperature as an accompani-

ment with roasted game birds, such as pheasant or quail, or other poultry, perhaps roasted turkey or spit-roasted chicken on the rotisserie (see page 139).

*See page 492 for fresh pineapple peeling and cubing directions.

Servings	Calories	Protein (g) (%)	Fat (g) (%)	Cholesterol (mg)	Carbohydrates (g) (%)	Fiber (g)	Sodium (mg)
1	171	4.7 (11%)	4.1 (21%)	0	30.3 (68%)	1.2	123

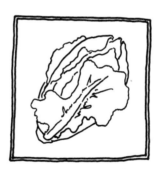

Red Beets Pickled German-Style

In Germany, root vegetables such as beets, carrots, turnips, and parsnips are as popular as green beans and peas in the United States. Like many vegetable salads of German origin, the red beets in this recipe are coated with a tart vinegar dressing. Offer it German-style along with meat and hot vegetables rather than as a first course or following the main course.

Serving: 24 Serving Size: ½ c
Yield: 3 qt

Beets, cooked without salt or canned, drained, rinsed in cold water, thin slices	4½ lb	Cloves, whole	1 t
		Allspice, whole	1 t
		Bay leaves	2
Onion, grated	6 oz	Cinnamon sticks	2
Vinegar, red wine	1 pt	Salt	To taste
Apple or fruit juice concentrate, unsweetened	½ c	Pepper, freshly ground	To taste

1. Place the beets and onions in a nonreactive container.
2. In a saucepan, add the vinegar and remaining seven ingredients. The whole spices can be placed in a sachet for easy removal but flavor extraction will be enhanced if allowed to mix in the marinade. Heat to a boil; reduce the heat to low. Simmer for 5 minutes.
3. Pour the marinade over the beets. Cover; refrigerate for at least 24 hours, stirring gently every so often. Drain to serve. Remove the bay leaves and whole spices if desired. Discard. Season with salt and pepper to taste. Offer German-style along with the main course selection. Store refrigerated in the liquid up to 1 month.

Servings	Calories	Protein (g) (%)	Fat (g) (%)	Cholesterol (mg)	Carbohydrates (g) (%)	Fiber (g)	Sodium (mg)
1	42	1.5 (13%)	0.2 (3%)	0	9.7 (84%)	2.8	66.9

Shredded Cabbage with Corn and Bell Pepper Tossed in Pineapple Tofu Dressing

In this salad, shredded cabbage takes on a new dimension by combining with grilled corn kernels, diced, green, bell peppers, sliced green onions, and grated carrots. A creamy, tofu, mayonnaise-like dressing hinting of pineapple rounds out the medley nicely.

Servings: 24   *Serving Size: ⅔ c*
Yield: 1 gal

Cabbage, shredded	2 lb	Green onion, white and 1-in.	
Carrot, washed, shredded	6 oz	green, thin slices	4 oz
Pepper, green, bell, small dice	8 oz	Pineapple tofu dressing (see	
Corn kernels, fresh, grilled		page 313)	1 recipe
(see page 201) or frozen,			
blanched	8 oz		

1. Place all the ingredients in a bowl; toss gently until the vegetables are well mixed and moistened with the dressing.
2. Serve this colorful salad as an appetizer course or vegetable dish along with a sandwich or main course meat, seafood, or poultry item. It's a natural with either Cajun turkey-tofu burgers (see page 110) or crispy baked mustard chicken breasts (see page 134).

Servings	Calories	Protein (g) (%)	Fat (g) (%)	Cholesterol (mg)	Carbohydrates (g) (%)	Fiber (g)	Sodium (mg)
1	43	2.3 (20%)	0.8 (16%)	0	7.5 (64%)	1.5	24.7

Soba Noodle Salad Tossed with Red and Yellow Bell Peppers, Snow Peas, Carrots, Mushrooms, and Water Chestnuts

The primary ingredient in this salad is soba noodles, sand-colored, spaghetti-like noodles of medium thickness made from buckwheat and wheat flours. When combined with red and yellow bell pepper strips, sliced mushrooms, carrots, snow peas, and water chestnuts, and toasted slivered almonds and tossed with a sesame-flavored ginger soy dressing, the fiber-, vitamin-, and mineral-rich medley becomes a flavorful and textural sensation.

Servings: 24　　　　*Serving Size: 1 c*
Yield: 1½ gal

*Soba noodles, dry	1½ lb	Mushrooms, thin slices	1 lb
Bell peppers, red and yellow, matchstick strips	1 lb each	Green onions, white and 1-in. green, thin slices	8 oz
Water chestnuts, thin slices, canned, drained, rinsed in water	1 lb drained	Sesame-flavored ginger soy dressing (see page 318)	2 qt
		Almonds, slivered, toasted without fat	6 oz
Carrots, thin diagonal slices	1 lb		
Snow peas, trimmed, strings removed, blanched to set color, refreshed in cold water, drained	1 lb		

1. In a sauce pot, heat 1½ gal of water to a boil. Add the soba noodles; stir to separate. Boil, stirring occasionally until tender, or about 5 minutes.
2. Drain the noodles; refresh in cold water; drain. Pat dry.
3. In a serving container, gently toss the red and yellow bell peppers and next six ingredients with the noodles to thoroughly mix. Serve, sprinkled with the almonds.

*Soba noodles are available at stores offering Japanese food ingredients.

Servings	Calories	Protein (g) (%)	Fat (g) (%)	Cholesterol (mg)	Carbohydrates (g) (%)	Fiber (g)	Sodium (mg)
1	216	8.4 (14%)	6.6 (26%)	0	34.9 (60%)	4.6	398

Spinach and Red Leaf Lettuce Salad Dressed with Walnut Vinaigrette*

Spinach is a good source of vitamins and minerals including vitamin C, B vitamins, beta-carotene (vitamin A value), iron, and calcium. For a tasty, low-fat salad, offer this mixture of spinach and red leaf lettuce tossed with ripe tomato chunks, sliced button mushrooms, crisp water chestnuts, and garbanzo beans, coated in a light, walnut-flavored vinaigrette dressing and garnished with thinly sliced red onion rings.

Servings: 24   *Serving Size: ½ c*
Yield: 3 qt

Spinach, leaves, bite-sized pieces, washed	12 oz	Mushrooms, thin slices	6 oz
Lettuce, red leaf, bite-sized pieces, washed	8 oz	Water chestnuts, thin slices, canned, drained, rinsed in water	4 oz
Garbanzo beans, dried, cooked without salt or canned, drained, rinsed in water	8 oz cooked or canned, drained	Tomatoes, small dice	1 lb + 2 oz
		Walnut-flavored vinaigrette dressing (see page 320)	1 recipe
		Onion, red, very thin rings	4 oz

1. Combine the first five ingredients in a large bowl or storage container; toss gently to mix. At service, toss gently with the tomatoes and dressing until the vegetables are moistened.
2. Serve on chilled plates, garnished with the red onion rings.

*Adapted from a recipe by Chris Cuffari.

Servings	Calories	Protein (g) (%)	Fat (g) (%)	Cholesterol (mg)	Carbohydrates (g) (%)	Fiber (g)	Sodium (mg)
1	68	2.0 (11%)	2.5 (31%)	0	10.6 (58%)	2.0	16.3

Vegetable Slaw Coated in Ranch-Style Dressing

This vegetable slaw isn't just any cabbage salad. It's a mixture of shredded cabbage garnished with diced bell peppers and tomatoes, corn kernels, and minced red onion. The colorful medley is coated in a creamy, ranch-style dressing prepared from low-fat dairy products and fresh herbs.

Servings: 24 Serving Size: 1 c
Yield: 1½ gal

Green cabbage, shredded	3 lb	Onion, red, minced	8 oz
Bell peppers, green, small dice	1 lb	Tomatoes, small dice	1 lb
Corn kernels, fresh or frozen, cooked without salt	8 oz	Ranch-style dressing (see page 314)	1 qt

1. Combine the cabbage, bell peppers, corn, and onions in a storage container. Chill.
2. At service, add the tomatoes and ranch-style dressing; gently toss until well mixed and moistened with the dressing. Serve as a salad, side dish, or sandwich topping with selections such as Cajun turkey-tofu burgers (see page 110) or extra-lean ground beef burgers seasoned with onions, bell peppers, and Worcestershire (see page 69).

Servings	Calories	Protein (g) (%)	Fat (g) (%)	Cholesterol (mg)	Carbohydrates (g) (%)	Fiber (g)	Sodium (mg)
1	62	3.8 (22%)	1.7 (22%)	4.9	9.6 (56%)	2.1	48.4

FRUIT SALADS

Fresh Fruit Salad Tossed with Beets, Pomegranate Seeds, and Roasted Peanuts

One of Mexico's most popular salads is the Christmas Eve salad, a combination of fresh fruits and beets sprinkled with pomegranate seeds and chopped, roasted peanuts. It is traditionally eaten on Christmas Eve at midnight or following midnight mass when a special supper is served and gifts are opened. This is a light and healthy variation of this favorite.

Servings: 24   *Serving Size:* $1\frac{1}{8}$ c
Yield: $1\frac{1}{2}$ *gal* $+$ $1\frac{1}{2}$ *pt*

Vinegar, red wine	$\frac{1}{4}$ c + 2 T	§Pomegranate seeds	1 large pomegranate
Apple juice concentrate, unsweetened	$\frac{1}{4}$ c	Lettuce, leaves, red leaf	1 lb (24)
Pineapple juice concentrate, unsweetened	$\frac{1}{4}$ c	Beets, fresh, cooked without salt, peeled or canned, drained, rinsed in cold water, matchstick strips	$1\frac{1}{2}$ lb drained
*Pineapple, fresh or canned without sugar, large dice	3 lb		
†Oranges, peeled, sectioned	2 lb		
Banana, peeled thin slices	$1\frac{1}{2}$ lb		
‡Jicama, or tart apple, peeled, large dice	1 lb + 2 oz	Peanuts, dry roasted, unsalted, coarsely chopped	5 oz

1. In a small bowl, mix the wine vinegar and juice concentrates. Set aside.
2. In a large bowl or storage container, combine the pineapple, oranges, bananas, jicama, and pomegranate seeds. Pour the juice and vinegar syrup over; mix to coat. Refrigerate until chilled, or about 2 hours.
3. Line 24 chilled salad plates with lettuce leaves. Top with the salad mixture. Serve with the beets and peanuts sprinkled over.

*To cube a fresh pineapple, first remove the leaves by holding with one hand and twisting in the opposite direction with the other. Next, trim the top and cut a thin slice from the bottom so it sits level. Cutting in wide strips from top to bottom, remove the peel. Remove the eyes by cutting thin wedge-shaped grooves diagonally around the fruit following the pattern of the eyes. Remove the hard center core and cube.

†To section an orange, cut thin slices from each end so that it sits level. Cutting from top to bottom and following the shape of the fruit, remove the peel and white membrane. Working over a container to catch the juices, cut from the exterior of the fruit to the center between the fruit of one section and its membrane. Repeat on the other side of the same section. Continue until all the orange sections are removed. Remove any seeds from the sections.

‡Jicama is available at stores offering Mexican food ingredients. For more information, see page 505.

§Pomegranates are available August to December, reaching their peak in October. To remove the seeds from the pomegranate, cut off its crown end and cut into fourths. Place the pomegranate in a bowl; cover with cold water. Using your fingers, break the submerged pomegranate quarters apart and pull the seed clusters from the bitter membranes. The membranes and rinds will float to the top of the water; skim them off and discard. The seeds will sink to the bottom. Using a strainer, drain the water from the pomegranate seeds; pat dry with paper towels. The pomegranate seeds are now ready to use.

Servings	Calories	Protein (g) (%)	Fat (g) (%)	Cholesterol (mg)	Carbohydrates (g) (%)	Fiber (g)	Sodium (mg)
1	146	3.4 (9%)	3.5 (20%)	0	28.5 (71%)	4.4	27.1

Fresh Peaches and Grapes Waldorf-Style

Traditionally, Waldorf salad was associated with a mixture of apples, celery, and possibly walnuts, all well coated with mayonnaise. For a healthier, innovative approach, this salad is prepared with cubes of fresh peaches, grape halves, and crisp, diced celery. To minimize fat and calories without reducing flavor, the salad is coated with honey and lime-flavored tofu dressing and garnished with a small amount of toasted, chopped walnuts.

Servings: 24 **Serving Size:** $\frac{2}{3}$ c
Yield: 1 gal + 1 c

*Peaches, peeled, small dice	3 lb	Walnuts, chopped, toasted	
Grapes, green, seedless, halves	2 lb	without fat (divided)	4 oz
Celery, small dice	1½ lb	Lettuce, red leaf, leaves	1 lb (24)
Dressing:			
Honey, clover	2 T		
Lime juice, freshly			
squeezed	2 T		
Pineapple-flavored creamy			
tofu dressing (see page			
313)	1 c		

1. Combine the peaches, grapes, and celery in a bowl. Refrigerate until chilled.
2. In a small bowl, blend the honey and lime juice together until the honey is dissolved. Beat in the tofu dressing until well mixed.
3. Drain the peach mixture. Reserve the fruit juice for another use. At service, toss the peach mixture with half of the walnuts (2 oz) and the honey lime salad dressing. Serve on lettuce leaf-lined chilled plates garnished with the remaining walnuts.

*For peach peeling directions, see page 16.

Servings	Calories	Protein (g) (%)	Fat (g) (%)	Cholesterol (mg)	Carbohydrates (g) (%)	Fiber (g)	Sodium (mg)
1	100	2.1 (8%)	3.5 (28%)	0	17.7 (64%)	2.5	31.7

Malaysian-Inspired Tropical Fruit and Crisp Vegetable Salad

This salad is a variation of Malaysian Rojak, a favorite of street vendors throughout the Malaysian Peninsula and in Singapore. The combination of the crisp to tender and tart to sweet medley of fruits and vegetables is complemented by the sweet and salty flavors of a reduced-sodium soy sauce and fruit juice based dressing. Nutritionally, the salad is rich in vitamins, especially C and beta-carotene, a good source of fiber and minerals, and contains no cholesterol.

Servings: 24   *Serving Size:* $1\frac{1}{3}$ c
Yield: 2 gal

Peanuts, raw, shelled, skinned, coarsely chopped	4 oz	Lime juice, freshly squeezed	$\frac{1}{2}$ c
Sesame seeds	2 T	Orange juice, freshly squeezed	$\frac{1}{2}$ c
Shrimp broth (see page 8) or rich white chicken stock (see page 7)	$\frac{1}{2}$ c	*Pineapple, peeled, cored, large dice	4 lb
*Hoisin sauce	$\frac{1}{2}$ c	*Guava, ripe, peeled, seeded, large dice	2 lb
Soy sauce, low-sodium	$\frac{1}{2}$ c	*Mango, ripe, peeled, pitted, large dice	2 lb
Chilies, fresh, serrano, or other hot, green, seeds and membranes removed, minced	3	*Jicama, peeled, matchstick strips	2 lb
Garlic, minced	1 T	*Cucumbers, European or peeled slicing, thin slices	12 oz
Apple or fruit juice concentrate, unsweetened	2 T	*Star fruit (carambola), thin crosswise slices	12 oz

1. Place a nonstick skillet over medium-high heat until hot. Add the peanuts; cook, stirring constantly, until the nuts are brown, or about 3 minutes. Transfer to a small container.
2. Add the sesame seeds to the skillet. Place over medium-high heat; cook, stirring constantly, until brown, or about 2 minutes. Transfer to the container with the peanuts. Set aside.
3. In a saucepan, combine the shrimp broth (or chicken stock) and hoisin sauce. Heat to a boil, stirring. Reduce the heat to low. Simmer until slightly thickened, or about 5 minutes.
4. Add the soy sauce, chilies, garlic, and juice concentrate to the saucepan. Simmer, stirring about a minute. Remove from the heat; stir in the lime and orange juices.

5. In a serving container, combine the pineapple, guava, mango, jicama, cucumber, and star fruit. Pour the sauce over the fruits and vegetables; toss gently to mix.
6. Serve immediately sprinkled with the toasted peanuts and sesame seeds.

*Ingredient Information:

Hoisin Sauce is a sweet and spicy reddish-brown sauce made from a mixture of soybeans, garlic, chili peppers, and spices. It is available in stores offering Chinese food ingredients.

Pineapples do not continue to get sweeter once picked, only softer and juicier. Purchase them at the peak of ripeness and use immediately. Thumping or peeling a leaf from a pineapple's crown does not indicate its ripeness. Select large, plump, fresh-looking pineapples with fresh, green leaves and a sweet fragrance for best results. Pineapples are available year round but prices tend to be lowest from April through June. See page 492 for fresh pineapple peeling and dicing directions.

Guavas have a shocking pink to salmon-colored flesh and flowery flavor. Their seeds are edible. They are ripe when their shells give to gentle pressure and they have a fragrant aroma. They are available August through October.

Mangoes have a peach-like flavor and flowery aroma. When ripe, they give to gentle pressure. They are available sporadically January through September. See page 493 for mango peeling and dicing directions.

Jicamas have a crisp, slightly sweet flesh similar in texture and taste to water chestnuts. They can be stored in a cool (50°F, 10°C), dark, dry place for up to 3 weeks. Once cut, refrigerate. They are available at stores offering Mexican food ingredients.

European Cucumbers, unlike slicing cucumbers, are nearly seedless. Select firm, dark green ones with slender shapes.

Star Fruit, also known as carambolas, produce star shapes when sliced crosswise, as their nickname suggests. The yellow-gold colored fruit has an edible waxy skin and crisp flesh. Their flavor ranges from sweet-tart to quite sour. They are available September through February.

Servings	Calories	Protein (g) (%)	Fat (g) (%)	Cholesterol (mg)	Carbohydrates (g) (%)	Fiber (g)	Sodium (mg)
1	153	4.0 (10%)	3.6 (20%)	0	29.6 (71%)	5.8	398

Naturally Sweet Fresh Fruit Medley

The Center for Science in the Public Interest ranked fruits on the basis of nine nutrients and fiber content. Three of the four in this salad made the top ten: strawberries, kiwi fruit, and oranges. The other seven are papaya, cantaloupe, tangerine, mango, apricot, persimmon, and watermelon.

Servings: 24   *Serving Size: ½ c + 1⅓ T*
Yield: 3½ qt

Strawberries, ripe, washed, hulled, sliced	1⅓ lb	†Pineapple, fresh or canned without sugar, large dice	2 lb
Kiwi fruit, ripe, peeled, sliced	1⅓ lb	Lettuce, red leaf, leaves	1 lb
*Oranges, peeled, sectioned	1⅓ lb		(24)

1. In a mixing container, place all the fruits. Toss gently to mix.
2. Serve on chilled plates lined with lettuce leaves. Let diners enjoy the naturally sweet flavor of the fruits or coat them with creamy-peach poppy seed dressing (see page 308).

*See page 494 for orange sectioning directions.

†See page 492 for fresh pineapple peeling and dicing directions.

Servings	Calories	Protein (g) (%)	Fat (g) (%)	Cholesterol (mg)	Carbohydrates (g) (%)	Fiber (g)	Sodium (mg)
1	57	1.1 (6%)	0.4 (6%)	0	13.8 (87%)	2.8	3.6

Pineapple Cubes, Orange Sections, and Jicama Strips Glazed with Orange Pineapple Soy Dressing

Some of the simplest things in life are the most enjoyable. This salad is a good example. Cubes of ripe, sweet pineapple are tossed with juicy sections of orange and crisp strips of jicama, all drizzled with a light soy sauce dressing.

Servings: 24　　　*Serving Size: 1 c*
Yield: 1½ gal

*Pineapple, large dice, fresh or canned without sugar	3 lb	Orange pineapple soy salad dressing (see page 312)	1 pt
†Oranges, peeled, sectioned	2½ lb	Lettuce, red leaf, leaves	1 lb (24)
‡Jicama, peeled, matchstick strips	2 lb		

1. Gently toss the pineapple, orange sections, and jicama with the dressing.
2. Serve on chilled plates lined with red leaf lettuce leaves.

*See page 492 for fresh pineapple peeling and dicing directions.

†See page 494 for orange peeling and sectioning directions.

‡Jicama is available at stores offering Mexican food ingredients. For more information, see page 505.

Servings	Calories	Protein (g) (%)	Fat (g) (%)	Cholesterol (mg)	Carbohydrates (g) (%)	Fiber (g)	Sodium (mg)
1	92	1.7 (7%)	2.0 (18%)	0	18.8 (75%)	3.4	75.6

OILS AND VINEGARS

Basil and Garlic Scented Extra-Virgin Olive Oil

The possibilities for flavoring oils are endless, ranging from fruits and spices to herbs, alone or in combinations. In the case of this basil and garlic scented extra-virgin olive oil, the basil and garlic marry well with the olive oil. However, since the objective is usually to taste the flavoring ingredients, bland-flavored oils like safflower, corn, sunflower, soybean, grapeseed, cottonseed, or canola are recommended as bases for most flavored oils.

Servings: 24   *Serving Size: 2⅔ T*
Yield: 1 qt

Basil leaves, washed	3 oz	Basil, sprigs, washed	As needed
Garlic, minced	2 oz		
*Oil, olive, extra-virgin, cold-pressed (divided)	1 qt	Garlic, cloves, peeled	As needed

1. Blanch the basil leaves in boiling water for 10 seconds; drain. Shock in cold water; drain; pat dry.
2. In a blender, puree the basil leaves and minced garlic with ½ c of the oil to form a paste. Place the basil paste in a jar or other covered container; add the olive oil; shake or whip to mix well. Let stand 30 minutes. Refrigerate 24 hours.
3. Filter through a paper coffee filter or china cap lined with cheesecloth. Discard the basil-garlic paste. Pour into a clean, airtight container or serving bottles. Add 1 sprig of fresh basil and a clove of peeled garlic to garnish each serving container. Store tightly covered, refrigerated. Serve as a condiment or use as a flavoring agent in dishes such as grilled portobello mushrooms glazed with herb marinade (see page 343).

Servings	Calories	Protein (g) (%)	Fat (g) (%)	Cholesterol (mg)	Carbohydrates (g) (%)	Fiber (g)	Sodium (mg)
1	323	0.2 (< 1%)	36 (99%)	0	0.9 (1%)	0.3	0.6

Variations

Chervil-Scented Canola Oil or Other Tender Herb-Scented Oil: Substitute 3 oz of tender herbs, such as chervil, cilantro, parsley, or tarragon, for the basil and garlic, alone or in combinations. Replace the olive oil with a bland-flavored oil, such as canola, corn, cottonseed, grapeseed, safflower, soybean, or sunflower.

*Olive oils are graded on the basis of their acidity. Cold-pressed or those pressed cold from fresh, ripe fruit are the best. They are naturally low in acid. Extra-virgin olive oil, generally the most expensive and considered the most desirable and fruitiest of the olive oils, is from the first pressing of cold-pressed olives. It is a maximum of 1% acid. While its color can range from pale, clear yellow to bright green, usually the deeper the color, the more intense its olive flavor. Lesser quality olive oil is extracted from subsequent pressings using heat and chemical solvents. It tends to be paler in both color and flavor.

Orange- and Ginger-Flavored Safflower Oil

Flavored oils are delicious, cholesterol-free alternatives to butter-rich sauces. They can be used to dress a wide variety of dishes but are especially nice tossed with steamed vegetables, brushed lightly over grilled meat, poultry, and seafood selections, or served as accompaniments to warm whole grain breads and rolls.

Servings: 24 *Serving Size: 2⅔ T*
Yield: 1 qt

Orange zest, finely grated	1½ oz (¼ c + 2 T)	Orange zest, strips	As needed
Gingerroot, finely grated or minced	1 oz	Gingerroot, peeled, thin slices	As needed
Safflower, sunflower, soybean, canola, corn, grapeseed, cottonseed, or other bland oil	1 qt		

1. Combine the finely grated orange zest, finely grated gingerroot, and oil in a jar or other covered container. Shake or whip well to blend. Stand at room temperature for 30 minutes.
2. Refrigerate for 48 hours. Strain through a paper coffee filter or china cap lined with cheesecloth; discard the orange zest and gingerroot.
3. Pour into a clean, airtight container or serving bottles. Add a strip of orange zest and a slice of gingerroot to garnish each serving container. Store tightly covered, refrigerated. Serve as a condiment or use as a flavoring agent.

Servings	Calories	Protein (g) (%)	Fat (g) (%)	Cholesterol (mg)	Carbohydrates (g) (%)	Fiber (g)	Sodium (mg)
I	323	< 0.1 (< 1%)	36.3 (99%)	0	0.6 (1%)	0.1	0.2

Variations

Garlic-Flavored Oil: Substitute 2 oz of minced garlic for the grated orange zest and gingerroot and whole, peeled garlic cloves for the zest strips and ginger slices.

Herb-Flavored Oil: Substitute 3 oz of strong herbs, such as oregano, rosemary, sage, or thyme, alone or in combinations, for the grated orange zest and gingerroot and herb sprigs for the zest strips and ginger slices.

Horseradish-Flavored Oil: Substitute 2 oz of grated fresh horseradish for the grated orange zest and gingerroot and thin slices of peeled horseradish for the zest strips and ginger slices.

Shallot-Flavored Oil: Substitute 2 oz of minced shallots for the grated orange zest and gingerroot and peeled shallots for the zest strips and ginger slices.

Raspberry-Infused White Wine Vinegar

Fruit-infused vinegars can be sprinkled on much more than just raw vegetables and salad greens. They can give spark to cooked potatoes and vegetables, add pizzaz to grilled and roasted meat, seafood, and poultry selections, unleash the flavor of seafood, vegetable, and bean soups, and liven up the taste of fresh fruit salads and desserts.

Servings: 24 *Serving Size: 2⅔ T*
Yield: 1 qt

Raspberries, washed	1 lb + 6 oz	Vinegar, white wine (good quality)	1 qt

1. Place the raspberries and vinegar in a nonreactive saucepan. Heat to a simmer. Remove from the heat. Let stand to reach room temperature.
2. Pour into a jar or other covered container; cover. Let steep in a cool, dark place for 3 weeks. Strain through a china cap lined with cheesecloth. Store in sterile, corked bottles or other airtight containers, refrigerated, or in a cool, dark place. Serve with salad greens in pretty bottles along with a high-quality oil or enhance the flavor of cooked vegetable, meat, poultry, or seafood dishes, soups, or sauces.

Servings	Calories	Protein (g) (%)	Fat (g) (%)	Cholesterol (mg)	Carbohydrates (g) (%)	Fiber (g)	Sodium (mg)
1	18	0.2 (4%)	0.1 (5%)	0	5.3 (91%)	1.2	0.4

Variations

Blackberry-Infused White Wine Vinegar: Substitute 1 lb + 6 oz of washed blackberries for the raspberries.

Blueberry-Infused White Wine Vinegar: Substitute 1 lb + 6 oz of washed blueberries for the raspberries.

Peach-Infused White Wine Vinegar: Substitute 2 lb of peeled, pitted, and cubed peaches for the raspberries.

Pear-Infused White Wine Vinegar: Substitute 1¾ lb of peeled, cored, and cubed pears for the raspberries.

Strawberry-Infused White Wine Vinegar: Substitute 1 lb + 6 oz of washed, hulled, and halved, small, or quartered, large strawberries for the raspberries.

Rosemary- and Thyme-Infused White Wine Vinegar

Flavored vinegars can be made by steeping fruits, herbs, flowers, and spices in vinegar for several weeks. Good-quality white wine vinegars have a pleasing flavor for steeping herbs. Good-quality red wine vinegars are too strong for most herbs but their flavor marries well with garlic.

Servings: 24   *Serving Size: 2⅔ T*
Yield: 1 qt

Rosemary sprigs, about 5 in.	3	Peppercorns, black	1 t
Thyme sprigs	2	Vinegar, white, wine or cider	
Lemon zest, 2 × ¼-in. thick		(good quality)	1 qt
strips	2		

1. Place the rosemary, thyme, lemon zest, and peppercorns in a jar or other covered container; pour the vinegar over; cover. Place in a cool, dark place to steep for at least 3 weeks.
2. Strain through a china cap lined with cheesecloth. Store in sterile, corked bottles or other airtight containers refrigerated, or in a cool, dark place. Splash on bland lettuces such as butter, Bibb, red leaf, or iceberg, or add zip to sauces, stews, meat, seafood, poultry, and vegetable dishes.

Servings	Calories	Protein (g) (%)	Fat (g) (%)	Cholesterol (mg)	Carbohydrates (g) (%)	Fiber (g)	Sodium (mg)
1	17	0.3 (4%)	0.5 (16%)	0	4.9 (80%)	1.4	2.3

Variation

Rosemary-, Thyme-, and Garlic-Infused Red Wine Vinegar: Replace the lemon zest with 2 cloves of peeled garlic and substitute good-quality red wine vinegar for the white wine or cider vinegar.

DRESSINGS

Asian-Inspired Lime Dressing

Many Southeast Asian countries serve fish sauce as a condiment as well as make it into a variety of dipping sauces by adding chilies, sugar, and other ingredients. In this recipe, the strongly flavored, pungent seasoning sauce is transformed into a light salad dressing by blending it with lime juice and unsweetened white grape juice concentrate.

Servings: 24   *Serving Size: 2⅓ T*
Yield: 3½ c

Lime juice, freshly squeezed	1½ c	*Fish Sauce	¾ c
White grape or apple juice			
concentrate, unsweetened	1¼ c		

1. In a small container, combine all the dressing ingredients. Mix to blend. Serve over salads such as beefalo and shrimp Thai-style cellophane noodle salad (see page 270).

*Fish sauce is available at stores offering Southeast Asian food ingredients.

Servings	Calories	Protein (g) (%)	Fat (g) (%)	Cholesterol (mg)	Carbohydrates (g) (%)	Fiber (g)	Sodium (mg)
1	40	2 (19%)	0.2 (4%)	5.2	8 (78%)	0.4	78.2

Balsamic-Rice Vinegar Dressing

The sharp, clean taste of rice vinegar is balanced with the intense, sweet-tart, barrel-aged balsamic vinegar in this dressing. Hints of the mild licorice flavored tarragon and garlic round out its flavor.

Servings: 24   *Serving Size: 2⅔ T*
Yield: 1 qt

Vinegar, rice	1¼ pt	Salt	To taste
Vinegar, balsamic	1¼ c	Pepper, freshly ground	To taste
Garlic, minced	2 oz		
Tarragon, fresh, minced or dried	¼ c or 1 T + 1 t		

1. Place all the ingredients in a storage container; mix together.
2. Refrigerate until the flavors are mellowed, or at least 8 hours. Serve with grilled or roasted vegetables such as roasted Idaho potato chips (see page 347) or grilled summer vegetable salad (see page 281).

Servings	Calories	Protein (g) (%)	Fat (g) (%)	Cholesterol (mg)	Carbohydrates (g) (%)	Fiber (g)	Sodium (mg)
1	9	0.2 (5%)	< 0.1 (1%)	0	3 (94%)	0.2	0.8

Citrus-Flavored Cranberry Vinaigrette

Traditionally, vinaigrette or basic French dressing is prepared with 3, sometimes 4 or 5 parts of oil to vinegar. For more healthful dressings, offer ones with 1 to 2 parts of oil per 14 to 15 parts of vinegar or other fat-free ingredients. In this vinaigrette, there is a mere 1 part of oil to 9 parts of fat-free ingredients.

Servings: 24   *Serving Size: 1½ T*
Yield: 1 pt + ⅓ c

Cranberries, fresh, or frozen without sugar	4 oz	Oil, canola, sunflower, or corn	¼ c
Orange juice, freshly squeezed	1 c	Honey, clover	¼ c
Vinegar, red wine	¾ c	Mustard, Dijon-style	¼ c

1. Combine all the ingredients in a blender. Puree until smooth.
2. Stir well before serving. Serve with mixtures of salad greens, vegetables, and/or fruits.

Servings	Calories	Protein (g) (%)	Fat (g) (%)	Cholesterol (mg)	Carbohydrates (g) (%)	Fiber (g)	Sodium (mg)
1	41	0.2 (2%)	2.4 (50%)	0	5.2 (48%)	0.3	33

Creamy-Peach Poppy Seed Dressing

Nutritionally, nonfat, plain yogurt is low in fat and cholesterol. Further, it's a good source of protein and calcium. Its slightly tart flavor and smooth and creamy texture make it an ideal salad dressing base. In this dressing, it's blended with a puree of ripe peaches, sweetened with a small amount of honey, and enhanced with poppy seeds. The dressing is a lovely complement with fresh fruit or mixtures of salad greens and fruits.

Servings: 24　　　*Serving Size: 1⅔ T*
Yield: 1¼ pt

*Peaches, ripe, peeled, coarsely chopped	10 oz	Honey, clover	2 T
Yogurt, plain, nonfat	¾ c	Poppy seeds	1 T

1. In a blender, puree the peaches and yogurt until smooth. Mix in the honey and poppy seeds. Serve chilled over naturally sweet fresh fruit medley (see page 296); offer as a dip on a fresh fruit platter; or toss with combinations of greens and fruits.

*See page 16 for peach peeling directions.

Servings	Calories	Protein (g) (%)	Fat (g) (%)	Cholesterol (mg)	Carbohydrates (g) (%)	Fiber (g)	Sodium (mg)
1	14	0.6 (16%)	0.2 (11%)	0.1	2.7 (73%)	0.2	6.0

Freshly Squeezed Lime and Vegetable Dressing

This dressing is so good, it's hard to believe it is made without oil or egg yolks. Flavorful vegetable stock is blended with freshly squeezed lime juice and thickened and flavored at the same time with a puree of tender, fresh vegetables. Prepared mustard rounds out its garden-fresh taste.

Servings: 24   *Serving Size: $\frac{1}{4}$ c + 1 T*
Yield: $1\frac{3}{4}$ qt + $\frac{1}{2}$ c

Tomatoes, peeled, coarsely chopped	8 oz	Lime juice, freshly squeezed	$\frac{3}{4}$ c
Corn kernels, fresh or frozen	8 oz	Mustard, prepared	$\frac{1}{4}$ c
Onion, minced	6 oz	Salt	To taste
Garlic, minced	1 T	Pepper, freshly ground	To taste
Flavorful vegetable stock (see page 2) or rich white chicken stock (see page 7)	1 qt		

1. In a saucepan, combine the first five ingredients. Heat to a boil; reduce the heat to low. Simmer the vegetables until tender, or about 5 minutes.
2. In a blender, puree the mixture until smooth. Blend in the remaining ingredients. Return to the saucepan. Reheat to serve. It makes a great dressing for hot potato, sausage, and broccoli salad (see page 273), or offer it with salads of assorted greens and vegetables.

Servings	Calories	Protein (g) (%)	Fat (g) (%)	Cholesterol (mg)	Carbohydrates (g) (%)	Fiber (g)	Sodium (mg)
1	21	0.7 (12%)	0.3 (11%)	0	4.7 (77%)	0.9	38.9

Nonfat Creamy Curry Dressing

Nonfat sour cream by itself may be rather tasteless, but blended with minced garlic, a splash of honey, and lime juice, and seasoned with ginger and curry powder, it takes on a whole new life. This creamy, east meets west dressing can add punch to salads, spark up sandwiches, and transform vegetable platters to gourmet fare.

Servings: 24   *Serving Size: 2⅔ T*
Yield: 1 qt

Sour cream, nonfat	2 lb	Curry powder	1 T +
Garlic, minced	1 T +		1 t
	1 t	Ginger powder	1 t
Honey, clover	1 T +	Salt	To taste
	1 t	Pepper, freshly ground	To taste
Lime juice, freshly squeezed	1 T +		
	1 t		

1. Place all the ingredients in a mixing bowl. Mix until well blended. Spread on poultry sandwiches such as grilled, skinless chicken breast or poached skinless, sliced turkey breast or substitute for mayonnaise in sandwich fillings such as tuna, shrimp, or salmon salad. It's also excellent on fruit and fruit and seafood or poultry combination salads like cashew chicken salad with grapes and water chestnuts (see page 272).

Servings	Calories	Protein (g) (%)	Fat (g) (%)	Cholesterol (mg)	Carbohydrates (g) (%)	Fiber (g)	Sodium (mg)
1	47	2.5 (22%)	0.1 (1%)	5.9	8.6 (77%)	0.2	29.9

Oil-Free Mayonnaise-Like Dressing

This dressing does contain egg yolks but in comparison to "real" mayonnaise, its total fat and calories are reduced substantially. To achieve the creamy consistency of mayonnaise without the fat, nonfat milk is thickened with cornstarch, enriched with egg yolks, and blended into stiffly beaten egg whites. A splash of cider vinegar, a sprinkle of mustard powder, and pinch of red pepper give the dressing a slight tang.

Servings: 24   *Serving Size:* $1\frac{5}{6}$ T
Yield: $2\frac{3}{4}$ c

Cornstarch	1 T + 2 t	Apple or fruit juice concentrate, unsweetened	2 T
Mustard, dry	$\frac{1}{2}$ t	Vinegar, cider	$\frac{1}{4}$ c
Salt	To taste or $\frac{1}{2}$ t	Egg yolks, large, lightly beaten	3 ($2\frac{1}{4}$ oz)
		Margarine, unsalted, corn oil	$\frac{1}{2}$ oz
Red pepper, ground	Pinch	Egg whites, large, stiffly beaten	3 ($3\frac{3}{4}$ oz)
Milk, nonfat	$\frac{3}{4}$ c		

1. In a saucepan, mix the dry ingredients with enough of the nonfat milk to make a smooth paste.
2. Beat the remaining milk and juice concentrate into the paste. Heat to a boil, stirring. Reduce the heat and simmer a few minutes until thickened. Remove from the heat.
3. Mix the vinegar with the beaten egg yolks. Temper by adding a spoonful of the hot mixture to the egg yolk mixture and stirring quickly. Repeat twice. Stir the egg yolk mixture back into the dressing.
4. Cook over very low heat, stirring constantly until thick or a few minutes. Remove from the heat. Stir in the margarine to melt. Cool.
5. Fold the sauce into the stiffly beaten egg whites. Transfer to a storage container. Refrigerate until chilled. Offer the dressing as a spread on sandwiches or as an ingredient in dishes calling for mayonnaise or salad dressing such as cashew chicken salad with grapes and water chestnuts (see page 272).

Servings	Calories	Protein (g) (%)	Fat (g) (%)	Cholesterol (mg)	Carbohydrates (g) (%)	Fiber (g)	Sodium (mg)
1	22	1.1 (20%)	1.1 (48%)	26.6	1.7 (32%)	< 0.1	12.1

Orange Pineapple Soy Salad Dressing

A tablespoon of some salad dressings can add as much as 100 calories and 10 grams of fat. For a healthful dressing, aim for 30 to 50 calories and $\frac{1}{2}$ to $1\frac{1}{2}$ grams of fat per tablespoon. To reach this goal, select high-quality oils with distinctive flavors such as extra-virgin olive, or a nut oil, perhaps walnut, hazelnut, or almond. For example, in this dressing, a nice balance of flavor is achieved with only 1 part sesame oil to a 10-part mixture of fruit juice and low-sodium soy sauce. As a result, this pleasantly tart dressing yields only 19 calories and $1\frac{1}{4}$ grams of fat per tablespoon.

Servings: 24   *Serving Size: $2\frac{3}{4}$ T*
Yield: 1 qt + 2 T

Orange juice, freshly squeezed	1 pt	Pineapple juice concentrate,	
Lime juice, freshly squeezed	1 c	unsweetened	$\frac{1}{4}$ c
Soy sauce, low-sodium	$\frac{1}{2}$ c	Gingerroot, minced	2 t
Sesame oil, light colored	$\frac{1}{4}$ c +	Garlic, minced	2 t
	2 T	Pepper, freshly ground	To taste

1. Combine all the ingredients in a storage container; mix.
2. Refrigerate until the flavors are blended, or about 3 hours.
3. Serve with vegetable, fruit, and/or grain salads such as a salad of pineapple cubes, orange sections, and jicama strips (see page 297) or quinoa salad decorated with pineapple, mandarin oranges, and water chestnuts (see page 284).

Servings	Calories	Protein (g) (%)	Fat (g) (%)	Cholesterol (mg)	Carbohydrates (g) (%)	Fiber (g)	Sodium (mg)
1	52	0.7 (5%)	3.5 (58%)	0	5.0 (37%)	0.1	160

Pineapple-Flavored Creamy Tofu Dressing

Tofu, the primary ingredient in this dressing, is made from dried soybeans which have been soaked, pureed into a milky substance, and then mixed with a coagulant until curds form. The longer the curds are drained, the firmer they become. Chinese chefs transform tofu into a variety of dishes by stir-frying, grilling, braising, and deep-frying until dense and meaty, or frying into puffs which can be stuffed. In this recipe, the high-protein curds are blended with pineapple juice and Dijon-style mustard to become a creamy mayonnaise-like dressing.

Servings: 24 *Serving Size: 2 T*
Yield: 1½ pt

Tofu, firm	1¼ lb	Salt	To taste
Pineapple juice, unsweetened	¾ c	Pepper, freshly ground	To taste
Mustard, Dijon-style	1½ T		or ½ t
Lemon juice, freshly squeezed	1 T		

1. Place all the ingredients in a blender; puree until smooth.
2. Serve as a dressing with salads of greens and/or vegetables such as shredded cabbage with corn and bell pepper (see page 287) or as a spread for sandwiches.

Servings	Calories	Protein (g) (%)	Fat (g) (%)	Cholesterol (mg)	Carbohydrates (g) (%)	Fiber (g)	Sodium (mg)
12	18	1.2 (26%)	0.7 (34%)	0	1.9 (40%)	< 0.1	13.9

Ranch-Style Salad Dressing

Ranch-style salad dressing typically is a seasoned blend of buttermilk with mayonnaise and/or sour cream. To cut the fat without the flavor, nonfat sour cream is blended with nonfat buttermilk (naturally low in fat), fresh herbs, green onions, and garlic in this version. The green speckled, creamy dressing makes a superb low-fat, low-calorie house dressing.

Servings: 24 **Serving Size: $2\frac{1}{3}$ T**
Yield: $3\frac{1}{2}$ c

Sour cream, nonfat	1 lb	Oregano, minced or dried	$1\frac{1}{2}$ t or $\frac{1}{2}$ t
Buttermilk, nonfat	1 pt		
Lemon juice, freshly squeezed	2 t	Tarragon, minced or dried	$\frac{3}{4}$ t or $\frac{1}{4}$ t
Green onion, white only, minced	4 oz	Salt	To taste
Parsley, minced	$\frac{1}{4}$ c	Pepper, freshly ground	To taste
Garlic, minced	2 t	Red pepper	To taste
Basil, minced or dried	$1\frac{1}{2}$ t or $\frac{1}{2}$ t		

1. In a bowl or storage container, mix the sour cream, buttermilk, and lemon juice until well blended.
2. Add all the remaining ingredients; mix well; chill to mellow the flavors, at least 6 hours. Serve as a dressing for salads composed of vegetables and/or greens such as vegetable slaw coated in ranch-style dressing (see page 290).

Servings	Calories	Protein (g) (%)	Fat (g) (%)	Cholesterol (mg)	Carbohydrates (g) (%)	Fiber (g)	Sodium (mg)
1	23	2.1 (35%)	0.2 (7%)	0.7	3.5 (58%)	0.2	35.9

Raspberry-Infused Honey Vinaigrette Dressing

The ideal salad dressing is one that has well-balanced flavors, a pleasant tartness, as well as one that harmonizes and complements the ingredients it accompanies. This dressing receives high scores when tossed with a medley of tender salad greens. Furthermore, it's nearly fat-free and is cholesterol-free.

Servings: 24   *Serving Size: 2½ T*
Yield: 3¾ c

Raspberry-infused white wine vinegar (see page 302)	1 c	Garlic, minced	1 T
Honey, clover	¼ c + 3 T	Salt	To taste
		Pepper, freshly ground	To taste
Lime juice, freshly squeezed	¼ c	Flavorful vegetable stock (see page 2) or rich white chicken stock (see page 7)	1 pt
Worcestershire sauce, very low sodium	1½ T		
Mustard, Dijon-style	1 T		

1. In a storage container, place all the ingredients but the stock. Whip until blended. Add the stock; mix until blended. Refrigerate at least 4 hours for the flavors to mellow. Dress salad greens or fresh fruit with or use as a marinade for game or poultry selections.

Servings	Calories	Protein (g) (%)	Fat (g) (%)	Cholesterol (mg)	Carbohydrates (g) (%)	Fiber (g)	Sodium (mg)
1	26	0.2 (2%)	0.1 (2%)	0	7.2 (96%)	0.3	14

Rice Wine Vinaigrette

In this dressing, the mildly tart and subtly sweet taste of rice wine vinegar is balanced with the salty flavor of soy sauce and the sweetness of concentrated fruit juice. It is enriched with a splash of sesame oil.

Servings: 24   *Serving Size: 2¼ t*
Yield: 1 c + 2 T

Vinegar, rice wine	¾ c	Oil, sesame, light colored	1 T
Soy sauce, low-sodium	3 T		
White grape or apple juice concentrate, unsweetened	2 T		

1. In a bowl, mix all the ingredients. Serve over vegetable salads such as broccoli marinated in rice wine vinaigrette (see page 275).

Servings	Calories	Protein (g) (%)	Fat (g) (%)	Cholesterol (mg)	Carbohydrates (g) (%)	Fiber (g)	Sodium (mg)
1	10	0.2 (6%)	0.6 (47%)	0	1.3 (47%)	< 0.1	60

Saffron and Basil Orange Vinaigrette Dressing

While vinaigrettes were traditionally prepared with 3 parts of oil to 1 part vinegar, saffron and basil orange vinaigrette dressing contains only about 10% oil and 6% vinegar. For a healthier approach, orange juice concentrate, red wine vinegar, and lemon juice are blended with fresh vegetable stock and a small amount of extra-virgin olive oil. Freshly minced basil, chives, and garlic, saffron threads, and finely grated orange zest enliven this elegant, light, and fresh-tasting dressing.

Servings: 24   *Serving Size: $2\frac{2}{3}$ T*
Yield: 1 qt

Flavorful vegetable stock (see page 2) or rich white chicken stock (see page 7)	1 c	Vinegar, red wine	3 T
		Basil, minced or dried	$\frac{1}{2}$ c or 2 T + 2 t
Orange juice concentrate, unsweetened	$\frac{3}{4}$ c + 2 T	Chives, minced	1 oz
		Garlic, minced	2 t
Lemon juice, freshly squeezed	$\frac{3}{4}$ c	Orange zest, finely grated	$\frac{1}{2}$ t
Oil, olive, extra-virgin	$\frac{1}{4}$ c + 1 T	Saffron, threads	$\frac{1}{4}$ t
		Salt	To taste
		Pepper, freshly ground	To taste

1. Combine all the ingredients in a storage container; whip until thoroughly blended. Cover; chill until service. At this time, mix well again. It makes a nice addition to green salad tossed with vegetables (see page 280) or toss it with greens of choice.

Servings	Calories	Protein (g) (%)	Fat (g) (%)	Cholesterol (mg)	Carbohydrates (g) (%)	Fiber (g)	Sodium (mg)
1	47	0.5 (4%)	2.9 (52%)	0	5.7 (45%)	0.5	2.4

Sesame-Flavored Ginger Soy Dressing

This full-bodied, cholesterol-free, low-fat, low-calorie dressing is prepared by blending a puree of vegetables simmered in chicken stock with low-sodium soy sauce, rice wine vinegar, white grape and orange juice concentrates, freshly squeezed lime juice, and a small amount of sesame oil. It's charming with pasta, grain, and vegetable salads.

Servings: 24   *Serving Size: $4\frac{5}{8}$ T*
Yield: $1\frac{3}{4}$ qt $+ \frac{1}{4}$ c

Onion, coarsely chopped	$9\frac{1}{2}$ oz	White grape juice concentrate, unsweetened	$\frac{1}{2}$ c
Tomato, ripe, coarsely chopped	$3\frac{1}{2}$ oz	Orange juice concentrate, unsweetened	$\frac{1}{2}$ c
Celery, coarsely chopped	$2\frac{1}{2}$ oz	Sesame oil, light-colored	$\frac{1}{4}$ c
Gingerroot, coarsely chopped	$2\frac{1}{2}$ oz	Lime juice, freshly squeezed	$\frac{1}{4}$ c
Rich white chicken stock (see page 7)	$1\frac{1}{2}$ c	Salt	To taste
Vinegar, rice wine	1 c	Pepper, freshly ground	To taste
Soy sauce, low-sodium	1 c		

1. In a blender, place the first 11 ingredients; process until smooth. Season with salt and pepper to taste. Serve with pasta and/or vegetable salads such as soba noodle salad tossed with red and yellow bell peppers, snow peas, carrots, mushrooms, and water chestnuts (see page 288).

Servings	Calories	Protein (g) (%)	Fat (g) (%)	Cholesterol (mg)	Carbohydrates (g) (%)	Fiber (g)	Sodium (mg)
1	58	1.5 (10%)	2.5 (36%)	0	8.2 (54%)	0.4	329

Vegetable-Thickened Oil-Free Vinaigrette

For this nearly fat-free tasty vinaigrette, vegetables are simmered in a flavorful vegetable stock, pureed, and mixed with red wine vinegar, a splash of lemon juice, and freshly minced herbs.

Servings: 24   *Serving Size: 1½ T*
Yield: 2¼ c

Flavorful vegetable stock (see page 2) or rich white chicken stock (see page 7)	1 pt	Lemon juice, freshly squeezed	¼ c + 2 T
Onions, coarsely chopped	3 oz	Parsley, minced	¼ c + 2 T
Celery and carrots, coarsely chopped	2 oz each	Chives, minced or dried	3 T or 1 T
Mushrooms, coarsely chopped	1 oz	Garlic, minced	1 T
Vinegar, red wine	¼ c + 2 T	Salt	To taste
		Pepper, freshly ground	To taste

1. Place the stock, onions, celery, carrots, and mushrooms in a saucepan; heat to a boil. Boil until the vegetables are tender and the broth reduced to 1 c, or about 15 minutes.
2. Transfer the vegetables and broth to a blender; blend until the mixture is smooth.
3. Add the vinegar, lemon juice, and seasonings to the mixture; blend well. Serve over vegetable salads such as potato, kidney bean, and bell pepper salad (see page 283).

Servings	Calories	Protein (g) (%)	Fat (g) (%)	Cholesterol (mg)	Carbohydrates (g) (%)	Fiber (g)	Sodium (mg)
1	7	0.2 (10%)	< 0.1 (5%)	0	1.9 (85%)	0.4	5.5

Walnut-Flavored Vinaigrette Dressing*

The principal ingredient in this vinaigrette dressing is rice vinegar. It's so mild in flavor, it takes only a tad of walnut oil to balance its light flavor.

Servings: 24   *Serving Size: 2 T*
Yield: 1½ pt

Vinegar, rice	1¼ c	Oil, walnut	3½ T
White grape or apple juice		Onion, red, minced	10 oz
concentrate, unsweetened	½ c +	Salt	To taste
	2 T	Pepper, freshly ground	To taste

1. Combine all the ingredients in a storage container. Whip to mix. Serve over green salads such as spinach and red leaf lettuce salad (see page 289).

*Adapted from a recipe by Chris Cuffari.

Servings	Calories	Protein (g) (%)	Fat (g) (%)	Cholesterol (mg)	Carbohydrates (g) (%)	Fiber (g)	Sodium (mg)
1	37	0.2 (3%)	2 (47%)	0	4.9 (51%)	0.4	0.9

9

Egg and Cheese Dishes

EGG DISHES

Broccoli Timbales Enhanced with Swiss Cheese

While timbales are typically prepared with only whole eggs, these custard-like broccoli molds call for a ratio of 2 whites per yolk.

Servings: 24   *Serving Size: 6-oz timbale*
Yield: 24 6-oz timbales

Broccoli florets and stems, washed, pared	2¼ lb	Swiss cheese, low-fat, shredded	12 oz
Vegetable cooking spray, butter-flavored	—	Parsley, minced	¼ c
		Paprika, sweet, Hungarian	2 t
Shallots, minced	6 oz	Nutmeg, freshly ground	¼ t
Garlic, minced	1 T	Salt	To taste
Margarine, unsalted, corn oil	1 oz	Pepper, white or black, freshly ground	To taste
Flour, cake, or all-purpose, unbleached	1 oz	Egg yolks, large	6 (4½ oz)
Milk, evaporated, skim	1 pt	Egg whites, large	12
Rich white chicken stock (see page 7)	1 c		(15 oz)

1. Steam or boil the broccoli in unsalted water until tender. Drain; refresh in cold water. Drain.
2. Coat a nonstick skillet with cooking spray. Place over medium heat until hot. Add the shallots and garlic. Saute until tender.
3. In a blender or food processor, add the broccoli, shallots, and garlic; blend into a chunky paste. Set aside.
4. Melt the margarine in a saucepan. Stir in the flour. Cook over low heat a few minutes until frothy, without browning. Gradually beat in the evaporated milk and stock. Heat to a boil, stirring. Reduce the heat to low; simmer, stirring occasionally until thickened to medium consistency and the starch flavor is cooked out, or about 10 minutes. Add stock or evaporated skim milk to thin and thicken by reducing or adding a cornstarch slurry.
5. Stir in the Swiss cheese and seasonings. Continue heating until the cheese has melted. Set aside to cool slightly. Blend in the egg yolks and broccoli mixture.
6. Beat the egg whites until stiff. Fold them lightly into the sauce and broccoli mixture.

7. Coat 24 6-oz custard cups or timbale molds with cooking spray. Fill with the custard mixture. Place the cups on a rack in a 4-in. counter pan of hot but not boiling water. The water should be as high as the filling in the molds. Bake in a 325°F (165°C) oven until set, or about 25 minutes.
8. Remove the timbales from the water. Cool 5 minutes before unmolding. Loosen the edges of the timbales with a spatula. Invert on plates to serve. Serve with a light tomato sauce such as tomato coulis seasoned with garlic and basil (see page 39) if desired.

Servings	Calories	Protein (g) (%)	Fat (g) (%)	Cholesterol (mg)	Carbohydrates (g) (%)	Fiber (g)	Sodium (mg)
1	100	10 (39%)	3.4 (30%)	58.7	8.0 (31%)	1.4	112

Fiesta Scrambled Eggs

Current dietary recommendations do not suggest Americans eliminate whole eggs from their diets but rather limit consumption from 3 to 4 per week. For about one-third of their weekly allotment, diners can enjoy fiesta scrambled eggs, creamy, whole eggs and whites blended with diced tomatoes, bell peppers, and onions.

Servings: 24   *Serving Size: 1⅓ each whole large eggs and whites + vegetables*
Yield: 1¾ gal + ½ c eggs + vegetables

Eggs, large	32 (4 lb)	Onions, minced	2 lb
Egg whites, large	32 (2½ lb)	Peppers, bell, green and red, small dice	1¼ lb each
Mustard, prepared	2 T	Garlic, minced	1½ T
Salt	To taste	Tomatoes, small dice	2½ lb
Pepper, freshly ground	To taste		
Vegetable cooking spray, olive-flavored	—		

1. In a mixing bowl, beat to completely blend the whole eggs, whites, mustard, and salt and pepper to taste. Set aside.
2. Coat a large nonstick skillet with cooking spray or cook the vegetables and eggs in batches. Place over medium heat until hot. Add the onions, green and red bell peppers, and garlic. Cook until the vegetables are tender.
3. Add the tomatoes; cook until the mixture is thick and well blended. Drain any liquid from the mixture. Season with salt and pepper to taste.
4. Reduce the heat to medium. Pour the eggs into the skillet; cook, stirring occasionally, so that the eggs cook in fairly large pieces without becoming brown. Cook until all the portions are coagulated.
5. Serve immediately with toasted triangles of whole grain bread.

Servings	Calories	Protein (g) (%)	Fat (g) (%)	Cholesterol (mg)	Carbohydrates (g) (%)	Fiber (g)	Sodium (mg)
1	175	15.8 (36%)	7.9 (41%)	320	10.2 (23%)	2.1	195

Spinach Mushroom Souffle

To minimize the fat and cholesterol in this souffle, half of the egg yolks are replaced with whites and then blended with a low-fat and low-cholesterol white sauce. For flavor without fat, minced mushrooms and shallots are reduced in madeira wine and added to the fluffy mixture with fresh, chopped spinach.

Servings: 24   *Serving Size: 1 c souffle*
Yield: 24 1-c souffles

Vegetable cooking spray, butter-flavored	—	Low-fat white sauce, thick consistency (see page 36)	1 qt
Bread crumbs, whole wheat, fresh	2 oz	Egg yolks, large	8 (6 oz)
Mushrooms, minced	12 oz	Egg whites, large, room temperature	16 (20 oz)
Shallots, minced	3 oz		
Madeira wine	½ c	Cream of tartar	1 t
Spinach, leaves, washed, chopped	12 oz		

1. Coat 24 1-c souffle dishes lightly with cooking spray. Sprinkle with the bread crumbs to coat the sides and bottoms. Shake out the excess crumbs.
2. Place the mushrooms in a ricer and press out the juice. Reserve the juice for seasoning in other cooking.
3. Coat a nonstick skillet with cooking spray. Saute the mushrooms and shallots over medium-high heat until the mushrooms give up the rest of their juices. Add the madeira; cook until it evaporates. Set aside.
4. Add the spinach to a saucepan; place over medium-high heat. Cook, steaming the spinach in its own moisture until tender. Drain; squeeze out the excess liquid. Stir the spinach and mushroom mixture into the white sauce. Simmer until heated through. Remove from the heat to cool slightly.
5. Pour the yolks into the sauce, beating constantly.
6. In a mixing bowl, beat the egg whites for about 30 seconds; add the cream of tartar. Continue to beat until the egg whites are stiff. Fold the egg whites into the cheese mixture.
7. Pour the mixture into the prepared souffle dishes. Place the dishes in a 350°F (175°C) oven. Bake for 30 minutes without opening the oven door. At this time, check for doneness by very gently shaking the dishes. If the centers are firm and do not jiggle, the souffles are done. If necessary, bake another 5–10 minutes.

8. Remove from the oven; serve immediately with a glass of chilled fruit juice and a chunk of freshly baked, whole grain bread.

Servings	Calories	Protein (g) (%)	Fat (g) (%)	Cholesterol (mg)	Carbohydrates (g) (%)	Fiber (g)	Sodium (mg)
1	97	6.6 (27%)	4.7 (43%)	91.5	7.2 (30%)	0.4	101

No alcohol is listed in the nutrition analysis. It is assumed to be cooked off during preparation.

CHEESE DISHES

Bean- and Cheese-Filled Whole Wheat Tortillas

These meatless, whole grain tortilla-wrapped packages have many attributes. Nutritionally, they are packed with protein; rich in minerals, notably iron and calcium; a good source of vitamins and fiber; and contain little fat and cholesterol. In addition to their healthful qualities, they can be assembled in minutes from purchased tortillas, and the beans and salsa can be prepared in advance. They are economical, and like sandwiches, can be picked up and eaten with the fingers.

Servings: 24   *Serving Size: 1 filled tortilla*
Yield: 24 filled tortillas

Tortillas, whole wheat, prepared without lard, 8-in.	24	Cheddar cheese, shredded, low-fat and low-sodium	12 oz
Freshly fried pinto beans simmered in broth without the radishes or lettuce, heated (see page 181)	$2\frac{1}{4}$ qt	Fresh tomato salsa seasoned with cilantro and chilies (see page 44)	$1\frac{1}{2}$ pt

1. Wrap the tortillas tightly in foil; place in a 350°F (175°C) oven until heated through, or about 10 minutes.
2. Spoon $\frac{1}{4}$ c + 2 T (6 T) of beans, 2 T of cheese, and 2 T of salsa down the center of each tortilla. Lap ends of the tortilla over the filling and roll up. Serve on heated plates or wrapped to go.

Servings	Calories	Protein (g) (%)	Fat (g) (%)	Cholesterol (mg)	Carbohydrates (g) (%)	Fiber (g)	Sodium (mg)
1	187	11.5 (22%)	1.9 (8%)	3.0	37.6 (70%)	7.4	188

Fresh Low-Fat Milk Paneer Cheese
Fresh Low-Fat Milk Chenna Cheese

Fresh Asian Indian cheese in curd form is called chenna. When chenna is compressed into a cake it is called paneer. These cheeses are similar to American pot or Italian ricotta cheeses except much drier. These reduced-fat versions are prepared by heating low-fat milk with lemon juice until curds form. Once formed, they are separated from the liquid whey by draining. Finally, the curds (chenna) are compressed into a light, smooth, and velvety cheese (paneer).

Servings: 24   *Serving Size: 2 oz paneer cheese*
Yield: 3 lb paneer cheese

*Low-fat milk	3 gal	Lemon juice, freshly squeezed	¾ c

1. In a deep heavy-bottomed sauce pot, heat the milk to a boil. Stir often to prevent sticking and scorching.
2. Reduce the heat to medium. Add the lemon juice. Stir gently until white curds form and separate from the greenish-yellow whey (watery part), or about 10 seconds. Sometimes the curd forms before all the lemon juice has been added. If this occurs, do not add the full amount. It will only harden the curd. If the curd does not form after 10 seconds or it only partially forms, add a little more lemon juice until there are lumps of white curd and a clear greenish yellow whey.
3. Once the curd begins to form, immediately turn off the heat, continuing to stir the mixture very slowly and gently. The curds are very fragile and break easily.
4. Pour the cheese and whey through a colander or china cap lined with 4 layers of cheesecloth, discarding the liquid whey.
5. Rinse the curds in the colander or china cap under a gentle stream of cold water to remove any remaining smells of lemon juice.
6. Bring up the four corners of the cheesecloth and tie them together. Gently twist to extract as much whey as possible.
7. Drain additional whey from the curd by hanging the curd in the cloth from a refrigerator shelf over a pan for a few hours.

Fresh Low-Fat Milk Chenna Cheese:
8. Remove the drained, crumbly cheese from the cheesecloth. Place it on a smooth, clean work surface. Break it apart and press with paper towels to extract any excess whey.
9. With the palm of the hand, knead the cheese by pressing and spreading it out a small bit at a time. Gather up all the cheese with a spatula and repeat the process again and

again until the cheese is light and velvety smooth and no longer grainy, or up to 10 minutes.

10. Serve blended with minced fresh herbs, such as cilantro, parsley, or basil and/or spices, like freshly ground black pepper. Shape into a log and serve on a fresh vegetable or cracker tray or offer as an alternative to butter for bread. Another option is to blend minced fresh herbs, freshly ground pepper, minced green chilies, and salt with the soft cheese. Shape the seasoned soft cheese into small patties; brown in a nonstick skillet coated with cooking spray and serve between bread garnished with sliced raw vegetables as a sandwich. It can be stored, wrapped in plastic, refrigerated for up to 3 days.

Fresh Low-Fat Milk Paneer Cheese:

11. Tightly wrap the drained curds in cheesecloth. Place in a colander with a weight, such as a pot filled with water or a brick wrapped in plastic, on it for $\frac{1}{2}$ hour or longer if refrigerated. Remove the compressed cheese.

12. Use as a substitute for cream cheese or as directed in recipes such as green peas and fresh cheese in tomato sauce (see page 332). It can be stored refrigerated, wrapped in plastic for up to 4 days.

*Nonfat milk can be substituted for the low-fat milk if an even lower fat cheese is desired. The yield on the cheese will be less due to the loss of fat.

Servings	Calories	Protein (g) (%)	Fat (g) (%)	Cholesterol (mg)	Carbohydrates (g) (%)	Fiber (g)	Sodium (mg)
1	244	16.3 (27%)	9.4 (34%)	36.6	24.1 (39%)	< 0.1	242

Fresh Nonfat Milk White Cheese

This fresh cheese, like ricotta and farmer cheeses, doesn't keep for long. It is best to use the same day it is made or within a day or two. For a simple but light dessert, offer the cheese dusted lightly with brown sugar and topped with sliced, sweet, ripe fruit, perhaps mango, kiwi, banana, or berries, alone or in combination.

Servings: 24   *Serving Size: 1 oz*
Yield: 1½ lb

Milk, nonfat	3 qt	**Buttermilk, nonfat**	3 qt

1. In a saucepan, heat the milk and buttermilk over low heat. Stir occasionally. As curds form, skim them off with a slotted spoon. Drain off the final curds with a fine mesh strainer.
2. Pat the curds into a circular or square shape or puree in a blender to use as an ingredient in dips, salad dressings, desserts, or sauces.

Servings	Calories	Protein (g) (%)	Fat (g) (%)	Cholesterol (mg)	Carbohydrates (g) (%)	Fiber (g)	Sodium (mg)
1	92	8.2 (36%)	1.3 (13%)	6.5	11.8 (51%)	0	192

Fresh Nonfat Yogurt Cheese
Thickened Yogurt Flavored with Fresh Herbs

A healthy substitute for sour cream is thickened nonfat yogurt and one for cream cheese is nonfat yogurt cheese. Both are easy to make. Liquid is simply drained from nonfat yogurt by refrigerating in a cheesecloth-lined china cap until the desired consistency. Thickened yogurt seasoned with vegetables and/or herbs and spices makes a tasty topping for baked potatoes or dip for roasted potato chips (see page 347) or raw vegetables. Yogurt cheese might be used as an ingredient in low-fat cheese cakes or as a base for frostings or spreads.

Servings: 24   *Serving Size:* 3½ T *yogurt cheese*
Yield: 1¼ *qt* + ¼ *c yogurt cheese*

Yogurt, nonfat, plain   1 gal

1. Line a china cap with 2 or 3 layers of cheesecloth rinsed in cold water and wrung out. Let the yogurt drain refrigerated until it is the consistency of cream cheese, holds its shape, retains the mark of a finger indentation, and about 2½ quarts of the whey have drained off. Substitute for cream cheese in recipes.
2. To prepare thickened yogurt, let the yogurt drain as described in step 1 until it is thick but still soft, or 1 hour. Use as an ingredient in sauces, salad dressings, or desserts. Blend with chives or a combination of fresh herbs and serve as a baked potato topping or a dip for roasted potatoes.

Servings	Calories	Protein (g) (%)	Fat (g) (%)	Cholesterol (mg)	Carbohydrates (g) (%)	Fiber (g)	Sodium (mg)
1	91	9.3 (41%)	0.3 (3%)	2.9	12.5 (56%)	0	125

Green Peas and Fresh Cheese in Tomato Sauce

In this dish, moist pieces of freshly prepared, low-fat cheese and tender, green peas are coated with a savory tomato sauce. It will likely be a favorite of both your vegetarian and meat eaters.

Servings: 24   *Serving Size: $\frac{9}{10}$ c*
Yield: 1 gal + 1$\frac{1}{2}$ qt

Fresh low-fat paneer cheese (see page 328) or other low-fat fresh cheese	1 recipe (3 lb)	Pepper, freshly ground	To taste or 1 t
Parchment paper	—	Red pepper, ground	To taste or $\frac{1}{2}$ t
Vegetable cooking spray	—	Tomatoes, peeled, coarsely chopped	3$\frac{1}{2}$ lb
Onions, minced	2 lb	Green peas, fresh, shelled or frozen	3 lb
Gingerroot, minced	1$\frac{1}{3}$ oz ($\frac{1}{4}$ c)	Indian-inspired spice blend (see page 58)	2$\frac{1}{2}$ T
Garlic, minced	2 t	Cilantro, minced	1 oz
Coriander, freshly ground	1 T	Salt	To taste
Paprika, Hungarian, sweet	1 T		
Turmeric powder	2 t		

1. Cut the fresh cheese into $\frac{1}{2} \times \frac{1}{2} \times \frac{1}{2}$-in. pieces; spread the pieces on parchment paper to dry.
2. Coat a large nonstick skillet with cooking spray or cook in batches. Place over medium-high heat until hot. Add the cheese, cooking and gently turning until light brown. Transfer to a holding container. Set aside.
3. Coat a sauce pot with cooking spray. Place over medium-high heat until hot. Add the onions, ginger, and garlic; cook until light brown.
4. Add the coriander, paprika, turmeric, and black and red peppers; mix together.
5. Add the tomatoes. Reduce the heat to medium. Cook until the mixture thickens to a pulpy sauce, stirring often.
6. Add 1 qt of water or as needed. Heat the sauce to a boil; reduce the heat to low; cover and cook until it reaches sauce consistency and the flavors are mellowed.
7. In a blender, puree the mixture until a chunky sauce consistency. Return to a clean sauce pot.
8. Add the peas and fresh cheese. Heat to a boil; reduce the heat to low; cook until the peas are tender, or about 10 minutes for fresh and 5 for frozen. Stir gently.

9. Stir in the Indian-inspired spice blend, cilantro, and salt to taste. Serve with whole wheat tortillas prepared without lard or boiled brown basmati rice (see page 235).

Servings	Calories	Protein (g) (%)	Fat (g) (%)	Cholesterol (mg)	Carbohydrates (g) (%)	Fiber (g)	Sodium (mg)
1	322	20.6 (25%)	10 (27%)	36.6	39.4 (48%)	4.6	253

Spinach and Swiss Cheese Phyllo Strudel

Phyllo leaves, also spelled filo, are tissue-thin pastry sheets, prepared by kneading wheat flour and water together and stretching. In fact, the dough is stretched so thin, it is difficult and time consuming to make in one's own kitchen.

Traditionally, several layers of phyllo leaves were liberally coated with melted butter and baked filled with ingredients to form crisp, flaky wrappers for turnovers and other baked dishes. In spinach and Swiss cheese phyllo strudel, the dough sheets are lightly coated with butter-flavored cooking spray rather than butter to form light packets for their vegetarian filling.

Servings: 24   Serving Size: two 1-in. wide slices
Yield: three 17-in. strudels

Filling:		Dough:	
Vegetable cooking spray, butter-flavored	—	*Phyllo dough sheets, frozen, thawed (12 × 17 in.)	12 oz (18)
Onions, minced	12 oz		
Garlic, minced	1 T	Vegetable cooking spray, butter-flavored	18 3-second sprays
Spinach, leaves, washed, chopped	2 lb		
Salt	To taste		
Pepper, freshly ground	To taste	Bread crumbs, whole wheat, dried, corn or wheat flake cereal crumbs, or wheat germ (divided)	2 oz
Swiss cheese, low-fat, shredded	6 oz		
Parmesan cheese, freshly grated, part-skim milk	3 oz		
Bread crumbs, whole wheat, dried, corn or wheat flake cereal crumbs, or wheat germ	1 oz		

1. Coat a nonstick skillet with cooking spray. Add the onions and garlic. Cook until tender without browning.
2. Add the spinach; cook until wilted, or about 3 minutes. Drain, pressing to remove any liquid.
3. Season with salt and pepper to taste. Toss with the Swiss and parmesan cheeses and the 1 oz of bread crumbs.
4. Unfold the sheets of phyllo dough so that they lie flat. Cover with plastic wrap and then a damp towel to keep them from drying.

5. Spread a large piece of parchment paper or plastic wrap on a work surface. Spread 1 dough sheet on the parchment or plastic-lined work surface with the longest side nearest. Coat the dough with a 3-second spray of cooking spray. Sprinkle about 1 t of the crumbs over the dough. Repeat 5 times by placing another sheet of dough over and coating with cooking spray and crumbs.
6. Spread one-third of the filling on top of the dough leaving a 1½-in. border of dough uncovered.
7. Lift the longest edge of the dough nearest with the parchment or plastic to fold over the dough. Replace the parchment or plastic and roll up like a jelly roll.
8. Seal the dough seam with water. Do not seal the ends. Place seam side down on a baking sheet coated with cooking spray.
9. Repeat steps 5–8 two more times.
10. Bake in a 375°F (190°C) oven until golden brown, or about 35 minutes. Let stand to firm up, or about 10 minutes. Slice each roll into 16 1-in. slices. Serve as an appetizer or main course offering.

*Replace the wheat phyllo dough sheets with whole wheat sheets for a higher fiber option.

Servings	Calories	Protein (g) (%)	Fat (g) (%)	Cholesterol (mg)	Carbohydrates (g) (%)	Fiber (g)	Sodium (mg)
1	97	6 (24%)	2.5 (23%)	4.9	13 (53%)	1.6	205

Variation

Broccoli, Corn, and Cheddar Cheese Phyllo Strudel: Substitute 8 oz of sliced green onions for the 12 oz of minced onions, 2 lb of broccoli florets, and 1 lb of fresh or frozen corn kernels for the spinach, and 9 oz of low-fat, low-sodium cheddar cheese for the Swiss and parmesan cheeses.

Toasted Open-Face Swiss Cheese Sandwich with Tomatoes and Caraway

To minimize the fat, cholesterol, and calories in this sandwich without losing flavor, slices of whole grain bread are dipped in nonfat milk, topped with ripe sliced tomatoes and a combination of low-fat and regular shredded Swiss cheese, and baked. A sprinkle of caraway seeds gives this open-face sandwich a charming finish. It is top of the line.

Servings: 24 *Serving Size: 1 open-face sandwich*
Yield: 24 open-face sandwiches

Milk, nonfat	1 pt + ¼ c	Tomato, thin slices	4 lb (96)
Bread, whole grain, slices	1½ lb (24)	Swiss cheese, low-fat, shredded	1 lb
Vegetable cooking spray, butter-flavored	—	Swiss cheese, shredded	12 oz
		Caraway seeds	1 T

1. In a shallow container, add the milk. Dip the bread into the milk, coating both sides. Drain off excess milk. Place the slices on a nonstick baking sheet well coated with cooking spray.
2. Place the tomato slices overlapping one another on the bread. Cover with the shredded cheese. Sprinkle with the caraway seeds.
3. Bake in a 400°F (205°C) oven until the cheese is melted, or about 8 minutes. Serve for lunch or supper along with a cup of soup or a salad.

Servings	Calories	Protein (g) (%)	Fat (g) (%)	Cholesterol (mg)	Carbohydrates (g) (%)	Fiber (g)	Sodium (mg)
1	181	13.6 (29%)	6.4 (31%)	20	18.9 (41%)	3.0	254

10

Hors d'Oeuvres and Beverages

S N A C K S

Crispy Whole Wheat Cheese Wafers

Unlike most wafers, these aren't covered with salt. Rather, they are seasoned with fresh basil and parsley, freshly ground pepper, and minced garlic. While their fat content exceeds the recommended 30% level, each whole wheat wafter contains only 2.2 g of fat and 1.3 mg of cholesterol. To keep the total fat below the 30% level, serve the wafers with clear soups filled with grains, pasta, and/or vegetables, and small amounts of lean meat, seafood, or poultry, such as a whole wheat chicken noodle soup with garden vegetables or salads coated with low-fat dressings like grilled vegetable salad sprinkled with balsamic vinegar.

Servings: 24   *Serving Size: 1 wafer*
Yield: 24 wafers

Margarine, unsalted, corn oil	2 oz	Salt	To taste
Milk, nonfat	2 T	Pepper, freshly ground	To taste
Basil, minced or	1 T	Swiss cheese, low-fat,	
dried	or 1 t	shredded	3 oz
Parsley, fresh, minced	1 T	Flour, whole wheat, pastry	
Garlic, minced	1 t	(divided)	4 oz +
			1 T

1. Beat the margarine with the nonfat milk and seasonings through pepper until light and fluffy.
2. Mix in the Swiss cheese.
3. Add 4 oz of the flour; blend to mix and form a dough. If the dough is sticky, add more whole wheat flour. The additional flour will not be included in the nutrition analysis.
4. Coat a rolling pin with $\frac{1}{2}$ t of the remaining flour. Roll the dough on a work surface sprinkled with the remaining $2\frac{1}{2}$ t of flour into a 9 × 10-in. rectangle $\frac{1}{4}$-in. thick. Use more flour as needed.
5. Cut the dough 4 × 6 into twenty four $2\frac{1}{4}$ × $1\frac{2}{3}$-in. bars. Transfer to an ungreased baking sheet.
6. Place in a 375°F (190°C) oven; bake until golden brown, or about 12–14 minutes.
7. Remove to a wire rack to cool. Serve along with a cocktail, soup such as black

mushroom and pearl barley soup (see page 9), or salad such as green salad tossed with vegetables and dressed with saffron and basil orange vinaigrette (see page 280).

Servings	Calories	Protein (g) (%)	Fat (g) (%)	Cholesterol (mg)	Carbohydrates (g) (%)	Fiber (g)	Sodium (mg)
1	41	1.7 (17%)	2.2 (46%)	1.3	3.9 (37%)	0.6	10.3

Cucumber Slices with Fresh Mint and Cilantro Chutney Sandwiches

Sandwiches were named for their creator, the Earl of Sandwich. Lord Sandwich's obsession with gambling would not allow him to leave the gambling table long enough to eat a meal. His solution was the invention of the sandwich. Traditionally, the criteria for a good sandwich were that it be delicate, thin, and fresh, all of which can be said of this light vegetable sandwich.

Servings: 24   *Serving Size: one-half sandwich*
Yield: 24 ½ sandwiches

Margarine, unsalted, corn oil	2 oz	*Cucumber, English, peeled,	
Mustard powder	¾ t	thin slices	2½ lb
Bread, whole grain, thin slices,		Salt	To taste
crusts removed	1 lb (24)	Pepper, freshly ground	To taste
Fresh mint and cilantro chutney (see page 43)	1 pt		

1. Mix the margarine and mustard powder in a small bowl. Whip until light, airy, and almost double in size.
2. Spread the whipped margarine on the bread.
3. Spread the chutney over the margarine.
4. Place the cucumbers on half of the coated bread slices. Sprinkle with the salt and pepper to taste. Cover with the remaining bread slices.
5. Cut the sandwiches into triangles or other interesting shapes. Serve as hors d'oeuvres or combine with a cup of soup for a light lunch or supper.

*English cucumbers are nearly seedless. Replace with slicing cucumbers if they are not available.

Servings	Calories	Protein (g) (%)	Fat (g) (%)	Cholesterol (mg)	Carbohydrates (g) (%)	Fiber (g)	Sodium (mg)
1	79	2.9 (14%)	2.9 (30%)	0.2	11.8 (56%)	1.9	109

Gingered Apricot Farm-Raised Venison Jerky

Health-conscious diners need feel no guilt when nibbling on this low-fat, high-protein venison jerky. Venison's low-fat meaty flavor makes it a great choice for these chewy snacks.

Servings: 24   *Serving Size: 2 sticks*
Yield: 48 sticks

Venison, saddle, trimmed of fat and silverskin	5 lb	Honey, clover	¼ c
		Garlic, minced	1 oz
Beer, flat	1¼ pt	Gingerroot, minced	1 oz
Apricot puree from dried fruit (see page 389) or apricot spread, fruit-sweetened	¼ c	Mustard, powder	1½ T
		Salt	To taste or 1 t
Soy sauce, low-sodium	¾ c	Hot pepper sauce	To taste or 1 t

1. Partially freeze the meat to firm it for easy cutting.
2. Slice the meat on the bias into 48 pieces, each 6 in. long, 3 in. wide, and ⅛ to ¼-in. thick.
3. Combine the beer and remaining ingredients in a nonreactive container large enough to hold the meat. Add the meat; marinate refrigerated 24 hours, turning occasionally.
4. Lay the meat over the bars of an oven rack in a 175°F (80°C) oven, turning occasionally. Place a sheet pan underneath to catch any dripping juices. Leave the door slightly ajar to allow steam to escape and drying to occur. When the jerky is very dry (not more than 2% moisture or bacteria will grow) and slightly flexible, or 4–5 hours, remove the meat from the oven. Serve as a snack with beverages. Cool. If not used immediately, place in an airtight container; store refrigerated.

Servings	Calories	Protein (g) (%)	Fat (g) (%)	Cholesterol (mg)	Carbohydrates (g) (%)	Fiber (g)	Sodium (mg)
1	35	5.8 (71%)	0.6 (17%)	21.2	0.8 (10%)	0.1	40.4

No alcohol is listed in the nutrition analysis. It is assumed to be cooked off during preparation.

Note: The nutrition analysis is based on the estimated absorption of the marinade and the dried weight of the meat.

Ginger Sesame Chicken Wings

These baked, skinless chicken wings are "finger-lickin'" good. Their secret is a light ginger, garlic, and soy sauce glaze and a coat of toasted sesame seeds.

Servings: 24   *Serving Size: 1 wing drum*
Yield: 24 wing drums

Soy sauce, low-sodium	¼ c + 2 T	Pepper, freshly ground	To taste
Garlic, minced	¼ c	Chicken wings, drums only, skinless	3¾ lb
Gingerroot, minced	¼ c		(24)
Red pepper, ground	To taste or 1 t	Sesame seeds	1 oz
Salt	To taste	Vegetable cooking spray	—

1. In a bowl, add the first six ingredients; mix well.
2. Place the chicken wings in a nonreactive container large enough to hold them. Pour the mixture over. Turn to coat. Marinate refrigerated for 4 hours, turning occasionally.
3. Dredge the wings in the sesame seeds; place on a baking sheet coated with cooking spray. Bake in a 400°F (205°C) oven, turning once, until the wings are browned and cooked through, or about 15 minutes. Serve immediately as an hors d'oeuvre or appetizer course.

Servings	Calories	Protein (g) (%)	Fat (g) (%)	Cholesterol (mg)	Carbohydrates (g) (%)	Fiber (g)	Sodium (mg)
1	100	16.3 (66%)	3.2 (29%)	40.3	0.8 (4%)	0.1	178

Grilled Portobello Mushrooms Glazed with Herb Marinade

Until recently, the only mushrooms commonly available were the button variety. Today, a myriad are marketed which can add excitement and elegance to the menu. For an exquisite hors d'oeuvre, offer grilled portobello mushrooms (dense-fleshed creminis) glazed with herb marinade.

Servings: 24   *Serving Size: 1 medium-sized portobello mushroom*
Yield: 24 mushrooms

Sauce:		Garlic, minced	1½ T
Flavorful vegetable stock		Thyme, minced	1½ oz
(see page 2)	1 c	Basil, minced	1½ oz
Basil- and garlic-scented extra-virgin olive oil (see page 298)	2 T + 2 t	Oregano, minced	1½ oz
		Salt	To taste
Lemon juice, freshly squeezed	¼ c	Pepper, freshly ground	To taste
		Portobello mushroom caps, medium-sized, cleaned	6 lb (24)
Mushrooms:			
Flavorful vegetable stock		Vegetable cooking spray, olive-flavored	—
(see page 2)	1½ pt	Basil leaves	For garnish
Shallots, minced	6 oz		

1. Combine the sauce ingredients in a saucepan. At service, heat.
2. Combine the first eight ingredients for the mushrooms in a mixing bowl. Mix to blend.
3. Place the mushrooms in a nonreactive container. Pour the marinade over. Marinate, turning to coat occasionally for 2 hours.
4. Cook on a grill coated with vegetable oil. Season the mushroom caps with additional salt and pepper to taste. Slice into strips. Serve fanned out on plates, garnished with basil leaves. Accompany by the warm sauce and chunks of whole wheat French bread (see page 383) to sop it up.

Servings	Calories	Protein (g) (%)	Fat (g) (%)	Cholesterol (mg)	Carbohydrates (g) (%)	Fiber (g)	Sodium (mg)
1	54	2.8 (18%)	2 (30%)	0	8.1 (52%)	1.9	9.4

Mushrooms Stuffed with a Chunky Mixture of Sauteed Fresh Vegetables

For a trimmer form of stuffed mushroom caps, replace traditional fillings of high-fat ground meats and refined, white bread crumbs with stuffings of lightly sauteed, fresh vegetables.

Servings: 24   *Serving Size: 2 stuffed mushrooms*
Yield: 48 stuffed mushrooms

Rich white chicken stock (see page 7) or flavorful vegetable stock (see page 2)	$\frac{1}{4}$ c	Tomatoes, small dice	6 oz
		Carrots, shredded	2 oz
		Spinach, leaves, washed, chopped	2 oz
Brandy	2 T	Marjoram, minced or dried	2 t or $\frac{1}{2}$ t
Shallots or onions, minced	3 oz		
Garlic, minced	1 t	Fennel seeds	$\frac{1}{4}$ t or to taste
Mushrooms, very large, cleaned, stems removed and minced	2 lb as purchased (48)	Salt	To taste
		Pepper, freshly ground	To taste
		Vegetable cooking spray, olive-flavored	—
Zucchini, washed, very small dice	6 oz		

1. In a nonstick skillet, add the stock and brandy. Heat to a boil. Reduce the heat to medium. Add the shallots or onions and garlic. Cook until tender and the liquid is evaporated.
2. Add the minced mushroom stems and next six ingredients; braise-deglaze adding water if needed until tender. The mixture should resemble a semi-chunky paste. Season with salt and pepper to taste and additional fennel seeds if needed.
3. Place the mushrooms on a sheet pan coated with cooking spray. Fill with the vegetable mixture.
4. Place in a 350°F (175°C) oven; bake until the mushrooms are tender, or about 20

minutes. Serve as hors d'oeuvres, a vegetable side dish, or one component on a vegetable plate.

Servings	Calories	Protein (g) (%)	Fat (g) (%)	Cholesterol (mg)	Carbohydrates (g) (%)	Fiber (g)	Sodium (mg)	Alcohol (g) (%)
1	17	1.1 (22%)	0.2 (10%)	0	3.3 (65%)	0.9	5.8	0.1 (3%)

Roasted Corn Tortilla Chips

Traditionally, tortilla chips were prepared by deep frying triangular-shaped tortilla pieces in lard. Fat, cholesterol, and calories are cut in this version by toasting tortilla wedges until crisp in the oven. Serve them along with dips like chili cheese dip with tomatoes and onions (see page 354), fresh tomato salsa seasoned with cilantro and chilies (see page 44), or guacamole-like avocado dip with diced red, yellow, and green bell peppers (see page 357), or offer them as scoops with freshly fried pinto beans simmered in broth (see page 181).

Servings: 24   *Serving Size: 4 chips*
Yield: 8 dozen chips

| Salt | To taste or 1½ t | Water | ½ c |
| | | Tortillas, corn, 6-in. | 12 |

1. In a small bowl, add the salt to taste and water. Stir to dissolve. Brush the tortillas with the salt solution or place it in a spray bottle and spray the tortillas.
2. Stack and cut each into eight wedges. Arrange in a single layer on nonstick baking sheets.
3. Bake in a 450°F (230°C) oven, turning once, until crisp and light brown, or about 6 minutes per side. Serve with low-fat dips or salsas such as tomato bell pepper salsa (see page 51). For later use, store the chips in an airtight container and "refresh" a little in the oven before serving.

Servings	Calories	Protein (g) (%)	Fat (g) (%)	Cholesterol (mg)	Carbohydrates (g) (%)	Fiber (g)	Sodium (mg)
1	33	0.8 (10%)	0.4 (10%)	0	7 (80%)	0.8	24.3

Roasted Idaho Potato Chips

These roasted potato chips are not easy to prepare but they are definitely worth the trouble. Best yet, there's no need to feel guilty after eating a large serving of these paper-thin, skin-on, oven-browned, crisp chips.

Servings: 24   *Serving Size: 6 chips*
Yield: 12 doz chips

Potatoes, Idaho or baking, washed	12 oz	Salt	To taste
Vegetable cooking spray, olive-flavored	16 2-second sprays	Pepper, freshly ground	To taste

1. With a food slicer, evenly slice the potatoes paper thin. Immerse in cold water until needed. Pat dry to use.
2. Cover a baking sheet with parchment paper or aluminum foil. Spray with cooking spray.
3. Place a layer of potatoes on the parchment or aluminum foil so they are not overlapping one another. Leave a $1\frac{1}{2}$-in. border around all the edges.
4. Cover the potatoes with another piece of parchment or aluminum foil. Place another baking sheet on top of the potatoes to keep them flat.
5. Bake in a 400°F (205°C) oven until tender, or about 15 minutes.
6. Remove the top baking sheet and top piece of parchment or foil.
7. Place the potatoes under a broiler or in a very hot oven until brown. Turn the potatoes over and brown the other side.
8. Combine the salt and pepper in a small bowl. Sprinkle over the chips to taste. Serve with balsamic-rice vinegar dressing (see page 306), tomato bell pepper salsa (see page 51), ranch-style chip dip (see page 358), or other low-fat dips.

Servings	Calories	Protein (g) (%)	Fat (g) (%)	Cholesterol (mg)	Carbohydrates (g) (%)	Fiber (g)	Sodium (mg)
1	11	0.3 (10%)	<0.1 (1%)	0	2.5 (89%)	0.2	0.8

Variations

Cajun-Style Roasted Potato Chips: Replace the salt and pepper with spicy cajun-style seasoning blend (see page 62).

Roasted Parsnip, Sweet Potato, or Yam Chips: Substitute parsnips, sweet potatoes, or yams for the potatoes. Substitute butter-flavored vegetable cooking spray for the olive-flavored spray. Serve with an appropriate chutney or salsa.

Stone-Ground Whole Wheat Caraway Pretzels

Pretzels were brought to the United States by a German colonist. The crisp, crunchy snacks are an American favorite. In this healthy version, part of the all-purpose flour is replaced by stone-ground whole wheat flour, the amount of fat is reduced, margarine is substituted for butter, and the pretzels are coated in caraway seeds rather than the traditional coarse salt. For additional flavor, freshly ground pepper is blended into the dough.

Servings: 24   Serving Size: 1 small pretzel
Yield: 24 small pretzels

Water, lukewarm (105– 115°F) (40–45°C)	1 c	Pepper, freshly ground	To taste or $\frac{1}{2}$ t
Apple or fruit juice concentrate, unsweetened	1 t	Caraway seeds (divided)	1 T + 2 t
Yeast, active dry	$\frac{1}{4}$ oz (1 package)	Flour, bread or all-purpose, unbleached (divided)	5 oz + 2 T
Flour, whole wheat, stone- ground	6 oz	Vegetable cooking spray, butter-flavored	—
Margarine, unsalted, corn oil, soft	1 t	Egg white, large, lightly beaten	1 ($1\frac{1}{4}$ oz)
Salt	To taste or $\frac{1}{2}$ t		

1. Combine the water, juice concentrate, and yeast in a large mixing bowl. Stir until dissolved. Let the yeast rest 10 minutes.
2. Mix in the whole wheat flour, next three ingredients, and 2 t of the caraway seeds. Beat until well mixed, or at least 3 minutes. Stir in all but 2 T of the bread or all-purpose flour. Add more bread or all-purpose flour as needed if the dough is sticky. It will not be recorded in the nutrition analysis. Lightly sprinkle 1 T of the remaining bread or all-purpose flour on a work surface; add the dough; knead until smooth and elastic, or about 8 minutes.
3. Shape the dough into a ball. Place it in a clean bowl coated with cooking spray. Turn the dough once. Cover; set in a proof box or warm place (72–80°F) (22–27°C) until doubled in size, or about 45 minutes.
4. Punch the dough down. Lightly sprinkle the remaining 1 T flour on a work surface. Add the dough; shape into a roll about 12 in. long. Cut the dough into 24 equal pieces.

With the palms of your hands, roll each piece into 6-in. lengths of about pencil thickness. Taper the ends slightly.

5. On a flat surface, curve the ends toward you. Cross the loop halfway along each side once. Bend the ends back and press firmly onto the curve of the loop. Place the pretzels on a baking sheet coated with cooking spray. Let rise until almost double in size.

6. Half-fill a large saucepan with water; heat to a boil. With a slotted spoon, carefully place a few pieces of the dough into the water. Cook until they rise to the surface, or about 1 minute; remove with a slotted spoon, draining well. Return the pretzels to the baking sheet. Brush with the egg white; sprinkle with the remaining 1 T caraway seeds.

7. Bake in a 375°F (190°C) oven until golden brown and crispy, or about 15 minutes. Serve immediately alone or accompanied by prepared mustard, or cool completely and store in an airtight container. They will keep for about 1 week.

Servings	Calories	Protein (g) (%)	Fat (g) (%)	Cholesterol (mg)	Carbohydrates (g) (%)	Fiber (g)	Sodium (mg)
1	53	2.0 (15%)	0.4 (7%)	0	10.6 (78%)	1.3	3.5

Toasted Mustard Rounds

A crunchy accompaniment to any salad, these reduced-fat toasted mustard rounds are delicious. They work great as a base for hors d'oeuvres or as a garnish for soups. While individually their fat content exceeds the 30% recommended level, when served with low-fat and complex carbohydrate-rich vegetable soups or salads, the percentage of fat drops.

Servings: 24   *Serving Size: 1 crouton*
Yield: 24 croutons

Onion, finely grated	3 T	Garlic cloves, peeled, halves	4
Mustard, Dijon-style	1½ T	Bread, seven grain, slices,	
Salt	To taste	2-in. circle cutouts	24
Margarine, unsalted, corn oil	1¾ oz		(9 oz)
	(3½ T)		

1. Mix the onion, mustard, and salt to taste in a bowl. Set aside.
2. In a nonstick skillet, melt the margarine over low heat. Add the garlic cloves; cook until golden.
3. Remove the garlic; discard.
4. Place the croutons on a sheet pan. Brush half of the melted margarine on the croutons. Turn the croutons over and repeat.
5. Toast in a salamander or a very hot oven until both sides are golden brown, turning once.
6. Spread the croutons with the onion-mustard mixture.
7. Return the croutons to the salamander or very hot oven until golden and crisp. Serve as a base for hors d'oeuvres or along with soups or salads.

Servings	Calories	Protein (g) (%)	Fat (g) (%)	Cholesterol (mg)	Carbohydrates (g) (%)	Fiber (g)	Sodium (mg)
1	43	1.1 (10%)	2.2 (43%)	0	5.2 (47%)	0.8	68.3

DIPS AND TOPPINGS

Buttermilk Sour Cream Potato Topping

It is well recognized that potatoes are not "fattening," but rather it is the calorie-concentrated butter, gravies, and sour cream served with them. This topping solves the dilemma. It is a blend of calcium- and protein-rich, low-fat and nonfat dairy products seasoned with minced garlic, green onions, and fresh herbs.

Servings: 24
Yield: 1½ pt

Serving Size: 2 T

Cream cheese, nonfat	8 oz	Garlic, minced	1½ T
Sour cream, fat-free	1 c	Salt	To taste
Buttermilk, low-fat	½ c	Pepper, freshly ground	To taste
Green onion, white and 1-in.			or 1 t
green, minced	4 oz	Red pepper, ground	To taste
Parsley, minced	¼ c		or ¼ t

1. In a blender, process the cream cheese, sour cream, and buttermilk until smooth; add the remaining ingredients and mix until blended. Serve immediately or refrigerate to chill. Offer this healthy topping in lieu of butter or sour cream on baked russet potatoes (see page 218).

Servings	Calories	Protein (g) (%)	Fat (g) (%)	Cholesterol (mg)	Carbohydrates (g) (%)	Fiber (g)	Sodium (mg)
1	19	2.3 (50%)	0.1 (3%)	1.8	2.1 (47%)	0.2	69.8

Cannellini Bean Dip Adorned with Green Onions, Bell Peppers, and Tomatoes

Many Americans eat several small meals or a variety of snacks throughout the day rather than three more substantial ones. Offer low-fat and high-protein and fiber dips like this one along with fresh vegetables or low-fat whole grain chips to accommodate these diners.

Servings: 24　　　*Serving Size: 5⅓ T*
Yield: 2 qt

*Cannellini beans (white beans), canned, drained, rinsed with water or dried, cooked without salt, cooking broth reserved	1 lb + 6 oz canned or cooked, drained	Lemon juice, freshly squeezed	2 t
		Hot pepper sauce	To taste or 1½ t
		Salt	To taste
		Pepper, freshly ground	To taste or ¾ t
		Tomato, ripe, small dice	8 oz
		Pepper, green, bell, small dice	8 oz
Garlic, minced	1 T	Green onion, white and 1-in. green, minced	3 oz

1. In a blender, puree the beans with the garlic, lemon juice, and hot pepper sauce, salt, and pepper to taste until smooth. Add a small amount of the reserved bean cooking broth or water if needed to blend.
2. Mix in the tomato, green pepper, and green onion. Serve at room temperature, warm, or chilled with low-fat crackers or fresh vegetables.

*If cannellini beans are not available, use navy beans, also known as Great Northern beans, Michigan beans, or pea beans. If dried beans are used, follow these procedures to cook: Soak the beans in unsalted cold water to cover overnight or 8 hours; drain. Cover with fresh cold water; heat to a boil; reduce the heat to low. Simmer partially covered until tender, or about 1½ to 2 hours. Drain to use.

Servings	Calories	Protein (g) (%)	Fat (g) (%)	Cholesterol (mg)	Carbohydrates (g) (%)	Fiber (g)	Sodium (mg)
1	43	2.6 (23%)	0.2 (5%)	0	8.2 (72%)	2.4	2.2

Chili Cheese Dip with Tomatoes and Onions

Cheese and chilies have a natural affinity for one another. This zesty, reduced-fat and reduced-cholesterol, melted cheddar cheese dip provides the proof.

Servings: 24   *Serving Size:* $2\frac{2}{3}$ T
Yield: 1 qt

Vegetable cooking spray	—	*Chilies, canned, seeds and	
Onions, minced	12 oz	membranes removed,	
Tomatoes, peeled, coarsely		rinsed with water,	
chopped	$1\frac{1}{4}$ lb	chopped	$1\frac{1}{2}$ T
Cheddar cheese, shredded,		Salt	To taste
low-fat and low-sodium	12 oz		

1. Coat a nonstick skillet with cooking spray. Place over medium heat until hot. Add the onions; saute until tender, or about 5 minutes. Add the tomatoes; cook 5 minutes longer.
2. Transfer the onions and tomatoes to a double boiler. It may be a stainless steel bowl placed over a saucepan of steaming water. Add the cheese, chilies, and salt if desired; cook, stirring constantly, until the cheese is melted. Transfer to a heat-proof dish on a heating tray or other device to keep the cheese melted. Serve with raw vegetables or low-fat chips such as roasted corn tortilla chips (see page 346).

*Add more chilies if a spicier (hotter) dip is desired.

Servings	Calories	Protein (g) (%)	Fat (g) (%)	Cholesterol (mg)	Carbohydrates (g) (%)	Fiber (g)	Sodium (mg)
1	35	3.8 (43%)	1.1 (28%)	3.0	2.6 (30%)	0.5	5

Fruit-Sweetened Nonfat Strawberry Yogurt
Strewn with Strawberry Chunks

Historically, yogurt has been a mainstay in the diet of many populations. In the United States, its popularity is relatively new. In fact, the first commercial yogurt was not produced until 1946 by Dannon in New York. While today, yogurt is readily available plain and in a variety of flavors commercially, fresh yogurt is easy to make and many diners consider it to be superior to the store-bought type.

Servings: 48   *Serving Size: nearly 1 cup*
Yield: $2\frac{7}{8}$ gal + $\frac{1}{2}$ c (2 gal + $14\frac{1}{2}$ c)

Milk, nonfat	2 gal	White grape or apple juice	
Dry milk, nonfat	10 oz	concentrate, unsweetened	$1\frac{1}{4}$ pt
*Yogurt, plain, nonfat, active		Strawberries, ripe, washed,	
culture	1 c	hulled, crushed	$5\frac{1}{4}$ lb

1. In a sauce pot, heat the nonfat milk to 180°F (82°C), or almost boiling. Stir constantly to prevent a skin from forming on the surface. Add the nonfat dry milk; mix. Cool to 110°F (43°C). If a skin forms on the surface, carefully remove it with a spoon.
2. Place the yogurt in a mixing bowl. Add about $\frac{1}{4}$ c of the warm milk and stir gently to dilute the yogurt. Add a little more milk and stir to mix thoroughly. Add this to the rest of the milk. Mix gently to blend the yogurt thoroughly with the milk.
3. Remove 1 c of the mixture to a small container. It can be used in place of plain yogurt as a starter for the next recipe.
4. Add the juice concentrate and strawberries to the large quantity of yogurt mixture only. Cover the bowl and small container with foil; wrap towels around. Set in a warm place that is at least 80°F (27°C) but not more than 115°F (45°C). An oven with a pilot light works well, or place in an insulated cooler. Let stand until the yogurt is firm when shaken gently, or 3–5 hours.
5. Store the yogurt and starter in covered containers, refrigerated until chilled. Serve in goblets or dessert dishes as an introduction, accompaniment, or conclusion to any meal, or offer as a topping for whole grain pancakes or waffles.

*The nonfat plain yogurt used in this recipe must contain an active culture to work. Review the commercial yogurt's ingredient list for this information. Once the fresh yogurt is made, use it as the culture for future batches.

Servings	Calories	Protein (g) (%)	Fat (g) (%)	Cholesterol (mg)	Carbohydrates (g) (%)	Fiber (g)	Sodium (mg)
1	206	16.4 (31%)	1.0 (4%)	8.2	33.5 (64%)	2.3	242

Variations

Nonfat Plain Yogurt: Omit the juice concentrate and strawberries. It will set up in about 6–8 hours.

Blueberry-, Raspberry-, Cantaloupe-, Peach-, Banana-, Kiwi-, or Other Fruit-Flavored Nonfat Yogurt Strewn with Fruit Chunks: Replace the strawberries with small pieces of the appropriate fruit.

Guacamole-Like Avocado Dip with Diced Red, Yellow, and Green Bell Peppers*

Traditionally, this creamy, spicy dip is prepared primarily from avocados. In this recipe, part of the high-fat (86%) and high-calorie (322 each) avocados are replaced with a puree of roasted, low-fat, low-calorie green bell peppers and nonfat, plain yogurt. For flavor, texture, and color, red and yellow bell peppers are blended into the smooth, green sauce along with diced onions and tomatoes and minced cilantro.

Servings: 24   *Serving Size:* $3\frac{2}{3}$ T
Yield: $1\frac{1}{4}$ qt $+\frac{1}{2}$ c

Avocado, peeled, pitted	1 lb + 6 oz	Tomato, small dice	8 oz
Pepper, green, bell, roasted,† peeled, seeds and membranes removed	8 oz	Onion, minced	8 oz
		Chilies, jalapeno or other hot green, seeds and membranes removed, minced	3
Yogurt, plain, nonfat	$1\frac{1}{4}$ pt		
Lime juice, freshly squeezed	$\frac{1}{4}$ c	Garlic, minced	1 T
Pepper, red and yellow bell, small dice	12 oz each	Cilantro, minced	4 oz
		Salt	To taste
		Pepper, freshly ground	To taste

1. In a blender, puree the avocado and next three ingredients until smooth. Mix in all the remaining ingredients. Cover and refrigerate until chilled.
2. Serve as a dip with fresh vegetables or low-fat and low-cholesterol chips such as roasted corn tortilla chips (see page 346) or as a condiment with meat, fish, poultry, or vegetarian dishes such as tacos, tostadas, or quesadillas.

*Adapted from a recipe by Byron Takeuchi.

†See page 493 for roasting bell pepper directions.

Servings	Calories	Protein (g) (%)	Fat (g) (%)	Cholesterol (mg)	Carbohydrates (g) (%)	Fiber (g)	Sodium (mg)
1	75	2.6 (13%)	4.2 (46%)	0.4	8.4 (41%)	1.8	23.8

Ranch-Style Chip Dip

While the flavor and creaminess of this dip mirror that of typical mayonnaise and sour cream-based chip dips, its fat and cholesterol content are substantially less. It is prepared by blending nonfat sour cream with minced green onions, garlic, and fresh herbs. When served with raw vegetables or chips such as roasted Idaho potato chips (see page 347), weight reducers can enjoy this dip without concern for fat or calories.

Servings: 24   Serving Size: $1\frac{1}{3}$ T
Yield: $2\frac{1}{8}$ c

Sour cream, nonfat	1 lb	Oregano, minced or	
Lemon juice, freshly squeezed	2 t	dried	$1\frac{1}{2}$ t
Green onions, minced, white			or $\frac{1}{2}$ t
only, tops reserved for		Tarragon, minced or	
garnish	3 oz	dried	$\frac{3}{4}$ t
Parsley, minced	3 T		or $\frac{1}{4}$ t
Garlic, minced	2 t	Salt	To taste
Basil, minced or		Pepper, freshly ground	To taste
dried	$1\frac{1}{2}$ t or $\frac{1}{2}$ t		

1. In a bowl or storage container, mix the sour cream with all the remaining ingredients.
2. Chill to blend the flavors, at least 3 hours.
3. Slice the green onion tops thin. Sprinkle over the dip. Serve with a medley of colorful, crisp, raw vegetables or a selection of low-fat chips.

Servings	Calories	Protein (g) (%)	Fat (g) (%)	Cholesterol (mg)	Carbohydrates (g) (%)	Fiber (g)	Sodium (mg)
1	14	1.4 (36%)	0.02 (1%)	0	2.5 (62%)	0.1	14.2

Roasted Elephant Garlic

For a healthy alternative to garlic bread laden with fat, offer warm rounds of whole grain bread broken into pieces with roasted elephant garlic. When garlic is roasted, it becomes buttery soft, sweet, and delicate tasting.

Servings: 24   Serving Size: ½ head elephant garlic
Yield: 12 heads elephant garlic

*Garlic, elephant, heads	12 (12 oz as purchased)	Salt	To taste
		Pepper, freshly ground	To taste
		Rosemary, branches	12

1. Remove the pointed top from each garlic head. Cut in half crosswise, halfway between the top and bottom.
2. Sprinkle each cut surface with salt and pepper to taste. Place a sprig of rosemary on each bottom half.
3. Place the garlic halves back together and wrap tightly in foil. Place on a sheet pan. Bake in a 400°F (205°C) oven until the garlic is soft.
4. Remove the foil and rosemary. Serve with warm, whole wheat French bread (see page 383) or dark pumpernickel, country style bread and a small dish of extra-virgin olive oil. To eat, squeeze each clove to extract the soft flesh from the skin and spread on the bread. Dip in olive oil if desired.

*Elephant garlic has a sweeter and milder taste than American garlic and is about eight times its normal size. When not available, replace with the white-skinned, strongly-flavored American garlic or the somewhat milder-flavored Mexican or Italian garlic, both with mauve-colored skins.

Servings	Calories	Protein (g) (%)	Fat (g) (%)	Cholesterol (mg)	Carbohydrates (g) (%)	Fiber (g)	Sodium (mg)
1	17	0.7 (15%)	0.1 (5%)	0	3.7 (80%)	0.8	1.9

BEVERAGES

Chardonnay and Cranberry Spritzer*

Current dietary guidelines recommend moderate consumption of alcohol. One way to cut intake is to blend beers with vegetable juices (my favorite is tomato juice and beer) and wines with fruit juices and waters. Both red and white wine make good bases for spritzers. In this spritzer, full-bodied chardonnay is blended with cranberry juice and soda water and sweetened with juice concentrate.

Servings: 1 and 24   Serving Size: $\frac{9}{10}$ c
Yield: $\frac{9}{10}$ c and $1\frac{1}{4}$ gal + $1\frac{1}{4}$ pt

	1 serving	24 servings
Wine, full-bodied chardonnay	$\frac{1}{4}$ c + 2 t	$1\frac{3}{4}$ qt
Cranberry juice, unsweetened	$\frac{1}{4}$ c + 2 t	$1\frac{3}{4}$ qt
Soda water	$\frac{1}{4}$ c + 2 t	$1\frac{3}{4}$ qt
White grape juice concentrate, unsweetened	1 T	$1\frac{1}{2}$ c
Ice, crushed	—	—
Orange slices	1	24

1. Mix the first four ingredients in a mixing container. Fill stemmed glasses with crushed ice. Pour or ladle the spritzer mixture over. Serve garnished with orange slices or other fresh ripe fruit in season.

*Adapted from a recipe by KC Knauer.

Servings	Calories	Protein (g) (%)	Fat (g) (%)	Cholesterol (mg)	Carbohydrates (g) (%)	Fiber (g)	Sodium mg	Alcohol (g) (%)
1	128	0.3 (1%)	0.1 (1%)	0	21 (65%)	1.0	20.2	6.4 (34%)

Freshly Prepared Spicy Tomato Cocktail

With everyone being so health conscious, this tomato cocktail is ideal at breakfast or brunch but equally as good for a nutritious pre-lunch or dinner cocktail. Offer it chilled in frosted stemmed glasses, garnished with a rib of crisp celery.

Servings: 24   *Serving Size: 1 c*
Yield: 1½ gal

Tomatoes, ripe, eighths	12 lb	Worcestershire sauce, very	
Flavorful vegetable stock (see		low sodium	1½ T or
page 2) or water	1 pt		to taste
Onion, peeled, 1-in. pieces	1 lb	Apple juice concentrate,	
Celery, ½-in. pieces	8 oz	unsweetened	1 T or
Carrots, washed, ½-in. pieces	8 oz		to taste
Bay leaf	1	Salt	To taste
Parsley sprigs	1 oz	Pepper, freshly ground	To taste
Garlic cloves, peeled	1	Hot pepper sauce	To taste

1. Simmer the tomatoes with the next seven ingredients until the vegetables are very tender, or about 40 minutes.
2. Remove the bay leaf. Puree in a blender until smooth. Strain through a china cap, stirring and pressing to extract all but the very fibrous vegetable components. Discard the small amount of vegetable pulp remaining. To adjust the consistency, thicken by reducing over heat or thin with stock or water.
3. Season with the remaining ingredients. Serve warm or chilled garnished with lemon slices or celery sticks.

The following nutrition analysis is based on the ingredients listed in this recipe. It does not reflect that some of the pulp is strained from the cocktail before serving. As a result, the calories and nutrients are likely less than the listed figures.

Servings	Calories	Protein (g) (%)	Fat (g) (%)	Cholesterol (mg)	Carbohydrates (g) (%)	Fiber (g)	Sodium (mg)
1	64	2.2 (13%)	0.8 (10%)	0	14.2 (77%)	3.8	37.6

Spicy Minted Orange Iced Tea

There is much debate about the origin of iced tea. One theory contends it was invented in New Orleans some time around 1868—this being the reported place and time commercial ice manufacturing began in the United States. The following adaptation of the exceedingly popular drink makes a refreshing warm weather beverage.

Servings: 24   *Serving Size: 1⅛ c concentrated tea*
Yield: 1½ gal + 1½ pt concentrated tea

Water, fresh tap or bottled	1½ gal	Allspice berries	2 t
Mint leaves	3 oz	Orange juice concentrate,	
*Black tea leaves, Darjeeling	2 oz	unsweetened	1½ c
Cinnamon sticks	1½ oz	White grape or apple juice	
	(16)	concentrate, unsweetened	1 c
Cloves, whole	1½ t	Lemon juice, freshly squeezed	½ c

1. Heat the water to a boil in a nonreactive container.
2. Add the mint leaves and next four ingredients. Turn off the heat; cover the pan and let the tea brew. Steep 5 minutes. Strain through a fine mesh nonreactive strainer or one lined with cheesecloth.
3. Add the remaining ingredients. Chill and serve over ice in tall glasses garnished with colorful straws or lemon or orange twists. Add more grape or apple juice concentrate for a sweeter beverage.

*Darjeeling is a distinctive, delicate-flavored black tea from northern India. Replace it with the leaves of a similar flavored black tea if not available.

Servings	Calories	Protein (g) (%)	Fat (g) (%)	Cholesterol (mg)	Carbohydrates (g) (%)	Fiber (g)	Sodium (mg)
1	57	0.7 (4%)	0.2 (3%)	0	14.2 (93%)	1.4	9.4

Strawberry, Banana, and Kiwi Orange Shake*

This dairy-free fruit shake is big on flavor without the fat and calories found in ice cream shakes. It can be offered as a healthy beverage at breakfast, lunch, or dinner or promoted as a snack any time of the day.

Servings: 24 *Serving Size: $1\frac{1}{8}$ c*
Yield: $1\frac{1}{2}$ gal + $2\frac{1}{2}$ c

Strawberries, ripe, washed, hulled	2 lb	Orange juice, freshly squeezed	2 qt
Bananas, ripe, peeled, large dice	$1\frac{3}{4}$ lb	White grape juice concentrate, unsweetened	$\frac{1}{2}$ c
Kiwi fruit, ripe, peeled, large dice	$1\frac{1}{4}$ lb	Crushed ice	$2\frac{1}{4}$ qt
		Strawberry fans (see page 447)	12 oz (24)

1. In a large blender or in batches, combine the first six ingredients. Process until smooth. Adjust the sweetness with more white grape juice concentrate if needed. The addition will not be reflected in the nutrition analysis. Serve immediately in stemmed glasses garnished with strawberry fans.

*Adapted from a recipe by Shelly Doonan.

Servings	Calories	Protein (g) (%)	Fat (g) (%)	Cholesterol (mg)	Carbohydrates (g) (%)	Fiber (g)	Sodium (mg)
1	107	1.5 (5%)	0.6 (5%)	0	25.9 (90%)	3.0	3.2

11

Breads, Cakes, Frostings, and Sweet Sauces

BREADS AND CAKES

Angel Spice Cake

This cake combines the best of two classics. The flavors of spice cake are blended with the light and airy-textured angel food cake. The end result is a luscious cake without fat or cholesterol.

Servings: 24   *Serving Size: 1 piece (one-twelfth of a 10-in. cake)*
Yield: 2 10-in. tube cakes

Sugar, granulated, fine	10 oz	Egg whites, large, room	
Flour, cake	8 oz	temperature	16
Cinnamon, freshly ground	2 t		(1¼ lb)
Nutmeg, freshly ground	¾ t	Cream of tartar	1 t
Clove, freshly ground	½ t	Vanilla extract	2 t

1. Sift the sugar twice into a bowl.
2. In another bowl, combine about half the sugar with the flour, cinnamon, nutmeg, and clove; sift 3 times.
3. In a mixing bowl, beat the egg whites until foamy; add the cream of tartar. Continue beating until soft peaks form. Gradually add the sugar that wasn't mixed with the flour, beating until the whites are stiff but not dry.
4. Fold in the flour-sugar mixture. Fold in the vanilla. Pour into 2 10-in. tube cake pans. Bake in a 350°F (175°C) oven until the cakes spring back lightly when touched, or about 45 minutes.
5. Remove from the oven and invert the pans on a rack. Let rest until thoroughly cooled, or about 1½ hours. The cakes should come out of the pans on their own when cooled. If they don't, run a knife around the edges to loosen.
6. Serve glazed or infused with apple syrup flavored with calvados (see page 385), coated with thick and fluffy maple cooked frosting (see page 401), topped with a scoop of nonfat, frozen yogurt, or simply as is. To cut, saw gently into pieces with a serrated knife.

Servings	Calories	Protein (g) (%)	Fat (g) (%)	Cholesterol (mg)	Carbohydrates (g) (%)	Fiber (g)	Sodium (mg)
1	94	3.2 (14%)	0.1 (1%)	0	19.8 (85%)	0.4	39.3

Variations

Candy Cane Angel Cake: Eliminate the cinnamon, nutmeg, and clove. Reduce the vanilla to 1 t and add 6 oz of crushed candy canes. Follow steps 1–5 above, folding in the crushed candy canes with the vanilla in step 4. Serve frosted with thick and fluffy flavored frosting prepared with corn syrup and no additional flavorings (see page 401) and sprinkled with an additional 1 oz of crushed candy canes.

Cocoa Angel Cake: Eliminate the cinnamon, nutmeg, and clove and decrease the cake flour to 7 oz. Follow steps 1–5 above adding 2 oz of cocoa in step 2 with one-half of the sugar.

Coffee-Flavored Angel Spice Cake: Follow steps 1–5, adding 1 T of instant coffee granules with the cinnamon, nutmeg, and cloves in step 2. Serve with choice of frosting.

Licorice-Flavored Angel Cake: Eliminate the cinnamon, nutmeg, and clove. Reduce the vanilla to 1 t and add 2 t anise flavoring. Follow steps 1–5 above, folding in the anise flavoring with the vanilla in step 4. Serve infused (see directions on page 385) or glazed with melted fruit-sweetened raspberry spread or naturally sweetened raspberry sauce (see page 394).

Vanilla Angel Cake: Eliminate the cinnamon, nutmeg, and clove. Reduce the vanilla to 1 t and add 1 t almond extract. Follow steps 1–5 above, folding in the almond extract with the vanilla in step 4. Use as a base for baked banana-strawberry alaska (see page 422) or as a component in berries encased in angel cake (see page 459) or top with orange fruit glaze (see page 395).

Angel Spice Cupcakes: Coat the bottoms of deep muffin tins with cooking spray. Fill about two-thirds full with angel spice cake batter or one of its variations. Bake until the cakes spring back lightly when touched, or about 20 minutes.

Fruit-Filled Angel Cake: With a serrated knife, using a sawing motion, cut horizontally a 1 in. high section from the top of the angel spice cake or one of its variations. Set aside. In the remaining cake section, cut a pocket to hold the filling. Using a serrated knife, cut away the center of the cake to within 1 in. of the sides and base. Ladle a fruit filling such as blueberry, blackberry, currant, gooseberry, huckleberry, loganberry, raspberry, or strawberry into the pocket. Replace the lid; cover the cake with the frosting of choice.

The cake which is removed can be shredded and mixed with the filling, cut into cubes, and served for dipping into fruit sauces such as naturally sweetened raspberry sauce (see page 394), orange fruit glaze (see page 395), or fruit-sweetened strawberry sauce (see page 392), made into crumbs and used as an ingredient in recipes, such as cherry phyllo strudel (see page 455) or sprinkled on fruit or frozen desserts.

Apple Crumb Cake

Apple crumb cake is not really a cake at all. Rather, it is glazed, baked apple slices layered with graham cracker crumbs and flavored with hints of rum, orange, and cinnamon.

Servings: 24   *Serving Size: 3⅓ × 3-in. piece*
Yield: 12 × 20 × 2-in. counter pan

Margarine, unsalted, corn oil	4 oz	Orange juice concentrate,	
Graham cracker crumbs	1 lb +	unsweetened	¾ c
	2 oz	Rum	¼ c
Cinnamon, freshly ground	3 T	Vegetable cooking spray,	
Apple or fruit juice		butter-flavored	—
concentrate, unsweetened	1 pt +	*Apples, tart, peeled, thin	
	1¼ c	slices	6 lb

1. In a nonstick skillet, melt the margarine over low heat; add the graham cracker crumbs and cinnamon. Cook, stirring until evenly browned.
2. In a small bowl, mix the juice concentrates and rum.
3. Coat a 12 × 20 × 2-in. counter pan with cooking spray. Layer the apples and graham cracker crumb mixture; repeat, ending with the crumbs on top.
4. Pour the juice concentrate mixture over. Bake in a 350°F (175°C) oven until the apples are tender, or about 1 hour. Cover the top of the cake with aluminum foil near the end of cooking if needed to prevent overbrowning.
5. Cool; cut the pan 6 × 4 into 24 3⅓ × 3-in. pieces. Serve with a scoop of nonfat, frozen vanilla yogurt.

*Examples of tart or slightly acidic varieties of apples are Gravenstein (yellow-green with red stripes), Granny Smith (green), Grimes Golden (gold), Jonathan (brilliant red), McIntosh (red to green), Newton Pippin (green), Northern Spy (red), Rhode Island Greening (green), Stayman (red), Winesap (red), and York Imperial (red).

Servings	Calories	Protein (g) (%)	Fat (g) (%)	Cholesterol (mg)	Carbohydrates (g) (%)	Fiber (g)	Sodium mg	Alcohol (g) (%)
1	273	2.1 (3%)	65 (21%)	0	52.9 (75%)	3.3	139	0.8 (2%)

Banana Apricot Whole Wheat Cake with No Added Fat

Besides being tasty, this cake has lots of nutritional goodies in it—high-potassium bananas, beta-carotene rich apricots, calcium- and protein-filled yogurt, and B vitamin and fiber-rich whole wheat flour.

Servings: 16   *Serving Size: 1 wedge (one-eighth of a 9-in. cake)*
Yield: two 9-in. rounds

Flour, whole wheat, pastry	5 oz	Bananas, very ripe, mashed	
Flour, cake or all-purpose,		(see page 491)	1¼ c
unbleached	4 oz	Apricot puree from dried fruit	
Sugar, light brown	12 oz	(see page 389)	¾ c
Baking soda	¾ t	Yogurt, nonfat, plain	¼ c
Baking powder	½ t	Vanilla extract	1 t
Salt	To taste	Vegetable cooking spray,	
	or ½ t	butter-flavored	—
Egg whites, large, lightly		Bananas, ripe, ¼-in. thick slices	12 oz
beaten	4 (5 oz)	Sugar, confectioners'	2 T

1. Place the whole wheat flour in a mixing bowl. Sift the cake flour and next four ingredients into the mixing bowl; mix well. Add the beaten egg whites, mashed bananas, apricot puree, yogurt, and vanilla. Stir until blended.
2. Pour into two 9-in. round cake pans coated with cooking spray. Bake in a 350°F (175°C) oven until a wooden pick inserted in the center comes out clean, or about 25 minutes. Place on a rack to cool.
3. Slice each cake into two layers. Place the sliced bananas between the layers. If served immediately, there is no need for icing. Simply sprinkle with confectioners' sugar. Cut each cake into eight wedges to serve. If icing is desired, coat with apricot-flavored powdered sugar frosting (see page 386). The sliced bananas can be omitted if the cake is to be frosted.

Servings	Calories	Protein (g) (%)	Fat (g) (%)	Cholesterol (mg)	Carbohydrates (g) (%)	Fiber (g)	Sodium (mg)
1	192	3.6 (7%)	0.4 (2%)	<0.1	45.5 (91%)	2.3	79.1

Banana Bran Walnut Muffins

Dishes once stereotyped as breakfast, lunch, or dinner foods are successfully crossing over this divide. For example, these muffins are to be expected on a breakfast menu but are equally tasty with a salad at lunch or in a bread basket for dinner.

Servings: 30   *Serving Size: 1 muffin*
Yield: 30 muffins

Bananas, unpeeled, very ripe	1 lb + 14 oz as purchased	Baking powder	2½ t
		Baking soda	1½ t
		Buttermilk, nonfat	1¾ c + 2 T
Flour, cake or all-purpose, unbleached	10 oz	Egg whites, large, lightly beaten	5 (6¼ oz)
Bran cereal, shredded (All-Bran)	5 oz		
Sugar, light brown	5 oz	Oil, canola, vegetable, or salad	¼ c + 1 T
Walnuts, chopped	2 oz		
Cinnamon, freshly ground	2½ t	Vegetable cooking spray, butter-flavored	—

1. To ripen the bananas further if not the desired ripeness, place them on a baking pan in a 350°F (175°C) oven. Bake until their skins turn completely black, or about 10 minutes. Cool. Peel. Mash the bananas. Set aside.
2. In a mixing bowl, combine the flour and next six ingredients.
3. In another bowl, blend the mashed bananas, buttermilk, egg whites, and oil.
4. Pour the liquid ingredients over the dry mixture; fold until just incorporated.
5. Spoon the batter into muffin cups coated with cooking spray. Do not place in paper liners. They will stick. Bake in a 400°F (205°C) oven until the muffins are golden brown and a wooden pick inserted in their centers comes out clean, or about 25 minutes.
6. Cool slightly in the tins. Transfer to a rack for additional cooling. Serve the muffins warm or at room temperature accompanied by whipped honey margarine if desired.

Servings	Calories	Protein (g) (%)	Fat (g) (%)	Cholesterol (mg)	Carbohydrates (g) (%)	Fiber (g)	Sodium (mg)
1	123	3.2 (10%)	3.8 (26%)	0.5	21 (64%)	2.4	158

Buckwheat Stone-Ground Yellow Corn Bread

Commercially ground buckwheat flour is available in two forms, dark and light. While the dark flour contains a larger percentage of the grain's fine milled seed hull particles, the light flour may be preferred for its less pungent flavor. Both types of buckwheat flour are 100% buckwheat.

Servings: 24　　　　*Serving Size: 1 wedge (one-twelfth of a 9-in. round)*
Yield: two 9-in. rounds

Flour, cake or all-purpose, unbleached	12 oz	Egg whites, large, lightly beaten	8
Baking powder	1½ oz		(10 oz)
Salt	To taste or 1½ t	Oil, canola, vegetable, or salad	3 oz
Cornmeal, yellow, stone-ground	1 lb	Apple or fruit juice concentrate, unsweetened	3 oz
Flour, buckwheat	8 oz	Vegetable cooking spray, butter-flavored	—
Milk, nonfat	1 qt		

1. In a mixing bowl, sift the cake flour, baking powder, and salt. Add the cornmeal and buckwheat flour; toss to mix.
2. In another bowl, beat the milk, eggs, oil, and juice concentrate together. Add half the liquid ingredients to the dry mixture; stir just until blended. Add the remaining liquid ingredients; stir just until blended.
3. Pour the batter into two 9-in. baking rounds coated with cooking spray. Bake in a 425°F (220°C) oven until the top is golden and a wooden pick inserted in the center comes out clean, or about 25 minutes. Cool slightly in the pans before cutting. Serve warm with whipped honey neufchatel cheese* or use as an ingredient in stuffings such as buckwheat stone-ground corn bread, spinach, and ham stuffing (see page 237) or as a topping on vegetable, meat, poultry, or fish selections such as spicy catfish with garlic and cilantro corn bread topping (see page 158).

*Whipped honey neufchatel cheese: Whip 8 oz of neufchatel cheese in a mixing bowl until light and airy. Mix in 2 oz of honey until well blended.

Servings	Calories	Protein (g) (%)	Fat (g) (%)	Cholesterol (mg)	Carbohydrates (g) (%)	Fiber (g)	Sodium (mg)
1	210	6.8 (13%)	4.7 (20%)	0.7	36.1 (67%)	3.2	237

Carrot, Raisin, and Pineapple Whole Wheat Cake

When hearty cakes with more body such as this one are prepared, a combination of whole grain cake or pastry flours can replace refined flours to produce nutritionally superior cakes, ones with more vitamins, trace minerals, and fiber.

Servings: 36　　　*Serving Size: 1 wedge (one-ninth of a 9-in. round)*
Yield: four 9-in. rounds

Flour, whole wheat, pastry	6 oz	Eggs, large	2 (4 oz)
Flour, cake or all-purpose, unbleached	14 oz	Carrots, washed, shredded	1 lb + 6 oz
Sugar, light brown	8 oz	Pineapple, crushed, packed without sugar, drained (reserve juice for frosting or other use)	1 lb drained
Baking soda	1 oz		
Cinnamon, freshly ground	1 T ($\frac{1}{4}$ oz)		
Allspice, freshly ground	1½ t		
Nutmeg, freshly ground	½ t	Raisins, seedless, or dried currants	5 oz
Date puree (see page 391)	1 qt + 1½ c	Vegetable cooking spray, butter-flavored	—
Egg whites, large	4 (5 oz)		

1. In a mixing bowl, place the whole wheat pastry flour; sift in the next six ingredients; mix until well blended.
2. Add the date puree; mix to blend.
3. Add the egg whites and eggs; mix well.
4. Stir in the carrots, pineapple, and raisins. Pour the batter into four 9-in. round baking pans coated with cooking spray. Bake in a 350°F (175°C) oven until a wooden pick comes out clean, or about 40–45 minutes. Cover the cake tops with aluminum foil after 30 minutes to prevent overbrowning. Set on a rack to cool. Cut each cake into nine wedges. Serve sprinkled with confectioners' sugar or frost with creamy light cheese frosting (see page 390).

Servings	Calories	Protein (g) (%)	Fat (g) (%)	Cholesterol (mg)	Carbohydrates (g) (%)	Fiber (g)	Sodium (mg)
1	200	3.7 (7%)	0.9 (4%)	11.8	46.8 (89%)	5.0	239

Cornmeal Cake with Anise and Cinnamon

This cake contains no refined sugar, egg yolks, or added butter. Applesauce and concentrated fruit juice sweeten the cake and keep it moist. Freshly ground cinnamon and crushed anise seeds add a nice touch.

Servings: 16   *Serving Size: 1 wedge (one-eighth of a 9-in. round)*
Yield: two 9-in. rounds

Vegetable cooking spray, butter-flavored	—	Granny Smith and McIntosh applesauce (see page 393) or unsweetened commercial applesauce	12 oz
Flour, cake or all-purpose, unbleached	12 oz		
Baking powder	1 T + 2 t	Margarine, corn oil, softened, unsalted	4 oz
Baking soda	½ t	Apple or fruit juice concentrate, unsweetened	½ c + 2 T
Salt	To taste or ¾ t		
Cornmeal, yellow, stone-ground	8 oz	Anise seeds, crushed	1 T
Egg whites, large	6 (7½ oz)	Cinnamon, freshly ground	¼ t

1. Coat two 9-in. round baking pans with cooking spray. Set aside.
2. Sift the flour and next three ingredients into a bowl; mix in the cornmeal; set aside.
3. In a mixing bowl, beat the egg whites until foamy. Beat in half of the flour mixture.
4. Add the applesauce, margarine, juice concentrate, and anise seeds; beat until blended.
5. Add the remaining flour mixture; beat until blended. Pour into the prepared cake pans. Sprinkle with the cinnamon.
6. Bake in a 350°F (175°C) oven until a wooden pick inserted in the center comes out clean, or about 20 minutes.
7. Cool 10 minutes in the pans on a wire rack; remove from the pans; cool completely on the wire rack. Cut each cake into eight wedges; serve with whipped honey neufchatel cheese (see page 371).

Servings	Calories	Protein (g) (%)	Fat (g) (%)	Cholesterol (mg)	Carbohydrates (g) (%)	Fiber (g)	Sodium (mg)
1	137	2.7 (8%)	5.9 (38%)	0.3	19.1 (54%)	1.5	171

Cranberry Orange-Flavored Upside Down Cake

Pineapple upside down cake was a specialty of my Mother, but there's no need to limit upside down cakes to pineapple toppings. For an innovative touch, this cake is topped with an orange-flavored chunky cranberry topping. Best yet, it contains no butter, margarine, shortening, or oil and no egg yolks, whole milk, or cream.

Servings: 24   Serving Size: 1 wedge (one-twelfth of a 9-in. round)
Yield: two 9-in. rounds

Vegetable cooking spray, butter-flavored	—	Salt	To taste or $\frac{3}{4}$ t
Cranberries, fresh or frozen without sugar	1 lb	Granny Smith and McIntosh applesauce (see page 393) or unsweetened commercial applesauce	12 oz
White grape juice concentrate, unsweetened	$\frac{1}{4}$ c		
Orange juice concentrate, unsweetened	$\frac{1}{4}$ c	Egg whites, large	6 ($7\frac{1}{2}$ oz)
Sugar, light brown (divided)	$1\frac{1}{4}$ lb	Orange zest, finely grated	1 T
Flour, whole wheat pastry	12 oz	Vanilla extract	$1\frac{1}{2}$ t
Baking powder	1 T + $1\frac{1}{2}$ t		

1. Lightly coat the bottom and sides of 2 9-in. round baking pans with vegetable cooking spray.
2. Combine the cranberries with the grape and orange juice concentrates and 8 oz of the brown sugar in a saucepan. Heat to a boil. Reduce the heat to a simmer; cook until it reaches syrupy consistency. Pour into the prepared cake pans.
3. Place the remaining brown sugar, flour, baking powder, and optional salt in a mixing bowl. Blend to mix. In another bowl, stir the applesauce, egg whites, orange zest, and vanilla until blended.
4. Mix the moist ingredients into the dry ingredients just until blended. Pour over the cranberry mixture. Bake in a 350°F (175°C) oven until the top is golden and a wooden pick inserted in the center comes out clean, or about 30 minutes. If further baking is required, cover the cake tops with aluminum foil to prevent overbrowning. Let the cakes cool on a rack about 5 minutes.
5. Loosen the edges of the cakes from the pan; place inverted serving platters over the cakes; turn upside down. Let set a few minutes before removing the pans so that the

cakes can absorb all the juices. Serve warm or at room temperature, each cut into 12 wedges.

Servings	Calories	Protein (g) (%)	Fat (g) (%)	Cholesterol (mg)	Carbohydrates (g) (%)	Fiber (g)	Sodium (mg)
1	169	3 (7%)	0.4 (2%)	0	40.4 (91%)	2.8	105

Gingerbread Cake Topped with Bananas

While gingerbread is often topped with whipped cream or a rich lemon sauce, this whole wheat, homestyle cake flavored with molasses, ginger, and other sweet spices is topped with sliced bananas glazed in fruit syrup. It's delicious served warm or at room temperature.

Servings: 24   *Serving Size: 3 × 3⅓-in. piece*
Yield: two 10 × 12 × 2½-in. counter pans

Apple juice concentrate, unsweetened (divided)	1½ pt	Flour, cake or all-purpose, unbleached	8 oz
Vanilla extract	2 t	Baking soda	1 T
Vegetable cooking spray, butter-flavored	—	Ginger, ground	1 T
		Cinnamon, freshly ground	2 t
Bananas, ripe, peeled, ¼-in. thick slices	2 lb	Cloves, freshly ground	¼ t
		Nutmeg, freshly ground	¼ t
Molasses, light	½ c	Egg whites, large, lightly beaten	8
Margarine, unsalted, corn oil	4 oz		
Flour, whole wheat, pastry	12 oz		(10 oz)

1. Blend 1 c of the juice concentrate with the vanilla. Pour ½ into each of two 10 × 12 × 2½-in. counter pans coated with cooking spray.
2. Lay the banana slices evenly over the juice concentrate mixture. Set aside.
3. In a saucepan, heat the remaining pint of juice concentrate, molasses, and margarine to a boil, stirring constantly. Remove from the heat; transfer to a mixing bowl; set aside to cool.
4. Place the whole wheat pastry flour in another bowl. Sift the cake flour and next five ingredients into the whole wheat flour; mix to blend.
5. Alternately, add the dry ingredients and egg whites to the juice concentrate mixture, beating after each addition. When smooth, pour the batter evenly over the bananas.
6. Bake the cakes in a 350°F (175°C) oven until a wooden pick inserted in the center comes out clean, or about 30 minutes. If further baking is required, cover with aluminum foil to prevent overbrowning and continue baking. Let stand 10 minutes.
7. Place inverted serving platters over the cakes; turn the cakes upside down. Let stand a

few minutes before removing the pans. Cut the cakes 3 × 4 into 12 $3\frac{1}{3}$ × 3-in. pieces. Serve warm or at room temperature with the bananas decorating the cakes' tops.

Servings	Calories	Protein (g) (%)	Fat (g) (%)	Cholesterol (mg)	Carbohydrates (g) (%)	Fiber (g)	Sodium (mg)
1	235	4.7 (8%)	4.5 (17%)	0	46.1 (76%)	3.0	134

Hot Fudge Pudding Cake

There's no need to prepare a frosting for this low-fat and low-cholesterol chocolate cake. During baking, a creamy fudge pudding forms on the bottom of the cake. Upon inverting, it becomes the cake's topping.

Servings: 24 *Serving Size: 3 × 3⅓-in. piece*
Yield: 12 × 20 × 2-in. counter pan

Sugar, granulated	1 lb	Baking powder	1 oz
Margarine, unsalted, corn oil	4 oz	Walnuts, chopped	4 oz
Milk, nonfat	1 pt	Vegetable cooking spray,	
Vanilla extract	1 T	butter-flavored	—
Flour, cake or all-purpose,		Sugar, light brown	1¼ lb
unbleached	1 lb	Water, boiling	1¾ qt
Cocoa powder (divided)	4½ oz		

1. In a mixing bowl, cream the granulated sugar and margarine.
2. Add the milk and vanilla extract; mix well.
3. Sift the flour, 1½ oz of the cocoa, and baking powder into another bowl. Add to the sugar-margarine mixture; mix well.
4. Stir in the walnuts. Pour the batter into a 12 × 20 × 2-in. counter pan coated with cooking spray.
5. Mix the brown sugar and remaining 3 oz of cocoa together; sprinkle over the batter.
6. Pour the boiling water over the batter. Bake in a 350°F (175°C) oven until the cake springs back when touched lightly, or about 45 minutes. Cool the cake. Cut the cake 4 × 6 into 24 3 × 3⅓-in. pieces. Serve upside down with the hot fudge sauce spooned over the cake.

Servings	Calories	Protein (g) (%)	Fat (g) (%)	Cholesterol (mg)	Carbohydrates (g) (%)	Fiber (g)	Sodium (mg)
1	314	4 (5%)	9.6 (26%)	0.8	57.4 (69%)	2	212

Low-Fat and Low-Cholesterol Chocolate Cake

Promote "healthy meal deals" on your menu by offering complementary dessert with selected entrees. When the dessert is one like this chocolate cake prepared without egg yolks or added fat (that's no butter, oil, shortening, or margarine), diners can literally "have their cake and eat it too."

Servings: 24   *Serving Size: 1 wedge (one-eighth of a 9-in. round)*
Yield: three 9-in. rounds

Flour, cake or all-purpose, unbleached	9 oz	Date puree (see page 391)	1 pt + ¼ c
Cornstarch	5 oz	White grape or apple juice	
Cocoa powder	4 oz	concentrate, unsweetened	1½ pt
Baking powder	1 T	Vanilla extract	2 t
Baking soda	1½ t	Vegetable cooking spray,	
Salt	To taste or ¾ t	butter-flavored	—
		Sugar, confectioners'	1½ oz
Egg whites, large	6 (7½ oz)		

1. In a bowl, sift together the first six ingredients; mix. In a mixing bowl, beat the egg whites with the date puree, juice concentrate, and vanilla. Add the dry mixture to the egg white mixture; mix together until blended.
2. Coat three 9-in. cake rounds with cooking spray. Divide the cake batter equally among the cake pans. Bake in a 350°F (175°C) oven until a wooden pick inserted in the center comes out clean, or 30–35 minutes. Cover the cake tops with aluminum foil after 30 minutes to prevent overbrowning. Cool on a rack.
3. To serve, sift confectioners' sugar over; cut into wedges and garnish with fresh berries or other fruit in season. Another delicious option is to serve the cakes laced with raspberry sauce. To prepare: Cut each cake into two layers; coat the bottom layer with naturally sweetened raspberry sauce (see page 394); cover with the top cake layer; cut into wedges; serve with the raspberry sauce napped over the center of each cake wedge.

Servings	Calories	Protein (g) (%)	Fat (g) (%)	Cholesterol (mg)	Carbohydrates (g) (%)	Fiber (g)	Sodium (mg)
1	204	3.5 (7%)	1.0 (4%)	0	48.3 (89%)	3.7	130

Peach Meringue Mousse Cake

Some desserts are traditionally cholesterol-free and contain only a tad of fat. Peach meringue mousse cake, a sweet, light, and airy egg white filling laced with bits of ripe peaches baked in a ramekin on an angel cake base and topped with meringue, is one such star of a dessert. It looks as good as it tastes.

Servings: 24   *Serving Size: 1-c ramekin*
Yield: 24 1-c ramekins

Vanilla angel cake, 3 ½-in. rounds, ½ in. thick (see page 367)	24	Egg whites, pasteurized	1 lb + 6½ oz
*Peaches, ripe, peeled, slices, fresh or frozen without sugar (divided)	5½ lb	Cream of tartar	3 T
		Sugar, light brown, sifted	8 oz
		Vanilla extract	1 T

1. Fit the angel cake rounds into the bottom of 24 1-c baking ramekins.
2. In a blender, puree 2½ lb of the peaches. Finely chop the remaining 3 lb of peaches; mix with the peach puree.
3. In a large mixing bowl, beat the egg whites with the cream of tartar until foamy; gradually add the sugar, beating until stiff and glossy. Fold in the vanilla.
4. Fold one-third of the meringue into the peach mixture. Spoon the peach mixture over the cake rounds in the ramekins.
5. Divide the remaining meringue among the ramekins; spread to completely cover the peach mixture. Broil 3 in. from the heat or cook using a torch until the meringue is light brown. Serve on saucers lined with doilies.

*See page 16 for peach peeling directions.

Servings	Calories	Protein (g) (%)	Fat (g) (%)	Cholesterol (mg)	Carbohydrates (g) (%)	Fiber (g)	Sodium (mg)
1	161	5.9 (14%)	0.1 (1%)	0	34.7 (85%)	1.9	131

Pumpkin Whole Wheat Pancakes

For cholesterol- and fat-conscious diners who want to squeeze a variety of vitamins and minerals into breakfast, these pancakes are a great way to start the day. Top with melon ball scoops of maple syrup-flavored nonfat frozen vanilla yogurt and diners will wonder why they ever skipped breakfast.

Servings: 24　　　　*Serving Size: three 3-in. pancakes*
Yield: 6 doz 3-in. pancakes

Flour, whole wheat, pastry	9 oz	Pumpkin, cooked without salt,	
Flour, cake or all-purpose,		cold, mashed, or canned	12 oz
unbleached	6 oz	Milk, nonfat	1 qt
Baking powder	2 T	Apple or fruit juice	
Cinnamon, freshly ground	1½ t	concentrate, unsweetened	¾ c
Nutmeg, freshly ground	1 t	Oil, canola, vegetable, or salad	2 T
Ginger, ground	½ t	Vegetable cooking spray,	
Cloves, freshly ground	¼ t	butter-flavored	12 two-
Egg whites, large	12		second
	(15 oz)		sprays

1. In a mixing bowl, place the whole wheat flour; sift in the next six ingredients; mix to blend.
2. In another bowl, place the egg whites; beat lightly. Add the pumpkin, milk, juice concentrate, and oil; mix until smooth.
3. Mix the liquid ingredients into the dry ingredients until moistened; there may be some lumps. Stand loosely covered for 30 minutes.
4. Coat a nonstick skillet with cooking spray. Place over medium-high heat until hot. Cooking to order, gently pour ⅛-c portions of the batter into the pan. Cook until bubbles appear on the surface of the pancakes and the bottoms are golden, or about 2 minutes. Turn and cook until the other sides are golden, or about 2 minutes. Repeat, using all the batter. Serve the pancakes with Granny Smith and McIntosh applesauce (see page 393), whipped honey neufchatel cheese (see page 371), warm maple syrup, or a dollop of frozen nonfat yogurt.

Servings	Calories	Protein (g) (%)	Fat (g) (%)	Cholesterol (mg)	Carbohydrates (g) (%)	Fiber (g)	Sodium (mg)
1	114	5.5 (19%)	1.6 (12%)	0.7	20 (69%)	1.9	158

Whole Wheat and Onion Sage Drop Biscuits

Lard, shortening, and butter or combinations of these depending on the flavor desired are generally the preferred choices of fat for preparing biscuits. In these biscuits, canola oil, a fat high in monounsaturated ("good") fat replaces these high cholesterol and/or saturated ("bad") fat options. To reduce the need for salt, the biscuits are flavored with minced onions and fresh sage.

Servings: 24   *Serving Size: 1 biscuit*
Yield: 24 biscuits

Flour, whole wheat, pastry	6 oz	Onions, minced	3 oz
Flour, cake or all-purpose, unbleached, sifted	6 oz	Oil, canola or vegetable	¼ c + 2 T
Baking powder	1½ T	Milk, nonfat	1 c + 2 T
Salt	To taste		
Sage, minced or dried	1½ T or 1½ t		

1. In a mixing bowl, mix the first six ingredients. Pour the oil and milk over the dry ingredients; mix only until the mixture leaves the sides of the bowl.
2. Drop 24 evenly divided portions from a spoon onto an ungreased, nonstick baking sheet. Bake in a 475°F (245°C) oven until golden brown, or about 15 minutes. Serve hot or at room temperature with a light (low-fat) vegetable salad or soup such as corn chowder garnished with roasted red bell pepper (see page 17).

Servings	Calories	Protein (g) (%)	Fat (g) (%)	Cholesterol (mg)	Carbohydrates (g) (%)	Fiber (g)	Sodium (mg)
1	86	2.1 (10%)	3.6 (38%)	0.2	11.5 (53%)	1.2	33.1

Whole Wheat French Bread

It is difficult to duplicate the hard, glossy crusted bread produced by the bakeries in France. To create similar results, spray these bread loaves with water throughout baking.

Servings: 24   *Serving Size: 3 slices*
Yield: 4 loaves

Yeast, active dry	½ oz (2 pkg)	*Flour, unbleached, all-purpose (divided)	1 lb
Water, lukewarm (105–115°F or 40–45°C) (divided)	1½ pt	Salt	To taste or 1 T
Honey, clover	1 T + 1 t	Vegetable cooking spray, butter-flavored	—
Flour, whole wheat, stone-ground	1 lb	Cornmeal, yellow, stone-ground	2 T

1. In a mixing bowl, dissolve the yeast in ½ c of the lukewarm water. Let the yeast rest for 10 minutes.
2. Stir in the remaining water and honey.
3. Add the whole wheat flour, all the unbleached flour except 2 T, and the salt. Using the dough arm attachment of the mixer, mix until the dough is smooth and elastic. If the dough hasn't lost its stickiness, add a little more all-purpose flour.
4. Place the dough in a bowl coated with cooking spray. Turn the dough once. Cover the bowl with plastic wrap; let the dough rise in a proof box or warm place (72–80°F or 22–27°C) until double in volume, or about 1 hour. If fermentation is complete, a dent will remain when a hand is pressed into the dough.
5. Punch down the dough. Divide it into four (14-oz) equal pieces. Shape each piece into a smooth round ball. Using the remaining 2 T of flour, lightly flour a work surface and rolling pin. On the floured surface, roll each dough ball into a 12 × 6-in. rectangle. Starting with the longer side, roll up tightly, pressing the dough into the roll with each turn. Pinch the edges and ends to seal. Roll the loaves with the palm of the hand to produce long thin loaves with tapered rounded ends.
6. Place well apart seam side down on sheet pans sprinkled with cornmeal. Brush or spray the loaves with cold water as they are going into the oven and several times during baking if a crisp crust is desired. Bake in a 425°F (220°C) oven until golden brown, or about 25 minutes. Slice each loaf into 18 pieces. Serve hot or at room temperature.

Offer with extra-virgin olive oil, a fruit spread, whipped margarine, or topping such as whipped creamy cranberry spread (see page 55).

*Additional flour may be required in this recipe. Use it as required. This will not have been accounted for in the nutrient analysis.

Servings	Calories	Protein (g) (%)	Fat (g) (%)	Cholesterol (mg)	Carbohydrates (g) (%)	Fiber (g)	Sodium (mg)
1	139	4.8 (13%)	0.6 (4%)	0	29.6 (83%)	3.1	2.7

FROSTINGS AND
SWEET SAUCES

Apple Syrup Flavored with Calvados

What makes this apple syrup special is calvados, a smooth and dry brandy with a deep woody flavor. It is produced by aging the fermented juices of Normandy apples in oak casks. It is a favorite of the French and considered to be one of their best.

Servings: 24   *Serving Size: 2 t*
Yield: 1 c

Calvados or applejack (brandy)	1½ c	Lemon juice, freshly squeezed	1 T
Apple juice concentrate, unsweetened	1½ c	Lemon zest strips, 3 × ½-in.	6

1. In a saucepan, combine all the ingredients. Place over low heat; simmer until the consistency of syrup, or reduced to 1 c. It will thicken further when cool. Set aside for 15 minutes. Strain to remove the lemon zests; discard.
2. Serve as a topping with pancakes, waffles, French toast, or nonfat frozen yogurt. To infuse a cake with the syrup, prick the cake all over with a wooden skewer; brush the top and sides of the cake until the syrup has been absorbed. It makes a nice complement to angel spice cake (see page 366).

Servings	Calories	Protein (g) (%)	Fat (g) (%)	Cholesterol (mg)	Carbohydrates (g) (%)	Fiber (g)	Sodium (mg)
1	29	0.1 (< 1%)	0.1 (< 1%)	0	7.3 (100%)	0.1	4.5

No alcohol is listed in the nutrition analysis. It is assumed to be cooked off during preparation.

Apricot-Flavored Powdered Sugar Frosting

This is an easy-to-make frosting, simply confectioners' sugar blended with heated milk and a splash of apricot brandy.

Servings: 24   Serving Size: 2 t
Yield: 1 c

Confectioners' sugar	10 oz	*Apricot brandy	3 T
Milk, nonfat, hot	2 T		

1. Place the sugar in a bowl. Add the hot milk and apricot brandy. Beat until smooth. Use as icing for cakes such as banana apricot whole wheat cake with no added fat (see page 369).

*Barack Palinka is the European name for apricot brandy.

Servings	Calories	Protein (g) (%)	Fat (g) (%)	Cholesterol (mg)	Carbohydrates (g) (%)	Fiber (g)	Sodium (mg)	Alcohol (g) (%)
1	50	<0.1 (< 1%)	< 0.1 (< 1%)	< 0.1	11.8 (91%)	0	0.8	0.6 (8%)

Buckwheat Honey Glaze

There are many types of honey, each with its own unique flavor and appearance. Because of its strong flavor, dark brown buckwheat honey, also known as "California sage honey," is a good choice for this recipe. When not readily available, the more common, pale, and delicate clover honey may be substituted.

Servings: 24   **Serving Size: $\frac{1}{2}$ T**
Yield: $\frac{3}{4}$ c

Honey, buckwheat or clover $\frac{1}{2}$ c   **Sugar, light brown**   2 oz

1. In a small saucepan, combine the honey and brown sugar. Heat to a boil.
2. To serve, pour the hot glaze over cakes. If decorations such as candied orange zests or flowers are to be placed on the cake, set them on immediately after the glaze is applied. When it dries, the glaze will hold the decorations in place.

Servings	Calories	Protein (g) (%)	Fat (g) (%)	Cholesterol (mg)	Carbohydrates (g) (%)	Fiber (g)	Sodium (mg)
1	30	< 0.1 (< 1%)	0 (0%)	0	8.1 (100%)	0	1.2

Butterscotch Sauce

There's no cream or butter in this easy-to-make dessert topping. Rather, evaporated skim milk, brown sugar, and corn syrup are transformed into a thick and creamy sauce. With a splash of vanilla flavoring, it's ready to spoon over a scoop of frozen nonfat yogurt.

Servings: 24   *Serving Size: 2 T*
Yield: 1½ pt

| Sugar, light brown | 15 oz | Milk, evaporated, skim | 1½ c |
| Corn syrup, light | 1½ c | Vanilla extract | 1 t |

1. Place the brown sugar and corn syrup in a saucepan. Simmer over low heat, stirring until it reaches a thick syrup consistency, or about 5 minutes. Set aside to cool. Stir in the evaporated milk and vanilla extract. Serve over baked fruit or nonfat, frozen yogurt (see banana split with frozen yogurt and butterscotch sauce on page 444). To serve warm, reheat in a double boiler.

Servings	Calories	Protein (g) (%)	Fat (g) (%)	Cholesterol (mg)	Carbohydrates (g) (%)	Fiber (g)	Sodium (mg)
1	138	1.2 (3%)	< 0.1 (< 1%)	0.6	34.8 (96%)	0	50

Chilled Apricots in Light Fruit Juice Syrup
Apricot Puree from Dried Fruit

Beta-carotene, a chemical precursor of vitamin A, is believed to prevent several types of cancer, heart disease, and cataracts. It might even boost the immune system and extend the life span. These chilled apricots are prepared from dried apricots. They are rated number 1 on the list of top beta-carotene sources.*

Servings: 24
Yield: 2⅛ qt puree

Serving Size: ⅓ c puree

Apricots, dried	2 lb	White grape juice concentrate,	
Water	3½ pt	unsweetened	¾ c

1. Place all the ingredients in a saucepan. Heat to a boil; reduce the heat to low. Simmer until the fruit is tender, or about 40 minutes. Adjust the amount of liquid with more water and the sweetness by adding more juice concentrate. The additional juice concentrate will not be reflected in the nutrition analysis. Serve warm or chilled as a dessert placed in goblets on decorative saucers.
2. To prepare pureed apricots, strain the apricots from the liquid. Reduce the strained liquid over heat or add water to the liquid to yield 1½ pt. Place the apricots and liquid in a blender; puree until smooth. Serve as a sauce over frozen, nonfat yogurt, a frosting on low-fat cakes, or a topping with whole grain pancakes or French toast, or use as a flavoring ingredient in other dishes such as warm fruit-sweetened apricot souffle (see page 467).

*Source: Human Nutrition Center, U.S. Department of Agriculture.

Servings	Calories	Protein (g) (%)	Fat (g) (%)	Cholesterol (mg)	Carbohydrates (g) (%)	Fiber (g)	Sodium (mg)
1	104	1.6 (6%)	0.2 (2%)	0	26.7 (93%)	3.0	5.5

Creamy Light Cheese Frosting

This reduced-fat version of cream cheese frosting is especially nice with moist and dense, high-fiber cakes filled with fruits and vegetables such as carrot, raisin, and pineapple whole wheat cake (see page 372), or maybe with a zucchini oat cake studded with dried cherries and apricot bits.

Servings: 36   *Serving Size:* $1\frac{1}{8}$ T
Yield: $1\frac{3}{4}$ c

Cream cheese, nonfat, or		*Pineapple juice, unsweetened	1 oz
neufchatel cheese	12 oz	Vanilla extract	1 t
Sugar, confectioners'	5 oz		

1. Combine all the ingredients in a mixing bowl. Beat until light and creamy. Use as frosting for cakes, such as carrot, raisin, and pineapple whole wheat cake.

*Use fresh, frozen, or canned pineapple juice (see page 492) or the juice reserved from carrot, raisin, and pineapple whole wheat cake.

Servings	Calories	Protein (g) (%)	Fat (g) (%)	Cholesterol (mg)	Carbohydrates (g) (%)	Fiber (g)	Sodium (mg)
1	22	1.2 (23%)	< 0.1 (< 1%)	1.5	4.2 (76%)	< 0.1	7

Date Puree

Most dried fruits can be pureed and served as a substitute for fat in cakes and other baked goods. Dates, dried plums (prunes), and raisins are the three types described in this recipe.

Servings: 24   *Serving Size: 1½ T*
Yield: 1⅛ pt

| Dates, pitted, unsweetened | 14 oz | Vanilla extract | 1 T |
| Water | ¾ c | | |

1. Place the dates in a blender; puree, adding the water and vanilla slowly, until smooth. Use as a replacement for fat and to add sweetness to baked goods such as carrot, raisin, and pineapple whole wheat cake (see page 372) and low-fat and low-cholesterol chocolate cake (see page 379).

Servings	Calories	Protein (g) (%)	Fat (g) (%)	Cholesterol (mg)	Carbohydrates (g) (%)	Fiber (g)	Sodium (mg)
1	47	0.3 (3%)	0.1 (1%)	0	12.3 (96%)	1.4	0.7

Variations

Dried plum and raisin purees: Substitute prunes (dried plums) and seedless raisins for the dates.

Fruit-Sweetened Strawberry Sauce

Lightly sweetened fruit purees make refreshing, fat-free, and cholesterol-free alternatives to butter-rich frostings on cakes and sauces on frozen dairy desserts. They are delicious laced over whole grain waffles and pancakes too. A special feature of this sauce is it contains no refined sugar either. It is sweetened with a puree of ripe banana and concentrated white grape juice.

Servings: 24   *Serving Size:* $3\frac{1}{3}$ *T*
Yield: $1\frac{1}{4}$ *qt*

Strawberries, fresh, hulled, or frozen without sugar	2 lbs	White grape juice concentrate, unsweetened	$\frac{1}{2}$ c
*Banana, very ripe, pureed	1 c		

1. In a blender, add all the ingredients; puree until smooth.
2. Serve as a sauce with healthy cakes such as vanilla angel cake (see page 367), fresh fruit, frozen, nonfat yogurt, or low-fat, whole grain waffles and pancakes.

*To ripen bananas further in the oven, see procedure on page 491.

Servings	Calories	Protein (g) (%)	Fat (g) (%)	Cholesterol (mg)	Carbohydrates (g) (%)	Fiber (g)	Sodium (mg)
1	30	0.4 (4%)	0.2 (6%)	0	7.3 (90%)	1.2	1.9

Granny Smith and McIntosh Applesauce

This isn't just any applesauce. In this recipe, unpeeled tart, green Granny Smith apples are simmered in apple juice with red- and green-toned, sweet-tart McIntosh apples, pureed, and strained of their skins. It is a treat, warm or cold.

Servings: 24   *Serving Size: ⅝ c*
Yield: 1¼ gal

*Apples, McIntosh or other sweet-tart apples, washed	6 lb as purchased	Apple juice, unsweetened	1 qt + ½ c
Apples, Granny Smith or other tart apples, washed	6 lb as purchased	Lemon juice, freshly squeezed	¼ c

1. Core the apples and cut into chunks. Place in a sauce pot with the apple juice. Heat to a boil; reduce the heat to low; simmer covered until the apples are tender, stirring occasionally, or about 10 minutes.
2. In a blender, process the cooked apples until pureed. Press through a strainer to remove the apple skins.
3. Stir in the lemon juice. Serve warm or chilled as a dessert or salad sauce, as a condiment with pork dishes, or a topping for desserts or breakfast items like whole grain pancakes and waffles.

*Other tart apples are listed in the Introduction under "Ingredient Specifications."

Servings	Calories	Protein (g) (%)	Fat (g) (%)	Cholesterol (mg)	Carbohydrates (g) (%)	Fiber (g)	Sodium (mg)
1	140	0.4 (1%)	0.7 (4%)	0	36.2 (95%)	4	3.2

Naturally Sweetened Raspberry Sauce

This puree of sweet, wine-tasting, ruby red raspberries looks and tastes elegant laced over a scoop of vanilla, nonfat, frozen yogurt, soaking into whole wheat pancakes, or napped over rolled crepes filled with sauteed fruit.

Servings: 24   *Serving Size: 2¾ T*
Yield: 1⅛ qt

| Raspberries, fresh, washed or frozen without sugar | 3 lb | Raspberry liqueur | Optional (3 T) |
| White grape or apple juice concentrate, unsweetened | 1¾ c | | |

1. In a blender, puree all the ingredients until smooth. Strain through cheesecloth or a fine mesh strainer to remove the seeds. Serve as a topping for nonfat, frozen yogurt, low-fat cakes such as vanilla angel cake (see page 367) and low-fat and low-cholesterol chocolate cake (see page 379), or whole grain waffles or pancakes.

Servings	Calories	Protein (g) (%)	Fat (g) (%)	Cholesterol (mg)	Carbohydrates (g) (%)	Fiber (g)	Sodium (mg)
1	62	0.6 (4%)	0.4 (5%)	0	14.9 (91%)	2.7	5.1

No alcohol is listed in the nutrition analysis. It is assumed to be cooked off during preparation.

Orange Fruit Glaze

This easy-to-prepare, orange-flavored fruit sauce makes a tasty, fat-free topping for whole grain pancakes and waffles. It's equally good laced over low-fat cakes and nonfat, frozen vanilla yogurt.

Servings: 24   *Serving Size: 2 T*
Yield: 1½ pt

White grape juice concentrate, unsweetened	1 c + 2 T	Cornstarch	1 oz
		Orange zest, finely grated	1½ t
		Orange juice, freshly squeezed	2¼ c

1. Place the first three ingredients in a saucepan. Stir to form a smooth paste. Stir in the orange juice. Stirring, heat to a boil; reduce the heat to low; simmer until thickened, or about 3 minutes. Serve over whole grain waffles or pancakes and low-fat cakes like vanilla angel cake (see page 367).

Servings	Calories	Protein (g) (%)	Fat (g) (%)	Cholesterol (mg)	Carbohydrates (g) (%)	Fiber (g)	Sodium (mg)
1	39	0.3 (3%)	0.1 (2%)	0	9.5 (95%)	0.4	1.3

Orange-Pineapple Yogurt Topping

Baked and fresh fruit is often delicious served without additional accouterments. But, to give them a special touch, they might be served with this fruity yogurt topping. It is also charming with whole grain waffles and pancakes.

Servings: 24   *Serving Size: 2 T*
Yield: 1½ pt

Yogurt, plain, nonfat	1 pt	Orange juice concentrate,	
Pineapple juice concentrate,		unsweetened	¼ c
unsweetened	¾ c	Orange zest, finely grated	1 t

1. Place all the ingredients in a bowl; mix until well blended. Serve over warm, sauteed, or baked fruit such as baked bananas coated in graham cracker crumbs (see page 457), sliced fresh fruit, or whole grain waffles and pancakes.

Servings	Calories	Protein (g) (%)	Fat (g) (%)	Cholesterol (mg)	Carbohydrates (g) (%)	Fiber (g)	Sodium (mg)
1	32	1.4 (17%)	< 0.1 (1%)	0.4	6.7 (82%)	0.1	15.9

Pineapple-Orange Flavored Seven-Minute Frosting

Seven-minute frosting was always my favorite birthday cake icing as a child. Unlike my Mother's though, this one is sweetened with concentrated orange and pineapple juices rather than refined sugar.

Servings: 24   *Serving Size: $2\frac{1}{3}$ T*
Yield: $3\frac{1}{2}$ c

Egg whites, pasteurized	5 oz	Pineapple juice concentrate,	
Cream of tartar	$\frac{1}{2}$ t	unsweetened	$\frac{3}{4}$ c
Orange juice concentrate,		Vanilla extract	2 t
unsweetened	$\frac{3}{4}$ c		

1. In a mixing bowl, place the egg whites and cream of tartar. Beat with an electric mixer on high speed until well mixed and foamy. Scrape the sides of the bowl. Beat in the juice concentrates until well mixed.
2. Place the mixture over a boiling water bath and continue beating rapidly until the frosting is thick and stands in peaks when the whip is lifted. Remove from the heat. Add the vanilla and continue beating until the frosting is thick enough to spread. Serve with cakes such as vanilla angel cake (see page 367).

Servings	Calories	Protein (g) (%)	Fat (g) (%)	Cholesterol (mg)	Carbohydrates (g) (%)	Fiber (g)	Sodium (mg)
1	34	0.9 (11%)	< 0.1 (1%)	0	7.6 (89%)	0.1	9.7

Pureed Fresh Pineapple Sauce
Fresh Pineapple Juice

This recipe was created on one of my first attempts at making fruit juice. After pureeing and straining the juice, it seemed such a waste to discard the remaining fruit puree. Upon tasting, I discovered that by sweetening the puree with unsweetened pineapple juice concentrate, it could be transformed into a heavenly sauce.

Servings: 24   *Serving Size: 5 fl oz juice and ¼ c + 3 T sauce*
Yield: 3¾ qt juice and 2½ qt + ½ c sauce

*Pineapple, ripe, peeled, cored, 1-in. cubes	12 lb (24 lb as purchased, or 5–7 pineapples)	Pineapple juice concentrate, unsweetened	1 pt

1. Puree the pineapple cubes in a blender until smooth.
2. Strain the mixture through a fine mesh strainer. Serve the clear liquid chilled as juice in chilled goblets.
3. Mix the pineapple juice concentrate with the puree until well blended. Serve the sauce chilled as a dessert sauce, condiment with meat, fish, or poultry selections, or as a topping for low-fat cakes or whole grain pancakes or waffles. Garnish the juice or sauce with strawberry fans† or mint leaves.

The pineapple puree in its natural unsweetened form might also be used fresh or dried as a thickening and flavoring agent in salad dressings like Asian-style ginger dressing, sweet sauces such as naturally sweetened cranberry pineapple coulis, sweet quick breads such as carrot pineapple bread, or vegetable dishes like sweet potato timbales.

*See page 492 for fresh pineapple peeling and cubing directions.
†See page 447 for directions on making strawberry fans.

Servings	Calories	Protein (g) (%)	Fat (g) (%)	Cholesterol (mg)	Carbohydrates (g) (%)	Fiber (g)	Sodium (mg)
1	154	1.2 (3%)	1.0 (5%)	0	38.7 (92%)	2.8	3.0

The nutrition analysis reflects one serving of juice and one serving of sauce.

Raspberry Glaze Finished with Kirsch

Kirsch, the fruit brandy flavoring this raspberry glaze, is also known as kirschwasser. It is a colorless liquid made from a mash of wild black cherries that grow in the Rhine Valley. When seedless fruit-sweetened raspberry spread is simmered briefly with water and finished with a splash of this best-known nongrape brandy, the result is an easy-to-make, refined sugar-free topping.

Servings: 24   *Serving Size: 1 T*
Yield: 1½ c

| Raspberry spread, fruit-sweetened | ¾ c | Water | ¾ c |
| | | *Kirsch | 2 t |

1. Place the fruit spread and water in a small saucepan. Heat to a boil. Reduce the heat to low; simmer briefly until it reaches sauce consistency. Remove from the heat. Stir in the kirsch. Serve drizzled over low-fat cakes, high-fiber pancakes or waffles, or dessert souffles like warm fruit-sweetened apricot souffle (see page 467).

*Substitute ½ t almond extract for the kirsch if desired.

Servings	Calories	Protein (g) (%)	Fat (g) (%)	Cholesterol (mg)	Carbohydrates (g) (%)	Fiber (g)	Sodium (mg)	Alcohol (g) (%)
1	15	< 0.1 (1%)	< 0.1 (1%)	0	3.7 (93%)	0.1	1.7	0.1 (6%)

Rhubarb Sauce with a Splash of Orange

Stewed fruits like this rhubarb sauce may be served for dessert but also as a meat accompaniment or topping for dishes such as pancakes, waffles, puddings, frozen dairy desserts, and cakes. When served as the final course of a meal, a dollop of creamy sweet topping makes a nice finishing touch. If prepared to complement a meat selection, a little vinegar, wine, or lemon juice may be added to sharpen the flavor of the stewed rhubarb.

Servings: 24 *Serving Size: 3⅓ T*
Yield: 1¼ qt

Rhubarb, ¾-in. pieces	4 lb	Wine, white	1 pt
Strawberry fruit spread, fruit-sweetened	1½ pt + ¼ c	Orange zest, 2 × ½-in. strips	3

1. Add all the ingredients to a saucepan. Heat to a boil; reduce the heat to very low. Cover and simmer until the rhubarb is softened and the mixture thickened, or about 35–40 minutes. Add water if needed.
2. Remove the orange zest; discard. Serve warm or chilled as a fruit sauce for dessert, a meat accompaniment, or as a topping ladled over a scoop of frozen, nonfat yogurt, whole grain French toast, pancakes or waffles, or low-fat cakes.

Servings	Calories	Protein (g) (%)	Fat (g) (%)	Cholesterol (mg)	Carbohydrates (g) (%)	Fiber (g)	Sodium (mg)
1	82	0.8 (4%)	0.2 (2%)	0	19.7 (94%)	2.3	11.2

No alcohol is listed in the nutrition analysis. It is assumed to be cooked off during preparation.

Thick and Fluffy Maple Cooked Frosting

What makes this thick and fluffy, egg white frosting unique is its maple flavor. It's a treat! Spread it on banana-, apple-, spice-, ginger-, or coffee-flavored cakes.

Servings: 24
Yield: 1½ qt

Serving Size: ¼ c

Syrup, maple	1¼ pt	Egg whites, pasteurized	5 oz
Cream of tartar	1 t		

1. Place the maple syrup and cream of tartar in a saucepan. Heat to a boil; cook until it reaches 240°F (115°C) or the soft ball stage on a candy thermometer.
2. In a mixing bowl, beat the egg whites until stiff but not dry. Gradually pour the cooked maple syrup in a fine stream into the beaten egg whites, beating constantly until thick and fluffy. Spread on cakes such as angel spice cake (see page 366). It makes enough to frost two 2-layer cakes.

Servings	Calories	Protein (g) (%)	Fat (g) (%)	Cholesterol (mg)	Carbohydrates (g) (%)	Fiber (g)	Sodium (mg)
1	90	0.6 (3%)	0.1 (1%)	0	22.5 (97%)	< 0.1	12.2

Variations

Thick and Fluffy Cooked Frosting in flavor of choice: Replace the maple syrup with light corn syrup. Add several drops of any flavoring extract desired, perhaps lemon, orange, peppermint, or almond.

Yogurt Honey Topping Dashed with Almond

Offer this blended yogurt and ricotta cheese sauce, lightly sweetened with honey, napped over a dish of berries or as a dip on a fruit plate. It's equally lovely as a topping on fruit tarts.

Servings: 24　　　　*Serving Size:* $\frac{5}{6}$ *T*
Yield: $1\frac{1}{4}$ c

Ricotta cheese, part-skim milk	6 oz	Honey, clover	2 T
Yogurt, plain, nonfat	$\frac{1}{4}$ c	Almond extract	$\frac{1}{4}$ t

1. In a blender, process all the ingredients until smooth. Serve as a topping with fruit or desserts such as raspberry snow tart (see page 433).

Servings	Calories	Protein (g) (%)	Fat (g) (%)	Cholesterol (mg)	Carbohydrates (g) (%)	Fiber (g)	Sodium (mg)
1	17	1.0 (22%)	0.6 (30%)	2.2	2.0 (48%)	0	10.8

12

Cookies, Bars, Pies, and Pastries

COOKIES AND BARS

Apricot and Coconut Wheat Flake Cereal Bonbons*

To provide the flavor of coconut without its saturated fat, these cereal bonbons are flavored with coconut extract. They are the answer to a sweet craving but at the same time rich in beta-carotene, B vitamins, and fiber.

Servings: 24   *Serving Size: 1 cereal bonbon*
Yield: 24 cereal bonbons

Apricots, dried, minced	6 oz	Coconut extract	1¼ t
Wheat flake cereal, coarsely crushed	7½ oz	Lemon zest, finely grated	¾ t
Milk, sweetened, condensed, low-fat	1¼ c		

1. In a bowl, combine the apricots, crushed wheat flakes, condensed milk, and coconut extract; mix together. Refrigerate for about ½ hour for easier handling.
2. Portion the wheat flake mixture into 24 small balls; place on a sheet pan lined with parchment.
3. Sprinkle the lemon zest on the cereal balls. Chill until firm, or about 1 hour. Serve with a glass of nonfat milk or cup of freshly brewed decaffeinated coffee.

*Adapted from a recipe by Leticia Gonzales and Jeff Haines.

Servings	Calories	Protein (g) (%)	Fat (g) (%)	Cholesterol (mg)	Carbohydrates (g) (%)	Fiber (g)	Sodium (mg)
1	99	2.4 (9%)	0.8 (7%)	6.2	21.1 (85%)	1.5	79.8

Variations

Substitute other dried fruits or combinations of dried fruits for the apricots, maybe dates, papaya, mango, cherries, or cranberries. Replace the wheat flakes with other cereals, perhaps bran or corn flakes.

Candied Orange Zests

Candied orange zests are prepared without fat and are rich in fiber too. They are a delicious alternative to a high-fat, high-cholesterol dessert. Served as a condiment with a cup of freshly ground and brewed decaffeinated coffee, they hit the spot after a filling meal. When feeling artistic, cut the orange peels in decorative shapes rather than the simple strips suggested here.

Servings: 24   *Serving Size: 2 t*
Yield: 1 c

Orange peel with pulp removed, 1-in. × $\frac{1}{8}$-$\frac{1}{4}$-in. strips	5$\frac{1}{2}$ oz	Honey, clover	$\frac{1}{4}$ c + 2 T
Sugar, light brown (divided)	4 oz	Pineapple juice concentrate, unsweetened	2 T

1. In a saucepan, place the orange peel strips; cover with cold water.
2. Heat the water to a boil; reduce the heat to medium; simmer for 5 minutes; drain; rinse with cold water. Repeat the process; set aside.
3. In a small saucepan, add all but 2 T of the brown sugar, the honey, juice concentrate, and 1 pt of water. Place over low heat, stirring until the sugar dissolves.
4. Add the peels. Increase the heat to medium; gently boil 15 minutes. The sugar liquid should be syrup consistency. Continue boiling gently if further thickening is required. Remove from the heat. Loosely cover; stand at room temperature at least 12 hours.
5. Remove the peels from the syrup; place on a wire rack over a sheet pan to drain. Once drained, place the peels and remaining brown sugar in a plastic bag; shake to coat.
6. Set aside to dry at room temperature for 2–3 days, or for several hours in an oven that has just been turned off and is still warm. Use immediately as a sweet condiment, garnish, or flavoring. The candied strips can be stored in an airtight container between layers of parchment for up to 1 month.

Servings	Calories	Protein (g) (%)	Fat (g) (%)	Cholesterol (mg)	Carbohydrates (g) (%)	Fiber (g)	Sodium (mg)
1	42	0.1 (1%)	< 0.1 (< 1%)	0	11.2 (99%)	0.2	2.3

Note: The nutrition analysis reflects all the ingredients used in the recipe. Since much of the syrup drips off the orange zests and some of the brown sugar does not cling to the zests, likely the nutrient content of each serving is only about one-third the amount indicated.

Variations

Substitute lemon, lime, or grapefruit peel for the orange peel and unsweetened orange juice concentrate for the pineapple juice concentrate.

Crisp Spiced Ginger Cookies

Cookies hot out of the oven are one of the childhood favorites Americans never out-grow. These crisp spiced ginger cookies make perfect nibbling along with a scoop of sorbet, cup of freshly brewed decaffeinated coffee, or chilled glass of nonfat milk.

Servings: 24   Serving Size: 2 cookies
Yield: 4 dozen cookies

Flour, unbleached, all-purpose (divided)	$1\frac{1}{4}$ lb + $\frac{1}{2}$ oz*	Cinnamon, freshly ground	1 T + 1 t
Ginger, ground	2 T + 2 t	Baking powder	2 t
		Margarine, unsalted, corn oil	8 oz
		Sugar, light brown	8 oz
Allspice, freshly ground	2 T + 2 t	†Banana, very ripe, pureed	1 c
		Vegetable cooking spray, butter-flavored	—

1. In a mixing bowl, sift together $1\frac{1}{4}$ lb of the flour, the spices, and baking powder.
2. Cream the margarine with the sugar until light and soft in another bowl. Blend in the banana puree.
3. Add the flour mixture to the margarine mixture in three batches, mixing until thoroughly blended.
4. Use the remaining flour to coat a work surface. Turn the dough onto the floured area. Work it until smooth. Shape it into a brick measuring 10 × 4 × 2 inches. Wrap in plastic film; chill until firm, or at least 2 hours.
5. With a slicing machine or a sharp knife, cut the dough into the thinnest possible slices, or 48. Place on nonstick baking sheets coated with cooking spray.
6. Bake in a 400°F (205°C) oven until golden, or about 7–10 minutes.
7. Remove the cookies from the pans while still warm. Serve along with a glass of nonfat milk or a cup of freshly brewed decaffeinated coffee or tea or offer as an accompaniment to fresh fruit or frozen, nonfat yogurt. Store the cooled cookies in an airtight container.

*$\frac{1}{2}$ oz = 2 T.

†To oven-ripen bananas, see procedure on page 491.

Servings	Calories	Protein (g) (%)	Fat (g) (%)	Cholesterol (mg)	Carbohydrates (g) (%)	Fiber (g)	Sodium (mg)
1	204	2.8 (5%)	8.0 (35%)	0	31.2 (60%)	1.4	40.8

Honey-Baked Whole Grain Bread Strips in Custard Coating

Sherry's merits in cooking are well recognized. Its delightful flavor can elevate simple peasant-style dishes like this one to nobility status. This easy but elegant sweet is prepared by baking strips of whole grain bread, enriched with an egg white custard in a sherry-enhanced syrup.

Servings: 24   *Serving Size: 4 baked bread strips*
Yield: 8 doz baked bread strips

Honey, clover	1½ c	Egg whites, large	12
Sherry, dry	1½ c		(15 oz)
*Bread, whole grain, crusts removed	1 lb (24 slices)	Vegetable cooking spray, butter-flavored	—
Milk, low-fat	1½ qt		

1. In a sheet pan, combine the honey and sherry; mix well.
2. Cut each slice of bread into 4 thick strips; arrange in two 12 × 20 × 2-in. counter pans. Pour 3 c of milk over each pan; turn to coat. Let stand until the bread is well soaked, or about 5 minutes.
3. Place the egg whites in a bowl; beat lightly. Coat the bread strips with the egg whites.
4. Coat a large nonstick skillet with cooking spray or cook in batches. Place over medium-high heat until hot. Add the strips to the hot skillet; cook until light brown, turning once. Coat the skillet with cooking spray when the bread strips begin to stick, or as needed. Place the browned bread strips on top of the honey syrup in the sheet pan; turn to coat.
5. Bake in a 350°F (175°C) oven uncovered until the bread is golden brown, or about 20 minutes, turning once. Remove from the oven; serve warm or at room temperature with the syrup spooned over. Offer for dessert or in lieu of a sweet morning pastry.

*Reserve crusts for another use like bread crumbs.

Servings	Calories	Protein (g) (%)	Fat (g) (%)	Cholesterol (mg)	Carbohydrates (g) (%)	Fiber (g)	Sodium (mg)
1	143	5.8 (15%)	0.9 (5%)	1.1	29.4 (79%)	1.3	160

No alcohol is listed in the nutrition analysis. It is assumed to be cooked off during preparation.

Little Almond Meringue Bites

These very sweet, tiny rounds are prepared from an almond-flavored egg white and sugar dough. They pop when baked and resemble open accordions. While they are high in sugar, these little morsels are prepared with no fat or egg yolks. One or two will satisfy the sweet tooth of most diners.

Servings: 38   *Serving Size: 2 meringue bites*
Yield: 6⅓ doz meringue bites

| Sugar, confectioners' (divided) | 1 lb + ½ oz | Almond extract | ½ t |
| Egg whites, large | 2 (2½ oz) | | |

1. In a mixing bowl, combine all but about 3 T of the sugar with the remaining ingredients. Beat until a very stiff dough is formed. Add more confectioners' sugar if needed to form a stiff dough. It will not be included in the nutrition analysis. Sprinkle the remaining confectioners' sugar over a work surface. Turn out the dough onto the surface. Roll out to about ⅓-in. thickness.
2. Using the center of a doughnut cutter, cut the dough into 1-in. rounds. Place on a baking pan lined with parchment paper. Roll the dough scraps a second time to about ⅓-in. thickness; cut into rounds. Bake in a 375°F (190°C) oven until the meringues pop, or about 10 minutes. Serve with a glass of cold nonfat milk or steaming cup of low-fat hot cocoa.

Servings	Calories	Protein (g) (%)	Fat (g) (%)	Cholesterol (mg)	Carbohydrates (g) (%)	Fiber (g)	Sodium (mg)
1	49	0.2 (1%)	< 0.1 (< 1%)	0	12.3 (98%)	0	3

Orange-Scented Custard Strips

Orange-scented custard strips are similar to French toast but prepared from whole grain bread coated in egg whites and a combination of evaporated, skim, and nonfat milk. For a unique flavor, grated lemon and orange zests are added.

Servings: 24   Serving Size: 4 thick custard strips
Yield: 8 doz thick custard strips

Egg whites, large	12 (15 oz)	Bread, whole grain, oven dried	1½ lb (24 slices)
Milk, nonfat	1½ pt		
Milk, evaporated, skim	¾ c	Vegetable cooking spray, butter-flavored	6 3-second sprays
Lemon and orange zest, finely grated	1 T each		

1. Beat the egg whites with the nonfat milk in a shallow container.
2. Mix in the evaporated milk and citrus fruit zests until well blended.
3. Soak both sides of the bread slices in the milk mixture a few minutes.
4. Coat a large nonstick skillet with cooking spray or cook in batches. Place over medium heat until hot. Cook the soaked bread until nicely browned on both sides, or about 3 to 4 minutes per side.
5. Cut into thick strips, triangles, or quarters. Serve hot topped with whipped creamy cranberry spread (see page 55), whipped honey margarine, fruit-sweetened fruit spread, a fruit sauce like naturally sweetened raspberry sauce (see page 394), or sliced, fresh fruit.

Servings	Calories	Protein (g) (%)	Fat (g) (%)	Cholesterol (mg)	Carbohydrates (g) (%)	Fiber (g)	Sodium (mg)
1	95	6.2 (25%)	1.3 (12%)	0.8	15.7 (64%)	2	201

PASTRY CRUSTS

Chocolate Meringue Shells

Offer chocolate meringue shells filled with frozen, nonfat vanilla yogurt and drizzled with raspberry sauce. They make an impressive presentation and taste so good, it's hard to believe they are low in fat and cholesterol.

To ensure success when preparing meringues from fresh eggs:

1. Make sure utensils are scrupulously clean and free of grease.
2. Separate the eggs while cold (it's easier).
3. Use the three-bowl system to separate the eggs. One egg at a time, separate the white from the yolk into bowl 1; place the yolk in bowl 2; transfer the egg white from bowl 1 to bowl 3. Separate the remaining eggs using the three-bowl procedure.
4. Use clear egg whites with firm jelly-like consistency, containing no egg yolk or particles.
5. Beat the egg whites until shiny and very stiff but not dry.
6. Once the meringues are baked, store them in an airtight container immediately, as they absorb moisture easily.

Servings: 24 *Serving Size: 1 meringue*
Yield: 24 meringues

| Egg whites, large, room temperature | 19 ($1\frac{1}{2}$ lb) | Sugar, superfine preferred | $1\frac{1}{2}$ lb |
| Cream of tartar | $\frac{1}{8}$ t | Cocoa powder | $2\frac{1}{2}$ oz ($\frac{3}{4}$ c) |

1. Place the egg whites in a mixing bowl. Beat until foamy. Add the cream of tartar; continue beating until the whites hold soft peaks.
2. Add the sugar slowly while beating. Continue beating until the meringue holds stiff peaks. Sift the cocoa powder over the meringue; fold in gently.
3. Using a pastry bag, pipe the meringue into 24 $4\frac{1}{2}$-in. circles on baking sheets lined with parchment paper, building the sides up for shells. For puff-shaped meringues, pipe the meringue into dollops (candy kiss shapes) with $4\frac{1}{2}$-in. diameters or using a spoon, drop dollops of the meringue on parchment-lined baking sheets. A larger number of smaller meringues can be made if desired.

4. Bake the meringues in the middle of a 275°F (135°C) oven for 1 hour. Turn off the oven, leaving the meringues to bake an additional hour while the oven cools.
5. Cool on the baking sheets. They may be kept up to 1 week stored at room temperature in an airtight container separated with sheets of parchment or wax paper.
6. To serve, arrange each meringue on a plate. Cut off the tops of the puff-shaped meringues; fill with a scoop of nonfat, frozen vanilla yogurt and drizzle with naturally sweetened raspberry sauce (see page 394) or fruit-sweetened strawberry sauce (see page 392). Simply top the shell-shaped meringues with the frozen yogurt and fruit sauce.

Servings	Calories	Protein (g) (%)	Fat (g) (%)	Cholesterol (mg)	Carbohydrates (g) (%)	Fiber (g)	Sodium (mg)
1	131	3.6 (10%)	0.4 (3%)	0	30.1 (87%)	0.9	47.4

Variation

Chocolate Meringue Sticks: Using a pastry bag, form the meringue mixture into sticks rather than shells.

Feathery Light Crepes

Crepe is the French word for pancake. That is precisely what these paper-thin, feathery light wrappers are. They can be rolled, folded, or topped with savory meat, cheese, and vegetable mixtures, sweet jams, fruit fillings, or frozen, nonfat yogurts.

Servings: 24   *Serving Size: 2 crepes*
Yield: 4½ doz crepes

Flour, cake or all-purpose, unbleached	12 oz	Oil, canola or vegetable	2 T
		*Almond extract	1 t
Salt	To taste or ½ t	Vegetable cooking spray, butter-flavored	24 2-
Milk, nonfat	1¼ qt		second
Egg whites, large	12 (15 oz)		sprays

1. In a food processor or blender, combine the flour, salt to taste, milk, egg whites, oil, and almond extract; process until smooth, scraping down the sides of the container as needed. Refrigerate the batter at least 1 hour.
2. Coat a 6-in. nonstick skillet with cooking spray. Place over medium heat until hot. Remove the skillet from the heat. Portion about 2⅓ T batter into the skillet, quickly tilting the skillet in all directions so that the batter covers the entire surface. Return the skillet to the heat.
3. Cook until bubbles appear on the surface and the underside is light brown, or about 1 minute; turn over. Cook the second side until light brown, or about 30 seconds. Crepes will roll best if not overbrown.
4. Stack the crepes layered between wax or parchment paper. Repeat the cooking process until the batter is finished. Coat the skillet with more cooking spray as needed, or when the crepes begin to stick.
5. Serve rolled with meat, fish, poultry, vegetable, and cheese fillings,* sauteed and glazed fruit, such as glazed apples rolled in feathery light crepes (see page 413), frozen nonfat yogurt, fruit sauces such as fruit sweetened strawberry sauce (see page 392), or combinations of frozen nonfat yogurt and fruit sauces such as sweet cherry crepes with vanilla frozen yogurt (see page 466).
6. Crepes may be made ahead, layered between parchment or wax paper, wrapped airtight in heavy foil, and refrigerated for about 3 days or frozen up to 3 months. To

reheat, place stacked crepes wrapped tightly in foil in a 350°F (175°C) oven until warm, or 10–15 minutes.

*Omit the almond extract if the crepes are to be rolled, folded, or topped with savory fillings.

Servings	Calories	Protein (g) (%)	Fat (g) (%)	Cholesterol (mg)	Carbohydrates (g) (%)	Fiber (g)	Sodium (mg)
1	88	5.0 (23%)	1.4 (14%)	0.9	13.5 (63%)	0.4	53.9

Graham Cracker Crust

Crumb pie crusts can be made with many types of crumbs. They range from the most commonly used graham cracker crumbs to cookie crumbs like gingersnap or vanilla wafer and cereal crumbs like corn or bran flakes. Crumb crusts can even be prepared from leftover breads and cakes, perhaps corn bread, gingerbread, lemon sponge, or angel cake. Crumb crusts are equally nice with chiffon fillings and gelatin whips as custard or fruit fillings.

Servings: 24 *Serving Size: 1 slice (one-eighth of a 9-in. pie)*
Yield: three 9-in. crusts

Margarine, unsalted, corn oil	4 oz	Egg white, large, lightly beaten	1
Graham cracker crumbs	8 oz		($1\frac{1}{4}$ oz)
Sugar, light brown	2 oz	Water	$\frac{1}{2}$ T

1. Melt the margarine in a saucepan. Add the graham cracker crumbs, brown sugar, and egg white; mix. Sprinkle the water over; mix until the crumbs are evenly moistened.
2. Divide the crumb mixture equally in three 9-in. pie pans.
3. Use your fingers or press another pie pan firmly into the crumbs to produce crusts of uniform thickness.
4. Bake in a 350°F (175°C) oven until light brown, or about 10 minutes.
5. Cool the crusts before filling. Use as a base for fillings of choice, perhaps raspberry snow tart (see page 433).

Servings	Calories	Protein (g) (%)	Fat (g) (%)	Cholesterol (mg)	Carbohydrates (g) (%)	Fiber (g)	Sodium (mg)
1	83	0.8 (4%)	4.7 (51%)	0	9.6 (45%)	0.3	60.5

Variations

Vanilla or chocolate wafer crusts: Prepare as above except replace the cracker crumbs with wafer crumbs and omit the brown sugar, egg white, and water. Rather than bake, chill until firm, or about 1 hour.

Gingersnap, presweetened flaked or puffed type cereal, or toasted cake or muffin crusts: Prepare as above except replace the cracker crumbs with gingersnap, cereal, or toasted cake/muffin crumbs and omit the sugar.

Flaked or puffed type cereal or toasted unsweetened bread crumb crusts: Prepare as above except replace the cracker crumbs with cereal or bread crumbs.

Meringue Pastry Shells

To achieve success when preparing meringue pastry shells from fresh eggs, keep a few simple guidelines in mind:

1. Egg whites should be at room temperature (65–75°F or 18–24°C) before beating. The meringue will be lighter and higher.
2. For proper volume, egg whites should have no egg yolks mixed in them.
3. The beater and bowl must be free of any trace of fat. Even a small amount will prevent the whites from foaming properly.

Servings: 24   *Serving Size: one-sixth of a 9-in. pastry shell*
Yield: four 9-in. pastry shells

Egg whites, large, room temperature	9 ($11\frac{1}{4}$ oz)	Vanilla extract	1 t
		Sugar, superfine preferred	1 lb
Cream of tartar	$\frac{3}{4}$ t	Vegetable cooking spray, butter-flavored	—

1. In a mixing bowl, place the egg whites; beat until foamy. Add the cream of tartar and vanilla. While beating, slowly add the sugar. Continue beating until the sugar is dissolved and the meringue holds stiff peaks. Stop occasionally to scrape the sides of the bowl.
2. Coat four 9-in. pie plates with cooking spray. Using a pastry bag fitted with a large star tip, pipe the meringue into the pie plates; form decorative edges.
3. Alternatively, spread the meringue over the bottoms and sides of the prepared pie plates. Using the back of a spoon, form decorative rims.
4. Bake in a 275°F (135°C) oven until firm and crisp, or about 1 hour and 15 minutes. Cool on a wire rack. Serve with a filling such as fresh fruit melange coated with mimosa sauce (see page 425).
5. If prepared in advance, store the shells in an airtight container at room temperature. They absorb moisture and disintegrate easily.

Servings	Calories	Protein (g) (%)	Fat (g) (%)	Cholesterol (mg)	Carbohydrates (g) (%)	Fiber (g)	Sodium (mg)
1	80	1.3 (6%)	0 (0%)	0	19.1 (94%)	< 0.1	20.8

Philippine-Style Spring Roll Wrappers

These spring roll wrappers contain no eggs, butter, margarine, oil, or other added fat, whole milk, or cream, and salt is optional. When these delicate crepes are lined with lettuce leaves and wrapped around a garlic- and soy-flavored, stir-fried filling of beef, shrimp, tofu, and vegetables, they make a light and nutritious main course.

Servings: 24   *Serving Size: 8-in. wrapper*
Yield: 24 8-in. wrappers

Flour, cake, sifted	1 lb + 5 oz	Salt	To taste
Water	1½ qt + 2 T	Vegetable cooking spray, butter-flavored	—

1. Combine the first three ingredients in a mixing bowl. Beat until smooth. Set aside for 30 minutes. The batter should be the consistency of thick cream. Add more water if needed.
2. Coat a 10-in. nonstick skillet with cooking spray. Place over medium heat until hot. Remove the skillet from the heat. Ladle in ¼ c + 1 T of the batter; tilt the skillet in all directions to spread the batter evenly over the entire surface.
3. Return the skillet to the heat. Cook until light brown on the underside, or about 2 minutes. Flip over. Cook the second side briefly, or about 30 seconds. The wrappers will roll best if not overbrowned. Stack the wrappers between wax or parchment paper. Repeat until all the batter is finished, coating the skillet with cooking spray when the wrappers begin to stick, or as needed.
4. Use as an ingredient in Philippine-style spring rolls with beef, tofu, and shrimp (see page 76). The wrappers will keep refrigerated for about 3 days and frozen up to 3 months layered between parchment or wax paper and wrapped airtight in heavy foil.

Servings	Calories	Protein (g) (%)	Fat (g) (%)	Cholesterol (mg)	Carbohydrates (g) (%)	Fiber (g)	Sodium (mg)
1	90	2.0 (9%)	0.2 (2%)	0	19.4 (89%)	0.7	1.5

Phyllo Pastry Tart

Phyllo pastry is generally purchased frozen in boxes of 24 sheets but is available in some Middle Eastern markets fresh. For best results, the frozen dough should be thawed refrigerated overnight, or for about 8 hours. It may be refrigerated up to 3 weeks once thawed but after it is opened should be used within a few days. Since phyllo is fragile and dries out quickly, the packages should be opened only when ready to use and then handled quickly and carefully, always keeping the dough sheets covered when awaiting use.

Servings: 24   Serving Size: one-eighth of a 9-in. pastry shell
Yield: three 9-in. pastry shells

Vegetable cooking spray, butter-flavored	12 4-second sprays	*Phyllo pastry, frozen, thawed, 12 × 17-in. sheets	12

1. Coat a 9-in. pie pan with cooking spray.
2. Unfold the sheets of phyllo dough so they lie flat. Cover with plastic wrap and then a damp towel to keep from drying.
3. Spread a large piece of parchment paper or plastic wrap on a work surface. Spread 1 dough sheet on the parchment or plastic-lined work surface. Coat the dough with a 4-second spray of cooking spray. Place the dough into the pie pan, gently pressing into the tin. Allow the edges to drape over the rim of the pan.
4. Repeat the process with 3 more dough sheets, crisscrossing the sheets alternately.
5. Gently press the edges of the 4 layers together and roll under themselves; crimp to form the impression of wrinkled tissue paper. Prepare 2 more crusts following the same procedure.
6. Prick the bottom of the pastry shells with a fork. Bake in a 350°F (175°C) oven until golden, or about 10 minutes. Set aside to cool. Serve with filling of choice, perhaps fresh fruit melange coated with mimosa sauce (see page 425).

*Replace the wheat phyllo dough sheets with whole wheat sheets for a higher fiber option.

Servings	Calories	Protein (g) (%)	Fat (g) (%)	Cholesterol (mg)	Carbohydrates (g) (%)	Fiber (g)	Sodium (mg)
1	29	0.7 (10%)	0.6 (18%)	0	5 (72%)	0.1	45.6

Reduced-Fat and Cholesterol-Free Oat Pastry Crust

In order to cut the fat in this pastry crust, yet produce a flaky crust, a tad of baking powder is blended into the dough. Nonetheless, it is still essential to mix the margarine and flour only until small lumps are formed throughout the mixture. If overmixed, a mealy crust will result. Likewise, overmixing after the water is added will toughen the crust.

Servings: 24   Serving Size: one-twelfth of a 9-in. pie crust
Yield: two 9-in. pie crusts

Flour, whole wheat pastry	10 oz	Margarine, unsalted, corn oil,	
Flour, oat blend	3 oz	firm	$4\frac{1}{2}$ oz
Salt	To taste	Water, very cold	$\frac{1}{4}$ C + 2 T
Baking powder	$\frac{3}{8}$ t	Almond extract	1 t

1. Combine the flours, salt to taste, and baking powder in a mixing bowl.
2. Using a pastry blender, cut the margarine into the flour until the size of peas.
3. Slowly add the water and almond extract, tossing with a fork until the flour is moistened without being wet.
4. Divide the dough into 2 equal parts; gently, press the dough between 2 sheets of parchment paper or heavy duty plastic wrap into 2 flattened rounds. Chill for ease in handling.
5. Using a rolling pin, roll each dough piece between 2 sheets of parchment paper or plastic wrap until it forms a $10\frac{1}{2}$-in. round and is of equal thickness (about $\frac{1}{8}$-in.). Place in the freezer until the parchment paper or plastic wrap can be removed easily from each crust, or about 3 minutes.
6. Remove the bottom sheets of parchment paper or plastic wrap. Fit into two 9-in. pie plates. Remove the top sheets of parchment paper or plastic wrap. Fold the edges over and flute the crust if desired.

Unbaked Pastry Crust

7a. Do not prick the pastry shell. Bake with fillings as directed in individual recipes, such as old-fashioned pumpkin pie (see page 431).

Baked Pastry Crust

7b. With a fork, lightly prick the bottoms, sides, and where the sides and bottoms of each meet. Bake in a 400°F (205°C) oven until golden brown, or about 10–15 minutes. Serve with fillings such as blackberry, blueberry, currant, gooseberry, huckleberry, loganberry, raspberry, strawberry (see page 423).

Lattice Topping

7c. See blueberry dessert topped with oat pastry lattice style (page 423) for lattice preparation procedure.

Servings	Calories	Protein (g) (%)	Fat (g) (%)	Cholesterol (mg)	Carbohydrates (g) (%)	Fiber (g)	Sodium (mg)
1	92	1.1 (5%)	5.8 (55%)	0	9.4 (40%)	0.5	45.6

PASTRY FILLINGS AND TOPPINGS

Baked Banana-Strawberry Alaska

In the June 6, 1886 edition of *La Liberte,* cookery columnist Baron Brisse credits the creation of baked Alaska to the chef of a Chinese delegation visiting Paris. During their stay, the chefs of the Celestial Empire exchanged recipes with the chefs of the Grand Hotel. To the delight of the French pastry chef, he learned how to make this crisp, meringue-crusted ice cream dessert. In this healthy version, frozen nonfat yogurt is substituted for ice cream and angel cake replaces the more traditional sponge cake.

Servings: 24   *Serving Size: 1 baked Alaska*
Yield: 24 baked Alaskas

Vanilla angel cake (see page 367), 3-in. rounds, ½-in. thick, dried in the oven, or 3 days old	24	Egg whites, pasteurized	15 oz
		Cream of tartar	1½ t
		Sugar, superfine preferred	11 oz
		Vanilla extract	1½ t
Frozen banana-strawberry yogurt (see page 447)	3 qt		

1. Place the 3-in. rounds of cake on heat-proof dishes or a sheet pan. Form a ½ c level scoop of frozen yogurt on each cake base. Freeze until firm.
2. Make a meringue as follows. Beat the egg whites until frothy. Add the cream of tartar. Gradually begin adding the sugar, beating until almost stiff.
3. Add the vanilla and continue to beat until stiff.
4. With a spatula, quickly frost each serving with a thick layer of meringue. Completely cover the frozen yogurt and cake with meringue. Some of the meringue may be piped in a pattern or flutes on the edges.
5. Brown the meringues with a propane torch or place under a salamander or in a 450°F (230°C) oven until browned. Watch closely. Serve immediately.

Servings	Calories	Protein (g) (%)	Fat (g) (%)	Cholesterol (mg)	Carbohydrates (g) (%)	Fiber (g)	Sodium (mg)
1	231	9.0 (15%)	0.4 (2%)	1.1	48.5 (83%)	1.4	116

Blueberry Dessert Topped with Oat Pastry Lattice-Style

Whatever berries are in season are the perfect fat-free filling for pies. But rather than sandwich them between two high-fat, high-cholesterol pastry crusts, eliminate one of the crusts and cut the fat and cholesterol in half. In this recipe, the solution, and a satisfying one, is a lattice pastry top prepared with a low-fat whole grain pastry crust.

Servings: 24   *Serving Size: 3 × 3⅓-in. piece*
Yield: 12 × 20 × 2-in. counter pan

Cornstarch	4 oz	Vegetable cooking spray,	
White grape juice concentrate,		butter-flavored	—
unsweetened	1 pt	Reduced-fat and cholesterol-	
Lemon juice, freshly squeezed	¼ c	free oat pastry crust	
Blueberries, fresh or frozen		(see page 421)	1 recipe
without sugar	4 lb +		
	5 oz		

1. In a bowl, combine the cornstarch and juice concentrate; blend until smooth. Mix in the lemon juice.
2. In a mixing bowl, pour the juice concentrate mixture over the berries. Gently mix until well coated. Pour into a 12 × 20 × 2-in. counter pan coated with cooking spray.
3. To prepare a lattice top for the blueberry filling, divide the pie crust dough in half. Gently press the dough into 2 flattened rectangles between parchment paper or heavy duty plastic wrap. Chill for 4 to 24 hours. On a work surface, with a rolling pin, roll each dough piece between the 2 sheets of parchment paper or heavy duty plastic into rectangles 6 × 12 in. and 4 × 20 in. of even thickness (about ⅛ in.).
4. Remove the top parchment paper or plastic wrap. Using a sharp knife or pastry wheel, cut the 6 × 12-in. rectangle into 12½ × 12 in. and the 4 × 20-in. rectangle into 8½ × 20-in. strips. Cover with parchment paper or plastic wrap.
5. Place in the freezer until the parchment paper or plastic wrap can be easily removed, or a few minutes. Remove the top parchment paper or plastic wrap. Place the 20-in. dough strips lengthwise evenly spaced over the filling. Fold back every other strip halfway.
6. Place a 12-in. strip across the 4 unfolded 20-in. strips. Unfold the 4 remaining 20-in. strips. Fold back the alternate 20-in. strips. Place the next 12-in. strip about 1 in. from the last. Continue until half the pan is latticed. Then begin the process starting on the other side of the center line.
7. Bake in a 375°F (190°C) oven until golden brown, or about 50 minutes. Cool on a wire

rack. To serve, cut 4 × 6 into 24 3 × 3⅓-in. pieces. Top with a scoop of nonfat, frozen vanilla yogurt if desired.

Servings	Calories	Protein (g) (%)	Fat (g) (%)	Cholesterol (mg)	Carbohydrates (g) (%)	Fiber (g)	Sodium (mg)
1	191	1.6 (3%)	6.4 (29%)	0.2	33.5 (68%)	2.6	52.7

Variations

Blackberry, Currant, Gooseberry, Huckleberry, Loganberry, Raspberry, or Strawberry Dessert Topped with Oat Pastry Lattice-Style: Replace the blueberries with the appropriate berry and adjust the amount of juice concentrate according to the berry's sweetness.

Berry-Filled Angel Cake: Prepare the berry filling as described in steps 1 and 2. Place the filling in the pocket of an angel cake as described in fruit-filled angel cake (see page 459).

Fresh Fruit Melange Coated with Mimosa Sauce in Phyllo Pastry Shell

With a name like this, it's "gotta" be good. A crisp, crumbly phyllo shell forms the perfect basket for colorful circles of lime green kiwi dotted with black seeds, bright red strawberry halves, juicy yellow pineapple cubes, and slices of golden peaches all glazed in a champagne fruit juice sauce.

Servings: 24   Serving Size: 1 slice (one-eighth of a 9-in. fruit-filled pastry)
Yield: three 9-in. fruit-filled pastries

Mimosa Sauce:
Orange juice, freshly squeezed	1½ pt
Cornstarch	2 oz
Champagne, dry	1 c
White grape or apple juice concentrate, unsweetened	¼ c

Fruit Melange:
Peaches, ripe, peeled,* ¼-in. thick slices	2 lb

†Pineapple, fresh or canned without sugar, large dice	2 lb
Kiwi, ripe, peeled, ¼-in. thick slices	2 lb
Strawberries, ripe, washed, hulled, halves	1½ lb
Phyllo pastry tart (see page 419)	1 recipe

1. In a saucepan, mix a small amount of the orange juice with the cornstarch to form a smooth paste; add the remaining orange juice; mix to blend. Heat over high heat until the mixture boils, stirring constantly; reduce the heat to low; simmer until thickened, or another minute, stirring constantly.
2. Remove from the heat; stir in the champagne and juice concentrate; set aside to cool until it reaches room temperature.
3. In a bowl, combine the peaches, pineapple, kiwi, and strawberries. Add the cooled mimosa sauce; toss gently to coat.
4. Divide evenly between 3 phyllo pastry tarts. To serve, cut each into eight wedges.

*See page 16 for peach peeling directions.
†See page 492 for pineapple peeling, coring, and dicing directions.

Servings	Calories	Protein (g) (%)	Fat (g) (%)	Cholesterol (mg)	Carbohydrates (g) (%)	Fiber (g)	Sodium (mg)	Alcohol (g) (%)
1	126	1.9 (6%)	1.1 (8%)	0	27.2 (82%)	3.3	49.9	0.9 (5%)

Variations

Replace the phyllo pastry tarts with meringue pastry shells (see page 417).

Rather than coating in the mimosa sauce and placing in a pastry shell, serve the fruit melange in its own natural juice layered in stemmed glasses or plated on a swirl of naturally sweetened raspberry sauce (see page 394) or fruit-sweetened strawberry sauce (see page 392).

Hot Peach Tart on Oat Crust

Tarts are reported to be one of the top three most popular desserts among restaurant customers. For tarts on the healthy side, follow the techniques used to prepare these hot peach tarts. Begin with fresh, ripe, vitamin-rich fruit; arrange the fruit attractively on a low-fat, whole grain crust, and glaze with a fruit-sweetened fruit puree or spread.

Servings: 24   *Serving Size: one-half 5-in. tart*
Yield: 12 peach tarts

Reduced-fat and cholesterol-free oat pastry crust (see page 420)	1 recipe	Strawberry spread, fruit-sweetened, hot	1¾ c
Peaches, peeled,* ⅛-in. thick slices	2½ lb as purchased		

1. Divide the oat pastry crust dough into 12 equal pieces. Gently shape each dough piece into a flattened round. Chill 4–24 hours.
2. On a work surface, with a rolling pin, roll each dough piece between 2 pieces of parchment or wax paper into thin rounds of even thickness (⅛ in.). Peel off the top paper; using a 5-in. plate or pattern as a guide, cut the pastry with a sharp knife or pastry wheel into perfect 5-in. circles.
3. Cover and place in the freezer until the bottom sheet of paper can be easily removed, or about 5 minutes.
4. Remove the top sheet of paper. Pick each dough circle up with the paper; turn onto a baking sheet. Prick with a fork. Bake in a 400°F (205°C) oven to partially cook, or about 5 minutes. Let cool.
5. Arrange the peach slices tightly in pinwheel style on the pastry, covering almost to the edge. Return to the 400°F (205°C) oven until the peaches are tender and the pastry golden brown, or about 15 minutes. Drizzle the strawberry or flavor of choice spread over the tarts. Cut into wedges and serve hot.

*See page 16 for peach peeling procedure.

Servings	Calories	Protein (g) (%)	Fat (g) (%)	Cholesterol (mg)	Carbohydrates (g) (%)	Fiber (g)	Sodium (mg)
1	146	1.5 (4%)	5.9 (35%)	0.2	23.3 (61%)	1.5	49.6

Lemon Chiffon Angel Pie

Like its name suggests, this pie is heavenly. A high-fiber, crunchy graham cracker crust is topped with a light and fluffy lemon chiffon filling. As an added bonus, the pie contains very little fat and no egg yolks.

Servings: 24   *Serving Size: 1 slice (one-eighth of a 9-in. pie)*
Yield: three 9-in. pies

Gelatin, unflavored	1 oz	Lemon zest, finely grated	2 T
Water, cold	½ c	Egg whites, pasteurized	6 oz
White grape or fruit juice		Cream of tartar	¾ t
concentrate, unsweetened		*Graham cracker crust	
(divided)	1 pt + ¼ c	(see page 415)	1 recipe
Lemon juice, freshly squeezed	1 c		
Yogurt, nonfat, plain	1 lb +		
	14 oz		
	(3¾ c)		

1. In a saucepan, soften the gelatin in the cold water and 1 c of the juice concentrate for 5 minutes. Dissolve over low heat. Stir in the remaining juice concentrate, lemon juice, yogurt, and lemon zest to blend. Chill until the mixture mounds on a spoon.
2. In a mixing bowl, beat the egg whites and cream of tartar until stiff peaks form. Stop occasionally to scrape the sides of the bowl. Gently fold the whipped egg whites into the lemon yogurt mixture.
3. Spread the filling evenly in three 9-in. graham cracker crusts; cover lightly with plastic wrap. Chill until set, or about 3 hours. Cut each pie into eight slices to serve. Store refrigerated.

*Replace the graham cracker crusts with meringue pastry shells (see page 417) if desired.

Servings	Calories	Protein (g) (%)	Fat (g) (%)	Cholesterol (mg)	Carbohydrates (g) (%)	Fiber (g)	Sodium (mg)
1	157	4.8 (12%)	4.9 (28%)	0.6	24.2 (60%)	0.4	108

Meringue-Topped Key Lime Pie

This refreshing meringue-topped pie derives its name from the pungent Floridian key limes which flavor it. If not available, replace with another variety, naming the pie accordingly.

Servings: 24   *Serving Size: 1 slice (one-eighth of a 9-in. pie)*
Yield: three 9-in. pies

Milk, low-fat, sweetened, condensed	1¼ qt + 5 fl oz	Reduced-fat and cholesterol-free oat pastry crusts, baked (see page 420)	1½ recipes (3 9-in.)
Key lime juice, freshly squeezed	1½ c		
Key lime zest, finely grated	3 T	Meringue topping for pie (see page 430)	
Green food coloring	Optional		1 recipe

1. In a mixing bowl, combine the condensed milk, lime juice, lime zest, and if desired, food coloring. Mix together until thickened. Thickening occurs because of the reaction of the lime juice with the milk.
2. Pour the mixture into three 9-in. baked pie crusts.
3. Spread the meringue over the filling with a spatula, sealing it to the pastry shell. This helps prevent shrinkage. Bake the pie in a 350°F (175°C) oven until lightly browned, or about 10–15 minutes.
4. Cool on a rack. Refrigerate until chilled. To serve, cut each pie into eight slices.

Servings	Calories	Protein (g) (%)	Fat (g) (%)	Cholesterol (mg)	Carbohydrates (g) (%)	Fiber (g)	Sodium (mg)
1	441	9.1 (8%)	11.5 (23%)	9.4	75.4 (68%)	0.8	171

Meringue Topping for Pie

To prevent meringue topping from weeping on pie fillings, follow these rules:

1. If using fresh eggs, use ones with a gelatinous body. Watery whites with off colors or odors are signs that the eggs are poor quality. Pasteurized eggs may also be used.
2. Whip egg whites in a clean mixing bowl with beaters free of fat. During beating, fat will cut through the aerated whites and weaken them. As a result, the meringue may run and possibly weep during and after baking.
3. Don't overwhip the egg whites. Signs of overwhipping are lumps that tend to separate and a noticeable loss in volume.
4. Add the amount of sugar listed in the recipe. Lack of sugar causes free moisture or weeping to occur after baking.
5. Don't brown the meringues too quickly or undercook them. In both cases, moisture will be released after baking and cause weeping.

Servings: 24   Serving Size: topping for one-eighth of a 9-in. pie
Yield: topping for three 9-in. pies

Egg whites, large, room temperature or pasteurized	12 (15 oz)	Cream of tartar	1 t
		Vanilla extract	1½ t
		Sugar, superfine preferred	14 oz

1. In a mixing bowl, place the egg whites. Beat until foamy. Add the cream of tartar and vanilla. While beating, slowly add the sugar. Continue beating until the sugar dissolves and the mixture forms stiff, glossy peaks.
2. Spread the meringue immediately over three 9-in. pies such as meringue-topped key lime pie (see page 429). Baked as directed in the recipe.

Servings	Calories	Protein (g) (%)	Fat (g) (%)	Cholesterol (mg)	Carbohydrates (g) (%)	Fiber (g)	Sodium (mg)
1	74	1.7 (9%)	0 (0%)	0	16.8 (91%)	0	27.6

Old-Fashioned Pumpkin Pie in Oat Crust

Pumpkin pie is especially popular during the holiday season. For equally good flavor without all the fat and cholesterol of traditional pumpkin pie, blend pumpkin with evaporated skim milk and egg whites rather than the typical heavy cream and whole eggs. The fat content will decrease by nearly half.

Servings: 24 *Serving Size: 1 slice (one-eighth of a 9-in. pie)*
Yield: three 9-in. pies

Pumpkin or winter squash, cooked without salt or canned	3 lb	Cinnamon, freshly ground	1 T
		Ginger, ground	1½ t
		Allspice, freshly ground	¾ t
Milk, evaporated, skim	1¼ pt + 2 T (2½ c + 2 T)	Nutmeg, freshly ground	⅜ t
		Cloves, freshly ground	¾ t
		Egg whites, large	9 (11 oz)
Apple or fruit juice concentrate, unsweetened	1 pt + ¼ c	Reduced-fat and cholesterol-free oat pastry crusts, unbaked (see page 420)	1½ recipes (3 9-in.)
Molasses, light	¼ c + 2 T		

1. In a mixing bowl, combine the ingredients through the egg whites; mix until well blended.
2. Pour the mixture into the 3 unbaked pie crusts. Bake in a 425°F (220°C) oven for 15 minutes; reduce the heat to 350°F (175°C); bake until a knife inserted into the center comes out clean, or about 45 minutes longer. Cool completely.
3. Cut each pie into eight slices. Serve with a scoop of vanilla nonfat, frozen yogurt if desired.

Servings	Calories	Protein (g) (%)	Fat (g) (%)	Cholesterol (mg)	Carbohydrates (g) (%)	Fiber (g)	Sodium (mg)
1	237	5.7 (9%)	8.9 (33%)	1.4	34.9 (57%)	2.1	130

Variation

Proceed as above but substitute a crumb pie crust, perhaps graham, gingersnap, or vanilla wafer (see page 415) for the oat pie crust.

Raspberry Snow Tart

Pie can be more than just a dream for health-conscious diners. It's a matter of preparing them with the right ingredients as in this raspberry snow tart. A filling of pureed raspberries is blended with nonfat buttermilk and evaporated skim milk and thickened with gelatin. The chiffon filling is served in a high-fiber, graham cracker crust.

Servings: 24   *Serving Size: one-eighth of a 9-in. pie piece*
Yield: three 9-in. tarts

Pie Filling:				Milk, evaporated, skim, chilled		
Gelatin, unflavored	2 T			in freezer for 30 minutes	1 c	
	($\frac{2}{3}$ oz)			**Pie Shell:**		
Raspberries, fresh or frozen,				Graham cracker crust		
unsweetened	1½ lb			(see page 415)	three	
White grape or fruit juice					9-in.	
concentrate, unsweetened	1 c			**Pie Topping:**		
Sugar, light brown (divided)	4 oz			Yogurt honey topping dashed		
Orange zest, finely grated	1 t			with almond (see page		
Buttermilk, nonfat	1 c			402)	1 recipe	
Egg whites, pasteurized	3¾ oz			Raspberries, washed	8 oz	
Cream of tartar	¼ t			Mint leaves, washed	2 doz	

1. Sprinkle the gelatin over ½ c of cold water. Let stand until softened, or about 5 minutes.
2. Puree the raspberries and juice concentrate in a blender until smooth. Strain through a fine mesh china cap; discard the seeds.
3. Add half or 2 oz of the sugar and the grated orange zest to the puree. Heat to a boil to dissolve the sugar.
4. Stir in the gelatin, dissolving completely. Chill until lukewarm.
5. Stir in the buttermilk. Chill until the mixture mounds slightly, stirring occasionally.
6. In a mixing bowl, beat the egg whites and cream of tartar until soft peaks form. Beat in the remaining sugar gradually until stiff.
7. In another mixing bowl, beat the partially frozen evaporated milk until soft peaks form.
8. Fold the beaten egg whites into the whipped evaporated milk. Fold the evaporated milk-egg mixture into the raspberry mixture.
9. Pour into the 3 cooled graham cracker crusts. Chill until set, or at least 3 hours.

10. Cut each pie into eight slices. To serve, spoon the yogurt topping across. Decorate with raspberries and mint leaves.

Servings	Calories	Protein (g) (%)	Fat (g) (%)	Cholesterol (mg)	Carbohydrates (g) (%)	Fiber (g)	Sodium (mg)
1	173	4.4 (10%)	5.7 (29%)	3	27.1 (61%)	2.1	107

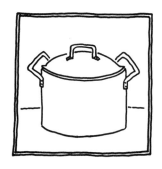

Reduced-Fat Pumpkin Cheesecake in a Graham Cracker Crust*

Pumpkin cheesecake might be featured as the dessert of the day on Halloween or replace pumpkin pie on Thanksgiving, but there's no need to limit this calcium- and beta-carotene-rich, reduced-fat dessert to two holidays a year. The ingredients are readily available year round and just waiting to be transformed into delicious, good-for-you dishes.

Servings: 36   *Serving Size: 1 wedge (one-twelfth of a 9-in. cake)*
Yield: three 9-in. cheesecakes

Graham cracker crust		Nutmeg, freshly ground	1 t
(see page 415)	1½	Cloves, freshly ground	1 t
	recipes	Ginger, ground	1 t
Cheese, nonfat cream	2 lb	Allspice, freshly ground	½ t
Ricotta cheese, nonfat	1 lb	Pumpkin, cooked without salt	
Egg whites, large	4 (5 oz)	or canned	2 lb
Sugar, light brown	13 oz	Egg whites, large	10
Flour, unbleached, all-purpose	2 oz		(12½ oz)
Cinnamon, freshly ground	1 T +	Cream of tartar	½ t
	1 t	Sugar, confectioners'	2 oz

1. Line three 9-in. springform pans with the graham cracker crust crumbs. Set aside.
2. In a food processor or blender, combine the cream cheese and next nine ingredients. Process until smooth. Place in a mixing bowl. Beat in the pumpkin until blended.
3. In another mixing bowl, beat the 10 egg whites until foamy. Add the cream of tartar. Gradually add the confectioners' sugar, continuing to beat until the sugar is dissolved and stiff peaks form. Stop occasionally to scrape the sides of the bowl.
4. Fold the egg white mixture into the pumpkin mixture. Pour into the 3 graham cracker crust-lined springform pans. Bake in a 450°F (230°C) oven for 15 minutes; lower the heat to 275°F (135°C) and bake until the cheesecake appears nearly set when shaken, or another 45 to 60 minutes. Remove from the oven; let cool to room temperature on a wire rack. Cover and chill 8 hours. Cut each cake into twelve wedges to serve.

*Adapted from a recipe by KC Knauer.

Servings	Calories	Protein (g) (%)	Fat (g) (%)	Cholesterol (mg)	Carbohydrates (g) (%)	Fiber (g)	Sodium (mg)
1	189	7.7 (16%)	5.9 (28%)	8.3	34.3 (55%)	1.2	313

13

Puddings, Frozen and Fruit Desserts

PUDDINGS

Baked Banana Whole Grain Bread Pudding

It is true, this banana-bread pudding contains no butter, cream, egg yolks, or sugar. Rather, ripe, sweet banana slices are tossed with cubes of whole grain bread and baked in a pudding prepared from evaporated skim milk, concentrated fruit juice, and egg whites. A pinch of freshly ground cinnamon and nutmeg give the pudding a charming finish.

Servings: 24   Serving Size: ½ c or 3⅓ × 3-in. pieces
Yield: two 12 × 10 × 2½-in. counter pans

Egg whites, large	8 (10 oz)	Apple or fruit juice concentrate, unsweetened	½ c
Bananas, ripe, peeled, ¼-in. thick slices	2 lb + 12 oz	Lime juice, freshly squeezed	¼ c
		Vanilla extract	2 T
		Nutmeg, freshly ground	½ t
*Bread, whole wheat, crusts removed, 1-in. cubes	15 oz	Cinnamon, freshly ground	½ t
Milk, evaporated, skim	1 pt	Vegetable cooking spray, butter-flavored	—

1. Place the egg whites in a mixing bowl; mix lightly. Add the bananas and next seven ingredients to the mixing bowl; gently mix until well blended.
2. Place the mixture in 2 12 × 10 × 2½-in. counter pans coated with cooking spray. Cover with aluminum foil.
3. Place the baking pans in larger baking containers. Pour an inch of hot water in the larger baking containers around the baking pans.
4. Bake in a 350°F (175°C) oven until the puddings are nearly set, or about 1¼ hours. Remove the baking pans from the water; cool.
5. Cut each pan 3 × 4 into 12 3⅓ × 3-in. pieces. To serve, invert the pudding onto shallow, brightly colored dishes placed on plates lined with doilies. Top with a dollop of frozen, nonfat vanilla yogurt if desired.

*Reserve crusts for another use.

Servings	Calories	Protein (g) (%)	Fat (g) (%)	Cholesterol (mg)	Carbohydrates (g) (%)	Fiber (g)	Sodium (mg)
I	128	5.1 (15%)	1.1 (7%)	0.8	25.9 (78%)	2.3	138

Baked Brown Rice Pudding Studded with Dried Cherries

Homestyle puddings, such as this baked brown rice pudding, are always popular with diners. There's no need to enrich them with egg yolks and whipped cream. Rather, garnish them with interesting dried fruits, perhaps dried cherries or cranberries.

Servings: 24   *Serving Size: ½ c*
Yield: two 10 × 12 × 2½-in. counter pans

*Brown rice, boiled without salt or fat	1¼ lb as purchased	Orange or lemon zest, finely grated	1 T
Sugar, light brown (divided)	8 oz	Egg whites, large, lightly beaten	20 (1 lb + 9 oz)
Milk, evaporated, skim	1½ pt	Vanilla extract	1½ T
Milk, nonfat	1 pt + ¼ c	Vegetable cooking spray, butter-flavored	—
†Cherries, dried	1 lb + 6 oz	Wheat flake cereal, coarsely crushed	4 oz

1. In a mixing bowl, mix the brown rice with 6 oz of the brown sugar and next six ingredients. Place in two 10 × 12 × 2½-in. counter pans coated with cooking spray.
2. In another bowl, mix the cereal crumbs with the remaining 2 oz of brown sugar; sprinkle over the rice. Bake in a 325°F (165°C) oven until set and golden brown, or about 45 minutes. Serve warm or chilled accompanied by a sweet, tart fruit sauce or spread.

*To cook the brown rice: Wash the rice; place in a saucepan with 1½ qt of water; heat to a boil; reduce the heat to low; stir; cover; simmer until the grains are tender and the water absorbed, or about 45–50 minutes. Do not remove the cover during cooking. Remove from the heat; stand covered for about 10 minutes; fluff.

†Replace the dried cherries with dried apples, apricots, blueberries, cranberries, dates, peaches, raisins, or other dried fruit.

Servings	Calories	Protein (g) (%)	Fat (g) (%)	Cholesterol (mg)	Carbohydrates (g) (%)	Fiber (g)	Sodium (mg)
1	255	9.3 (14%)	1.0 (4%)	1.7	53.3 (82%)	2.3	155

Sweet Potato Whole Grain Bread Pudding

When in need for basic comfort food, this moist pudding fills the bill. Whole grain bread is coated in a smooth pudding of mashed sweet potatoes enriched with molasses, brown sugar, egg whites, and evaporated skim milk.

Servings: 24   Serving Size: 1 wedge (one-twelfth of a 9-in. round)
Yield: two 9-in. rounds

Vegetable cooking spray, butter-flavored	—	Milk, evaporated, skim	1½ c
		Molasses, light	½ c
Bread, whole grain	12 oz (12 slices)	Sugar, light brown (divided)	½ lb
		Egg whites, large, lightly beaten	8 (10 oz)
Sweet potatoes, cooked without salt, mashed	1 lb	Cinnamon, freshly ground	1 T
Milk, nonfat	1½ c	Vanilla extract	2 t

1. Coat two 9-in. round cake pans with cooking spray.
2. Trim the crusts from the bread; reserve the crusts. Cut the bread into quarters. Cut each quarter in half. Arrange eight bread squares in a large circle around the edge of each of the cake pans. Place four bread squares at the point of every other placed bread square.
3. In a food processor or blender, process the crusts into bread crumbs; set aside.
4. Add the sweet potatoes, milk, evaporated milk, molasses, all but 2 T of the brown sugar, the egg whites, cinnamon, and vanilla to a mixing bowl; mix well.
5. Pour 1 c of the mixture over the bread in each cake pan. Arrange the remaining bread squares over the soaked bread. Pour the remaining sweet potato mixture over the bread. Spray two rounds of parchment paper, cut to cover the top of each pudding, with cooking spray. Place the coated side over each pudding. Let stand 30 minutes.
6. Meanwhile, in a nonstick skillet, toast 1 oz of the reserved bread crumbs. Stir in the remaining 2 T of brown sugar. Set aside. Use the remaining crumbs for another purpose.
7. Place the pans of sweet potato mixture in a 20 × 12 × 2-in. counter pan. Place in the center of a 350°F (175°C) oven. Add enough hot water to reach halfway up the side of the cake pans.
8. Bake until the custard appears nearly set, or about 45 minutes. Place the puddings on a rack for 15 minutes. Remove the paper.
9. Place a plate over each pudding; turn each pudding upside down and invert onto the

plate. Cut each pudding into twelve wedges. Serve warm or at room temperature sprinkled with the sweetened bread crumbs.

Servings	Calories	Protein (g) (%)	Fat (g) (%)	Cholesterol (mg)	Carbohydrates (g) (%)	Fiber (g)	Sodium (mg)
1	131	4.5 (13%)	0.7 (5%)	0.8	27.5 (82%)	1.6	122

FROZEN DESSERTS

Apricot Frozen Yogurt Sweetened with Fruit Juice

Beta-carotene has been touted for its merits. Dried apricots, the base of this healthy frozen yogurt, are a good source of it as well as fiber. Moreover, the egg whites in this frozen treat add cholesterol-free protein, the nonfat yogurt, B vitamins and calcium with minimal fat, and the freshly squeezed orange juice, vitamin C. It rates well on both taste and nutrition.

Servings: 24 *Serving Size: nearly ½ c (7½ T)*
Yield: 2¾ qt + ¼ c

Apricots, dried	15 oz	Orange juice, freshly squeezed	¾ c
White grape juice concentrate,		Yogurt, plain, nonfat	¾ c
unsweetened	1 pt +	Almond extract	½ t
	¾ c	Egg whites, pasteurized, stiffly	
Gelatin, unflavored	1 oz	beaten	6¼ oz

1. Place the apricots in a saucepan. Pour boiling water over them to cover. Let the apricots soak until soft, preferably 8 hours. Add more water if needed to cover the apricots. Heat to a boil. Reduce the heat; simmer until very soft, or 20–30 minutes. Remove from the heat; let the apricots cool slightly. Drain the apricots from their liquid, reserving 1½ pt liquid. Discard any remaining liquid. In a blender, puree the apricots with the 1½ pt apricot liquid and/or water to yield 1½ pt and the juice concentrate until smooth.
2. In a small saucepan, sprinkle the gelatin over the orange juice. Let stand about 5 minutes. Place over medium heat, stirring until the gelatin is completely dissolved. Cool.
3. Add the orange juice mixture to the apricot puree in the blender; blend well. Add the yogurt and almond extract to the blender. Blend until smooth. Transfer to a mixing bowl.
4. Fold the egg whites into the yogurt mixture.
5. Pour the mixture into the freezer container of an ice cream freezer. Freeze according to the manufacturer's directions.
6. To still freeze, pour a ¼-in. layer of the mixture into a nonreactive or counter pan. Cover tightly and freeze.

7. When it is almost firm, break into small chunks with a heavy spoon. Turn into a mixing bowl; beat until slushy, beginning the mixer on low speed and increasing to medium as the ice softens. Repeat the freezing and beating 3 times at half-hour intervals.
8. To serve, scoop into individual dessert dishes. If frozen hard, place in the refrigerator until slightly softened before serving.

Servings	Calories	Protein (g) (%)	Fat (g) (%)	Cholesterol (mg)	Carbohydrates (g) (%)	Fiber (g)	Sodium (mg)
1	111	3.0 (10%)	0.2 (2%)	0.1	25.6 (88%)	1.5	29.5

Banana Split with Frozen Yogurt and Butterscotch Sauce

Bananas, hot off the grill, topped with a small scoop of ice cold, vanilla, nonfat, frozen yogurt, all glazed with warm butterscotch sauce make this banana split one of a kind.

Servings: 24   *Serving Size: 1 banana split*
Yield: 2 doz banana splits

Bananas, ripe, medium-sized	4 lb as purchased (12)	Frozen yogurt, vanilla, nonfat	1½ qt
		Butterscotch sauce (see page 388), warm	1½ pt (1 recipe)

1. Cut the bananas in half lengthwise, leaving their skins on.
2. Coat a grill with vegetable oil. Grill, cut side down until the surface is golden brown, or 3–4 minutes. Remove the skins.
3. To serve, place one-half banana, grill marks up, in each banana split boat. Top with ¼ c (number 16) rounded scoop of frozen yogurt. Spoon 2 T of butterscotch sauce over.

Servings	Calories	Protein (g) (%)	Fat (g) (%)	Cholesterol (mg)	Carbohydrates (g) (%)	Fiber (g)	Sodium (mg)
1	231	4.1 (7%)	0.4 (1%)	1.3	56.1 (92%)	1.0	82.7

Chunky Pineapple Sherbet

Sherbet is believed to have originated with a popular Middle Eastern drink (charbet) made of sweetened fruit juice and water. Today, the term sherbet generally refers to a frozen version of these ingredients which is lighter than ice cream but richer than sorbet. In chunky pineapple sherbet, concentrated pineapple juice is blended with nonfat milk, and to make it stand out, is laced with chunks of fresh, juicy, crushed pineapple.

Servings: 24   *Serving Size: $\frac{2}{3}$ c*
Yield: 1 gal

Milk, nonfat, chilled	1$\frac{3}{4}$ qt	*Pineapple, crushed, fresh or	
Pineapple juice concentrate,		canned without sugar,	
unsweetened	1 pt +	drained, juice reserved for	
	3 T	another use	1 lb +
Orange juice, freshly squeezed	$\frac{1}{4}$ c +		5 oz
	3 T		drained

1. Combine all the ingredients in a mixing bowl; mix well.
2. Pour the mixture into a freezer container of an ice cream freezer. Freeze according to the manufacturer's directions.
3. To still freeze, pour the mixture into a $\frac{1}{4}$-in. thick layer in a nonreactive or counter pan. Cover; freeze.
4. When the sherbet is almost firm, break into small chunks with a heavy spoon. Turn into a mixing bowl; beat until slushy, beginning the mixer on low speed and increasing to medium as the ice softens.
5. Repeat the freezing and beating three times at half-hour intervals.
6. Freeze until firm. To serve, scoop into individual chilled dessert dishes placed on decorative plate liners. Garnish with pineapple leaves or orange zest (peel) curls. If the sherbet is frozen hard, place in the refrigerator until slightly softened before serving.

*For peeling and coring directions, see page 492.

Servings	Calories	Protein (g) (%)	Fat (g) (%)	Cholesterol (mg)	Carbohydrates (g) (%)	Fiber (g)	Sodium (mg)
1	86	2.9 (13%)	0.3 (3%)	1.3	18.6 (84%)	0.4	37.8

Frozen Banana Bonbons

Nutritionally, these bonbons are unlike most others. Thick slices of potassium-rich bananas are frozen in a coat of protein- and calcium-filled, pineapple-flavored yogurt and high-fiber, low-fat granola.

Servings: 24   *Serving Size: 3 bonbons*
Yield: 6 doz bonbons

Bananas, ripe but firm, peeled, medium-sized	3 lb (12)	Whole grain granola with sunflower seeds, cashews, almonds, dried apricots,	
Yogurt, plain, nonfat	1½ pt	and raisins (see page 248)	15 oz
Pineapple juice concentrate, unsweetened	¾ c		

1. Cut the bananas into 1-in. thick slices.
2. Mix the yogurt and pineapple juice concentrate in a bowl until well blended.
3. Dip the banana slices in the yogurt mixture to coat. Lay on a sheet pan lined with wax or parchment paper. Freeze until the yogurt coating is firm, or about 1 hour.
4. Dip the frozen yogurt-coated bananas in the yogurt mixture again.
5. Coat the banana slices evenly with granola. Return the slices to the lined tray and freeze until solid, or about 20 minutes. Defrost a few minutes. Serve as a breakfast, lunch, or dinner treat.

Servings	Calories	Protein (g) (%)	Fat (g) (%)	Cholesterol (mg)	Carbohydrates (g) (%)	Fiber (g)	Sodium (mg)
1	139	4.0 (11%)	1.4 (8%)	0.6	30 (81%)	2.5	27.4

Frozen Banana-Strawberry Yogurt

Frozen yogurt has around-the-clock appeal. Offer a scoop at breakfast over fruit or granola. Better yet, serve parfaits made with layers of frozen yogurt, granola, and sliced fresh fruit. Feature it solo on the lunch or dinner menu with mini scoops for light eaters, or use it as a filling in cakes. The list goes on: sandwich it between two cookies for a frozen yogurt sandwich; top it with a light sauce; "bowl it" with a sugar-coated phyllo basket; scoop it in a meringue shell; or garnish a fruit-topped whole grain waffle with it.

Servings: 24   *Serving Size:* $\frac{2}{3}$ c
Yield: 1 gal

Yogurt, plain, nonfat	2 qt	Vanilla extract	2 t
*Banana, very ripe, pureed	2 lb	White grape or fruit juice	
	(1 qt)	concentrate, unsweetened	1¼ c
Strawberries, ripe, hulled,		†Strawberry fans	Optional
crushed	1½ lb		garnish

1. In a mixing bowl, mix the first five ingredients until well blended.
2. Pour the mixture into the freezer container of an ice cream freezer. Freeze according to the manufacturer's instructions.
3. To still freeze, pour the mixture into a ¼-in. thick layer in a nonreactive or counter pan. Cover; freeze.
4. When it is almost firm, break into small chunks with a heavy spoon. Turn into a mixing bowl; beat until slushy, beginning the mixer on low speed and increasing to medium as the ice softens.
5. Repeat the freezing and beating 3 times at half-hour intervals.
6. Scoop into individual dessert dishes. Garnish with strawberry fans. If the frozen yogurt is frozen hard, stand at room temperature until slightly softened before serving.

*To oven ripen bananas, see page 491.

†To create strawberry fans, make several parallel, thin slices from the berry's root end almost through the stem end. Fan out.

Servings	Calories	Protein (g) (%)	Fat (g) (%)	Cholesterol (mg)	Carbohydrates (g) (%)	Fiber (g)	Sodium (mg)
1	104	5.3 (19%)	0.5 (4%)	1.5	20.8 (77%)	1.5	65.2

Frozen Raspberry Popsicles

Children and adults alike will line up for these frozen raspberry popsicles. Prepared from fresh, pureed raspberries, a medley of fruit juices, and just enough yogurt to balance the flavors, these sicles are what memories are made of.

Servings: 24　　　*Serving Size: ½ c + 1 T popsicle*
Yield: 2 doz popsicles

Raspberries, fresh or frozen without sugar	1 lb	Apple juice concentrate, unsweetened	¾ c
Raspberry juice, unsweetened	1 pt + 2 T	Yogurt, plain, nonfat	1½ pt
		Lime juice, freshly squeezed	2 t
Pineapple juice concentrate, unsweetened	1 c	Almond extract	½ t
		Paper cups, 5 oz	24
White grape juice concentrate, unsweetened	¾ c	Popsicle sticks or plastic spoons	24

1. In a blender, puree the raspberries with the raspberry juice and juice concentrates. Add the next three ingredients; mix until well blended.
2. Strain through a fine mesh china cap to remove the raspberry seeds.
3. Pour ½ c + 1 T into each paper cup. Cover with plastic wrap; freeze. When partially frozen, place a stick or plastic spoon into each cup to form a handle.
4. Freeze until hard. Unmold to serve.

Servings	Calories	Protein (g) (%)	Fat (g) (%)	Cholesterol (mg)	Carbohydrates (g) (%)	Fiber (g)	Sodium (mg)
1	87	2.2 (10%)	0.3 (3%)	0.6	19.4 (87%)	1	28.7

Papaya Banana Popsicles

These vitamin- and mineral-rich papaya banana popsicles are "lickin' good." The frozen fruit treats are a combination of frozen papaya and banana purees and concentrated fruit juices.

Servings: 24   *Serving Size: 1 popsicle*
Yield: 2 doz popsicles

Papaya, ripe, pureed	3½ lb	Orange juice concentrate,	
*Banana, very ripe, pureed	1¾ lb	unsweetened	¾ c
White grape or apple juice		Paper cups, 4 oz	24
concentrate, unsweetened	¾ c +	Popsicle sticks or plastic	
	2 T	spoons	24

1. In a mixing bowl, mix the papaya and next three ingredients until well blended.
2. Pour into 24 4-oz paper cups. Cover with plastic wrap; freeze.
3. When partially frozen, place a stick or plastic spoon into each cup to form a handle. Freeze until hard. Unmold to serve.

*To oven ripen bananas, see page 491.

Servings	Calories	Protein (g) (%)	Fat (g) (%)	Cholesterol (mg)	Carbohydrates (g) (%)	Fiber (g)	Sodium (mg)
1	87	1.0 (4%)	0.3 (3%)	0	21.8 (93%)	2.3	5

Smooth Freshly Prepared Low-Fat Peach Sherbet

For diners who prefer desserts prepared without refined sugar, recommend this low-fat peach sherbet. It derives its sweetness from naturally sweet ripe, fresh, juicy peaches and concentrated fruit juices. Meringue, folded in when the sherbet is partially frozen, gives this smooth and creamy dessert its light texture.

Servings: 24   *Serving Size: $\frac{9}{10}$ c*
Yield: $1\frac{1}{4}$ gal + 1 pt

Gelatin	1 oz	Orange juice concentrate,	
Water, cold	1 c	unsweetened	$\frac{1}{2}$ c
*Peaches, peeled, slices,		Peach juice, unsweetened	$1\frac{3}{4}$ qt
pureed	3 qt	Egg whites, pasteurized, stiffly	
	pureed	beaten	10 oz
	($5\frac{1}{4}$ lb as	Peach slices	For
	purchased)		garnish
Apple juice concentrate,			
unsweetened	1 c		

1. Sprinkle the gelatin over the cold water. Leave for 5 minutes without stirring until it swells to a spongy consistency.
2. In a mixing bowl, mix the peach puree and juice concentrates until well blended.
3. In a sauce pot, heat the peach juice to a boil. Add the gelatin mixture; stir to dissolve. Remove from the heat. Add the puree mixture; mix well. Set aside until cool. Fold in the egg whites until well blended.
4. Pour the mixture into the freezer container of an ice cream freezer. Freeze according to the manufacturer's instructions.
5. To still freeze the sherbet, pour a $\frac{1}{4}$-in. layer of the mixture into a nonreactive or counter pan. Cover tightly with plastic wrap; freeze until almost firm.
6. Break into small chunks with a heavy spoon. Turn into a mixing bowl. Beginning on low and increasing to medium speed as the mixture softens, beat until slushy.
7. Repeat the freezing and beating 3 times at half-hour intervals.
8. Freeze until firm. To serve, scoop into individual dessert dishes. Garnish with slices of

fresh peaches if desired. If the sherbet is frozen hard, place in the refrigerator until softened slightly before scooping.

*To remove peach skin, see procedure on page 16.

Servings	Calories	Protein (g) (%)	Fat (g) (%)	Cholesterol (mg)	Carbohydrates (g) (%)	Fiber (g)	Sodium (mg)
1	109	3.1 (11%)	0.1 (1%)	0	25.5 (88%)	1.7	29.1

Tropical Mango Sorbet Sweetened with Fruit Juice

Tropical mango sorbet makes a refreshing and light dessert but can also serve as a palate cleanser between courses, dressing for fruit salads, or garnish for fruit soups or fruit-flavored drinks. For a treat that will please both the eye and palate, layer a parfait glass with sorbets of three different colors, perhaps mango, kiwi, and strawberry.

Servings: 24   *Serving Size: ⅔ c*
Yield: 1 gal

Mango, very ripe, sweet, pureed	3 lb	Lime juice, freshly squeezed	¼ c + 2 T
Orange juice, freshly squeezed	1½ pt	Mint leaves or edible nasturtium flowers	For garnish
White grape or fruit juice concentrate, unsweetened	1½ c		

1. Mix the first four ingredients in a mixing bowl until well blended.
2. Pour into the freezer container of an ice cream freezer. Freeze according to the manufacturer's instructions.
3. To still freeze, pour a ¼-in. layer of the mixture into a nonreactive or counter pan. Cover tightly with plastic wrap and freeze.
4. When almost firm, break into small chunks with a heavy spoon. Turn into a mixing bowl; beat until slushy, beginning the mixer on low speed and increasing to medium as the ice softens.
5. Repeat the freezing and beating 3 times at half-hour intervals.
6. Freeze until firm. To serve, scoop into glass goblets placed on decorative plate liners. Garnish with mint leaves or nasturtium flowers. If the sorbet is frozen hard, place in the refrigerator until slightly softened before serving.

Servings	Calories	Protein (g) (%)	Fat (g) (%)	Cholesterol (mg)	Carbohydrates (g) (%)	Fiber (g)	Sodium (mg)
1	81	0.6 (3%)	0.3 (3%)	0	20.4 (94%)	1.3	5.9

Variations

Kiwi Sorbet Sweetened with Fruit Juice: Replace the mango puree with kiwi puree. Omit the lime juice. Adjust the juice concentrates as needed.

Strawberry Sorbet Sweetened with Fruit Juice: Replace the mango puree with strawberry puree. Omit the lime juice. Adjust the juice concentrates as needed.

FRUIT DESSERTS

Apple and Currant Phyllo Strudel

Phyllo dough is a natural for this low-fat version of strudel. Layers of the paper-thin dough are separated by light coats of butter-flavored vegetable oil and rolled around cubes of softened, tart apples, sprinkled with brown sugar and sweet currants. The pastries make elegant desserts.

Servings: 24   Serving Size: two 1-in. pieces of strudel
Yield: 4 doz 1-in. pieces of strudel

Filling:		Dough:	
Apples, Granny Smith or other baking apples, peeled, cored, small dice	2 lb	Phyllo dough sheets, frozen, thawed, 12-in. × 17-in.	6 oz (9)
Sugar, light brown	4 oz	Vegetable cooking spray, butter-flavored	9 3-
Currants, dried	6 oz		second
Cinnamon, freshly ground	¾ t		sprays
Nutmeg, freshly ground	¼ t	Graham cracker or gingersnap	
Lemon zest, finely grated	1 oz	crumbs	3 oz

1. In a bowl, combine the filling ingredients; toss gently to mix; set aside.
2. Unfold the sheets of phyllo dough so that they lay flat. Cover with plastic wrap and then a damp towel to keep from drying.
3. Spread a large piece of parchment paper or plastic wrap on a work surface.
4. Spread 1 dough sheet on the parchment or plastic-lined work surface with the longest side nearest. Coat the dough with a 3-second spray of cooking spray. Sprinkle about 1 T of the graham cracker crumbs over the dough. Placing the second dough sheet on the first, repeat the entire process twice.
5. Spread one-third of the filling on top of the dough leaving a 1½-in. border of dough uncovered.
6. Lift the parchment or plastic wrap under the longest edge of the dough nearest to fold the dough over the filling. Replace the parchment or plastic and roll up like a jelly roll.
7. Seal the seam with water. Do not seal the ends. Place seam side down on a baking sheet coated with cooking spray.
8. Repeat steps 3–7 two more times with the remaining ingredients.
9. Bake in a 375°F (190°C) oven until golden brown, or about 35 minutes. Let stand to

firm up for about 10 minutes. Slice each roll into 16 1-in. slices. Serve as a dessert, breakfast, or brunch offering.

Servings	Calories	Protein (g) (%)	Fat (g) (%)	Cholesterol (mg)	Carbohydrates (g) (%)	Fiber (g)	Sodium (mg)
1	81	0.9 (4%)	0.9 (10%)	0	18 (86%)	1.5	57.8

Variations

Apricot and Raisin Phyllo Strudel: Substitute 1 lb of apricots without their juice from chilled apricots in light fruit juice syrup (see page 389) for the apples and 6 oz of seedless raisins for the currants.

Cherry Phyllo Strudel: Substitute 3¼ lb pitted sour cherries for the apples and currants and 7 oz refined sugar for the brown sugar. Delete the lemon zest and replace the graham cracker crumbs with vanilla angel cake (see page 367) crumbs.

Apple Crisp with Raisins and Crumbly Oat Topping

Apple crisp is one of those classic dishes that appeals to all generations. In this version, sliced Granny Smith apples are sweetened with concentrated fruit juice and topped with a high-fiber, rolled oat crust.

Servings: 24   *Serving Size: 3 × 3⅓-in. piece*
Yield: 12 × 20 × 2-in. counter pan

Raisins, seedless	6 oz	Sugar, light brown	6 oz
Brandy	¼ c	Margarine, unsalted, corn oil	6 oz
Apples, Granny Smith, pippin,		Apple juice, unsweetened	¼ c
or other tart apples,*		Cinnamon, freshly ground	1 T
peeled, ⅛-in. thick slices	4 lb	Ginger, ground	1 T
Apple juice concentrate,		Nutmeg, freshly ground	1½ t
unsweetened	1 c	Salt	To taste
Rolled oats (long-cooking			or ½ t
oatmeal)	12 oz	Vegetable cooking spray,	
Flour, whole wheat, stone-		butter-flavored	—
ground	3 oz		

1. In a small saucepan, scald the raisins and brandy. Remove from the heat; set aside to cool.
2. Place the apple slices in a bowl and toss to coat with the juice concentrate. Set aside.
3. In another bowl, combine the oats and next eight ingredients. Work the mixture with a pastry blender or your fingertips until crumbly.
4. Add the plumped raisins to the apples.
5. Coat a 12 × 20 × 2-in. counter pan with vegetable cooking spray. Fill with the apple-raisin mixture. Spread the oat mixture over the fruit.
6. Bake in a 350°F (175°C) oven until the apples are softened and the top is lightly browned, or about 1 hour and 10 minutes. Serve the crisp warm or at room temperature. Cut the pan 4 × 6 into 24 3 × 3⅓-in. pieces. Top with a scoop of nonfat, frozen vanilla yogurt if desired.

*See the Introduction under "Ingredient Specifications" for listing of additional tart apples.

Servings	Calories	Protein (g) (%)	Fat (g) (%)	Cholesterol (mg)	Carbohydrates (g) (%)	Fiber (g)	Sodium (mg)	Alcohol (g) (%)
1	236	3.2 (5%)	7 (26%)	0	41.4 (67%)	3.9	7.8	0.8 (2%)

Baked Bananas Coated in Graham Cracker Crumbs with Orange-Pineapple Yogurt Topping

In this recipe, everyday bananas are transformed into a charming dessert. Slices are coated in graham cracker crumbs, broiled, and served warm, napped with chilled orange-pineapple yogurt sauce.

Servings: 24   *Serving Size: ½ banana + 2 T sauce*
Yield: 24 banana halves + 1½ pt sauce

Bananas, moderately ripe, peeled, medium-sized	3 lb (12)	Vegetable cooking spray, butter-flavored	—
Egg whites, pasteurized	4 oz	Orange-pineapple yogurt topping (see page 396)	1 recipe
Graham cracker or gingersnap crumbs	4 oz		

1. Cut the bananas in half horizontally and lengthwise.
2. Place the egg whites in a bowl; beat lightly. Dip the rounded side of each banana into the egg whites. Roll the rounded side in graham cracker crumbs to coat.
3. Lay the bananas flat side down on a sheet pan coated with cooking spray. If there are egg whites and crumbs remaining, repeat dipping the bananas in egg whites and rolling in crumbs.
4. Place the bananas in a salamander, broiler, or very hot oven until browned and crispy. Serve immediately with the yogurt topping napped over.

Servings	Calories	Protein (g) (%)	Fat (g) (%)	Cholesterol (mg)	Carbohydrates (g) (%)	Fiber (g)	Sodium (mg)
1	76	1.5 (7%)	0.8 (8%)	< 0.1	17.2 (85%)	1.2	37.6

Baked Peaches Stuffed with Grape Nuts and Walnuts

These baked peaches look good, taste good, and are good for you too. To create a crunchy filling for the peaches without all the fat of simply nuts, walnuts are mixed with grape nuts cereal and bound with egg whites. Glazed in a light brown sugar syrup, commonplace peaches are transformed into gourmet fare.

Servings: 24   *Serving Size: ½ stuffed peach*
Yield: 24 stuffed peach halves

Peaches, medium-sized, ripe	12	Grape nuts, cereal	3½ oz
Sugar, light brown (divided)	4 oz	Egg whites, large	1 (1¼ oz)
Walnuts, chopped	3½ oz	Water	1½ pt

1. Peel each peach;* cut in half; remove the pit; discard. Scoop out a bit more of the center to make a cavity. Cut a small slice off each peach's rounded edge so it sets flat. Place the peaches in a counter pan.
2. Finely chop the remaining peach. In a bowl, mix the chopped peaches and all but about 2 T of the brown sugar with the next three ingredients. Spoon the nut mixture into the peach cavities.
3. In a bowl, mix the remaining brown sugar and water; pour over the peaches. Bake in a 400°F (205°C) oven until the peaches are tender, or about 20 minutes. Spoon the sauce over the peaches' tops to glaze. Serve hot or chilled in decorative dessert dishes placed on plates lined with doilies.

*See page 16 for peach peeling directions.

Servings	Calories	Protein (g) (%)	Fat (g) (%)	Cholesterol (mg)	Carbohydrates (g) (%)	Fiber (g)	Sodium (mg)
1	98	1.8 (7%)	3.0 (26%)	0	17.8 (67%)	1.9	30.1

Berries Encased in Angel Cake

Vanilla angel cake and berries are naturals together. For an innovative presentation, cup-shaped molds of raspberries and strawberries wrapped in thin slices of angel cake are napped with a light berry coulis in this recipe.

Servings: 24   *Serving Size: 1 c berries in cake*
Yield: 24 c berries in cake

Strawberries, small, ripe, washed, hulled	3 lb	Vanilla angel cake (see page 367), oven dried, crusts removed, reserved for another use	2 10-in. tube cakes (1 recipe)
Raspberries, washed	3 lb		
White grape or fruit juice concentrate, unsweetened (divided)	2¼ c		
Orange juice concentrate, unsweetened (divided)	½ c + 3 T		

1. In a saucepan, simmer the berries with 1½ c white grape juice and ½ c orange juice concentrates, stirring until the berries soften and release their juices, or about 10 minutes.
2. Slice the angel cake into thin slices (⅛ in.). Using the top of an 8-oz custard cup, cut 24 rounds of cake from the slices. Set aside to cover the puddings.
3. Line 24 8-oz custard cups with the remaining cake slices and edges from the cutouts so that the cake pieces fit tightly together, totally covering the inside of the cups. Trim the cake as needed.
4. Using a perforated spoon, fill the custard cups with the fruit and enough juice to moisten the cake thoroughly. Reserve the remaining juice. Do not strain the raspberry seeds from the juice.
5. Cover the berries with the reserved cake cutouts.
6. Place the cups on a sheet pan. Place the bottoms of 24 empty 8-oz custard cups on top of the filled cups. Place a sheet pan over the empty custard cups; cover with 1-lb weights. Refrigerate for at least 24 hours and up to 48 hours.
7. In a blender, puree the reserved berry juice and seeds with the remaining ¾ c grape juice and 3 T orange juice concentrates until smooth and lightly thickened. To thicken the sauce further, add more berries and puree until smooth.

8. Unmold the puddings, inverting on decorative serving plates. Serve with the sauce ladled over. If desired, top with a dollop of nonfat frozen vanilla yogurt.

Servings	Calories	Protein (g) (%)	Fat (g) (%)	Cholesterol (mg)	Carbohydrates (g) (%)	Fiber (g)	Sodium (mg)
1	150	2.9 (7%)	0.7 (4%)	0	34.6 (89%)	4.4	27.8

Cantaloupe Balls Laced with Ouzo

In this beta-carotene- and vitamin C-rich fruit cup, cantaloupe balls are marinated in ouzo (anise-flavored) fruit syrup. The end result is a cool and light dessert. It makes an ideal conclusion to a warm-weather meal.

Servings: 24 **Serving Size: ½ c**
Yield: 3 qt

Cantaloupe, ripe	9 lb as purchased*	Ouzo, Pernod, or other anise-flavored liqueur	¼ c
Apple or fruit juice concentrate, unsweetened	½ c	Lime zest, finely grated	1½ T

1. Cut the melon in half. Remove the seeds. Using a melon ball cutter, remove the pulp in small balls. Place in a storage container.
2. In another bowl, combine the juice concentrate and ouzo. Pour over the melon balls, turning to coat. Cover and refrigerate.
3. Marinate the fruit about 3 hours, turning occasionally. Serve with the lime zest sprinkled over the cantaloupe balls in chilled, stemmed goblets. Place on saucers lined with doilies.

*Three medium-large and 4 medium sized cantaloupes equal 9 pounds.

Servings	Calories	Protein (g) (%)	Fat (g) (%)	Cholesterol (mg)	Carbohydrates (g) (%)	Fiber (g)	Sodium (mg)	Alcohol (g) (%)
1	42	0.6 (6%)	0.2 (4%)	0	9.2 (81%)	0.5	7.7	0.6 (9%)

Glazed Apples Rolled in Feathery Light Crepes

Apples are popular with just about everyone. Take them to new heights by serving them sauteed, glazed in warm fruit syrup, and rolled in feathery, light crepes with a scoop of nonfat, frozen vanilla yogurt.

Servings: 24   Serving Size: 2 crepes with 2⅔ T filling + 1⅓ T frozen yogurt each
Yield: 4 doz filled crepes

Sugar, light brown	3 T	Apple or fruit juice	
Cinnamon, freshly ground		concentrate, unsweetened	1½ c
(divided)	2¾ t	Brandy	½ c
Vegetable cooking spray,		Feathery light crepes	
butter-flavored	—	(see page 413)	1 recipe
*Apples, tart (Granny Smith)			(48)
cored, peeled, ⅛-in. thick,		Yogurt, frozen, vanilla, nonfat	1 qt
1-in. long slices	5 lb		

1. Combine the brown sugar and ¾ t of the cinnamon; mix well. Set aside.
2. Coat a large nonstick skillet with cooking spray or cook in batches. Add the apples; cook over medium heat, stirring frequently, until partially tender, or about 10 minutes.
3. Add the juice concentrate, brandy, and remaining 2 t cinnamon. Continue cooking until the apples are tender.
4. Spoon the warm filling (2⅔ T) on the edge of each crepe closest. Add a dollop (1⅓ T) of frozen yogurt. Roll the crepe up. Serve 2 crepes on black or colored plates. Sift the cinnamon brown sugar over to garnish.

*See the Introduction under "Ingredient Specifications" for listing of other tart apples.

Servings	Calories	Protein (g) (%)	Fat (g) (%)	Cholesterol (mg)	Carbohydrates (g) (%)	Fiber (g)	Sodium (mg)	Alcohol (g) (%)
1	220	9.6 (17%)	0.7 (2%)	2	44 (80%)	2.4	124	0.4 (1%)

Honeydew Melon Garnished with Ginger

This simple, refreshing, and healthy dessert can be a diner's delight if prepared from a properly ripened honeydew melon. To assess its ripeness, press your thumb into the melon's pointed end. When it yields about $\frac{1}{4}$ inch, the melon is ready to eat. Upon slicing, the honeydew's flesh should be a greenish-yellow.

Servings: 24   *Serving Size: $\frac{1}{8}$ honeydew*
Yield: 24 slices honeydew

Honeydew melon, large, ripe, chilled	20 lb as purchased (4)	*Orange, medium, sweet, juicy	1$\frac{1}{4}$ lb as purchased (4)
		Sugar, light brown	4 oz
		Gingerroot, minced	2 oz

1. Cut the melons in halves lengthwise; remove the seeds.
2. Cut the halves into 3 equal lengthwise slices.
3. Cut the skin from the flesh of each slice leaving the last inch attached.
4. Make one center lengthwise and 6 equally spaced crosswise cuts through the flesh of each slice, yielding 14 bite-sized pieces.
5. Slide cross-sections of each slice $\frac{1}{2}$-in. in alternating directions.
6. Cut each orange into 6 thin slices. Cut each slice from the center through the outer peel; twist and place onto the melon slices as garnish.
7. In a small bowl, mix the brown sugar and ginger. Serve the melon slices on decorative plates accompanied by the ginger-sugar mixture.

*Florida oranges tend to be thin-skinned and very juicy, while California oranges are generally thicker-skinned and less juicy than the Florida fruit.

Servings	Calories	Protein (g) (%)	Fat (g) (%)	Cholesterol (mg)	Carbohydrates (g) (%)	Fiber (g)	Sodium (mg)
1	93	1 (4%)	0.2 (2%)	0	24.1 (94%)	1.9	21.5

Oranges, Cherries, and Raspberries Layered in Cherry-Flavored Syrup

For a simple but elegant dessert, layer sliced oranges, black cherries, and raspberries in stemmed glasses, baste with kirsch-flavored (cherry) fruit syrup, and garnish with toasted, slivered almonds.

Servings: 24   *Serving Size:* ¾ c
Yield: 1 gal + 1 pt

Oranges, peeled, thin slices	3 lb	Kirsch (cherry-flavored	
Black cherries, washed,		liqueur)	½ c
halves, pitted	3 lb	Almonds, slivered, blanched	3 oz
Raspberries, washed	2 lb		
White grape juice concentrate,			
unsweetened	1 c		

1. Place the oranges, black cherries, and raspberries each in a separate container.
2. Mix the juice concentrate and kirsch together. Pour over the fruits; cover and refrigerate for at least 2 hours, basting occasionally with the kirsch marinade.
3. Saute the almonds in a nonstick skillet, stirring, until golden brown. Cool.
4. Layer the oranges, black cherries, and raspberries in stemmed glasses; top with an orange slice. Ladle the remaining marinade over the fruit. Garnish with a sprinkle of slivered almonds. Serve on saucers lined with doilies.

Servings	Calories	Protein (g) (%)	Fat (g) (%)	Cholesterol (mg)	Carbohydrates (g) (%)	Fiber (g)	Sodium (mg)	Alcohol (g) (%)
1	143	2.3 (6%)	2.7 (16%)	0	28.1 (73%)	4.2	3.6	1.2 (6%)

Steamed Pears with Cinnamon and Honey

Honey and cinnamon flavor the cavities of these whole, fresh, steamed pears. They are an easy but elegant dessert.

Servings: 24   *Servings Size: 1 pear*
Yield: 2 doz pears

Pears, Bartlett, ripe, medium-sized	8 lb as purchased (24)	Cinnamon, freshly ground	1½ T
		Honey, clover	½ c

1. Cut the tops off the pears, about 1 in. down; reserve as lids. Using a fruit corer, remove the cores. Do not cut through the bottoms of the pears.
2. Mix the cinnamon with the honey.
3. Fill each cavity with about a teaspoon of the cinnamon-honey. Replace the tops.
4. Place the pears upright in individual heat-proof dishes; steam in a commercial steamer or set in steaming vessels over boiling water until tender, or about 15 minutes.
5. Serve the pears hot in their steaming dishes.

Servings	Calories	Protein (g) (%)	Fat (g) (%)	Cholesterol (mg)	Carbohydrates (g) (%)	Fiber (g)	Sodium (mg)
1	105	0.6 (2%)	0.6 (4%)	0	27.2 (94%)	4.4	0.4

Sweet Cherry Crepes with Vanilla Frozen Yogurt

What can be more romantic than finishing an elegant candle-lit dinner with crepes? For a special, low-fat, Valentine's Day treat, offer feathery light crepes rolled with nonfat, frozen vanilla yogurt and topped with sweet dark red cherries in a light fruit sauce.

Servings: 24   *Serving Size: 1 filled crepe*
Yield: 24 filled crepes

Cornstarch	2½ T	Brandy	Optional
Water	¼ c		(¼ c)
White grape juice concentrate, unsweetened	¾ c	Vanilla extract	1½ t
Orange juice concentrate, unsweetened	¼ c	Feathery light crepes (see page 413)	24
Lemon juice, freshly squeezed	1½ T	Frozen yogurt, vanilla, nonfat	1 qt +
Cherries, dark, sweet, pitted, frozen or canned without sugar	2 lb		½ c

1. Blend the cornstarch with the water to make a smooth, thin paste.
2. In a saucepan, combine the white grape and orange juice concentrates and lemon juice. Heat to a boil. Beat in the cornstarch paste. Cook, beating, until thickened, or a few minutes.
3. Stir in the cherries; heat through. Add the optional brandy if desired; mix well. Remove from the heat. Stir in the vanilla.
4. To serve, place a crepe rolled with 3 T of frozen, vanilla yogurt on a decorative plate. Ladle 3⅓ T of the cherries and sauce over. The cherries and sauce are also delicious as a topping on whole grain pancakes, French toast, and waffles.

Servings	Calories	Protein (g) (%)	Fat (g) (%)	Cholesterol (mg)	Carbohydrates (g) (%)	Fiber (g)	Sodium (mg)
1	132	6.2 (19%)	0.3 (2%)	1.3	26.5 (80%)	0.8	73.5

No alcohol is listed in the nutrition analysis. It is assumed to be cooked off during preparation.

Warm Fruit-Sweetened Apricot Souffle

Souffles never cease to impress diners. These apricot souffles are a lovely way to end a meal. They contain neither egg yolks nor cream.

Servings: 24   *Serving Size: 1 c souffle*
Yield: 24 1 c souffles

Apricot puree from dried fruit (see page 389)	1½ pt	Cream of tartar	1 t
White grape juice concentrate, unsweetened	1¼ c	Vegetable cooking spray, butter-flavored	—
Lemon zest, finely grated	1 T	Raspberry glaze finished with kirsch (see page 399)	1 recipe (1½ c)
Egg whites, large	20 (1 lb + 9 oz)		

1. In a bowl, mix the apricot puree, juice concentrate, and lemon zest.
2. In a mixing bowl, beat the egg whites until frothy; add the cream of tartar. Continue beating until stiff but not dry.
3. Quickly and gently fold the apricot puree into the egg whites.
4. Fill 24 8-oz custard cups coated lightly with vegetable cooking spray.
5. Place the baking dishes in a 2-in. counter pan. Add hot water to reach one-third of the way up the sides of the molds. Bake in a 350°F (175°C) oven until puffed and firm but still moist inside, or about 35 minutes. Serve immediately on decorative plates drizzled with the raspberry glaze (1 T/souffle).

Servings	Calories	Protein (g) (%)	Fat (g) (%)	Cholesterol (mg)	Carbohydrates (g) (%)	Fiber (g)	Sodium (mg)	Alcohol (g) (%)
1	56	3.4 (23%)	0.1 (1%)	0	10.8 (74%)	0.8	48.8	0.1 (2%)

APPENDIX 1

Substitutes to Reduce the Total and/or Saturated Fat and/or Cholesterol

Dairy

Whipped cream
- Whipped, chilled, evaporated low-fat or skim milk
- Whipped tofu or skim ricotta cheese with a tad of oil, and if to be sweetened, honey and vanilla to taste
- Frozen low-fat or nonfat yogurt

Whole milk or half and half
- Evaporated low-fat or skim milk or low-fat or nonfat milk
- Reduced-fat milks enriched with nonfat milk powder

Ice cream
- Frozen, low-fat or nonfat yogurt, granita, sorbet, sherbet, or reduced-fat ice cream (ice milk) like layered raspberry, lime, and orange sherbet parfait

Ice cream bars or cones
◆ Popsicles, frozen low-fat or nonfat yogurt bars or sherbet or reduced-fat ice cream bars

Ice cream shakes or malts
◆ Fruit smoothies like banana strawberry whip or low-fat or nonfat yogurt or low-fat or nonfat frozen yogurt, sherbert, or reduced-fat ice cream (ice milk) shakes like peach melba shake

Coffee cream
◆ Milk prepared from triple strength nonfat dry milk powder
◆ Evaporated low-fat or skim milk

Sour cream
◆ Low-fat or nonfat yogurt (1 cup yogurt blended with 1 tablespoon cornstarch if to be cooked)
◆ "Lite" or nonfat sour cream
◆ Low-fat or nonfat sour cream made on premise from skim, or low-fat evaporated milk, or low-fat or nonfat milk
◆ Low-fat or nonfat fresh cheeses like cottage or farmer whipped with lemon juice or low-fat or nonfat milk or low-fat or nonfat buttermilk

Whole milk cheeses like cheddar, Swiss, cream, and colby
◆ Less whole milk cheese but visible
◆ Part-skim mozzarella, pot, farmer, sapsago, or hoop cheeses
◆ "Lite" or nonfat cream cheese or neufchatel cheese
◆ Low-fat or nonfat cheeses like cottage, ricotta, or processed cheeses
◆ Fresh low-fat or nonfat cheeses made on premise like yogurt, paneer, or white cheeses

Meat, Seafood, Poultry, and Eggs

Dark poultry meat with skin
◆ Poultry breast meat with skin removed before or after cooking
◆ Poultry simulated textured vegetable protein products

Packaged chicken parts
◆ Packaged poultry meat labeled without skin

Duck, goose, or squab
◆ Duck, goose, or squab cooked without fat and served without skin like roast duck melon and mango salad

- Pheasant, quail, cornish game hen, or chicken cooked without fat and served without skin

Fried fish or chicken
- Lean fish or skinless chicken breast meat preferably:
  - baked with a low-fat crust, like skinless chicken breasts baked in ginger-flavored mashed sweet potatoes
  - roasted with seasoning agents like whole chicken roasted with lemon, garlic, and rosemary with skin removed before serving
  - grilled or broiled flavored with a dry rub or low-fat marinade like scallops marinated in a raspberry peppercorn glaze and grilled on skewers with vegetables
  - poached in flavorful broth or wrapped in plastic with seasonings like monkfish poached wrapped in plastic with thyme, orange zest, fennel seeds, and Dijon mustard
  - steamed or cooked in parchment like red snapper steamed with ginger, green onions, garlic, and low-sodium soy sauce
  - simmered in flavorful stock skimmed of fat and later thickened with a fat-free starch slurry, bread or other crumbs, or vegetable puree like blanquette of skinless chicken legs and mushroom caps braise-deglazed in madeira wine and served in reduced fat-free cooking juices thickened with a slurry of browned flour and finished with evaporated skim milk and a tad of butter
- Lean fish and skinless breast meat of chicken deep fried in vegetable oil rather than hydrogenated vegetable oil (shortening)

Tuna packed in oil
- Tuna packed in water
- Fresh tuna cooked without fat

Prime grades of beef
- Lower grades of beef like choice or select

Regular ground beef
- Ground lean veal or skinless turkey or chicken breast meat
- Extra-lean ground beef or ground round
- One of the above meats extended with grains, vegetables, bread or low-fat cracker crumbs, legumes, textured vegetable protein, or other very low-fat ingredients like meat loaf studded with potato cubes and grated beets
- Ground beef analogs

Beef, pork, and lamb cuts
- Lean cuts of the listed meats trimmed of fat, cooked to no more than medium to prevent drying, marinated with low-fat mixtures or dry rubs for flavor, or cooked by moist methods

- Veal and low-fat game, skinless white poultry, meat, or lean fish
- Reduced portion sizes of the listed meats served with more vegetables and grains like lamb kebobs with mushrooms, red bell peppers, and zucchini
- Dried bean, pea, or lentil selections like Egyptian fava bean patties or lentil and brown rice salad with green onions and tomatoes
- Beef or pork analogs

Bacon
- Low-fat turkey bacon or lean Canadian bacon or ham
- Less bacon but more visible

Cold cuts
- Fresh lean meat trimmed of fat and cooked without fat or skinless poultry breast meat cooked without fat

Whole eggs
- Two egg whites per whole egg
- Two egg whites and one whole egg per two whole eggs
- Cholesterol-free, fat-free egg substitute
- Leaven baked goods with yeast, baking powder, or baking soda

Fats and Oils

Butter, lard, or shortening

In general use
- Whipped butter or polyunsaturated margarine
- Vegetable oil and butter blend
- Margarine (softest best)
- Poly- or monounsaturated oil (substitute $\frac{3}{4}$ tablespoon oil/1 tablespoon butter)
- Less butter or margarine but added at the end of cooking or browned first

As spread on bread products
- Jelly, jam, marmalade, honey, syrup, cinnamon and sugar, margarine or butter whipped with fruit puree and/or one of the previous sweeteners like strawberry butter
- Braise-deglazed, minced seasoning vegetables like glazed onions
- Roasted or grilled, flavorful vegetables like garlic
- Low-fat condiments like mustard, relish, or salsa
- Seasoned, whipped, low-fat or nonfat fresh cheese like farmer
- A flavorful oil, like extra-virgin olive, ideally extended with a flavorful vinegar like raspberry

+ Spreads from vegetables or legumes like grilled eggplant and red pepper spread or from flavorful ingredients high in unsaturated fats like tapenade (olive) or tahini (sesame seed)

To prevent sticking in pans
+ Ingredients simmered in liquids like stock or braise-deglazed instead of sauteed like wild mushroom leek compote
+ Nonstick pans
+ Vegetable cooking spray or vegetable oil sprayed from bottles

In cakes and baked goods
+ Fruit purees like dried plum (prune)
+ Light or dark corn syrup
+ Fruit purees, fruit butters, and corn syrup with a small amount of oil

Flavoring on cooked vegetables
+ Vegetables roasted or grilled for flavor like zucchini
+ Freshly minced herbs and freshly ground spices or low-fat condiments like low-sodium soy sauce
+ Butter or other flavored, vegetable cooking spray
+ Butter substitute powder
+ Small amounts of high-fat ingredients like toasted seeds or chopped browned nuts made visible

Salad dressings
+ A splash of citrus juice, vinegar, and/or sprinkle of herbs and spices
+ Dressings with oil reduced to 1–2 tablespoons/cup
+ Assertive vinegars like balsamic and flavorful oils like macadamia nut in low-fat dressings
+ Dressings extended with minced, raw, and roasted fruits and vegetables, their purees, juices, dried pulps, and juice concentrates, wines, liqueurs, sweet syrups, double strength stocks or low-fat condiments like chili sauce
+ Dressings from low-fat or nonfat yogurt, cheese, milk, or buttermilk like herbed cottage cheese dressing
+ Dressings in which oil is replaced with small amounts of mashed olives or anchovies, olive juice, tofu, black bean paste, or ground nuts
+ Low-fat dressings with body from starches or fruit or vegetable purees
+ High-fat dressings thinned with juice or stock
+ Low-fat commercial dressings
+ Reduced amounts of dressing sprayed on salads at service

- Low-fat salad dressings with vibrant flavoring agents like grated ginger or horseradish, minced garlic, or citrus zest
- Dressings offered on the side

Mayonnaise
- Low-fat or nonfat yogurt
- "Lite" commercial mayonnaise or other low-fat, low-cholesterol commercial or freshly prepared salad dressing
- Mayonnaise extended with low-fat ingredients like skim buttermilk
- Cholesterol-free and low fat condiments like vinegar, chili sauce, or pepper jam
- Blended tofu (high-fat, no cholesterol) or low-fat or nonfat fresh cheeses seasoned without fat
- Cold fruit or vegetable sauces like pineapple, papaya, onion, ginger, and cilantro salsa
- Salad dressing (thickened with starch not egg yolks so cholesterol-free but high in total fat)

Miscellaneous

Pan-fried, deep-fried, or sauteed ingredients
- Ingredients braised, poached, simmered, or boiled with fat skimmed from cooking liquids like poached eggs served on baked black bean patties with tomato jalepeno salsa
- Ingredients broiled, grilled, or roasted on racks or grids
- Ingredients baked, braise-deglazed, microwaved, or pan-broiled without fat and any formed during cooking removed
- Items baked coated in low-fat ingredients like zucchini slices baked coated in cereal crumbs like oat flakes or crisp crusts

High total and/or saturated fat and/or cholesterol crusts
- Pastries made with no or 1 crust like vegetarian pot pie topped with pastry cut outs
- Low-fat crumb, phyllo, bread, or meringue crusts like turkey tamale pie on corn bread crust
- Crusts with shortening, lard, butter, or margarine replaced with vegetable oil or frozen vegetable oil

Coconut
- Coconut extract
- Reduced amounts of freshly grated coconut toasted if appropriate to enhance flavor

Cream soups

- Clear soups filled with vegetables, grains, and small amounts of lean meat, seafood, or poultry like consomme brunoise (very small diced vegetables)
- Cream-style soups prepared with low-fat or skim evaporated milk or low-fat or nonfat milk or low-fat or nonfat yogurt and thickened with vegetable purees or starch slurries like cream of potato and leek soup thickened with potato puree

Gravies and high-fat sauces

- Fruit and vegetable sauces like tomato ginger preserve
- Items flavored with low-fat marinades or dry rubs
- Sauces thickened with starch slurries, crumbs, vegetable purees, or by reduction like cassoulet cooking broth thickened with cornbread crumbs
- Low-cholesterol and/or low-fat sauces finished with a tad of butter and/or polyunsaturated margarine
- Sauces prepared from fat-free stocks, wines, beers, liqueurs, or low-fat or nonfat milk, buttermilk, or yogurt like a red grape and zinfandel sauce
- Cooking juices reduced and skimmed of fat (refrigerate to solidify the fat and remove easily)

Frostings and high-fat toppings

- Fresh fruits, their purees or sauces or fruits baked on the bottom or top of cakes like peach upside down cake or gingerbread cake topped with bananas
- Frostings or toppings prepared with marshmallow creme, mostly sugar, and little or no fat like powdered sugar and orange juice glaze, or an egg white base like meringue
- Hard candy chips like peppermints
- Sprinkle of confectioners', brown, or granulated sugar mixed with sweet spices like cinnamon if appropriate
- "Light" sweet syrups
- Reduced amounts or no frostings or toppings
- Frozen low-fat desserts like nonfat frozen yogurt

Chocolate

- 3 tablespoons cocoa or carob powder and $\frac{3}{4}$ tablespoon vegetable oil or 1 tablespoon margarine for each ounce of chocolate like hot fudge (cocoa) pudding cake

Nuts or seeds

- Reduced amounts of nuts or seeds made visible, roasted to enhance flavor, and chopped to spread further if appropriate
- Nugget-style cereals like Grape Nuts
- Dried fruits like currants and banana chips

Desserts with egg yolks
- Desserts made from egg whites like floating islands and angel cake
- Desserts made from fruits or primarily sugar without eggs like plum compote with caramel crackle

APPENDIX 2

Substitutes to Reduce Sodium/Salt

Meat and Fish, Meat Substitutes, and Cheese

Sardines, anchovies, caviar, herring, smoked salmon, salt cod, smoked trout, or other smoked, canned, cured, or pickled fish
- Fresh or fresh frozen fish, canned tuna, salmon or crab, or shellfish cooked without salt like scallops poached in plastic with minced ginger, garlic and cilantro, grated orange zest, and a splash of drinking sherry
- Fish smoked or pickled on premise without salt or other high-sodium ingredients
- Canned, salt-free fish
- Smaller portions of the listed items made visible or served with larger ones of low-sodium grains or their products, vegetables, or fruits

Imitation crabmeat (surimi)
- Fresh or fresh frozen crabmeat cooked without salt or other high-sodium ingredients

Bacon; bacon bits; Canadian bacon; salt pork; canned or cured ham; corned, chipped, or dried beef; bologna; luncheon meat; pastrami; pickled pig's feet; or other kosher, canned, cured, pickled, or smoked meats or poultry
- Smaller amounts of the listed items made visible or served with larger ones of low-sodium grains or their products, vegetables, or fruits

- Fresh or fresh frozen meat or poultry cooked without salt or other high-sodium ingredients
- Meat or poultry smoked or pickled on premise without salt or other high-sodium ingredients
- Dried beans, peas, or lentils cooked without salt or other high-sodium ingredients, unsalted nuts or seeds or selections made from these ingredients

Hot dogs, bratwursts, or sausages from pork, beef, poultry, or other ingredients
- Sausages made on premise without salt or other high-sodium ingredients
- Fresh or fresh frozen meats or poultry cooked without salt or other high-sodium ingredients
- Smaller portions of the listed items made visible or served with larger ones of grains or their products, fruits, or vegetables

Low-cholesterol and/or low-calorie processed cheeses, blue cheese, or cheese spreads or sauces
- Smaller amounts of the listed cheeses made visible or served with larger ones of low-sodium ingredients
- Fresh, unsalted low-fat or nonfat cheeses
- Equal or smaller amounts of aged cheeses
- Commercial reduced-sodium cheeses

Aged cheeses like provolone or gouda
- Smaller amounts of aged cheeses made visible
- Grated tofu

Chip dips
- Dips or sauces prepared on premise from fresh fruits or vegetables or dried legumes cooked without salt like guacamole or red and white bean salsa with bell peppers
- Commercial low-sodium dips

Canned, packaged or frozen, main course dishes including breaded meat, fish, or poultry
- Main course dishes cooked from fresh ingredients without salt or other high-sodium ingredients

Canned soups or dehydrated soup mixes
- Soups made without salt from fresh ingredients, freshly prepared, salt-free stock, or low-sodium, commercial stock
- Commercial, reduced-sodium, or salt-free soups

Soy protein products
- Products cooked without salt, made from dried beans, peas, or lentils, grains or their

products, or vegetables, fruit, or unsalted nuts or seeds like kidney beans simmered in spicy tomato broth garnished with bell peppers, carrots, and celery

Vegetables and Their Juices

Canned lima beans, peas, corn, or sauerkraut
- Smaller portions of the listed vegetable rinsed with water or lower-sodium, canned vegetables rinsed with water
- Frozen lima beans, peas, or corn or better yet, these vegetables, fresh cooked without salt

Canned tomato, sauerkraut, or vegetable juices
- Fresh vegetable juices seasoned without salt or high-sodium condiments such as a garden vegetable juice
- Fruit juices or bottled waters
- Iced teas or coffees

Canned tomato sauce and other tomato products
- Tomato sauce or other tomato products made from fresh tomatoes without salt or from unsalted canned tomatoes
- Unsalted, commercial tomato sauce or other salt-free cooked or flavored tomato products

Canned legumes like kidney beans
- Dried legumes cooked without salt
- Canned legumes rinsed with water

Canned baked beans
- Baked beans made from dried beans, fresh tomatoes, no or less salt, and without salt pork or bacon (could smoke bacon on premise without salt or high-sodium ingredients or replace bacon with fresh meat)

Potato chips or other packaged potato products like instant mashed
- Potato chips or other potato dishes made from fresh, preferably, or frozen potato products with no added salt, like mashed potato pancakes accented with onion and garlic

Breads and Grains

Commercial bread stuffing
- Stuffings made on premise without salt from low-sodium breads, grains boiled without salt, fruits, or vegetables

Mixes for grain dishes
- Grain dishes prepared on premise without salt

Most commercial dry cereals or instant hot cereals
- Low-sodium, dry cereals like puffed wheat or rice or shredded wheat or regular or quick cooking hot cereals

Salted snack foods
- Unsalted forms of snack foods like unsalted pretzels or salt-free popcorn
- Snacks prepared on premise without salt and low-sodium or sodium-free baking powder
- Naturally low-sodium snacks like rice cakes, melba toast, or raw fruits or vegetables

Mixes for quick breads, cakes, cookies, or pastries
- Quick breads or other baked goods prepared on premise without salt and leavened with eggs or low-sodium or sodium-free baking powder

Chow mein noodles
- Rice steamed or boiled without salt
- Crispy noodles deep fried in vegetable oil (high fat) on premise without salt
- Soft noodles made and boiled without salt

Seasoned bread crumbs
- Bread crumbs made on premise without salt from low-sodium bread

Flavoring and Leavening Agents, Condiments, and Other Processed Foods

Salt or seasoned, flavored, or lite salt
- Herbs, fresh preferred
- Spices, freshly ground preferred
- Herb and spice blends made on premise without salt and whole spices toasted to enhance flavor if appropriate such as Caribbean curry powder
- Splash of angostura bitters, vinegar, wine, or citrus juice
- Commercial low-sodium seasoning blends like pumpkin pie seasoning
- Equivalent amounts of condiments with less sodium than table salt like soy sauce or low-sodium soy sauce
- Citrus zests in sauces or dressings
- See substitutions for condiments like worcestershire, etc. in chart below
- Ground dried fruit and vegetable pulp like beet, pineapple, ginger, and pepper with roasted game hen

Baking powder
- Low-sodium commercial baking powder
- Sodium-free baking powder made on premise
- Eggs

Cooking wine
- Drinking wine
- Fruit juices like tangerine-pineapple juice
- Flavor extracts like orange or almond extract

Monosodium glutamate (MSG) or Accent
- Herbs or spices
- Seasoning vegetables like lemongrass
- Splash of vinegar, lemon juice, or other acidic ingredient like grapefruit-orange-strawberry juice
- Sprinkle of sugar like powdered
- Flavor extracts like banana extract

Pickles, olives, or pickle relish
- Freshly chopped or sliced vegetables or fruits
- Chunky fruit or vegetable sauces made in house like mango chutney or corn relish

Commercial chili sauce
- Chili sauce made from fresh tomatoes seasoned with dried, fresh chilies, chili flakes, or ground red pepper

Condiments like worcestershire, soy, or teriyaki sauces, ketchup, or mustard
- Fruit, legume, or vegetable sauces made on premise like black-eyed pea and shallot relish or cranberry ketchup
- Minced seasoning vegetables cooked without salt like onions and garlic braise-deglazed in white wine
- Marinades or dry rubs prepared without salt or high-sodium ingredients like a south-western dry rub for lean beef of cilantro, garlic, hot chili pepper, cumin, pepper, and a tad of olive oil and lime juice
- See substitutions for salt, etc., in chart above
- Low-sodium commercial forms of condiments like ketchup with no salt added

Horseradish sauce
- Freshly grated horseradish root or a spicy radish like daikon

Meat tenderizer
- Meats cooked by moist methods like marinated spicy pot roast with gingersnap gravy
- Meats marinated in mixtures made in house without salt from low-sodium acidic and

other ingredients like vinegars, wines, citrus juices, oils, herbs, and spices; skip the dairy products like yogurt
- Meats with connective tissues broken down by mechanical methods like pounding, cubing, or grinding
- Meats with visible connective tissues like silverskin removed
- Tender meats which require no tenderizing

Bouillon or stock bases
- Stocks or bouillons made in house from raw ingredients without salt
- Commercial, low-sodium stocks or broths

Commercial barbecue sauce
- Barbecue sauce prepared from fresh tomatoes without salt or unsalted, canned tomato products
- Marinades or dry rubs made from low-sodium ingredients like wine, vinegar, lemon juice, oils, herbs, or spices like tropical marinade, or spicy Cajun rub
- Fruit, vegetable, or herb sauces like jalepeno-cilantro lime salsa

Commercial salad dressings or ones made from mixes
- Salad dressings made from fresh, nondairy ingredients and seasoned with herbs, spices, sugars, sweet syrups, and/or seasoning vegetables like very garlicky warm sherry vinaigrette

Commercial spaghetti or pizza sauces
- Spaghetti or pizza sauces made from fresh tomatoes or unsalted, canned ones, herbs, and spices
- Freshly made spaghetti or pizza sauce toppings without salt or tomatoes like cheese-free basil and pine nut pesto

Salted seeds or nuts
- Unsalted seeds or nuts
- Dried fruits such as cranberries or blueberries

Margarine or butter
- Unsalted butter or margarine
- Jams, jellies, marmalades
- Vegetable or nut oils like canola or pistachio
- Reduced portions of margarine or butter or reduced portions flavored with low-sodium seasoning agents like herbs or honey

Saccharin
- Sugar or one of its forms, sorghum molasses, honey, rice syrup, barley malt syrup, or fruit juice concentrates

Instant cocoa mix
- Low-fat or nonfat milk with chocolate syrup
- Chocolate drink

Pudding mix
- Pudding made in house without salt and unsalted butter or margarine and less or no milk like semolina pudding with raspberry sauce

Gravy mix
- Gravy made without salt from low-sodium stock freshly prepared without salt and an unsalted butter or margarine roux or thickened with a salt-free flour and water slurry or cooked vegetable puree
- Sauce made from fruits, vegetables, or legumes cooked without salt like apple cider sauce for pork

Gelatin mix
- Gelatins made from unsweetened, commercial gelatin, fruits, their juices or purees, and sugar if needed
- Chilled, fresh, canned, or cooked fruit selections like a fruit palette of pureed plums, grapes, bananas, strawberries, blueberries, and tangerines or other seasonal fruits

APPENDIX 3

Substitutes to Increase Fiber

Grains

White rice
- Unrefined rices like fluffy brown wild pecan or whole grains like rye berries

Wheat (white) flour
- Whole white wheat flour
- White flour + wheat germ, whole grain flours, whole grains, nuts, or seeds
- 1 pound whole wheat flour = about 14 ounces white flour

Wheat (white) cake flour
- Whole wheat pastry flour

Wheat (white) bread crumbs
- Whole grain bread, cake, cracker, or cereal crumbs, oats, wheat germ, or chopped nuts or seeds

Pasta from wheat flour
- Whole grain pastas
- Lupin pasta made with one-third bean flour
- Pastas topped, tossed, or filled with vegetables, seeds, or nuts or sauces made from them like pasta primavera
- Unrefined rices or whole grains like triticale berries

Refined wheat quick or yeast breads, rolls, or crackers
- Whole grain breads, rolls, or crackers like whole wheat tortillas, chive-flecked barley muffins, or graham crackers
- Breads, rolls, or crackers enriched with vegetables, fruits, seeds, or nuts like onion and garlic oat bread, pumpkin bread with walnuts, or pumpernickel raisin bread

Cereals from refined grains
- Cereals topped or enriched with dried, fresh, frozen, or canned fruits, preferably unpeeled
- Whole grain cooked or dry cereals like oatmeal or bran flakes
- Granola

Refined wheat cakes or other sweet baked goods
- Cakes baked with whole grain flours like whole wheat apple spice cake with coffee glaze
- Cakes with fat replaced by fruit purees like chocolate applesauce cupcakes
- Baked goods enriched with fruits, whole grains, vegetables, nuts, or seeds like chocolate zucchini cake or peanut butter oatmeal cookies
- Fresh, canned, frozen, or dried fruits preferably unpeeled, or desserts made from them like peach crisp with oat topping
- Cakes napped with fruit sauces, garnished with fresh fruit, or served with fruit on top like pineapple rum upside down cake

Pastry crusts
- Whole grain cracker, cookie, cake, or cereal crumb crusts like graham cracker, whole wheat phyllo crusts or crusts made from doughs with ground nuts or whole grain flours

Stuffings
- Stuffings prepared from whole grains or their breads or enriched with vegetables, dried fruits, and small amounts of nuts like bulgur stuffing with toasted walnuts, mixed dried fruit, and dried mushrooms

Fruits and Vegetables

Peeled fruits
- Unpeeled fresh, cooked, dried, or canned fruits like poached plums and cherries
- Fruits cooked, stuffed, or topped with seeds, nuts, or whole grains like baked apples stuffed with dried, mixed fruits and chopped nuts
- Fruits, cooked coated in whole grain cereal, cake, bread, or cracker crumbs, chopped nuts, seeds, or whole grain flour batters or doughs like banana slices rolled in peanut butter granola cookie crumbs and frozen

- Fruits served on crusts made from whole grain flours, cookies or crackers, cereals, cakes or their crumbs, or chopped nuts or seeds like whole wheat gingersnap fruit pizzas

Peeled fruit sauces
- Sauces made from unpeeled fruits like rhubarb or whole plums

Peeled potato dishes like mashed
- Baked, boiled, steamed, mashed, or roasted potatoes with their skins or cooked skins only

Fruit juices like grape or orange
- Fresh, canned, or dried fruits like grapes or sliced oranges (with membranes)

Raw or cooked peeled vegetables
- Unpeeled, cooked, fresh, frozen, or canned vegetables like steamed broccoli or asparagus with unpeeled stems
- Raw vegetables served unpeeled like cucumbers or combined with whole grains or their products like tomato and 3 whole grain bread salad
- Vegetables cooked, coated, or topped with whole grain flours; cereal, bread, or cracker crumbs; chopped nuts; seeds or whole grain flour batters like Mexican ratatouille topped with cubes of blue corn and flax seed bread

Meat, Fish, Poultry, and Dairy

Ice cream or other frozen desserts
- Ice cream or frozen desserts topped, coated, or enriched with fruit chunks or their purees, seeds, nuts, whole grain, sweet cereal, cracker or cake crumbs, or chunks of whole grain cookies (oatmeal raisin) or their doughs such as frozen low-fat yogurt balls rolled in whole grain gingersnap crumbs

Milk shakes and malts
- Shakes or malts from frozen yogurt, reduced-fat ice cream, or sherbert containing nuts, whole grain cookies, or fruits; for example, a cinnamon apple yogurt shake
- Fruit smoothies like a nutty banana shake

Meat and cheese sandwiches
- Sandwiches made with increased amounts of raw vegetables and whole grain breads
- Nut butter sandwiches on whole grain breads topped with fruits or vegetables
- Sandwiches with dried bean, pea, or lentils, or their spreads or patties like whole wheat tortillas with refried beans
- Sandwiches seasoned with fruit, vegetable, or legume chutneys, relishes, salsas, coulis, or sauces like mango mustard on a turkey ham sandwich

- High-protein salads emphasizing vegetables, legumes, fruits, nuts, or seeds like chicken salad with almonds, water chestnuts, celery, onions, and dried apricots in a whole wheat pita pocket

Entrees featuring meat, seafood, poultry, cheese, or eggs
- Entrees featuring increased amounts of whole grains, their pastas or breads, or vegetables like:
    Stir-fries
    Casseroles
    Soups
    Main course salads
    Stews
    Pizzas
    Pasta dishes
    Sandwiches
    Hot pots
    Ragouts
    Risottos
- Traditional entree plates with larger portions of grains and vegetables.
- Vegetable or fruit plates
- Meat, seafood, or poultry rolled, enriched, or filled with whole grains or vegetables like lettuce-wrapped spring rolls
- Entrees featuring dried beans, peas, lentils, nuts, or seeds along with vegetables and whole grains like black-eyed peas and barley casserole
- Meat, seafood, poultry, eggs, or cheese cooked, coated in whole grain bread, cereal, or cracker crumbs or doughs or batters made from whole grain flours like chicken sausage quiche in whole wheat crepe cups
- Meat, seafood, poultry, cheese, or egg entrees served with fruit or vegetable sauces like cumin mushroom sauce or sauces thickened with vegetable or fruit purees

APPENDIX 4

Substitutes to Reduce Calories, Add Nutrients, or Increase Portion Size without Calories

High-Fat Items

◆ See Appendix 1

Alcoholic Beverages

In Cooking

Rum, brandy, or sherry
◆ One teaspoon vanilla/tablespoon alcohol for first 2 tablespoons alcohol and then fruit juice to equal

Orange liqueur
- One-half teaspoon orange zest and orange juice to equal the volume of the listed liqueur

Kirsch or amaretto
- Dash of almond extract and peach or apricot nectar to equal the volume of the listed liqueur

Sweet dessert wine
- Fruit juice of the same color

Red or white wine
- Two tablespoons red or white wine vinegar and 7 fluid ounces stock for a cup of wine

In Cooking or Drinking

Beers or wines
- Nonalcoholic versions of beers and wines
- Light beers
- Beer blended with vegetable juices like tomato
- Wines blended with fruit juices like mimosas with peach and tangerine juices and orange-flavored sparkling water
- See the substitutions for sodas following

Nonalcoholic Sweet Beverages

Sodas
- Fresh or bottled waters
- Hot or cold, regular or decaffeinated, flavored or unflavored teas or coffees like minted iced tea slush
- Bouillons, consommes, or broths
- Bottled waters blended with fruit juices like melonade sipper
- Artificially sweetened sodas
- Vegetable juices
- Low-fat or nonfat milk or fruit juices (comparable in calories to sodas but more nutritious) like fresh citrus cooler

Fruit juices
- See the preceding substitutions listed for sodas
- Fruit itself such as half grapefruit for grapefruit juice (more filling because negligible calories from its fiber)

Ingredients High in Sugar

Presweetened breakfast cereal
- Cooked or dry sugar-free cereals sprinkled with sweet spices like cinnamon, reduced amounts of sugar, artificial sweetener, or sweet, ripe fresh fruit, or canned fruit packed without sugar
- Cereals high in volume but low in weight like puffed rice (perception of more created)

Jams, jellies, marmalades, or syrups
- Smaller portions of jams, jellies, marmalades, or syrups
- "Light" or low-calorie jams, jellies, marmalades, or syrup like ones flavored with artificial sweeteners
- Naturally sweet high-fiber and/or water fruit toppings like strawberry puree or pear and apple salsa

Sweet desserts
- Smaller dessert portions
- Desserts artificially sweetened
- Desserts with less sugar served warm or at room temperature like bread pudding with rum-flavored sauce
- Desserts deriving part of their perceived sweet flavor from sweet spices like nutmeg or extracts such as vanilla
- Decaffeinated or regular coffees flavored with sweet spices or extracts
- Naturally sweet fruits high in water and/or fiber like cantaloupe
- High-fiber and/or water fruits perceived to be sweeter by sprinkling with salt or an acid like lemon juice such as watermelon, cantaloupe, or apples
- A high-calorie dessert shared with another diner

Fruits, Vegetables, and Grains

High-starch vegetables
- Vegetables high in fiber and water like broccoli for corn

High-starch fruits
- Fruits high in fiber and water like honeydew melon for banana

Grains or dishes made from them
- Grains or dishes made from them replaced with smaller portions of grains and larger ones of high-fiber and water fruits and vegetables like open-faced sandwiches topped with lots of shredded vegetables or stir-fried rice with a mixture of vegetables and a smaller amount of rice

Flour as a thickening agent

- Cornstarch or arrowroot (thickening power of 1 tablespoon cornstarch or arrowroot = 2 tablespoons flour and calories similar)
- Fruit or vegetable purees

APPENDIX 5

Healthy Cooking Procedures

Adding salt to dishes is often reserved for the end of cooking. If salt/sodium is not of concern to diners, it may be added with other seasoning agents during cooking. This will allow the salt to blend better with other ingredients in dishes.

Banana ripening will occur naturally at room temperature. To speed up the softening and sweetening processes, bake the bananas in their skins. Depending on their size and state of ripeness, baking in a 350°F (175°C) oven will turn their skins black and their fruit will become soft and sweet in about 10 minutes.

Boiling potatoes is performed as follows. Place washed potatoes in unsalted cold water to cover. Starting with cold water allows for more even cooking. Heat the water to a boil; reduce the heat to medium; simmer until tender. Drain the potatoes. Steam dry in a colander for a few minutes. Serve immediately. If the potatoes are to be served at room temperature or chilled, place the potatoes on a sheet pan to cool. Do not cool in cold water. They will become soggy.

Braise-deglazing is to cook in a fat-free liquid, stirring, until the liquid evaporates and the ingredients begin to brown and stick to the pan. Add more liquid to the pan as needed and continue stirring, repeating the process until the ingredients are tender and browned. Braise-deglazing works well when recipes call for browning-seasoning ingredients like garlic, ginger, mushrooms, onions, and bell peppers. Liquids for braise-deglazing should be selected to match the flavors in dishes, such as red wine to braise-deglaze mushrooms in a beef dish.

Cooking in parchment or en papillote is a steaming method of cooking in parchment packages that concentrates the flavors and aromas of ingredients without adding fat. The procedure is as follows. Cut out heart-shaped pieces of parchment paper. One-half of each heart should be large enough to hold the designated ingredients and still allow room to crimp the edges. To cut, fold the parchment paper in half and cut half of a heart from the folded side. Place the ingredients in the center of one side of each heart. To seal the packages, fold the empty half of the parchment paper over the mixture. Then, starting at the top of the fold, make a small crimp in the edge. Continue crimping around the edge. Each crimp should hold the previous one in place. When the bottom of the heart is reached, fold the point under to hold it in place. Spray the packages with cooking spray. Place the packages on a baking pan and bake.

Cooking pasta is performed as follows. Heat 1 gallon of unsalted water to a boil for each pound of pasta. Add the pasta, stirring as it softens to keep it from sticking together and to the bottom of the pan. Boil, stirring occasionally, until the pasta is al dente. Drain in a colander and serve the steaming pasta immediately with a low-fat sauce. If the pasta is to be served later or offered chilled, drain and rinse with cold running water until the pasta is completely cooled. In cold dishes like salads, incorporate the cooled pasta with other ingredients. This will prevent it from sticking together. To prevent sticking when the pasta is to be held for later use, toss it with a small amount of vegetable oil.

Cubing a pineapple can be performed as follows. Remove the leaves by holding the pineapple with one hand and twisting in the opposite direction with the other. Next, trim the top and cut a thin slice from the bottom so that it sits level. Cutting in wide strips from top to bottom, remove the peel. Remove the eyes by cutting thin wedge-shape grooves diagonally around the fruit following the pattern of the eyes. Finally, cut out the pineapple's hard center core and cube.

Deglazing the pan is to loosen small browned bits of food from its bottom by adding a liquid such as broth or wine and stirring. The deglazing juices are often made into a sauce to accompany the item cooked in the pan.

Dicing is to cut into cubes with 6 equal sides. The following are common dice sizes:

small dice	$\frac{1}{4}$ inch $\times$ $\frac{1}{4}$ inch $\times$ $\frac{1}{4}$ inch cubes
medium dice	$\frac{1}{2}$ inch $\times$ $\frac{1}{2}$ inch $\times$ $\frac{1}{2}$ inch cubes
large dice	$\frac{3}{4}$ inch $\times$ $\frac{3}{4}$ inch $\times$ $\frac{3}{4}$ inch cubes

Dicing a mango can be performed as follows. Begin by slicing down either side of the unpeeled mango's stem, next to the pit. Repeat on the other side, yielding two nearly half mango sections. A band of fruit will remain around the pit. Cut cubes in the flesh of each section down to but not through the peel. Push the peel up to separate the cubes. Sliding the knife under the mango cubes and next to the inside of the peel, cut the mango cubes free from the peel. Cut away the band of fruit remaining on the pit; peel off its skin and dice the fruit.

Grinding spices can be done with a mortar and pestle or in a pepper mill, clean coffee grinder, or electric mini-processor. For some whole spices, it may be desirable to toast them before grinding. This helps bring out their flavors.

Making a sachet is tying a mixture of herbs and/or spices in a cheesecloth bag.

Making a slurry is mixing a starch such as flour, cornstarch, or arrowroot with a small amount of cold liquid like water or stock to form a smooth paste. This fat-free mixture can serve as a thickening agent for liquids in dishes such as soups, sauces, gravies, and salad dressings.

Mincing vegetables is to finely chop ones such as onions and garlic.

Peeling a tomato can be performed by following this procedure. Using a paring knife, cut an X through the skin (only) on the bottom of the tomato. Blanch the tomato in boiling water for about 20 seconds; refresh in cold water. Next, cut out the core and peel the tomato. If the seeds and juice are to be removed from the tomato, cut the tomato in half horizontally and squeeze out the seeds and juice. Finish by chopping or dicing the tomato as required in the recipe. Use this brief boiling (blanching) and refreshing in cold water procedure to peel *peaches* and *apricots*.

Presoaking dried beans can help them to cook more evenly and shorten their cooking time. To presoak, place washed beans in 4 parts of water, cover, and let stand 8 hours or overnight. When time is limited, place washed beans in 4 parts of water and heat to a boil. Cook for 2 minutes, cover, and turn the heat off. Let stand 1 hour.

Refreshing in cold water is to quickly cool ingredients in cold water. For example, vegetables like green beans might be partially cooked by boiling, refreshed in cold water to stop the cooking, and held for later use. At service, saute in a nonstick skillet lightly coated with vegetable cooking spray.

Roasting a bell pepper can be done over a hot grill or the open flame of a gas range, or under a hot broiler. Proceed as follows. Cook, turning as needed, until the skin is charred and looks blistered. At this point, remove from the heat, wrap tightly in plastic wrap or place in a plastic or heavy paper bag, and seal tightly. Set aside to sweat for 15 minutes. Peel off the skin, rinsing under cold water. Trim off the ends, remove the seeds and core, cut away the ribs, and slice into the desired shape.

Tempering yogurt with a small amount of hot liquid will help to prevent it from curdling when it is to be blended into the hot liquids of soups, sauces, and other dishes. Further strategies to prevent curdling are: mixing 1 cup of yogurt with 2 tablespoons of flour or 1 tablespoon of cornstarch before stirring it into hot liquids; holding hot liquids enriched with yogurt on low heat; and adding yogurt to hot liquids at the end of cooking.

Sectioning an orange or other citrus fruit can be performed as follows. First, cut thin slices from each end of the fruit so that it sits level. Next, cutting from the top to bottom and following the shape of the fruit, remove the peel and white membrane. Working over a container to catch the juices, cut from the exterior of the fruit to the center between the fruit of one section and its membrane. Repeat on the other side of the same section. Continue until all the fruit's sections are removed. Remove any seeds from the sections.

Sweating without fat is to cook ingredients in fat-free liquids or their own moisture until tender without browning. Sweating works well with seasoning vegetables such as onions and garlic when they require softening without browning.

Washing, rather than peeling, *fruits and vegetables* such as apples, pears, carrots, and potatoes may be specified in recipes. The peels of fruits and vegetables are retained for the fiber, vitamins, and minerals they can add to dishes.

Whipping evaporated skim milk works best if it is partially frozen and beaten at high speed with chilled beaters in a chilled bowl. A little unflavored gelatin, about 3 tablespoons per pint, can prevent it from deflating. To add the gelatin, heat a small amount of the evaporated milk, stir in the gelatin until dissolved, and whip with the remaining chilled evaporated milk.

APPENDIX 6

Sources for Food Ingredients in Healthy Cooking

Dried Beans and Lentils

Bean Bag
818 Jefferson Street
Oakland, CA 94607
(800) 845-BEAN

Dean & Deluca
560 Broadway
New York, NY 10012
(800) 221-7714

Phipps Ranch
P.O. Box 349
Pescadero, CA 94060
(415) 879-0787

Dried Fruits and Nuts

Chukar Cherries
320 Wine Country Road
Prosser, WA 99350
(800) 624-9544

Hadley Fruit Orchards
P.O. Box 495
Cabazon, CA 92230
(800) 854-5655

Flours, Baking Products, and/or Grains

Arrowhead Mills
P.O. Box 2059
Hereford, TX 79045-2059
(806) 364-0730

King Arthur's Flour
(The Baker's Catalogue)
Rural Route 2, P.O. Box 56
Norwich, VT 05055
(800) 827-6836

Montana Flour & Grains
P.O. Box 517
Fort Benton, MT 59442
(406) 622-5436

Morgan's Mills
Rural Route 2, P.O. Box 4602
Union, ME 04862
(207) 785-4900

Fruits and Vegetables

Diamond Organics
P.O. Box 2159
Freedom, CA 95019
(800) 922-2396
(*Fresh, organically grown fruits and vegetables*)

Underwood Ranches
P.O. Box 607
Somis, CA 93066
(800) 447-7746
(*Baby specialty vegetables and lettuces*)

Fruit Juice Concentrates

Wax Orchards
22744 Wax Orchards Road, S.W.
Vashon, WA 98070
(800) 634-6132

Game Meat

Broadleaf Venison (USA, Inc.)
11030 Randall Street
Sun Valley, CA 91352
(800) 336-3844

Faire Game, Inc.
2707 West Eisenhower Boulevard
Number 5
Loveland, CO 80538
(800) 889-6328

Herbs and Spices

Penzeys Spice House
1921 South West Avenue
Waukesha, WI 53186
(414) 574-0277
(*Garam Masala [Indian-Inspired Spice Blend. See page 58] and other spices*)

Spice House
P.O. Box 1633
Milwaukee, WI 53201
(414) 768-8799

Mail-Order Food Companies

Mail Order Gourmet
P.O. Box 1085
New York, NY 10011
(800) 989-5996
(*150 companies offering unusual food items*)

Mushrooms

Delftree Farm
234 Union Street
North Adams, MA 01247
(800) 769-3742
(*Fresh and dried wild mushrooms*)

Pasta

Pasta Just For You By Sue
111 West Main Street
West Dundee, IL 60118
(800) 727-8287 or (800) PASTA-US
(*52 pasta flavors*)

Phyllo Dough

Athens Foods
13600 Snow Road
Cleveland, OH 44142-2596
(800) 837-5683
(*Whole wheat and wheat phyllo dough*)

Tofu Products

Morinaga Nutritional Foods, Inc.
2050 West 190th Street
Suite 110 A
Torrance, CA 90504
Mori-Nu at (800) NOW-TOFU
(*Reduced-fat tofu products available too*)

Vegetable Cooking Spray

Tryson House
15635 Alton Parkway
Suite 260
Irvine, CA 92718
(800) 222-6820
(*Assorted flavors of cooking sprays*)

Wild Pecan Rice

Conrad Rice Mill Inc.
P.O. Box 296
307 Ann Street
New Iberia, LA 70560
(318) 364-7242

Wild Rice

Black Duck Company
9640 Vincent Avenue South
Bloomington, MN 55431
(612) 884-3472

APPENDIX 7

Healthy Cooking Tools, Equipment, and Sources

Tools and Equipment

Bulb basters can help remove the fat from soups, sauces, and other cooking liquids. Updated models with regular round tips and interchangeable flat tips that separate the fat from flavorful liquids are now available.

Defatting pitchers make it easy for chefs to lose the fat but keep the flavor in liquid-based dishes. When fatty liquids are poured into a defatting pitcher, the fat rises quickly to the top and the rich juices can be poured off through a spout cleverly placed at the pitcher's bottom, leaving the grease behind.

Fat-off ladles are useful for removing fat from cooking juices, stocks, broths, soups, gravies, sauces, and stews. When a fat-off ladle is dipped in a fatty liquid, the fat rises to the top and flows through small slots around its raised rim. The fat collects in its bowl and is ready to be discarded.

Nonstick meat loaf pans have two parts. The inner part is perforated so that grease drains off during cooking, reducing calories, fat, and cholesterol.

Nonstick pans allow ingredients to be cooked using less fat without sticking.

Sources

Commercial Aluminum Cookware
(Calphalon)
Box 583
Toledo, OH 43697
(419) 666-8700
(*Nonstick pans*)

The Vollrath Company, Inc.
1236 North 18th Street
Sheboygan, WI 53082-0611
(414) 457-4851
(*Nonstick pans*)

The Wooden Spoon
Route 6
Box 852
Mahopac, NY 10541-0851
(800) 431-2207
(*Assorted cooking tools and equipment*)

Williams Sonoma Catalog
P.O. Box 7044
San Francisco, CA 94120-7044
(800) 541-2233
(*Assorted cooking tools and equipment*)

GLOSSARY

Ingredients in Healthy Cooking

Amaranth is a tiny, pale-yellow, whole grain about the size of a poppy seed with a pronounced, earthy, sweet flavor and a gelatinous texture when cooked.

Arugula, also known as rugula or rocket, is a very perishable, green-colored lettuce with round and slightly elongated leaves. It has a bitterish flavor.

Barley is available in hulled, pearl, and pot or Scotch forms. It may contain a cholesterol-inhibiting substance and is a good source of protein, fiber, iron, and other nutrients even in its refined form. Hulled barley has its inedible hull removed but not its bran. These brown grains have a mild, nutty flavor and chewy texture. Pearl barley is the refined form of barley. These ivory-colored grains are missing their hull, bran, and most of their germ. Pot or Scotch barley is less refined than pearl barley with part of its bran layer remaining.

Beefalo is a cross between Black Angus beef and bison. It contains less fat and fewer calories than beef and has a unique taste and texture.

Black beans, also known as black turtle beans, are sturdy, black-skinned beans with a cream-colored flesh and mildly sweet taste. They are delicious with the spicy flavors in the cuisines of Mexico, Central and South America, and the Caribbean, where they have long been popular.

Belgian endive has small, narrow, white to pale-green-colored, pointed spearhead-like leaves. It has a slightly bitter flavor and waxy texture.

Boston lettuce has sweet, soft, buttery-textured leaves and small, round, loosely formed heads.

Brown sugar is white sugar crystals coated with molasses. While it contains a few extra nutrients not found in refined sugar, the quantity is so minuscule that, for all practical purposes, they are useless.

Buckwheat flour comes in two forms. Dark buckwheat flour is grayish in color with little black flecks. It is ground from the unhulled buckwheat groat. Buckwheat flour's light form is ground after the hull is removed. Both of these flours are low in gluten and have strong earthy tastes, the dark flour being the strongest.

Bulgur is whole-wheat kernels that have been steamed, dried, and then cracked into coarse, medium, or fine granules.

Butter-flavored powders can add butter flavor to healthy dishes with little or no fat and cholesterol. The spray-dried powders can be sprinkled on hot foods such as baked potatoes and other vegetables or liquified by mixing with hot water.

Cake flour is milled from the endosperm of soft wheat kernels. It is low in protein and gluten, and, thus, especially suitable for making high-starch cakes, cookies, and crackers and using as a thickening agent in sauces.

Cannellini beans are large, white, Italian, oval-shaped beans with a creamy texture. They can be made into purees and spreads but are good in salads and soups too. They are available dried and canned.

Canola oil is a bland-tasting oil pressed from rape seeds. It is lower in saturated fats (about 6%) than any other oil, contains Omega-3 fatty acids (polyunsaturated fat believed to lower both cholesterol and triglycerides), and is high in monounsaturated fat.

Cayenne pepper is a hot, pungent powder ground from several varieties of hot, red chili peppers. The spice industry is gradually replacing the term cayenne pepper with the more general term red pepper.

Cellophane noodles, also known as bean thread vermicelli, jelly noodles, and transparent vermicelli, are thin, semi-translucent noodles made from mung beans. They are almost pure starch with little protein.

Chanterelle (shang-tee-rell) mushrooms are golden-orange-colored, apricot-scented, trumpet-shaped, wild mushrooms with ruffled edges and a somewhat chewy texture.

Chinese cabbage, also known as Chinese celery cabbage, napa cabbage, and Peking cabbage, has tightly furled leaves with wide, white ribs and soft, pale-green tips. It has a mild flavor and crunchy texture.

Chinese dried mushrooms, also known as black mushrooms (dried), are pale buff to brown in color with a unique flavor and distinctive aroma. Prior to using, the mushrooms require soaking in lukewarm water for at least 25 minutes and removal of their tough stems.

Cornmeal is made from finely ground, dried, white and yellow corn. Commercially, it is generally ground from the corn kernel with the hull and germ removed. The higher fiber unbolted cornmeal, which retains its bran and germ, is available at some health-food stores. The rich-tasting, yellow cornmeal contains a bit more beta-carotene than the white cornmeal.

Cocoa powder can give cakes, baked goods, and other desserts a chocolate flavor, yet is much lower in saturated and total fat than solid chocolate. While both chocolate and cocoa powder come from cocoa beans, cocoa powder is what remains after most of the cocoa butter is pressed from unsweetened chocolate. Three tablespoons of cocoa powder along with 1 tablespoon of polyunsaturated vegetable margarine can be substituted in healthy recipes for each square or ounce of chocolate required. Cocoa powders with 10–12% fat should be selected when cooking healthy. Some gourmet cocoa varieties yield twice this amount.

Couscous is tiny pellets of moistened and rolled semolina, popular in North African cuisine. Couscous is also the name for the dish in which the semolina grains steam in the perforated top part of a special pot called a couscoussiere, while chunks of meat, vegetables, chickpeas, and raisins simmer in the bottom part.

Cracked wheat is wheat berries that have been cracked into coarse, medium, or fine granules for faster cooking.

Dried green or yellow peas, unlike common green peas, are dried from field peas. They are available in whole and split forms and are wonderful in soups and purees.

Edible flowers are a lovely way to add color, flavor, texture, and interest to dishes. When choosing flowers, be sure to use only edible blossoms. Popular ones include anise hyssop, borage, calendula, chrysanthemums, lavender, miniature roses, marigolds, nasturtiums, pansies, squash and zucchini blossoms, and violas. Also, ensure that the flowers selected have been grown without the use of pesticides or other chemical sprays. A reliable source is essential. If in doubt about a flower's safety, check with a local horticultural society or poison control center.

Egg substitutes have been formulated as substitutes for real eggs. A whole range of products is available with varying levels of fat and cholesterol. Most of them are made from egg whites and other ingredients, including oils, milk products, tofu, artificial color, vitamins, minerals, emulsifiers, and antioxidants, that simulate the yolk's color, flavor, texture, nutritional value, and mouth feel. There are also egg substitutes that contain blends of whole eggs and whites and even products that contain a small amount of egg yolk from which the cholesterol has been extracted. Egg substitutes are not used in the recipes in this book.

Egg whites contain no fat or cholesterol and only 17 of the 76 calories in a whole egg. Two egg whites can be substituted for one whole egg, or a combination of two egg whites and one whole egg for every two whole eggs required in many dishes. Adding one teaspoon of polyunsaturated vegetable oil to every four egg whites will help prevent sticking and add some flavor when preparing dishes like omelets.

Egg yolks have less cholesterol than previously thought. The yolk of a large egg contains only 213 milligrams of cholesterol rather than the 275 still listed in some references. This is still a significant amount, given that current recommendations suggest cholesterol consumption be limited to 300 milligrams per day. The yolk is also the source of all the egg's fat and most of its calories, 59 of the 76 calories in a large whole egg.

Enoki mushrooms are small, delicate-flavored mushrooms that look like oversized straight pins. They are common in Japanese cuisine.

European or English cucumbers are long, slender, nearly seedless cucumbers.

Evaporated skim milk is skim milk with 60% of its water removed. It can add the creaminess of whole milk or cream to dishes without their fat and cholesterol. It can be whipped and substituted for whipped cream.

Farmer cheese is a mildly tart-flavored, very low-fat fresh cheese with a firm but grainy texture that can be substituted for cream cheese.

Fermented black beans are dried, cooked, salted, and fermented, small black soybeans. They are also known as black beans, dried black beans, and preserved black beans. This pungent, salty-flavored Chinese specialty is available in cans or plastic bags at Asian grocery stores.

Filo (phyllo) dough can be used to make low-fat pastry crusts, shells, pouches, covers, and wrappers for sweet and savory ingredients by separating layers of the dough with vegetable cooking spray. Athens Foods at (800) 837-5683 offers phyllo dough in both wheat and whole wheat forms.

Fish sauce is a clear, amber to dark brown-colored, strong-flavored, pungent seasoning sauce used extensively in Southeast Asian cuisine.

Five spice powder is an aromatic, Chinese spice powder with a unique flavor. The blend of star anise, cassia bark, Sichuan peppercorns, wild fennel seeds, and cloves is used as a seasoning agent and condiment.

Flavor extracts in pure or imitation forms can make dishes sparkle without fat, cholesterol, or sodium. Readily available flavors include almond, anise, banana, brandy, butter, cherry, chocolate, coconut, lemon, maple, orange, peppermint, pineapple, rum, strawberry, and vanilla.

Fruit juice concentrates can be used to sweeten foods. The flavors readily available in unsweetened, frozen concentrate form are apple, pineapple, purple grape, and orange. Frozen, unsweetened, white grape juice concentrate can also be found in some locations. Blends of fruit juice concentrates can be purchased from specialty companies. Fruit Sweet, a combination of unsweetened peach and pear juices and pineapple syrup, is produced by Wax Orchards. Wax Orchards can be reached at (800) 634-6132. For each cup of sugar in a recipe, replace with about one cup of juice concentrate and reduce the liquid ingredients by about one-third cup. Frozen, unsweetened orange, pineapple, apple, and white grape juice concentrates and Wax Orchards' Fruit Sweet and unsweetened white grape juice concentrate replace refined white sugar in many of the recipes in this book.

Garbanzo beans, also known as chick-peas, are mild, nut-flavored, round, creamy, beige-colored beans with a firm texture. They are popular in Middle Eastern, Mediterranean, and Indian cuisines.

Gram beans, also known as urad dal, are ivory-colored, hulled, and split seeds popular in northern Indian cuisine. The beans are available at Indian grocery stores.

Green onions, also known as scallions, have white underdeveloped bulb bases and green, long, straight leaves. While both parts are edible, use only the white portion unless specified otherwise.

Guavas are available in many varieties. When ripe, the thin skin of this sweet and fragrant tropical fruit can range in color from yellow to red to purple-black, and its flesh from shocking pink to salmon.

Hoisin sauce is a sweet and spicy, reddish-brown sauce made from a mixture of soybeans, garlic, chili peppers, and spices. It is available in stores offering Chinese food ingredients.

Honey is comprised predominantly of fructose along with glucose, the two sugars in sucrose, and about 18% water. Some believe it is more nutritious than white sugar. It is true—honey does provide vitamins and minerals in very small amounts that white sugar doesn't, but basically both are empty calories. Since honey is much sweeter than sugar, in liquid form about $\frac{1}{2}$ cup of honey can be substituted for each cup of sugar called for in recipes and the amount of liquid can be reduced by about $\frac{1}{4}$ cup for each $1\frac{1}{2}$ cups of honey used. Vegans and some other types of vegetarians avoid honey because it is made by bees and, therefore, of animal origin. Clover honey, the most common type of honey, is mild-flavored, thick, pale, and amber-colored. It is well suited for general cooking purposes but there are more than 300 varieties of honey available, each with its own unique flavors and appearances.

Horseradish is grown primarily for its large, white, pungent, spicy roots, although its young, tender leaves can be used in salads too. For use, fresh horseradish root should be peeled. It is most commonly served grated or shredded and used in sauces or as a condiment with fish or meat. Once grated, fresh horseradish loses its pungency quickly, so it should be prepared only as needed. Dried horseradish, which must be reconstituted, is also available but horseradish is more commonly found in the form of a prepared sauce or relish.

Jicama is a root vegetable shaped like a deformed turnip with a thin, rough, earth-colored, brown skin; juicy, crisp, sweet, white flesh; and the texture of an apple. It can be eaten raw or cooked. Jicama is available at stores offering Mexican food ingredients.

Kidney beans are beans with a deep-red skin, cream-colored flesh, and robust flavor. They hold their shape well in cooking. They are most readily available dried and canned.

Lemongrass is an herb with long, tapering, pale-green, serrated-edged leaves and a green-onion like base used in Thai and Vietnamese cooking. This sour-lemon flavored and scented seasoning agent is available in food stores offering Southeast Asian ingredients.

Lentils are tiny, lens-shaped legumes available in many varieties. Brown lentils are the most common with a mild peppery taste; olive-green-colored lentils are a bit milder in taste; French or European lentils are sold with their seed coats on and have a delicate sweetness; red or Egyptian lentils are smaller and rounder than brown lentils but unfortunately turn brown when cooked.

Looseleaf lettuce is mild-flavored, ranging in color from medium to dark green with shades of red. Its ruffled-edged leaves form loose bunches. Popular types are red, green, and oak leaf and salad bowl lettuces.

Mangoes have a thin, tough skin which turns from green to yellow with red mottling as the fruit ripens. The very juicy and fragrant flesh is sweet with a peach-like flavor.

Margarine (unsalted, corn oil) replaces butter in many of the recipes in this book. Like butter, by law, margarine must contain 80% fat. However, while both butter and margarine obtain all of their calories from fat, the fat in margarine is primarily polyunsaturated. Further, margarine made from vegetable oils like corn, sunflower, and safflower (no animal fats) contains no cholesterol. To minimize the sodium in dishes, unsalted margarine is further specified. There is a wide variety of products such as "light taste" margarine, $\frac{1}{3}$-less-fat margarine, butter-margarine, blends, tubs, and squeeze bottles that have less fat and calories than regular margarine. Generally, these products are not acceptable for use in the recipes in this book, baked goods in particular. Reduced-fat margarines produce cookies which are less crisp, dry out faster, and don't brown as much. Likewise, cakes become more gummy, dry out faster, and don't brown as well. To be sure a product is true margarine, check its label. Margarine with no qualifiers like "lower fat" is 80% fat margarine. All other products contain the words "% oil spread" on the front of their packages. The lower the percentage of oil listed, the less fat and more water the product contains.

Masa, available at Mexican food stores, is sun- or fire-dried corn kernels that have been cooked in limewater, soaked in limewater overnight, and then ground into masa.

Milk in nonfat or skim form contains less than 0.5% fat, low-fat milk is 1% or 2% fat as specified on its label, and whole milk contains 3.3% fat. As a result, the calories drop from 150 to 85 for a cup of whole versus nonfat milk and fall somewhere in between for low-fat milk. While nonfat milk is the lowest fat form, the creamier, low-fat milk is often preferred by food service customers.

Mirin, a sweet, golden wine made from glutinous rice, is also known as rice wine. This low-alcohol wine, common to Japanese cuisine, is used as a cooking ingredient not a beverage. It can be found in Japanese food markets and supermarkets offering gourmet ingredients.

Molasses is what is left behind after sugar has been refined. Light molasses has gone through the extraction process only once. It has a fairly high sugar content. So-called dark molasses is a product of second boiling. Each time sugar is extracted, its sugar content decreases. Blackstrap molasses is third extraction molasses. It is a tarry looking, strong-tasting syrup, low in sugar, and a rich source of nutrients.

Mung beans are tiny, pea-shaped beans with a green color, available in split and hulled as well as whole forms. They are popular in Chinese and Indian cuisines. In the United States, they are commonly used to grow bean sprouts. The yellow-colored, split, and hulled forms used in the recipes in this book are available at Indian grocery stores. They are also known as moong dal.

Oats in rolled or old-fashioned form are oat groats that have been steamed and pressed flat to shorten their cooking time. Instant or quick rolled oats are processed further and then heat-treated for faster cooking. Oats have excellent nutritional qualities. They are well endowed with protein, B vitamins, calcium, and fiber.

Oat flour is ground from whole oat groats, retaining much of its bran. Its delicate, sweet flavor and ability to keep baked goods fresh make it a welcome addition to baked goods. Besides being rich in vitamins and minerals, this low-gluten flour is rich in soluble fiber, the compound recognized for its cholesterol-lowering effects.

Olive oil, labeled extra virgin, is obtained from the mechanical pressing of olives, using no chemical solvents, under controlled temperature conditions. It is the most expensive form, with a maximum of 1% acidity and the highest-quality flavor. Virgin olive oil is made in the same manner as extra virgin, with an acidity of more than 1% and less than 3% and high flavor. Olive oil, formerly known as pure olive oil, is a blend of refined and virgin olive oil with the terms pure or 100% pure often listed on the label. It has an acidity of less than 1.5%. Olive pomace oil is extracted with solvents from the olive pomace and then blended with virgin olive oil. It is relatively low in cost and most suited for use in cooking. Light olive oil is bland or lighter in taste, not lower in calories or fat.

Orzo is a tiny, rice-shaped pasta that works well in soups and can be offered pilaf-style in lieu of rice.

Papaya, a juicy, pear-shaped fruit with a golden-yellow skin and flesh (when ripe), has a sweet-tart flavor and creamy smooth texture. Its center cavity is filled with peppery-flavored, round, silver-black seeds which are edible but generally discarded.

Paprika is a powdered seasoning made by grinding sweet red pepper pods. The Hungarian variety, considered to be superior by many, is specified in the recipes in this book. Replace it with paprika from Spain, South America, or another location if Hungarian paprika is not available.

Pasteurized eggs are available in dried, frozen, and liquid forms. Dried eggs are inferior to frozen and liquid products and, generally, are not recommended for restaurants to use. Frozen eggs are created by a combination of pasteurization and blast freezing. Once thawed, frozen eggs can be used in recipes calling for beaten eggs. Liquid eggs have been pasteurized but not frozen. Likewise, they can be substituted for beaten eggs in dishes. Their drawback previously was their 7–10-day shelf life. Extended-life liquid eggs are now available, which can be stored at 40°F (5°C) or less for up to 8 weeks.

Pastry flour is milled from the endosperm of soft, low-gluten wheat and has a protein level similar to cake flour but contains less starch. It is desirable for preparing high-starch pastries.

Pink lentils also known as Masoor dal and Masar dal, are lens-shaped, salmon-colored lentils. They are available at Indian grocery stores. When cooked, the pink lentils turn yellow. The red Egyptian lentils, available at Middle Eastern stores, make good substitutes.

Pinto beans, also known as red Mexican beans, are pale pink beans with a deep reddish-brown streak. They are popular in the cuisines of Spanish-speaking countries and commonly used in refried beans and chili.

Plum tomatoes, also known as roma tomatoes, Italian tomatoes, and paste tomatoes, have a thick, meaty texture with few seeds that makes them well suited for use in sauces.

Porcini mushrooms, also known as bolete, cep, and cepe mushrooms, range in size from 1 to 10 inches. These pungent, woodsy-flavored, wild mushrooms have stout stems and a spongy surface underneath their brown caps. They are most commonly available in dried form. For use, they must be softened for about 25 minutes in hot water.

Portobello mushrooms are mature crimini mushrooms (Italian brown mushrooms) with a meaty flesh and robust flavor. When grilled, these large mushrooms (4 to 10 inches in length) taste like steak.

Potatoes fall into two basic groups. First are the thin-skinned, firm, and waxy-textured types, often called new potatoes. They include the round whites, long whites, and red rounds. They are ideal for boiling and steaming. When small ($1\frac{1}{4}$ to $2\frac{1}{2}$ inches in diameter), new, red potatoes are desired in a recipe, they are listed as very small or baby, new, red potatoes. The second group contains the thick-skinned, dry, mealy-textured russet potatoes. They are ideal for baking and frying. Potatoes with yellow fleshes and golden- to tan-colored skins come in both starchy and waxy forms. They are known for their exceptional flavor. They include Bintje, Carole, Yellow Finn, and Yukon Gold varieties.

Quinoa (keen-wa) is a pale yellow seed slightly larger than mustard seed with a sweet flavor and soft texture. Nutritionally, it's a winner. It is an excellent source of magnesium and is rich in iron, calcium, and copper. Furthermore, it is a good source of protein, B vitamins, and fiber.

Rice in its whole grain, brown form is rich in fiber, B vitamins, and minerals including iron, zinc, phosphorous, copper, and manganese. Brown rice is also the only form of rice that provides vitamin E. White rice is almost pure starch. Most of its vitamins, minerals, protein, and fiber are removed in the milling process.

Rye berries, also called whole kernels or groats, are similar in shape to wheat with a bluish-gray color and strong distinctive flavor.

Sake is a yellowish, slightly sweet, relatively low-alcohol Japanese wine made from fermented rice.

Sesame oil, pressed from sesame seeds, comes in two forms, one being light in color with a mild nutty flavor and the second, known as Oriental sesame oil, with a darker color and more pronounced flavor and fragrance. The light-colored sesame oil is specified in the recipes in this book. Sesame oil has a high level of polyunsaturated fats, ranking fourth behind safflower, soybean, and corn oil.

Shiitake mushrooms are large flat mushrooms with a woody odor and a rich mushroom flavor.

Soba noodles are Japanese, dark-brownish-gray spaghettilike noodles made from buckwheat flour or buckwheat flour in combination with wheat flour. Both fresh and dried forms of these protein-rich noodles are available. An interesting green-tinted variation of soba noodles is also available. It is created by adding green matcha tea powder to the buckwheat-based dough.

Star fruit, also known as carambola, become star-shaped when cut crosswise. This 3- to 5-inch-long fruit has an edible, thin, glossy, golden-yellow skin and, when ripe, a juicy, fragrant flesh of the same color with a sweet-tart to sour taste.

Tofu or bean curd is sold in white cakes of varying textures packed in water. Alone, tofu is very bland but it readily picks up flavor. Thus, it is a good choice in combination dishes along with a variety of flavorful ingredients. Hard or medium-firm tofu holds its shape best in preparation and cooking. Soft tofu can be blended to make cream pies, spreads, dips, puddings, and cream soups. Reduced-fat versions of tofu are now available.

Triticale (trit-i-kay-lee) is a hybrid of wheat and rye. The nut-flavored grain is a good source of B vitamins and provides a better balance of protein than either of its two parent grains. Triticale berries are about the size of wheat berries and contain their germ and bran. Cracked triticale is made from berries that have been cracked to shorten their cooking time. Triticale flakes are berries that have been steamed and flattened.

Vegetable cooking sprays are made from polyunsaturated oils like corn or soybean with lecithin added. Canola oil spray is also available. Vegetable cooking sprays are commonly sold in natural, butter, and olive flavors. Tryson House at (800) 222-6820 offers these flavors as well as Italian, garlic, Oriental, and mesquite mists. Vegetable cooking sprays can be used to lightly coat pans with oil and prevent sticking. A light 1- to 2-second spray of most adds about 2 calories, less than 1 gram of fat, and no cholesterol or sodium.

Wheat berries are unprocessed whole wheat kernels with a hearty, nutty flavor and chewy texture.

Wheat bran is the rough outer grain covering of wheat. It is primarily recognized for its high fiber content but it also adds B vitamins and protein to the diet.

Wheat germ is the nutrient-rich embryo of the wheat berry. It contains protein and polyunsaturated fat and is a source of vitamin E, B vitamins including thiamin, riboflavin, and niacin, minerals including zinc, and fiber. It must be refrigerated to prevent it from becoming rancid.

"White beans" is a generic term referring to several kinds of white beans including navy beans, marrow beans, pea beans, and great northern beans. They work well in salads, soups, and commonly appear in baked beans.

Whole wheat flour, also known as graham flour, is a coarse-textured flour ground from the entire wheat kernel. It contains the fiber, B vitamin, and trace-mineral-rich outer head, bran portion of the berry along with the protein-rich, fatty germ or embryo of the kernel, and the starch-filled endosperm. The endosperm is the part of the wheat kernel that yields white flour and provides the gluten necessary to make bread rise.

Whole wheat pastry flour has a nutty taste and more minerals and fiber than white cake or pastry flour. It produces excellent results in pastry making or baking powder-risen breads, such as muffins, cookies, or cakes when gluten is not necessary and, in fact, not desired.

Wild rice is really the seed of an aquatic grass. Its dark brown, slender grains have a nutty, earthy flavor. Wild rice is a better source of protein than other types of rice and adds fiber, zinc, magnesium, and B vitamins to the diet. It is available in giant (long), extra-fancy (medium), and select (short) forms.

Yellow lentils, also known as toor dal, toovar dal, and arhar dal, are seeds that have been hulled and split to yield golden yellow lentils. They are available at Indian grocery stores. Yellow lentils should not be confused with the common supermarket variety which are sold unhulled with a thin, brown skin.

Zest is the colorful, outermost skin layer of citrus fruits (commonly oranges and lemons), used for garnishing and flavoring dishes. The bitter white pith should be avoided.

Index

Abbreviations, listing of, xx-xxi
Almond(s):
    granola, whole grain, with sun-
        flower seeds, cashews, dried
        apricots, raisins and, 248
    meringue bites, 409
    wild rice with mushrooms and,
        251–252
Angel hair pasta, pancakes, carrot-
    flavored, with bell peppers,
    255–256
Angel spice cake, 366–367
Apple(s):
    cabbage, shredded green, with cin-
        namon and, 204
    sliced with baby carrots in fruit
        glaze with, 190–191
Apple crisp with raisins and oat top-
    ping, 456
Apple crumb cake, 368
Apple and currant phyllo strudel,
    454–455
Applesauce, 393
Apple syrup with calvados, 385
Apple yogurt, butternut squash bisque
    with, 11–12
Apricot(s):
    coconut wheat flake cereal bon-
        bons, 404

dried, granola, whole grain, with
    sunflower seeds, cashews, al-
    monds, raisins and, 248
frozen yogurt fruit juice and, 442–
    443
Apricot-flavored powdered sugar
    frosting, 386
Apricot fruit juice syrup puree, 389
Apricot glaze, lamb kebabs, grilled,
    85
Apricot souffle, fruit-sweetened, 467
Avocado dip, guacamole-like, with
    bell peppers, 357

Baked Alaska, banana-strawberry, 422
Balsamic-rice vinegar dressing, 306
Bamboo shoots, snow peas, stir-fried
    shiitake mushrooms and, 207–
    208
Banana:
    bread pudding, whole wheat, 438
    strawberry, and kiwi orange shake,
        363
Banana apricot whole wheat cake,
    369
Banana baked in graham cracker
    crumbs with orange-pineapple
    yogurt topping, 457

Banana bonbons, 446
Banana bran walnut muffins, 369
Banana split with butterscotch and
    frozen yogurt, 444
Barbecued:
    chicken, 122
    shrimp, spicy coconut, 167–168
Barbecue sauce, for fowl, 57
Barley and mushroom soup, 9
Barley risotto, with mushrooms and
    spinach, 233–234
Barley soup, with mushrooms and
    beef, 25
Bars, see Cookies and bars
Basil:
    oils and vinegars, 298–299
    tomato relish with garlic and, 53
Beans and lentils, 172–189
    black bean patties, with tomato
        bell pepper salsa, 172–173
    black beans, Puerto Rican-style,
        182–183
    cannellini bean dip with green on-
        ions, bell peppers, and toma-
        toes, 353
    garbanzo beans:
        in ginger sauce, 176
        turkey ball soup with, and vege-
            tables, 24

Beans and lentils (*Continued*)
  kidney beans:
    brown rice and, Jamaican-style,
      177
    with Indian seasonings, 184
    in tomato broth with bell pep-
      pers, carrots, and celery, 178–
      179
  lentils, pink, with roasted spices,
    280
  lentil sandwich spread, with Asian
    spices, 185–186
  mung beans, yellow split, with cau-
    liflower and spinach, 187
  pinto beans:
    fried and simmered in broth,
      174–175
    in vegetable broth, 181
  stew, three bean, lentil, and pea
    stew, 188–189
  tortillas, bean- and cheese-filled
    whole wheat, 327
Beef, 64–81
  burgers, with onions, bell peppers,
    and Worcestershire sauce,
    69
  cubes, braised in mustard beer
    sauce, 64–65
  flank steak, with mushroom and
    green onions, 70–71
  patties, with pickled beets and ca-
    pers, 66
  pot roast, marinated, with gin-
    gersnap gravy, 74–75
  roast round, with vegetables braised
    in red wine, 67
  roast tenderloin, Cajun-style, 68
  sirloin steak, sauteed, with red pep-
    per tomato sauce, 80
  spring rolls with tofu, shrimp and,
    Philippine-style, 76–77
  stew, with winter vegetables, 72–
    73
  tenderloin strips:
    sauteed, in Stroganoff-style
      sauce, 78–79
    stir-fried, in soy glaze, 81
  translucent noodles with vegetables
    and, in soy glaze, 265–266
Beefalo, salad with shrimp and cello-
    phane noodles, Thai-style,
    270–271
Beef soup, with mushrooms and bar-
    ley, 25
Beets:
  beef patties, capers and, 66
  fruit salad, pomegranate seeds, and
    roasted peanuts, 291–292
  glazed in orange and red wine vin-
    egar sauce, 192

  pickled, German-style, 286
  sliced gingered orange beets, 205
Belgian endive, *see* Endive
Bell peppers:
  angel hair pasta pancakes, carrot-
    flavored, with, 255–256
  avocado dip, guacamole-like, with,
    357
  beef burgers, with onions,
    Worcestershire sauce and, 69
  brown rice pilaf, with celery, on-
    ions and, 245–246
  cabbage, shredded, with corn and,
    in pineapple tofu dressing, 287
  chicken thighs, in tomato sauce
    with mushrooms and, 132–
    133
  corn chowder, with roasted red bell
    pepper garnish, 17–18
  crab cakes with toasted corn and,
    169
  gazpacho soup, 15
  kidney beans in tomato broth, car-
    rots, celery and, 178–179
  potato boats stuffed with mashed
    potatoes and, 228–229
  potato salad with kidney beans
    and, vinaigrette sauce, 283
  soba noodles with snow peas, car-
    rots, mushrooms, water chest-
    nuts and, 288
  stewed with zucchini and tomatoes
    with turkey ham, 215
  stuffed with ground turkey, brown
    rice and mozzarella cheese,
    116–117
  tomato bell pepper salsa, 51
    black bean patties with, 172–
    173
  tomato soup, creamed, with sweet
    red bell pepper, 20–21
  turkey tacos with cheese and toma-
    to bell pepper salsa, 120–121
  vegetable salad, grilled, 281
Beverages, 360–363
  chardonnay and cranberry spritzer,
    360
  orange iced tea, minted, 362
  strawberry, banana, and kiwi or-
    ange shake, 363
  tomato cocktail, spicy, 361
Biscuits, whole wheat and onion sage,
    382
Bisque, *see* Soups
Black bean patties, with tomato bell
    pepper salsa, 172–173
Black beans, Puerto Rican-style, 182–
    183
Black bean sauce, sea bass steamed
    whole with, 160–161

Blueberries:
  with oat pastry, 423–424
  wild rice with shiitake mushrooms
    and, 253–254
Braised beef, cubes, in mustard beer
    sauce, 64–65
Braised pork, cubes, with paprika and
    yogurt, goulash-style, 93–94
Bread pudding:
  baked banana and whole grain, 438
  sweet potato whole grain, 440–441
Breads and cakes, 366–384
  angel cake, berries encased in,
    459–460
  angel spice cake, 366–367
  apple crumb cake, 368
  banana apricot whole wheat cake,
    369
  banana bran walnut muffins, 369
  biscuits, whole wheat and onion
    sage, 382
  carrot, raisin, and pineapple whole
    wheat cake, 372
  chocolate cake, 379
  corn bread, buckwheat stone-
    ground yellow, 371
  cornmeal cake with anise and cin-
    namon, 373
  cranberry orange-flavored upside
    down cake, 374–375
  gingerbread cake with bananas,
    376–377
  hot fudge pudding cake, 378
  pancakes, pumpkin whole wheat,
    381
  peach meringue mousse cake, 380
  salt reduction, listed, 478–479
  whole wheat French bread, 383–
    384
Broccoli:
  marinated in rice wine vinaigrette,
    275
  potato salad with sausage and
    (hot), 273
  stir-fried, vegetable medley, 202
  stir-fried with wine, soy sauce, and
    ginger, 210
  timbales with Swiss cheese, 322–
    323
Broths, *see* Soups; Stocks
Brown rice:
  bell pepper stuffed with ground tur-
    key, mozzarella cheese and,
    116–117
  black beans, Puerto Rican-style
    with, 182–183
  with chicken, seafood, and vege-
    tables, paella-style, 243–244
  chicken brown rice and vegetable
    soup with curry, 13–14

fried, with vegetables, 241–242
kidney beans and, Jamaican-style, 177
pilaf, with bell peppers, celery, and onions, 245–246
pork tenderloin, stuffed with raisins, olives and, 101–102
pudding, baked with dried cherries, 439
in tomato broth, 236
turmeric-flavored, with tomatoes, 247
Buckwheat and corn bread, 371
Buckwheat cornbread stuffing, with spinach and ham, 237–238
Buckwheat honey glaze, 387
Bulgur salad, with garden vegetables, 276–277
Buttermilk, potatoes mashed with, 223
Buttermilk sour cream potato topping, 352
Butternut squash bisque with chunky apple yogurt, 11–12
Butterscotch sauce, 388

Cabbage:
    shredded, with apples and cinnamon, 204
    shredded, with corn and bell pepper in pineapple tofu dressing, 287
    stir-fried, vegetable medley, 202
Cakes, see Breads and cakes
Calorie need, explained, xxiv
Calorie reduction, substitutes for, 487–490
Cannellini bean dip with green onions, bell peppers, and tomatoes, 353
Cantaloupe balls with ouzo, 461
Capers, beef patties with pickled beets and, 66
Carrot(s):
    baby, in fruit glaze with apple slices, 190–191
    citrus-glazed, with parsley, 195
    kidney beans in tomato broth bell peppers, celery and, 178–179
    raisin and pineapple whole wheat cake with, 372
    soba noodles with bell peppers, snow peas, mushrooms, water chestnuts and, 288
    stir-fried:
        with coconut flavor, 209
        vegetable medley, 202
    tomatoes stuffed with zucchini and, 214

Carrot bisque, gingered, 23
Cashews:
    chicken salad with grapes, water chestnuts and, 272
    granola, whole grain, with sunflower seeds, almonds, dried apricots, raisins and, 248
Catfish, with garlic and cilantro cornbread topping, 158–159
Cauliflower:
    coated with cilantro and onions, 193
    mung beans, yellow split, with spinach and, 187
    stir-fried with tomatoes and turmeric, ginger, and cilantro, 194
Celery:
    brown rice pilaf, with onions, bell peppers and, 245–246
    chicken breasts braised with herbs, garlic and, 127–128
    kidney beans in tomato broth bell peppers, carrots and, 178–179
Chardonnay and cranberry spritzer, 360
Cheddar cheese, penne pasta baked in cheddar and Swiss cheese sauce, 262
Cheese:
    manicotti tubes with spinach, mushrooms, tomato sauce and, 259–260
    mashed potatoes with green onions and, 219
    mozzarella, pork cutlets, breaded, with filling of, 95
    penne pasta baked in cheddar and Swiss cheese sauce, 262
Cheese custard, sliced potatoes simmered in, 220
Cheese dishes, 327–336
    chenna and paneer cheese, 328–329
    green peas and cheese in tomato sauce, 332–333
    strudel, spinach and Swiss cheese with phyllo pastry, 334–335
    Swiss cheese sandwich, toasted open-face, with tomatoes and caraway, 336
    tortillas, bean- and cheese-filled whole wheat, 327
    white cheese, nonfat milk, 330
    yogurt cheese, nonfat, thickened with yogurt flavored with herbs, 331
Cheese frosting, 390
Cheese substitutes, salt reduction, listed, 476–478

Chenna cheese, 328–329
Cherries, oranges, and raspberries in cherry-flavored syrup, 464
Cherry crepes with vanilla frozen yogurt, 466
Chicken, 122–140
    barbecue sauce for, 57
    barbecue-style, 122
    breasts:
        baked, with mustard, 134
        braised in tomato port wine sauce, 123
        braised with celery, herbs, and garlic, 127–128
        braised with paprika, Hungarian-style, 125–126
        cubed, simmered in coconut sauce, 124
        sauteed, with oregano and mozzarella cheese, 137–138
        brown rice with, and seafood, and vegetables, paella-style, 243–244
        croquettes, with mushroom sauce, 129–130
        drumsticks, grilled, tandoori-style, 135–136
        spit-roasted, on rotisserie, 139–140
    thighs:
        in cinnamon crust, 131
        in tomato sauce with mushrooms and bell peppers, 132–133
    wings, ginger sesame, 342
Chicken brown rice and vegetable soup with curry, 13–14
Chicken gravy, with blended vegetables, 34
Chicken salad:
    with cashews, grapes, and water chestnuts, 272
    with orange-pineapple soy dressing, 274
Chicken soup, with whole wheat noodle and vegetables, 32
Chicken stock, white, 7
Chili cheese dip with tomatoes and onions, 354
Chilies, tomato salsa cilantro and, 44
Chili sauce, hot red, 46
Chocolate cake, 379
Chocolate meringue shells, 411–412
Cholesterol, substitutes for reduction of, 468–475
Chowder, see Soups
Christmas Eve salad, beets and fruit, pomegranate seeds, and roasted peanuts, 291–292
Chutney, see Condiment sauces

Cilantro:
cauliflower coated onions and, 193
tomato salsa chilies and, 44
Cilantro and mint chutney, 43
Cilantro cornbread topping, catfish with garlic and, 158–159
Cinnamon, cabbage, shredded green, with apples and, 204
Citrus-flavored cranberry vinaigrette, 307
Coconut sauce, chicken breast cubes simmered in, 124
Collard greens, mixed greens, with ground peanuts, 199
Condiment sauces, 41–56. See also Sauces
chili sauce, hot red, 46
cranberry pineapple relish, 42
cranberry spread, whipped creamy, 55
dipping sauce, Vietnamese-style, 54
horseradish and yogurt sauce with dillweed, 56
hot sauce, spicy, African-style, 41
lime ginger-garlic sauce, 47
mint and cilantro chutney, 43
papaya mango salsa, 48
peanut butter, chunky, 45
salt reduction, listed, 479–482
spring roll sauce, sweet, 50
tomato bell pepper salsa, 51
tomato cucumber relish, 52
tomato relish with basil and garlic, 53
tomato salsa with cilantro and chilies, 44
tomato sauce with spicy red peppers, 49
Cookies and bars, 404–410
almond meringue bites, 409
apricot and coconut wheat flake cereal bonbons, 404
candied orange zests, 405–406
crisp spiced ginger cookies, 407
custard strips, orange-scented, 410
whole grain bread strips, honey-baked, in custard coating, 408
Cooking equipment, descriptions and sources, 498–499
Cooking procedures, healthy strategies, 491–494
Corn:
cabbage, shredded, with bell pepper and, in pineapple tofu dressing, 287
zucchini stuffed with, and cheese and oat flake topping, 196
Cornbread:
buckwheat, stuffing, with spinach and ham, 237–238

buckwheat stone-ground yellow, 371
catfish with garlic and cilantro cornbread topping, 158–159
crab cakes with toasted corn and bell peppers, 169
Corn cake, 211
Corn chowder, with roasted red bell pepper garnish, 17–18
Cornish hens, broiled, Asian-inspired, 141–142
Cornmeal cake with anise and cinnamon, 373
Corn on the cob:
cooking methods, 201
grilled, 200
Corn soup, in creamy broth with cumin, 22
Couscous:
with ginger and soy, 239
lamb stew with vegetables and, 82–83
Crab cakes, with toasted corn and bell peppers, 169
Cranberry, chardonnay and cranberry spritzer, 360
Cranberry orange-flavored upside down cake, 374–375
Cranberry pineapple relish, 42
Cranberry sauce, turkey breast, sliced, with, 114–115
Cranberry spread, whipped creamy, 55
Cranberry vinaigrette, citrus-flavored, 307
Crepes, 413–414
apples glazed and rolled in, 462
cherry crepes with vanilla frozen yogurt, 466
Cucumber:
diced, red onion and tomato salad, 279
gazpacho soup, 15
onions and, marinated in sweet and sour dill dressing, 278
sliced with mint and cilantro chutney sandwich, 340
Cucumber tomato relish, 52
Curry, chicken brown rice and vegetable soup with, 13–14
Curry dressing, nonfat creamy, 310
Custard strips, orange-scented, 410

Dairy, substitutes to increase fiber in, 485–486
Dairy substitutes, fat reduction, listed, 468–469
Date puree, 391

Desserts, see Breads and cakes; Frozen desserts; Fruit desserts; Pastry
Dessert sauces, see Frosting and sweet sauces
Dillweed:
horseradish and yogurt sauce with, 56
sweet and sour dill dressing, cucumbers and onions marinated in, 278
Dipping sauce, Vietnamese-style, 54
Dips and toppings, 352–359. See also Snacks
avocado dip, guacamole-like, with bell peppers, 357
buttermilk sour cream potato topping, 352
cannellini bean dip with green onions, bell peppers, and tomatoes, 353
chili cheese dip with tomatoes and onions, 354
garlic bread, roasted elephant garlic, 359
ranch-style chip dip, 358
yogurt, fruit-sweetened nonfat strawberry, with strawberry chunks, 355–356
Dressings, 305–320. See also Oils and vinegars
balsamic-rice vinegar, 306
cranberry vinaigrette, citrus-flavored, 307
curry, nonfat creamy, 310
ginger soy, sesame-flavored, 318
honey vinaigrette, raspberry-infused, 315
lime, Asian-inspired, 305
lime and vegetable dressing, 309
mayonnaise-like, oil free, 311
orange pineapple soy, 312
peach poppy seed, creamy, 308
ranch-style, 314
red wine vinaigrette, 316
saffron and basil orange vinaigrette, 317
tofu, pineapple-flavored, creamy, 313
vegetable-thickened oil-free vinaigrette, 319
walnut-flavored vinaigrette, 320
Dried beans, see Beans and lentils

Egg dishes, 322–326
scrambled eggs, fiesta, 324
souffle, spinach mushroom, 324–326
timbales, broccoli, with Swiss cheese, 322–323

Egg drop soup, 26
Eggplant:
  baked, 197–198
  puree of, with green chilies, 206
  vegetable salad, grilled, 281
Egg substitutes, fat reduction, listed, 468–471
Elephant garlic, roasted, 359
Endive, vegetable salad, grilled, 281

Fat substitutes, fat reduction, listed, 471–473
Fennel seeds:
  pork tenderloin with, 103–104
  potatoes, sauteed cubes, with ginger, garlic and, 230
Fiber, substitutes to increase, 483–486
Fillings, see Pastry fillings and toppings
Fish, 150–164. See also Shellfish
  brown rice with chicken, seafood, and vegetables, paella-style, 243–244
  catfish, with garlic and cilantro cornbread topping, 158–159
  fiber substitutes to increase, 485–486
  listing of, xxiii
  mackerel, baked en papillote in soy-ginger glaze, 151–152
  red snapper, in tomato sauce Veracruz-style, 154
  salmon, baked in parchment on bed of vegetables with tarragon, 155–156
  sea bass, steamed whole, with black bean sauce, 160–161
  shark and vegetable kabob, with pineapple yogurt pepper sauce, 157
  shark fillets, broiled marinated, with papaya mango salsa, 153
  sole fillets, crispy crusted orange-flavored, 150
  swordfish steaks in tomato sauce, 162
  yellowfin tuna burgers with teriyaki ginger glaze, 163–164
Fish fumet, 6
Flank steak, with mushroom and green onions, 70–71
Flavorings, salt reduction, listed, 479–482
Fowl, barbecue sauce for, 57. See also Chicken; Game birds; Turkey
French bread, whole wheat, 383–384
Frosting and sweet sauces, 385–402
  applesauce, 393

apple syrup with calvados, 385
apricot-flavored powdered sugar frosting, 386
apricot fruit juice syrup puree, 389
buckwheat honey glaze, 387
butterscotch sauce, 388
cheese frosting, 390
date puree, 391
frosting, pineapple-orange flavored, 397
maple frosting, 401
orange fruit glaze, 395
pineapple sauce, 398
raspberry glaze with Kirsch, 399
raspberry sauce, 394
rhubarb sauce with orange, 400
strawberry sauce, 392
yogurt honey topping with almond, 402
yogurt topping, orange-pineapple, 396
Frozen desserts, 442–453
  banana bonbons with yogurt, 446
  popsicles:
    papaya banana, 449
    raspberry, 448
  sherbet:
    peach, 450–451
    pineapple, 445
    tropical mango with fruit juice, 452–453
  yogurt:
    apricot with fruit juice, 442–443
    banana split with butterscotch, 444
    banana-strawberry, 447
    cherry crepes with, 466
Fruit desserts, 454–467
  apple crisp with raisins and oat topping, 456
  apples glazed and rolled in crepes, 462
  apricot souffle, fruit-sweetened, 467
  bananas baked in graham cracker crumbs with orange-pineapple yogurt topping, 457
  berries encased in angel cake, 459–460
  cantaloupe balls with ouzo, 461
  cherry crepes with vanilla frozen yogurt, 466
  honeydew melon with ginger, 463
  oranges, cherries, and raspberries in cherry-flavored syrup, 464
  peaches baked and stuffed with Grape Nuts and walnuts, 458
  pears steamed with cinnamon and honey, 465
  strudel, apple and currant jelly with phyllo crust, 454–455

Fruit melange, with mimosa sauce in phyllo pastry, 425–426
Fruits:
  baby carrots in fruit glaze with apple slices, 190–191
  substitutes to increase fiber in, 484–485
  peaches, dried, triticale with, 240
Fruit salads, 291–297. See also Main course salads; Vegetable and grain salads
  beets and fruit, pomegranate seeds, and roasted peanuts, 291–292
  medley, naturally sweet, 296
  peaches and grapes, Waldorf-style, 293
  tropical fruit and vegetables, Malaysian-inspired, 294–295

Game birds:
  Cornish hens, broiled, Asian-inspired, 141–142
  Guinea hen, roast, with Madeira, 144–145
Game meats:
  beefalo, salad with shrimp and cellophane noodles, Thai-style, 270–271
  rabbit, braised in tomato wine sauce, with rosemary, 143
  red wine marinade for, 61
  venison, roast, with mushroom sauce, 146–147
Garbanzo beans:
  in ginger sauce, 176
  turkey ball soup with, and vegetables, 24
Garlic:
  catfish cilantro cornbread topping and, 158–159
  chicken breasts braised with herbs, celery and, 127–128
  lime ginger-garlic sauce, 47
  oils and vinegars, 298–299
  potatoes, sauteed cubes, with ginger, fennel seeds and, 230
  sliced baked potatoes with, 220
  tomato relish with basil and, 53
Garlic bread, roasted elephant garlic, 359
  dips and toppings, 359
Gazpacho, tomato, bell pepper, and cucumber soup, 15
Ginger:
  beets, sliced gingered orange beets, 205
  broccoli, stir-fried with wine, soy sauce and, 210
  couscous with soy and, 239

Ginger (*Continued*)
  honeydew melon with, 463
  lamb, leg of, roasted with mint,
    lemon and, 86–87
  lime ginger-garlic sauce, 47
  oils and vinegars, 300–301
Gingerbread cake with bananas, 376–
  377
Ginger cookies, 407
Ginger sauce, garbanzo beans in, 176
Ginger soy dressing, sesame-flavored,
  318
Glazes, *see* Rubs and marinades
Goulash, pork cubes, braised, with
  paprika and yogurt, 93–94
Graham cracker crust, 415–416
Grains, 233–254. *See also* Vegetable
  and grain salads
  barley risotto, with mushrooms and
    spinach, 233–234
  brown basmati rice, boiled, 235
  brown rice:
    with chicken, seafood, and vege-
      tables, paella-style, 243–244
    fried, with vegetables, 241–242
    pilaf, with bell peppers, celery,
      and onions, 245–246
    in tomato broth, 236
    turmeric-flavored, with tomatoes,
      247
  buckwheat-cornbread stuffing, with
    spinach and ham, 237–238
  couscous:
    with ginger and soy, 239
    lamb stew with vegetables and,
      82–83
  granola, whole grain, with sun-
    flower seeds, cashews, al-
    monds, dried apricots, and
    raisins, 248
  oat porridge, whole grain, with cin-
    namon and cardamom, 249
  salt reduction, listed, 478–479
  substitutes to increase fiber in,
    483–484
  triticale, with dried peaches, 240
  wild rice:
    with blueberries and shiitake
      mushrooms, 253–254
    with mushrooms and almonds,
      251–252
    pecan, with raisins and vege-
      tables, 250
Granola, whole grain, with sunflower
  seeds, cashews, almonds, dried
  apricots, and raisins, 248
Grapes:
  chicken salad with water chestnuts,
    cashews and, 272
  peaches and, Waldorf-style, 293

Gravies, *see* Sauces
Green beans:
  stir-fried:
    with coconut flavor, 209
    vegetable medley, 202
  with toasted sesame seeds, 213
Green chilies, eggplant puree with,
  206
Green onion:
  flank steak with mushrooms and,
    70–71
  mashed potatoes with cheese and,
    219
Green peas, *see* Pea
  cheese and, in tomato sauce, 332–
    333
  puree of, with sherry, 203
  stir-fried, with coconut flavor, 209
Green tossed salad, with vegetables
  and saffron basil orange vinaigrette, 280
Ground beef, with onions, bell peppers, and Worcestershire
  sauce, 69
Ground chicken, croquettes, with
  mushroom sauce, 129–130
Ground lamb, zucchini slices layered
  with, and cheese sauce
  Moussaka-style, 91
Ground turkey:
  bell peppers stuffed with brown
    rice, mozzarella cheese and,
    116–117
  macaroni with, in red wine mush-
    room sauce, 257–258
  meatballs, with allspice, 112–113
  tacos, with cheese and tomato bell
    pepper salsa, 120–121
  tamale casserole with cornmeal
    crust and filling of, 118–119
  with tofu, Cajun-style, 110–111
Guinea hen, roast, with Madeira,
  144–145

Ham, buckwheat-cornbread stuffing
  with spinach and, 237–238
Hamburger, with onions, bell peppers,
  and Worcestershire sauce, 69
Honeydew melon with ginger, 463
Honey vinaigrette dressing, raspberry-
  infused, 315
Hors d'oeuvres, *see* Dips and top-
  pings; Snacks
Horseradish and yogurt sauce, with
  dillweed, 56
Hot fudge pudding cake, 378

Iced tea, minted with orange, 362

Ingredients:
  measuring of, xix-xx
  sources for, 495–497
  specifications, xxi-xxii

Jerky, venison, gingerbread apricot
  flavored, 341
Jicama:
  oranges and, with lime juice and
    chili powder, 282
  pineapple cubes, orange sections
    and, with orange pineapple
    soy glaze, 297

Kale, mixed greens, with ground peanuts, 199
Kebabs, lamb, grilled, in apricot glaze,
  85
Key lime pie, with meringue, 429
Kidney beans:
  brown rice and, Jamaican-style,
    177
  with Indian seasonings, 184
  potato salad with bell pepper and,
    vinaigrette sauce, 283
  in tomato broth with bell peppers,
    carrots, and celery, 178–179
Kiwi, strawberry, and banana orange
  shake, 363

Lamb, 82–91
  ground, zucchini slices layered
    with, and cheese sauce
    Moussaka-style, 91
  kebabs, grilled, in apricot glaze, 85
  leg of:
    broiled with herb marinade, 84
    roasted rolled, with mint, 88
    roasted with ginger, mint, and
      lemon, 86–87
  stew:
    with potatoes and spinach in to-
      mato broth, 89–90
    with vegetables and couscous,
      82–83
Lasagna, spinach almond, with whole
  wheat noodles, 263–264
Leavening agents, salt reduction, listed, 479–482
Lemon chiffon angel pie, 428
Lentils:
  pink, with roasted spices, 280
  sandwich spread of, with Asian
    spices, 185–186
  stew, three bean, lentil, and pea
    stew, 188–189
Lentil soup with oregano, 10

Lime dressing:
   Asian-inspired, 305
   vegetable, 309
Lime ginger-garlic sauce, 47

Macaroni, with ground turkey in red
   wine mushroom sauce, 257–
   258
Mackerel, baked en papillote in soy-
   ginger glaze, 151–152
Main course salads, 270–274. *See also*
   Fruit salads; Vegetable and
   grain salads
   beefalo and shrimp, with cello-
      phane noodles, Thai-style,
      270–271
   chicken and cashew, with grapes
      and water chestnuts, 272
   chicken with orange-pineapple soy
      dressing, 274
   potato, sausage, and broccoli salad
      (hot), 273
Malaysian Rojak, tropical fruit and
   vegetables, 294–295
Mandarin oranges, quinoa salad with
   pineapple, water chestnuts
   and, 284–285
Mango papaya salsa:
   master recipe, 48
   shark fillets marinated and broiled
      with, 153
Mango sherbet with fruit juice, 452–
   453
Manicotti tubes, with spinach, mushrooms, cheese, and tomato
   sauce, 259–260
Maple frosting, 401
Marinades, *see* Rubs and marinades
Mayonnaise-like dressing, oil free,
   311
Measurement, of ingredients, xix-xx
Meats, *see* Beef; Game meats; Lamb;
   Pork; Veal
Meat substitutes:
   fat reduction, listed, 468–471
   fiber, 485–486
   salt reduction, listed, 476–478
Meringue:
   chocolate meringue shells, 411–
      412
   pastry shells, 417
   topping for pie, 430
Mimosa sauce, fruit melange with, in
   phyllo pastry, 425–426
Minestrone, vegetarian, 30–31
Mint and cilantro chutney, 43
Moussaka, ground lamb layered with
   zucchini slices and cheese
   sauce, 91

Mozzarella cheese:
   bell pepper stuffed with ground tur-
      key, brown rice and, 116–117
   chicken breasts sauteed with orega-
      no and, 137–138
   pork cutlets, breaded, with filling
      of, 95
Muffins, banana bran walnut, 369
Mung beans, yellow split, with cauliflower and spinach, 187
Mushrooms:
   barley risotto with spinach and,
      233–234
   chicken thighs, in tomato sauce
      with bell peppers and, 132–
      133
   flank steak with green onions and,
      70–71
   macaroni with ground turkey in
      red wine mushroom sauce,
      257–258
   manicotti tubes with spinach,
      cheese, tomato sauce and,
      259–260
   portobello mushrooms, grilled,
      glazed with herb marinade,
      343
   shiitake, wild rice with blueberries
      and, 253–254
   soba noodles with bell peppers,
      snow peas, carrots, water
      chestnuts and, 288
   stir-fried, vegetable medley, 202
   stuffed, with sauteed vegetables,
      344–345
   wild rice with almonds and, 251–
      252
Mushroom sauce:
   chicken croquettes with, 129–130
   with pureed vegetables, 38
   venison roast with, 146–147
Mushroom soup:
   with beef and barley, 25
   creamed, with sherry, 19
   pearl barley and, 9
Mustard:
   chicken breast, crispy baked, with,
      134
   orange-rosemary mustard rub, 59
Mustard rounds, 351

Nonfat milk white cheese, 330
Noodles, translucent, with beef and
   vegetables in soy glaze, 265–
   266
Noodle soup, chicken, whole wheat,
   and vegetables, 32
Nutrient enhancement, substitutes
   for, 487–490

Nutrient need, explained, xxii
Nutrient recommendation, recipes
   and, xxiv
Nutrients, computing of, xix-xxix

Oat flake topping, zucchini, corn-
   stuffed, with cheese and, 196
Oat pastry crust:
   blueberries with, 423–424
   master recipe, 420–421
   peach tart on, 427
Oat porridge, whole grain, with cinnamon and cardamom, 249
Oils and vinegars, 298–304. *See also*
   Dressings
   basil and garlic scented extra-virgin
      olive oil, 298–299
   orange- and ginger-flavored saf-
      flower oil, 300–301
   raspberry-infused white wine vine-
      gar, 302–303
   rosemary- and thyme-infused white
      wine vinegar, 304
Oil substitutes, fat reduction, listed,
   471–473
Olives, pork tenderloin, stuffed with
   brown rice, raisins and, 101–
   102
Onions:
   beef burgers, with bell peppers,
      Worcestershire sauce and,
      69
   brown rice pilaf, with celery, bell
      peppers and, 245–246
   cauliflower coated cilantro and,
      193
   cucumbers and, marinated in sweet
      and sour dill dressing, 278
   mixed greens, with ground peanuts,
      199
   red, diced cucumber, red onion and
      tomato salad, 279
   sliced baked potatoes with, 232
   stir-fried, vegetable medley, 202
   vegetable salad, grilled, 281
Orange fruit glaze, 395
Orange iced tea, minted, 362
Orange-pineapple soy dressing:
   chicken salad with, 274
   master recipe, 312
Orange-pineapple soy glaze, pineapple
   cubes, orange sections, and jicama strips with, 297
Orange-pineapple yogurt topping:
   bananas baked in graham cracker
      crumbs with, 457
   master recipe, 396
Orange-rosemary mustard rub,
   59

Oranges:
    cherries, and raspberries in cherry-flavored syrup, 464
    jicama and, with lime juice and chili powder, 282
    kiwi, strawberry, and banana shake with, 363
    oils and vinegars, 300–301
    pineapple cubes, jicama strips and, with orange pineapple soy glaze, 297
Oregano:
    chicken breasts sauteed with mozzarella cheese and, 137–138
    lentil soup with, 10
Orzo pilaf, with cloves and cinnamon, 261

Paella, brown rice with chicken, seafood, and vegetables, paella-style, 243–244
Pancakes, pumpkin whole wheat, 381
Paneer cheese, 328–329
Papaya banana popsicles, 449
Papaya mango salsa:
    master recipe, 48
    shark fillets marinated and broiled with, 153
Paprika:
    chicken breasts braised with, Hungarian-style, 125–126
    pork cubes, braised, with yogurt and, goulash-style, 93–94
Parsnip chips, 348
Pastas, 255–267
    angel hair pancakes, carrot-flavored, with bell peppers, 255–256
    lasagna, spinach almond, with whole wheat noodles, 263–264
    macaroni with ground turkey in red wine mushroom sauce, 257–258
    manicotti tubes, with spinach, mushrooms, cheese, and tomato sauce, 259–260
    noodles, translucent, with beef and vegetables in soy glaze, 265–266
    orzo pilaf, with cloves and cinnamon, 261
    penne, baked in cheddar and Swiss cheese sauce, 262
    spaghetti, whole wheat, with sauteed vegetables, 267
Pastry crusts, 411–421

chocolate meringue shells, 411–412
crepes, 413–414
graham cracker crust, 415–416
meringue pastry shells, 417
oat pastry crust, 420–421
phyllo pastry tart, 419
spring roll wrappers, Philippine-style, 418
Pastry fillings and toppings, 422–435
    baked Alaska, banana-strawberry, 422
    blueberries with oat pastry, 423–424
    fruit melange, with mimosa sauce in phyllo pastry, 425–426
    key lime pie, with meringue, 429
    lemon chiffon angel pie, 428
    meringue topping for pie, 430
    peach tart on oat crust, 427
    pumpkin cheesecake, in graham cracker crust, 435
    pumpkin pie in oat crust, 431–432
    raspberry snow tart, 433–434
Peaches:
    baked and stuffed with Grape Nuts and walnuts, 458
    dried, triticale with, 240
    grapes and, Waldorf-style, 293
    meringue mousse cake, 380
    tart on oat crust, 427
Peach poppy seed dressing, creamy, 308
Peach sherbet, 450–451
Peach soup, flavored with cinnamon and clove, chilled, 16
Peanut butter, chunky, 45
Peanuts:
    mixed greens with ground, 199
    roasted, beets and fruit salad, with pomegranate seeds and, 291–292
Pearl barley and mushroom soup, 9
Pears steamed with cinnamon and honey, 465
Peas, green, see Green peas
Pea soup, split, laced with spinach, 29
Pea stew, three bean, lentil, and pea stew, 188–189
Penne pasta, baked in cheddar and Swiss cheese sauce, 262
Phyllo pastry:
    fruit melange with mimosa sauce in, 425–426
    strudel, spinach and Swiss cheese with, 334–335
    tart, 419

Pilaf:
    brown rice with bell peppers, celery, and onions, 245–246
    orzo, with cloves and cinnamon, 261
Pineapple:
    cubed, orange sections, jicama strips and, with orange pineapple soy glaze, 297
    quinoa salad with mandarin oranges, water chestnuts and, 284–285
Pineapple cranberry relish, 42
Pineapple-flavored tofu dressing, creamy, 313
Pineapple-orange flavored frosting, 397
Pineapple sauce, 398
Pineapple sherbet, 445
Pineapple tofu dressing, cabbage, shredded, with corn and bell pepper in, 287
Pineapple yogurt pepper sauce:
    master recipe, 60
    shark and vegetable kabob with, 157
Pink lentils, with roasted spices, 280
Pinto beans:
    fried and simmered in broth, 174–175
    in vegetable broth, 181
Pomegranate seeds, beets and fruit salad, with roasted peanuts, 291–292
Popsicles:
    papaya banana, 449
    raspberry, 448
Pork, 93–104
    chops:
        grilled, lemon-scented with sage, 97
        pan broiled, citrus-flavored, 96
    cubes, braised, with paprika and yogurt, goulash-style, 93–94
    cutlets, breaded, with mozzarella cheese filling, 95
    tenderloin cubes, in soy and sherry glaze with green onions, 99–100
    tenderloin roast:
        with fennel seeds, 103–104
        Oriental-inspired, 98
        stuffed with brown rice, raisins and olives, 101–102
Porridge, oat, whole grain, with cinnamon and cardamom, 249
Portion size, substitutes for, 487–490
Portobello mushrooms, grilled, glazed with herb marinade, 343

Potato chips, roasted Idaho, 347–348
Potatoes, 218–232
  baked in parchment with Italian seasoning, 222
  baked russets, 218
  boats stuffed with mashed potatoes and bell pepper, 228–229
  boiled, with turkey bacon and rosemary, 231
  mashed:
    with buttermilk, 223
    with cheese and green onions, 219
    onion-flavored, 226
  new red, with parsley and chives, 225
  oven-roasted wedges, with rosemary, 227
  pancakes, with onion and garlic, 224
  sauteed cubes, with ginger, garlic, and fennel seeds, 230
  sliced, simmered in cheese custard, 220
  sliced baked:
    with garlic, 220
    with onions, 232
Potato salad:
  with kidney beans and bell pepper, vinaigrette sauce, 283
  with sausage and broccoli (hot), 273
Pot roast, marinated, with gingersnap gravy, 74–75
Poultry, see Chicken; Game birds; Turkey
  fat reduction substitutes, 468–471
  fiber substitutes, 485–486
Pretzels, stone-ground whole wheat caraway, 349–350
Processed foods, salt reduction, listed, 479–482
Puddings, 438–441
  bread pudding:
    baked banana and whole grain, 438
    sweet potato whole grain, 440–441
  rice pudding, baked with dried cherries, 439
Pumpkin cheesecake, in graham cracker crust, 435
Pumpkin pie in oat crust, 431–432
Pumpkin whole wheat pancakes, 381

Quinoa, with pineapple, mandarin oranges, and water chestnuts, 284–285

Rabbit, braised in tomato wine sauce, with rosemary, 143
Raisins:
  granola, whole grain, with sunflower seeds, cashews, dried apricots, almonds and, 248
  pork tenderloin, stuffed with brown rice, olives and, 101–102
  rice, wild pecan, with vegetables and, 250
Ranch-style chip dip, 358
Ranch-style dressing:
  master recipe, 314
  vegetable slaw in, 290
Raspberry:
  cherries, and oranges in cherry-flavored syrup, 464
  glaze with Kirsch, 399
  oils and vinegars, 302–303
  popsicles, 448
  sauce, 394
  snow tart, 433–434
Raspberry-infused honey vinaigrette dressing, 315
Recipe conversion, explained, xxv-xxix
Recipe nutrient analysis, explained, xxiv-xxv
Red leaf lettuce salad, with spinach and walnut vinaigrette, 289
Red pepper, see Bell peppers
  sirloin steak, sauteed, with red pepper tomato sauce, 80
  tomato sauce with, 49
Red snapper, in tomato sauce Veracruz-style, 154
Red wine marinade, for game, 61
Red wine vinaigrette, 316
Relishes, see Condiment sauces
Rhubarb sauce with orange, 400
Rice, see Brown rice; Grains
Rice pudding, baked with dried cherries, 439
Risotto, barley, with mushrooms and spinach, 233–234
Roasted corn tortilla chips, 346
Rock Cornish hens, broiled, Asian-inspired, 141–142
Rosemary:
  oils and vinegars, 304
  orange-rosemary mustard rub, 59
Rubs and marinades, 57–62
  barbecue sauce for fowl, 57
  orange-rosemary mustard rub, 59
  pineapple yogurt pepper sauce, 60
  red wine, for game, 61
  spice blend:
    Cajun-style, 62
    Indian-inspired, 58

Saffron and basil orange vinaigrette, 317
Saffron basil orange vinaigrette, green tossed salad with vegetables and, 280
Salads, see Fruit salads; Main course salads; Vegetable and grain salads
Salmon, baked in parchment on bed of vegetables with tarragon, 155–156
Salsa, see Condiment sauces
Salt, substitutes for reduction of, 476–482
Sandwiches, cucumber slices with mint and cilantro chutney, 340
Saturated fats, substitutes for reduction of, 468–475
Sauces, 34–40. See also Condiment sauces; Frosting and sweet sauces
  barbecue sauce for fowl, 57
  chicken gravy with blended vegetables, 34
  mushroom, with pureed vegetables, 38
  tomato, Italian-style, 35
  tomato coulis, with garlic and basil, 39
  vodka sauce, vegetable-thickened, 40
  white sauce, low-fat, 36–37
Sausage, potato salad with broccoli and (hot), 273
Scrambled eggs, fiesta, 324
Sea bass, steamed whole, with black bean sauce, 160–161
Seafood substitutes, fat reduction, listed, 468–471
Sesame-flavored ginger soy dressing, 318
Sesame seeds, green beans with toasted, 213
Shark:
  fillets, broiled marinated, with papaya mango salsa, 153
  vegetable kabob and, with pineapple yogurt pepper sauce, 157
Shellfish, 165–170. See also Fish
  crab cakes, with toasted corn and bell peppers, 169
  shrimp:
    barbecued spicy coconut, 167–168
    beefalo salad with cellophane noodles, Thai-style, 270–271
    Mediterranean-inspired, 170
  squid, steamed Asian-style, on bed of lettuce, 165–166

Sherbet:
  peach, 450–451
  pineapple, 445
  tropical mango with fruit juice,
    452–453
Shiitake mushrooms:
  snow peas, stir-fried bamboo shoots
    and, 207–208
  wild rice with blueberries and,
    253–254
Shrimp:
  barbecued spicy coconut, 167–168
  beefalo salad with cellophane noo-
    dles and, Thai-style, 270–271
  Mediterranean-inspired, 170
  spring rolls with beef, tofu and,
    Philippine-style, 76–77
Shrimp ball soup, with vegetables,
  27–28
Shrimp broth, 8
Sirloin steak:
  sauteed, with red pepper tomato
    sauce, 80
  veal, with vodka sauce, 105
Snacks, 338–351. See also Dips and
  toppings
  chicken wings, ginger sesame, 342
  mushrooms:
    portobello mushrooms, grilled,
      glazed with herb marinade,
      343
    stuffed, with sauteed vegetables,
      344–345
  mustard rounds, 351
  potato chips, roasted Idaho, 347–
    348
  pretzels, stone-ground whole wheat
    caraway, 349–350
  sandwiches, cucumber slices with
    mint and cilantro chutney,
    340
  tortilla chips, roasted corn, 346
  venison jerky, gingerbread apricot
    flavored, 341
  whole wheat cheese wafers, 338–
    339
Snow peas:
  soba noodles with bell peppers, car-
    rots, mushrooms, water chest-
    nuts and, 288
  stir-fried with bamboo shoots and
    shiitake mushrooms, 207–208
Soba noodles, with red and yellow
  bell peppers, snow peas, carrots, mushrooms, and water
  chestnuts, 288
Sodium, substitutes for reduction of,
  476–482
Sole fillets, crispy crusted orange-
  flavored, 150

Souffle, spinach mushroom, 324–326
Soups, 9–32. See also Stocks
  butternut squash bisque with
    chunky apple yogurt, 11–12
  carrot bisque, gingered, 23
  chicken, with whole wheat noodle
    and vegetables, 32
  chicken brown rice and vegetable,
    with curry, 13–14
  corn, in creamy broth with cumin,
    22
  corn chowder, with roasted red bell
    pepper garnish, 17–18
  egg drop, 26
  gazpacho, tomato, bell pepper, and
    cucumber, 15
  lentil with oregano, 10
  minestrone, vegetarian, 30–31
  mushroom:
    beef, and barley, 25
    creamed, with sherry, 19
    pearl barley and, 9
  peach, flavored with cinnamon and
    clove, chilled, 16
  shrimp ball, with vegetables, 27–28
  split pea, laced with spinach, 29
  tomato, creamed, with sweet red
    bell pepper, 20–21
  turkey ball, with garbanzo beans
    and vegetables, 24
Soy, couscous with ginger and, 239
Spaghetti, whole wheat, with sauteed
  vegetables, 267
Spice blend, see Rubs and marinades
  Cajun-style, 62
  Indian-inspired, 58
Spinach:
  almond lasagna and, with whole
    wheat noodles, 263–264
  barley risotto with mushrooms and,
    233–234
  buckwheat-cornbread stuffing with
    ham and, 237–238
  manicotti tubes with mushrooms,
    cheese, tomato sauce and,
    259–260
  mixed greens, with ground peanuts,
    199
  mung beans, yellow split, with cau-
    liflower and, 187
  mushroom souffle and, 324–326
  salad, with red leaf lettuce and
    walnut vinaigrette, 289
  split pea soup with, 29
  Swiss cheese strudel with phyllo
    pastry and, 334–335
Split pea soup, laced with spinach,
  29
Spreads, see Condiment sauces
Spring rolls, with beef, tofu, and

shrimp, Philippine-style, 76–
  77
Spring roll sauce, sweet, 50
Spring roll wrappers, Philippine-style,
  418
Squid, steamed Asian-style, on bed of
  lettuce, 165–166
Steak:
  flank steak, with mushroom and
    green onions, 70–71
  sirloin steak, sauteed, with red pep-
    per tomato sauce, 80
Stews:
  beef, with winter vegetables, 72–73
  lamb:
    with potatoes and spinach in to-
      mato broth, 89–90
    with vegetables and couscous,
      82–83
  three bean, lentil, and pea stew,
    188–189
  veal shanks braised in tomato
    sauce, Mediterranean-style,
    106–107
Stir-fry:
  broccoli, with wine, soy sauce, and
    ginger, 210
  cauliflower, with tomatoes, tur-
    meric, ginger, and cilantro,
    194
  snow peas, with bamboo shoots
    and shiitake mushrooms, 207–
    208
  tenderloin strips in soy glaze, 81
  vegetable medley, 202
  vegetables with coconut flavor, 209
Stocks, 2–8. See also Soups
  chicken, white, 7
  fish fumet, 6
  shrimp broth, 8
  veal, 4–5
  vegetable, 2–3
Strawberry, banana, and kiwi orange
  shake, 363
Strawberry sauce, 392
Stroganoff, beef tenderloin strips, sauteed, 78–79
Strudel:
  apple and currant jelly with phyllo
    crust, 454–455
  spinach and Swiss cheese with
    phyllo pastry, 334–335
Stuffing, buckwheat cornbread with
  spinach and ham, 237–238
Summer squash, vegetable salad,
  grilled, 281
Sunflower seeds, granola, whole grain,
  with cashews, almonds, dried
  apricots, raisins and, 248
Sweet and sour dill dressing, cucum-

bers and onions marinated in, 278

Sweet potato:
bread pudding, whole grain, 440–441
chips, 348
patties, with orange, 212

Swiss cheese:
broccoli timbales with, 322–323
penne pasta baked in cheddar and Swiss cheese sauce, 262
sandwich, toasted open-face, with tomatoes and caraway, 336
spinach strudel with phyllo pastry, 334–335

Swordfish steaks, in tomato sauce, 162

Tacos, turkey, with cheese and tomato bell pepper salsa, 120–121
Tamale casserole, with cornmeal crust and filling of ground turkey, 118–119
Tea, iced tea, minted with orange, 362
Tenderloin (beef):
roast, Cajun-style, 68
sautéed, in Stroganoff-style sauce, 78–79
stir-fried, in soy glaze, 81
Tenderloin (pork):
cubes, in soy and sherry glaze with green onions, 99–100
roast:
with fennel seeds, 103–104
Oriental-inspired, 98
Teriyaki ginger glaze, yellowfin tuna burgers with, 163–164
Thyme, oils and vinegars, 304
Timbales, broccoli, with Swiss cheese, 322–323
Tofu:
pineapple tofu dressing, cabbage, shredded, with corn and bell pepper in, 287
spring rolls with beef, shrimp and, Philippine-style, 76–77
turkey burgers with, Cajun-style, 110–111
Tofu dressing, pineapple-flavored, creamy, 313
Tomato:
brown rice, turmeric-flavored, with, 247
cauliflower stir-fried with, and turmeric, ginger, and cilantro, 194
diced cucumber, red onion and tomato salad, 279
gazpacho soup, 15

mixed greens, with ground peanuts, 199
stuffed with zucchini and carrots, 214
Swiss cheese sandwich, toasted open-face, with caraway and, 336
zucchini sautéed with herbs and, 216
Tomato cocktail, spicy, 361
Tomato coulis, with garlic and basil, 39
Tomato relish:
with basil and garlic, 53
with cucumber, 52
Tomato salsa:
with bell pepper:
black bean patties with, 172–173
master recipe, 51
with cilantro and chilies, 44
Tomato sauce:
chicken thighs in, with mushrooms and bell peppers, 132–133
Italian-style, 35
manicotti tubes with spinach, mushrooms, cheese and, 259–260
red snapper in, Veracruz-style, 154
sirloin steak, sautéed, with red pepper tomato sauce, 80
with spicy red peppers, 49
swordfish steaks in, 162
veal shanks braised in, Mediterranean-style, 106–107
Tomato soup, creamed, with sweet red bell pepper, 20–21
Tortilla chips, roasted corn, 346
Tortillas, bean- and cheese-filled whole wheat, 327
Total fats, substitutes for reduction of, 468–475
Translucent noodles, with beef and vegetables in soy glaze, 265–266
Triticale, with dried peaches, 240
Tropical fruit:
pineapple cubes, orange sections, and jicama strips, with orange pineapple soy glaze, 297
vegetables and, Malaysian-inspired, 294–295
Tropical mango sherbet with fruit juice, 452–453
Turkey, 110–121
bell peppers stuffed with brown rice, mozzarella cheese and, 116–117
breast, sliced, with cranberry sauce, 114–115

burgers, with tofu, Cajun-style, 110–111
ground, macaroni with, in red wine mushroom sauce, 257–258
meatballs, with allspice, 112–113
tacos, with cheese and tomato bell pepper salsa, 120–121
tamale casserole with cornmeal crust and filling of, 118–119
Turkey bacon, potatoes with, 231
Turkey ball soup, with garbanzo beans and vegetables, 24
Turkey ham, zucchini, bell peppers, and tomatoes stewed with, 215

Veal, 105–107
shanks, braised in tomato sauce, Mediterranean-style, 106–107
sirloin, roast, with vodka sauce, 105
Veal stock, 4–5
Vegetable and grain salads, 275–290. See also Fruit salads; Main course salads
beets, pickled, German-style, 286
broccoli, marinated in rice wine vinaigrette, 275
bulgur salad, with garden vegetables, 276–277
cabbage, shredded, with corn and bell pepper in pineapple tofu dressing, 287
cucumber, diced, red onion and tomato, 279
cucumbers and onions, marinated in sweet and sour dill dressing, 278
green tossed, with vegetables and saffron basil orange vinaigrette, 280
jicama and orange, with lime juice and chili powder, 282
potato, kidney bean, and bell pepper, with vinaigrette sauce, 283
quinoa with pineapple, mandarin oranges, and water chestnuts, 284–285
slaw, in ranch-style dressing, 290
soba noodles, with red and yellow bell peppers, snow peas, carrots, mushrooms, and water chestnuts, 288
spinach and red leaf lettuce with walnut vinaigrette, 289
vegetable salad, grilled, 281
Vegetables, 190–216. See also Main course salads; Vegetable and grain salads

Vegetables (*Continued*)
beets:
  glazed in orange and red wine
    vinegar sauce, 192
  sliced gingered orange beets, 205
broccoli, stir-fried with wine, soy
  sauce, and ginger, 210
cabbage, shredded green, with apples and cinnamon, 204
carrots:
  baby, in fruit glaze with apple
    slices, 190–191
  citrus-glazed, with parsley, 195
cauliflower:
  coated with cilantro and onions,
    193
  stir-fried with tomatoes and tur-
    meric, ginger, and cilantro,
    194
chicken brown rice soup with curry
  and, 13–14
corn cake, 211
corn on the cob:
  cooking methods, 201
  grilled, 200
eggplant:
  baked, 197–198
  puree of, with green chilies, 206
fiber substitutes to increase, 484–
  485
green beans, with toasted sesame
  seeds, 213
green peas, puree of, with sherry,
  203
green peas and cheese in tomato
  sauce, 332–333
mixed greens, with ground peanuts,
  199
salt reduction, listed, 478
sauteed, with whole wheat spaghetti, 267
snow peas, stir-fried with bamboo
  shoots and shiitake mushrooms, 207–208
stir-fried:
  with coconut flavor, 209
  medley of, 202
sweet potato chips, 348
sweet potato patties, with orange,
  212
tomatoes, stuffed with zucchini and
  carrots, 214
zucchini:
  bell peppers, and tomatoes
    stewed with turkey ham, 215
  corn-stuffed, with cheese and oat
    flake topping, 196
  sauteed with tomatoes and herbs,
    216

Vegetable stock, 2–3
Vegetable-thickened oil-free vinaigrette, 319
Venison:
  jerky, gingerbread apricot flavored,
    341
  roast, with mushroom sauce, 146–
    147
Vietnamese-style dipping sauce, 54
Vodka sauce:
  veal sirloin, roast, 105
  vegetable-thickened, 40

Waldorf salad, peaches and grapes,
  Waldorf-style, 293
Walnut vinaigrette:
  master recipe, 320
  spinach and red leaf lettuce salad
    with, 289
Water chestnuts:
  chicken salad with grapes, cashews
    and, 272
  quinoa salad with mandarin or-
    anges, pineapple and, 284–
    285
  soba noodles with bell peppers,
    snow peas, carrots, mushrooms
    and, 288
White cheese, nonfat milk, 330
White sauce, low-fat, 36–37
White wine spritzer, chardonnay and
  cranberry, 360
Whole grain bread strips, honey-
  baked, in custard coating, 408
Whole wheat cheese wafers, 338–339
Whole wheat French bread, 383–384
Whole wheat noodles, spinach almond lasagna with, 263–264
Whole wheat noodle soup, chicken
  and vegetables with, 32
Whole wheat spaghetti, with sauteed
  vegetables, 267
Wild pecan rice, with raisins and ve-
  getables, 250
Wild rice:
  with blueberries and shiitake mush-
    rooms, 253–254
  with mushrooms and almonds,
    251–252
Wine:
  apple syrup with calvados, 385
  chardonnay and cranberry spritzer,
    360
  chicken breasts braised in tomato
    port wine sauce, 123
  Guinea hen, roast, with Madeira
    wine, 144–145
  macaroni with ground turkey in

red wine mushroom sauce,
    257–258
peas green, puree of, with sherry,
    203
rabbit, braised in tomato wine
    sauce, with rosemary, 143
raspberry glaze with Kirsch, 399
red wine marinade, for game, 61
roast beef with vegetables braised
    in, 67
yellowfin tuna burgers with teriyaki
    ginger glaze, 163–164

Yam chips, 348
Yellowfin tuna burgers, with teriyaki
  ginger glaze, 163–164
Yellow split mung beans, with cauliflower and spinach, 187
Yogurt:
  butternut squash bisque with
    chunky apple yogurt, 11–12
  frozen:
    with apricot and fruit juice,
      442–443
    banana bonbons, 446
    banana split with butterscotch,
      444
    banana-strawberry, 447
    fruit-sweetened nonfat strawberry,
      with strawberry chunks, 355–
      356
  horseradish sauce with dillweed
    and, 56
  pineapple yogurt pepper sauce, 60
  pork cubes, braised, with paprika
    and, goulash-style, 93–94
  toppings:
    honey with almond, 402
    orange-pineapple, 396
Yogurt cheese, nonfat, thickened
    with yogurt flavored with
    herbs, 331

Zucchini:
  corn-stuffed, with cheese and oat
    flake topping, 196
  ground lamb layered with slices of,
    and cheese sauce Moussaka-
    style, 91
  sauteed with tomatoes and herbs,
    216
  stewed with bell peppers and toma-
    toes with turkey ham, 215
  tomatoes stuffed with carrots and,
    214
  vegetable salad, grilled, 281